ISSN 1557-5535

SPORTS IN AMERICA

RECREATION, BUSINESS, EDUCATION, AND CONTROVERSY

Robert Jacobson

INFORMATION PLUS® REFERENCE SERIES
Formerly Published by Information Plus, Wylie, Texas

GALE
CENGAGE Learning·

Detroit • New York • San Francisco • New Haven, Conn • Waterville, Maine • London

Sports in America: Recreation, Business, Education, and Controversy

Robert Jacobson

Kepos Media, Inc.: Paula Kepos and Janice Jorgensen, Series Editors

Project Editors: Elizabeth Manar, Kathleen J. Edgar

Rights Acquisition and Management: Kelly Quin, Edna Shy, Robyn Young

Composition: Evi Abou-El-Seoud, Mary Beth Trimper

Manufacturing: Cynde Lentz

Cover photograph: Image copyright Craig Barhorst, 2009. Used under license from Shutterstock.com.

Gale
27500 Drake Rd.
Farmington Hills, MI 48331-3535

ISBN-13: 978-0-7876-5103-9 (set)
ISBN-13: 978-1-4144-5379-8

ISBN-10: 0-7876-5103-6 (set)
ISBN-10: 1-4144-5379-5

ISSN 1557-5535

This title is also available as an e-book.
ISBN-13: 978-1-4144-7002-3 (set)
ISBN-10: 1-4144-7002-9 (set)
Contact your Gale sales representative for ordering information.

Printed in the United States of America
1 2 3 4 5 6 7 14 13 12 11 10

TABLE OF CONTENTS

PREFACE vii

CHAPTER 1

America's Sports Obsession 1

Why do people care so much about sports? This chapter defines sports and explores the depth of Americans' passion for them. It summarizes sports participation, attendance, and viewership statistics. The chapter also briefly surveys the major team and individual sports in the United States, as well as the Olympics, and examines the relationship between these sports and media. Finally, it touches on the connection between sports and health, as well as the sports gambling phenomenon.

CHAPTER 2

Sports Participation and Attendance 13

What sports do people like to play and what sports do they like to watch? Using data from a variety of sources, this chapter looks at the numbers for sports participation and attendance at sporting events, covering both the major team sports as well as newer and emerging sports, such as snowboarding and lacrosse. It also examines the money Americans spend on sports equipment, as well as which sports they spend it on.

CHAPTER 3

Sports and the Media 31

Given that business, sports, and the media are so intimately connected, it is sometimes difficult to determine where one ends and the other begins. This chapter outlines the financial relationship between big-time sports and television, from its roots in the early days of television to the present. It also covers viewership numbers, advertising issues, and public image concerns.

CHAPTER 4

Professional Team Sports 43

This chapter focuses on the major professional sports in the United States: baseball, football, basketball, and hockey, as well as soccer, which is on its way to joining the list. How did these sports rise to their current status, and where are they headed? The structure of the leagues and the often combative relationship between players and team owners are discussed.

CHAPTER 5

Other Professional Sports 59

Not every sports enthusiast is interested primarily in the major team sports. Many prefer, for example, the head-to-head competition of golf, tennis, auto racing, and/or boxing, which are all covered in this chapter. The chapter also discusses the leagues/structures of these sports and how they operate and how much money the top professionals compete for.

CHAPTER 6

College, High School, and Youth Sports 69

The role of school sports is a delicate one. College and high school athletics are at once both an element of a well-rounded education and a training ground for hard-core professional competition. These dual roles often come into conflict. College sports have become big business, and as a result high schools have not escaped the influence of money. This chapter examines participation in school sports, the influence of money on the academic institutions that sponsor them, and other issues such as gender equity and the benefits of participation. The growing intensity of school sports has trickled down to youth sports as well; this chapter explores related issues, such as the risks of single-sport specialization by very young athletes.

CHAPTER 7

The Olympics 99

The Olympic Games are an idealistic attempt to bring the world together to celebrate friendly athletic competition. Even though the movement seems to have fallen short of this goal, the Olympics are wildly popular across the planet. This chapter studies the history and business aspects of the Olympic Games, including both the Summer and Winter Olympics and the associated games for people with disabilities.

CHAPTER 8

Sports and Health 109

It is no secret that physical activity is an important part of a healthy lifestyle. This chapter investigates some of the specific health benefits of sports participation, both physical and mental/behavioral. It also covers the risks involved in athletic pursuits, from such physical ailments as bruises and broken bones to emotional injuries in children thrown into overly competitive environments.

CHAPTER 9

Performance-Enhancing Drugs 119

What are steroids? What are dietary supplements, and why are many of them banned in most sports? How are the governing bodies of sports fighting back? This chapter looks at the variety of substances athletes use in the belief—often correct—that the substances will make them stronger and faster. It reviews the history of performance-enhancing substances from herbal concoctions used in the ancient Olympics through the more recent BALCO scandal and problems that have plagued Major League Baseball and professional cycling.

to legal sports bookmaking in Nevada, to the office Super Bowl pool, to offshore Internet betting operations, this chapter surveys the scope of sports gambling in the United States. It also considers the problems sports gambling sometimes creates.

CHAPTER 10
Sports and Gambling. 129
   Americans like to bet on sports almost as much as they like to play them. Sports gambling is a huge business in the United States, and most of it is underground. From pari-mutuel betting on horse races,

IMPORTANT NAMES AND ADDRESSES 137

RESOURCES 139

INDEX 141

PREFACE

Sports in America: Recreation, Business, Education, and Controversy is part of the *Information Plus Reference Series*. The purpose of each volume of the series is to present the latest facts on a topic of pressing concern in modern American life. These topics include the most controversial and studied social issues in the 21st century: abortion, capital punishment, care for senior citizens, crime, the environment, health care, immigration, minorities, national security, social welfare, women, youth, and many more. Although written especially for the high school and undergraduate student, this series is an excellent resource for anyone in need of factual information on current affairs.

By presenting the facts, it is the intention of Gale, Cengage Learning, to provide its readers with everything they need to reach an informed opinion on current issues. To that end, there is a particular emphasis in this series on the presentation of scientific studies, surveys, and statistics. These data are generally presented in the form of tables, charts, and other graphics placed within the text of each book. Every graphic is directly referred to and carefully explained in the text. The source of each graphic is presented within the graphic itself. The data used in these graphics are drawn from the most reputable and reliable sources, in particular from the various branches of the U.S. government and from major independent polling organizations. Every effort has been made to secure the most recent information available. Readers should bear in mind that many major studies take years to conduct, and that additional years often pass before the data from these studies are made available to the public. Therefore, in many cases the most recent information available in 2010 dated from 2007 or 2008. Older statistics are sometimes presented as well, if they are of particular interest and no more-recent information exists.

Although statistics are a major focus of the *Information Plus Reference Series*, they are by no means its only content. Each book also presents the widely held positions and important ideas that shape how the book's subject is discussed in the United States. These positions are explained in detail and, where possible, in the words of their proponents. Some of the other material to be found in these books includes: historical background; descriptions of major events related to the subject; relevant laws and court cases; and examples of how these issues play out in American life. Some books also feature primary documents or have pro and con debate sections giving the words and opinions of prominent Americans on both sides of a controversial topic. All material is presented in an even-handed and unbiased manner; readers will never be encouraged to accept one view of an issue over another.

HOW TO USE THIS BOOK

Sports have an enormous presence in American life. Most Americans engage in sporting activities of one type or another and enjoy watching sports in person or on television. The American passion for sports has made it a major industry worth billions of dollars. It has also brought with it a host of problems. Illegal sports gambling is commonplace. Athletes at all levels have been caught using performance-enhancing drugs. Professional athletes and their teams squabble over their shares of the profits to the dismay of fans. The lure of money has also had a corrupting influence on major college sports and encouraged student athletes to quit school and turn professional at an increasingly young age. Meanwhile, less popular sports, including many women's sports, struggle for attention and funds.

Sports in America: Recreation, Business, Education, and Controversy consists of 10 chapters and 3 appendixes. Each of the chapters examines a particular aspect of sports and American society. For a summary of the information covered in each chapter, please see the synopses provided in the Table of Contents at the front of the book. Chapters generally begin with an overview of the basic facts and background information on the chapter's topic, then proceed to examine subtopics of particular interest. For example, Chapter 3: Sports and the Media begins with an extensive history of sports on television, from the early days of television to the current omnipresence of sports on cable. This is followed by a description of the big business of sports media in several major sports. Advertising on sports broadcasts is also examined. The chapter also covers gender difference in sports viewing and explores the rise of sports video games. The final section discusses current issues related to sports and the media, including the influence of advertising on young sports fans, controversy surrounding the use of Native American mascots by sports teams, and the link between violence and professional athletes as role models. Readers can find their way through a chapter by looking for the section and subsection headings, which are clearly set off from the text. They can also refer to the book's extensive index if they already know what they are looking for.

Statistical Information

The tables and figures featured throughout *Sports in America: Recreation, Business, Education, and Controversy* will be of particular use to readers in learning about this issue. These tables and figures represent an extensive collection of the most recent and important statistics on sports and their role in American society—for example, graphics in the book cover the earnings of professional sports leagues, the percentage of people who gamble on sports, the number of Americans who participate in various sports, and spending on athletic scholarships by gender. Gale, Cengage Learning, believes that making this information available to the reader is the most important way to fulfill the goal of this book: to help readers understand the issues and controversies surrounding sports in the United States and to reach their own conclusions.

Each table or figure has a unique identifier appearing above it for ease of identification and reference. Titles for the tables and figures explain their purpose. At the end of each table or figure, the original source of the data is provided.

In order to help readers understand these often complicated statistics, all tables and figures are explained in the text. References in the text direct the reader to the relevant statistics. Furthermore, the contents of all tables and figures are fully indexed. Please see the opening section of the index at the back of this volume for a description of how to find tables and figures within it.

Appendixes

In addition to the main body text and images, *Sports in America: Recreation, Business, Education, and Controversy* has three appendixes. The first is the Important Names and Addresses directory. Here readers will find contact information for a number of government and private organizations that can provide further information on sports and related issues. The second appendix is the Resources section, which can also assist readers in conducting their own research. In this section the author and editors of *Sports in America: Recreation, Business, Education, and Controversy* describe some of the sources that were most useful during the compilation of this book. The final appendix is the detailed index, which facilitates reader access to specific topics in this book.

ADVISORY BOARD CONTRIBUTIONS

The staff of Information Plus would like to extend its heartfelt appreciation to the Information Plus Advisory Board. This dedicated group of media professionals provides feedback on the series on an ongoing basis. Their comments allow the editorial staff who work on the project to make the series better and more user-friendly. The staff's top priority is to produce the highest-quality and most useful books possible, and the Information Plus Advisory Board's contributions to this process are invaluable.

The members of the Information Plus Advisory Board are:

- Kathleen R. Bonn, Librarian, Newbury Park High School, Newbury Park, California

- Madelyn Garner, Librarian, San Jacinto College, North Campus, Houston, Texas

- Anne Oxenrider, Media Specialist, Dundee High School, Dundee, Michigan

- Charles R. Rodgers, Director of Libraries, Pasco-Hernando Community College, Dade City, Florida

- James N. Zitzelsberger, Library Media Department Chairman, Oshkosh West High School, Oshkosh, Wisconsin

COMMENTS AND SUGGESTIONS

The editors of the *Information Plus Reference Series* welcome your feedback on *Sports in America: Recreation, Business, Education, and Controversy*. Please direct all correspondence to:

Editors
Information Plus Reference Series
27500 Drake Rd.
Farmington Hills, MI 48331-3535

CHAPTER 1
AMERICA'S SPORTS OBSESSION

WHAT ARE SPORTS?

A sport is a physical activity that people engage in for recreation, usually according to a set of rules, and often in competition with each other. However, such a simple definition does not capture the passion many Americans feel for their favorite sports. Sports are the recreational activity of choice for a huge portion of the U.S. population, both as spectators and as participants in sporting competitions. When enthusiasts are not participating in sports, they are flocking to the nation's arenas and stadiums to watch their favorite athletes play or tuning in to see games and matches broadcast on television. Table 1.1 gives a sport-by-sport view of spectator interest in the United States, based on polling data from the Gallup Organization examining individuals' responses when asked which sport is their favorite to watch.

There are two broad categories of sports: professional and amateur. A professional athlete is paid to participate; an amateur athlete is one who participates without receiving compensation. The word *amateur* comes from the Latin word for "love," suggesting that an amateur athlete plays simply because he or she loves the game.

SPORTS PARTICIPATION

Sports participation is difficult to measure because there are many different levels of participation, from backyard games to organized leagues, but analysts continue to refine research methods. The most direct approach is through surveys. Each year, the National Sporting Goods Association (NSGA, http://www.nsga.org), the trade association for sporting goods retailers, conducts an extensive nationwide survey about Americans' participation in sports. Key results of the survey are shown in Table 1.2. More Americans played basketball than any other team sport in 2008. The NSGA estimates that 29.7 million people aged seven and over played basketball more than once that year. Other popular team sports included soccer

(15.5 million participants), baseball (15.2 million), softball (12.8 million), volleyball (12.2 million), and tackle football (10.5 million). Of those team sports, soccer showed the most dramatic growth in participation from 2007, increasing 12.5%. Tackle football was the only one of those sports that saw a decline in participation from 2007, dropping by 3.7%

Americans love to participate in individual sports as well. The NSGA estimates that 49.5 million Americans went bowling in 2008, making it the most popular of all competitive sports nationally. The Sporting Goods Manufacturers Association (SGMA), another industry group that carefully tracks sports participation, also identifies bowling as the most popular competitive sport, and estimates the number of participants even higher, at about 58.7 million Americans in 2008, according to its *2009 SGMA Sports & Fitness Participation Topline Report* (Sporting Goods Manufacturers Association, 2009). Billiards is also popular as a recreational sport, though its appeal has decreased in recent years. According to the NSGA, 31.7 million people shot pool more than once in the United States in 2008, a 7.4% increase from 2007 (see Table 1.2) but still 100,000 shy of the 2006 figure. Proprietors of bowling and billiards facilities are attempting to overcome a seedy reputation to draw in a new generation of enthusiasts.

The NSGA estimates that 25.6 million Americans over age seven went golfing more than once in 2008. Tennis, while less popular now than at its peak during the late 1980s, has been enjoying a comeback since 2000. In 2008 about 12.6 million people got out on U.S. tennis courts at least a couple of times, according to the NSGA.

An interesting transition is taking place in youth sports participation. Generally, participation among youth in traditional team sports has been declining for several years. One exception is soccer, which is becoming a major sport in the United States. An increasing number of young Americans are also opting for extreme sports such as snowboarding. Golf has also enjoyed an increase in participation

TABLE 1.1

Poll respondents' rating of their favorite sport to watch, December 2008

WHAT IS YOUR FAVORITE SPORT TO WATCH?

	% mentioning
Football	41
Baseball	10
Basketball	9
Ice hockey	4
Soccer	3
Auto racing	3
Golf	2
Boxing	2
Tennis	1
Ice/figure skating	1
Gymnastics	1
Volleyball	1
Other	7
None/no opinion	14

SOURCE: Jeffrey M. Jones, "What Is Your Favorite Sport to Watch?" in *Football Remains Runaway Leader As Favorite Sport*, The Gallup Organization, December 29, 2008, http://www.gallup.com/poll/113503/Football-Remains-Runaway-Leader-Favorite-Sport.aspx (accessed June 3, 2009). Copyright © 2008 by The Gallup Organization. Reproduced by permission of The Gallup Organization.

TABLE 1.2

Sports participation, by total participation, 2008

[In millions]

Sport	Total	Percent change
Exercise walking	96.6	7.6%
Swimming	63.5	6.1%
Exercising with equipment	63.0	9.2%
Bowling	49.5	5.1%
Camping (vacation/overnite)	49.4	3.8%
Bicycle riding	44.7	11.4%
Fishing	42.2	2.7%
Workout at club	39.3	6.8%
Hiking	38.0	10.5%
Weight lifting	37.5	6.6%
Aerobic exercising	36.2	4.1%
Running/jogging	35.9	18.2%
Billiards/pool	31.7	7.4%
Basketball	29.7	5.7%
Boating, motor/power	27.8	−12.7%
Golf	25.6	2.6%
Target shooting	20.3	−3.2%
Hunting with firearms	18.8	−3.6%
Yoga	16.0	17.1%
Soccer	15.5	12.5%
Baseball	15.2	8.7%
Backpack/wilderness camp	13.0	−0.1%
Softball	12.8	3.6%
Tennis	12.6	2.9%
Volleyball	12.2	1.0%
Football (tackle)	10.5	−3.7%
Canoeing	10.3	na
Mountain biking (off road)	10.2	9.6%
Scooter riding	10.1	−4.6%
Skateboarding	9.8	−3.6%
In-line roller skating	9.3	−13.1%
Paintball games	6.7	−9.9%
Skiing (alpine)	6.5	1.9%
Hunting w/bow & arrow	6.2	7.5%
Snowboarding	5.9	15.6%
Water skiing	5.6	6.3%
Target shooting—airgun	5.0	−24.8%
Muzzleloading	3.4	−6.1%
Cheerleading	2.9	na
Hockey (ice)	1.9	−7.7%
Skiing (cross country)	1.6	−5.2%

Notes: Participated more than once. Seven (7) years of age and older. Percent change is from 2007.

SOURCE: "2008 Participation—Ranked by Total Participation," in *Information Center and Research: Sports Participation*, National Sporting Goods Association, Mount Prospect, IL © 2009, http://www.nsga.org/files/public/2008RankedByTotal_4Web_080423.pdf (accessed June 9, 2009)

among youth since the mid-1990s, as has lacrosse, a modern game derived from a Native American competition that became popular among French pioneers in Canada. U.S. Lacrosse reports in the *U.S. Lacrosse Participation Survey 2008* (2009, http://www.lacrosse.org/pdf/08participationsurvey.pdf) that 524,230 people played lacrosse in 2008, compared with 253,931 in 2001, and that over the previous decade the number of people playing lacrosse nationally had increased more than 10% per year.

Another way to gauge interest in sports is by examining how much money people spend on equipment. According to the NSGA, U.S. consumers spent just under $25 billion on sporting goods in 2006. Table 1.3 shows consumer purchases of sporting goods broken down by sport.

SPORTS ATTENDANCE

Besides participation, another measure of interest in sports is the number of people who attend games in person. Sports attendance in the United States is dominated by the four major team sports: baseball, football, basketball, and hockey. In professional team sports, attendance is affected by two main factors: the size of the market in which the team plays and the team's current success. Big-city teams and winning teams typically draw bigger crowds than small-town teams and losing teams.

The economy took a toll on attendance at major league sporting events in 2008, but the drop-off was relatively small. Major League Baseball (MLB) reports in the press release "National League, Seven Clubs Set All-Time Attendance Records" (October 1, 2008, http://mlb.mlb.com/news/press _releases/press_release.jsp?ymd=20081001&content_id= 3578727&vkey=pr_mlb&fext=.jsp&c_id=mlb) that over 78.6 million people attended MLB games during the 2008 regular season, about a million shy of the all-time record set in 2007. Average attendance at a Major League game in 2008 was over 32,000, second only to the all-time high set the previous year. According to the National Basketball Association (NBA) in "Regular Season Closes with Third-Highest Attendance All Time" (April 17, 2009, http://www.nba.com/2009/playoffs2009/04/17/attendance/index.html), the league also fell just short of its attendance record, set during the 2006–07 regular season, drawing 21.5 million spectators to its arenas, for an average of 17,520 per game. Professional football also saw a slight decline in attendance

TABLE 1.3

Consumer sports equipment purchases, by sport, 2004–08

[In millions of dollars]

			Forecast		
	2008	**2007**	**2006**	**2005**	**2004**
Archery	$396.0	$402.0	$396.2	$372.1	$331.6
Baseball & softball	396.0	401.4	388.3	372.4	352.0
Basketball	254.0	265.1	295.8	309.3	309.4
Billiards and indoor games	527.0	543.3	574.0	572.3	621.9
Bowling	179.0	182.8	181.5	183.5	181.6
Camping	1,410.0	1,452.6	1,526.3	1,446.5	1,531.2
Exercise	5,439.0	5,508.4	5,238.5	5,176.6	5,074.3
Fishing tackle	2,205.0	2,247.0	2,217.7	2,138.9	2,026.0
Football	94.0	95.9	97.0	95.2	88.0
Golf	3,770.0	3,824.0	3,668.6	3,465.5	3,198.2
Helmets, sport protective	165.0	142.7	142.0	153.3	na
Hockey & ice skates	140.0	143.0	142.2	138.5	140.5
Hunting and firearms	3,921.0	3,976.6	3,731.8	3,563.4	3,174.8
Lacrosse	38.0	37.5	32.5	na	na
Optics	1,033.0	1,049.2	1,013.9	886.9	858.8
Racquetball	32.0	33.6	38.4	45.4	39.2
Skin diving & scuba	367.0	376.4	369.0	358.3	351.3
Snow skiing	518.0	531.0	501.0	642.7	na
Snowboarding	320.0	325.0	314.0	301.0	268.9
Soccer balls	77.0	76.8	74.3	66.5	64.2
Tennis	442.0	439.7	417.9	397.1	361.7
Volleyball & badminton	31.0	31.3	30.8	32.1	33.7
Water skis	50.0	53.1	47.4	42.2	46.4
Wheel sports	435.0	433.5	422.1	407.7	541.9
Athletic team goods sales	2,645.0	2,671.3	2,618.9	2,567.5	2,517.2
Total equipment	**$24,884.0**	**$25,267.4**	**$24,497.0**	**$23,734.9**	**$22,112.8**

SOURCE: "Consumer Sports Equipment Purchases by Sport," in *Information Center and Research: Consumer Purchases/Sporting Goods Market*, National Sporting Goods Association, Mount Prospect, IL © 2009, http://www.nsga.org/files/public/ConsumerSportsEquipmentPurchasesbySport.pdf (accessed June 9, 2009)

for the 2008 regular season. According to data from the National Football League (NFL), total paid attendance for the NFL was 17.5 million—down from a record 17.6 million in 2007—with an average paid attendance of 68,241 per game. The National Hockey League (NHL) has rebounded since its 2004–05 season was canceled due to a labor dispute. The NHL reports in "NHL Says U.S. Hockey Interest Is Growing, With Attendance, TV Ratings Up" (April 30, 2009, http://www.nhl.com/ice/news.htm?id=420842) that attendance in 2008–09 was 21.4 million—an all-time high—for an average of 17,460 per game, also a new league record.

The other big sports draw in the United States is auto racing. The National Association for Stock Car Auto Racing (NASCAR), the nation's major stock car racing circuit, experienced substantial growth in attendance during the early years of the 21st century, but both attendance and television ratings for NASCAR races began to tail off around 2006. That decline accelerated as the economy faltered after 2007. Chapter 2 presents a more detailed discussion of major sports attendance in the United States.

PROFESSIONAL SPORTS

Team Sports

Throughout most of the 20th century, professional team sports in the United States meant baseball, football, basketball, and hockey. However, since the 1990s soccer has been gaining popularity and is often included in discussions of professional sports in the United States. Detailed information on professional team sports is provided in Chapter 4.

MLB has long been considered "America's national pastime." According to its Web site (2009, http://mlb.mlb.com/index.jsp), MLB consists of 30 teams, divided into the 16-team National League and the 14-team American League. Each league is in turn divided into three divisions. The MLB season consists of 162 games, running from early April through late September, followed by playoffs and finally the championship games known as the World Series. According to Plunkett Research in "Sports Industry Overview" (2009, http://www.plunkettresearch.com/Industries/Sports/SportsStatistics/tabid/273/Default.aspx), MLB was a $6.2 billion industry in 2009.

The premier professional football league in the United States is the NFL. Plunkett Research estimates in its "Sports Industry Overview" that the NFL generated league-wide revenue of $6 billion in 2009. There are 32 teams in the NFL (2009, http://www.nfl.com/), divided into two conferences: the National Football Conference (NFC) and the American Football Conference (AFC). The NFC and AFC are each divided into four divisions. NFL teams play a 16-game season, which begins around Labor Day in September. It ends with a single-elimination playoff series, culminating in the Super Bowl in February. The Super Bowl is the biggest sporting event in the country in terms of viewing audience. The Associated Press reported that according to data from Nielsen Media Research (2009, http://www.nfl.com/superbowl/story?id=09000d5d80e89a4f&template=without-video-with-comments&confirm=true), 98.7 million viewers on average were tuned in to the 2009 Super Bowl, making it the most-watched Super Bowl in history.

The NBA (2009, http://www.nba.com/), the top professional basketball league in the country, consists of 30 teams split into the Eastern and Western Conferences. Each conference has three divisions within it. The NBA season, which lasts for 82 regular-season games, begins in early November. The regular season is followed by the NBA playoffs, which begin in April. In "Sports Industry Overview," Plunkett Research notes that the NBA generated $3.2 billion in revenue during the 2008–09 season, placing it behind both football and baseball. Unlike football and baseball, however, basketball has a women's professional league, the Women's National Basketball Association (WNBA). There are 13 teams in the WNBA. They play a 34-game regular season, after which the top four teams in each conference compete in the championship playoffs.

Unlike any of the major men's professional sports, the WNBA typically loses money; the highly profitable men's league subsidizes operation of the WNBA. However, in March 2009 NBA Commissioner David Stern told Steve Ginsburg of Reuters that in the current bad economy, "The NBA is far less profitable than the WNBA" (http://www.reuters.com/article/sportsNews/idUSTRE52B07020090312?pageNumber=2&virtualBrandChannel=0). He explained, "We're losing a lot of money amongst a large number of teams. We're budgeting the WNBA to break even this year."

The top professional hockey league in North America is the NHL, which actually encompasses two countries, the United States and Canada, and is arguably more popular in the latter. The NHL (2009, http://www.nhl.com/) consists of 30 teams, divided into Eastern and Western Conferences. These conferences are in turn broken into three divisions each. The NHL season, like that of the NBA, is 82 games long. It is followed by the Stanley Cup playoffs, which ultimately determine the NHL champion. Even before the entire 2004–05 season was canceled due to a labor strike, the league's popularity was in decline. In the handful of seasons since the strike, however, interest in the NHL has rebounded considerably. According to Plunkett Research in "Sports Industry Overview," league-wide revenue was about $2.4 billion during the 2008–09 season, considerably less than any of the other major men's professional sports teams.

Even though only hockey has experienced a labor dispute that resulted in cancellation of an entire season, each of these sports is occasionally subject to disputes that threaten their continuity and that sometimes result in cancellation of part of a season. Labor disagreements in professional sports often pit the league, which represents the interests of the team owners, against the players, who are represented by a labor union.

Individual Sports

Team sports get most of the media attention in the United States, but professional sports that feature individual competitors are also of considerable interest.

The premier golf tour in the United States and in the world is the PGA Tour (2009, http://www.pgatour.com), which in 2009 consisted of 57 events offering more than $307 million in total prize money. The PGA Tour organization also runs a developmental tour called the Nationwide Tour and a tour for senior players called the Champions Tour. There are several other prominent regional professional golf tours based in other countries. Women's professional golf has a similar structure. The most prominent women's tour is the LPGA Tour, which is operated by the Ladies Professional Golf Association, and there are several other regional women's tours around the world.

Men's professional tennis is coordinated primarily by two organizations: the Association of Tennis Professionals (ATP), which operates the worldwide ATP Tour; and the International Tennis Federation, which coordinates the four international events that make up the Grand Slam of tennis (the Australian Open, the French Open, the Wimbledon Championships, and the U.S. Open). The highest level of play is called the ATP World Tour, which is in turn broken down into three tiers: ATP World Tour Masters 1000, ATP World Tour 500, and ATP World Tour 250. Together, the 2009 ATP World Tour (2009, http://www.atpworldtour.com) included 61 tournaments all over the world. Women's professional tennis is organized by the Women's Tennis Association, which runs the premier women's tour. Since 2005 Sony Ericsson has been the tour sponsor, with an $88 million agreement that extends for six years. According to the tour's official Web site (2009, http://www.sonyericssonwtatour.com/1/), the 2009 Sony Ericsson WTA Tour included 55 events in 31 countries, in which 2,200 players representing 96 nations competed for more than $86 million in total prize money.

Auto racing enjoyed a huge surge in popularity in the United States beginning in the mid-1990s. The most important racing circuit for stock cars—which resemble ordinary cars externally—is NASCAR. NASCAR (2009, http://www.nascar.com) sanctions more than 1,200 races per year at more than 100 tracks in 30 states, plus Canada and Mexico.

The other major type of race car is the open-wheeled racer. The main open-wheeled racing circuit in the United States is the Indy Racing League (IndyCar). The 2009 IndyCar Series (2009, http://www.indycar.com) featured 17 races between April and October, most in the United States with one in Japan. A second prominent open-wheeled race series, the Champ Car Series, was merged into the Indy Racing League in 2008.

Boxing is unique among professional sports in that it has no single commission that regulates or monitors it nationwide. A number of organizations sanction professional boxing matches, including the World Boxing Association (http://www.wbaonline.com/), the World Boxing Council (http://www.wbcboxing.com/), the World Boxing Organization (http://www.wbo-int.com/), and the International Boxing Federation (http://www.ibf-usba-boxing.com/). Each follows its own set of regulations, employs its own officials, and acknowledges its own champions. A fighter can be recognized as a champion by more than one organization simultaneously. Professional boxing in the United States has been plagued by corruption over the years, including tainted judging and fixed fights. Nevertheless, devoted fans tune in regularly to watch boxing on pay cable networks, and gamblers wager millions on the outcomes of boxing contests, injecting huge sums of money into the industry.

SPORTS AND THE MEDIA

For American sports enthusiasts, it is hard to separate the sports from the media industry that surrounds all aspects of professional and elite amateur sports. Leagues, teams, promoters, organizations, and schools make money through lucrative media contracts that give television networks the rights to broadcast sporting events over the public airwaves. For a full discussion of the intersection of sports and media, see Chapter 3.

The History of Sports on Television

The history of sports on television began with the 1939 broadcast of a college baseball game between Columbia and Princeton universities. Five years later the *Gillette Cavalcade of Sports* televised by the National Broadcasting Company (NBC) became the first network-wide television sports show. When single-company sponsorship became too expensive during the mid-1960s, sports programming developed a new model in which different companies bought advertising spots throughout the program.

The amount of sports programming and the amount of money in televised sports has continued to grow quickly since then. In "Sports and Television" (undated, http://www.museum.tv/archives/etv/S/htmlS/sportsandte/sportsandte.htm), Stanley J. Baran states that in 1970 the networks paid $50 million for the rights to broadcast NFL games, $18 million for MLB games, and $2 million for NBA games. By 1985 these totals had grown to $450 million, $160 million, and $45 million, respectively. During the 1980s the addition of cable television outlets extended the reach of televised sports even farther. However, television ratings for the four major team sports generally declined during the 1990s as competition for the same audience arose from other viewing options.

Major Sports on Television

During the 1950s baseball was the most popular televised sport. Since then, however, it has lost a large share of its audience to other sports, particularly football. Even though television ratings for World Series broadcasts declined for several years, they rebounded after 2002, but sank again after peaking in 2004. Television ratings for the 2008 World Series were the lowest ever for the fall classic, scoring an average rating of 8.4 (meaning 8.4% of all households were tuned in), well below the previous low of 10.1 set in 2006, according to Reuters reports of data from Nielsen Sports Marketing. MLB currently has television broadcast contracts lasting until 2013 with Fox, ESPN, and TBS.

Well before the close of the 20th century, football had supplanted baseball as the reigning king of televised sports. In *2001 ESPN Information Please Sports Almanac* (2000), Gerry Brown and Michael Morrison state that, as of the turn of the 21st century, five of the ten top-rated television shows of all time had been sports programs, and four of those were Super Bowls. Several more Super Bowl broad-

TABLE 1.4

Latest NFL TV contracts, by network or satellite provider

ESPN

Monday night
- 8 years, 2006–13
- $1.1 billion per year
- No Super Bowls

NBC

Sunday night
- 6 years, 2006–11
- $600 million per year
- Super Bowls in 2009 and 2012

Fox

Sunday afternoon NFC
- Originally 2006–11, extended through 2013
- $712.5 million per year
- Super Bowls in 2008, 2011 and 2014

CBS

Sunday afternoon AFC
- Originally 2006–11, extended through 2013
- $622.5 million per year
- Super Bowls in 2010 and 2013

DirecTV satellite

Sunday ticket
- 5 years, 2006–10
- $700 million per year
- No Super Bowls

SOURCE: Created by Robert Jacobson for Gale, 2009

casts were in the top 20. With 98.7 million viewers, Super Bowl XLIII in February 2009 was the most watched Super Bowl in history, and the second most watched television show of any kind ever, trailing only the 1983 series finale of *M*A*S*H*. The NFL signed a new round of television deals in April 2005, the most lucrative being a $1.1 billion contract resulting in the move of *Monday Night Football* from American Broadcasting Company (ABC) to ESPN beginning in 2006. (See Table 1.4.) The NFL received hundreds of millions of additional dollars from Fox, CBS, NBC, and DirecTV for various subsets of the NFL schedule.

Regular-season NBA basketball has never drawn as big a viewing audience as the NFL has—probably because there are so many more games—but viewership expands significantly during the playoffs. Of the major sports, the NHL has struggled the most to maintain its television audience. Even at its peak, hockey drew far fewer viewers than the other major sports, and the cancellation of the 2004–05 season hurt the NHL further. At the other extreme, NASCAR enjoyed a surge in its television audience around the turn of the 21st century, including an increased female audience and broader viewership in the Pacific Northwest and other regions of the country that had not traditionally favored auto racing.

AMATEUR SPORTS
College Sports

Most college sports take place under the auspices of the National Collegiate Athletic Association (NCAA). The NCAA describes itself on its Web site (2009, http://

www.ncaa.org/wps/ncaa?key=/ncaa/NCAA/About+The+NCAA/) as "a voluntary organization through which the nation's colleges and universities govern their athletics programs. It is comprised of institutions, conferences, organizations and individuals committed to the best interests, education and athletics participation of student-athletes." In *Composition & Sport Sponsorship of the NCAA* (2009, http://www.ncaa.org/wps/ncaa?key=/ncaa/NCAA/About+The+NCAA/Membership/Our+Members/), the NCAA counts a membership of 1,288 colleges, college athletic conferences, and other organizations and individuals. The NCAA is divided into Divisions I, II, and III based on size, athletic budget, and related variables. Division I is further divided into three subdivisions: Division I Football Bowl Subdivision (FBS, formerly Division I-A), Division I Football Championship Subdivision (Formerly Division I-AA), and the remaining Division I institutions that do not sponsor a football team (sometimes referred to informally as Division I-AAA). Within the NCAA many major sports colleges are grouped into conferences, which function like the divisions and leagues in professional sports.

According to the NCAA's annual *Sports Sponsorship and Participation Rates Report* (April 2009, http://www.ncaapublications.com/ProductsDetailView.aspx?sku=PR2009), more than 412,000 student-athletes participated in championship sports at NCAA member schools during the 2007–08 school year. The average NCAA institution had about 400 athletes—232 men and 168 women. However, women's teams actually outnumbered men's teams. Among men, the sport with the greatest number of teams in 2007–08 was basketball. However, in terms of number of players, football was the leader. Among women, soccer and outdoor track and field had the most participants in 2007–08, but more colleges had women's basketball teams than had either women's soccer or track and field teams.

For most of the 20th century, men's college teams and athletes far outnumbered women's teams and athletes, and far more money went into men's sports. However, the gap has been closing, largely because of the passage in 1972 of Title IX, a law mandating gender equity in federally funded education programs. Under Title IX, girls' sports were to be funded at the same rate as sports programs for boys. Since Title IX's mandatory compliance date of 1978, women's collegiate sports have experienced explosive growth.

Much to the discomfort of some in the academic world, college sports have become big business in the United States. Spending on sports programs has been rising at a faster rate than overall institutional spending across the NCAA. Even though college sports generate substantial revenue, this revenue does not cover the cost of running the entire athletic program at the vast majority of schools, largely because only a few sports—often only football and men's basketball programs—are actually profitable. The NCAA notes in *2004–06 NCAA Revenues and Expenses of Divisions I Intercollegiate Athletics Programs Report* (March 2008, http://www.ncaapublications.com/ProductsDetailView.aspx?sku=RE2008) that Division I-FBS athletic programs had median total revenues of $35.4 million and expenses of $35.8 million in 2006. Football and basketball accounted for a huge share of both revenues and expenses. A December 2007 report in *USA Today*, "The Money Game: College Football Coaches Calling Lucrative Plays," by Steve Wieberg and Jodi Upton, explored the escalation of university coaches' salaries, finding that at many major institutions the head football coach is paid several times as much as the university president. For example, Gary Klein reported in the *Los Angeles Times* (February 23, 2009) that University of Southern California football coach Pete Carroll (1951–) was paid $4.4 million during the 2006–07 school year, about four times the salary paid to university president Steven B. Sample (1940–).

High School Sports

The National Federation of State High School Associations (NFHS) conducts a detailed survey of high school sports participation each year. NFHS (2009, http://www.nfhs.org/content.aspx?id=3505&terms=participation+survey) data show that 7.5 million students participated in high school sports during the 2008–09 school year. This total was a record high. Participation among boys was 4.4 million, and 3.1 million girls participated. Based on these figures, the NFHS estimates that 55.2% of students who were enrolled in high school in the United States during the 2008–09 school year participated in a school-sponsored sport. The top states by student-athlete participation during the 2008–09 school year, according to the NFHS, were Texas (781,000), California (771,465), New York (380,870), Illinois (341,763), and Ohio (330,056).

For years, football has been the most popular high school sport for boys. According to the 2008–09 *NFHS High School Athletics Participation Survey*, 1.1 million boys played high school football during the 2008 season. Outdoor track and field was the second most popular sport for high school boys, with 558,007 participants, and basketball was third, with 545,145 participants. Among girls, outdoor track and field was the most popular sport, with 447,520 participants, followed by basketball (444,809) and volleyball (404,243).

BENEFITS TO STUDENT ATHLETES. Sociologist Beckett Broh of Wittenberg University noted several benefits of sports participation among high school students in an interview by Jeffrey Thomas on the U.S. State Department Web site America.gov (April 17, 2008, http://www.america.gov/st/educ-english/2008/April/20080417115316lCJsamohT0.6185572.html). According to Broh, student-athletes perform well academically but also "benefit developmentally in terms of building self-confidence and self-esteem and the ability to problem-solve; they develop socially in that they build relationships with students and teachers and parents that can act as resources for them in terms of their academics." Broh's research indicated further advantages for girls. Female athletes were found to be less likely to get pregnant outside of marriage, more likely to graduate from college, and more likely to achieve a higher income in their professional life than girls who did not participate in school athletics.

PROFESSIONALIZATION OF HIGH SCHOOL SPORTS. Such research shows that for the vast majority of student athletes, the experience provides positive outcomes. However, there is also evidence that the corrupting influence of money in big-time sports is beginning to trickle down to the high school level, including a series of reports in the *New York Times* in late 2005 of athletes buying diplomas and passing grades from bogus correspondence schools. The NCAA took measures in 2006 to crack down on these so-called diploma mills. That has not, however, stopped the spread of other questionable practices, such as specialty high schools established solely to field basketball teams composed of top players skimmed from all over the country, as detailed by Ron Jackson in the *Dayton Daily News* (May 20, 2009, http://www.daytondailynews.com/dayton-sports/high-school-sports/high-school-basketball-not-what-it-used-to-be-126354.html). Critics of such programs decry the introduction of the trappings of professional sports into high school athletics, including an extensive travel schedule, unconventional academic program, and, in the case of national champions Findlay Prep (http://www.findlayprep .com/), living together in a five-bedroom home in suburban Las Vegas. However, proponents note that since the athletes who comprise the team are likely headed to college and then to professional sports careers, the independence and travel associated with an elite academy team will better prepare them for their future success.

IMPACT OF ECONOMIC RECESSION ON HIGH SCHOOL SPORTS. The economic recession that began in late 2007 has presented serious problems for many high school sports programs. Sarah Larimer, in "Recession's Impact: High School Sports Face Cuts" (June 15, 2009, http://nbcsports.msnbc .com/id/31330906/ns/sports-msnbc_wire_services/), outlined numerous examples of financially strapped school districts across the country cutting back on the number of sports, shortening seasons, eliminating coaches' stipends, and raising student participation fees.

Officials in New York decided to trim back sports schedules in an effort to avoid cutting sports altogether. Michael Hill of the Associated Press reported in February 2009 that high school baseball seasons throughout the state would be cut from 24 games to 20, and football seasons would move from 10 games to 8 or 9 depending on the region (http://www.foxnews.com/wires/2009Feb10/0,4670, MeltdownSchoolSports,00.html). While the cuts to individual programs seemed small, the New York state athletic association estimated that at least $3 million in compensation

to referees and officials would be saved, and when transportation costs and other associated fees are included, the total cost savings to school districts statewide could reach nearly $10 million per year.

The Olympics

The concept behind the Olympic movement is to bring the world together through sports in the spirit of common understanding and noble competition. The Olympic Games are based on an athletic festival that took place in ancient Greece from about 776 BC until AD 393. The Olympics were revived in their modern form in 1896. The Summer Olympics take place every four years, the same years in which February has 29 days. According to the official Web site of the 2008 summer games in Beijing, China, (http:// en.beijing2008.cn/live/pressconference/mpc/n214494667 .shtml), 11,028 athletes from 204 countries competed in those games, and medals were awarded in 28 sports that encompassed 302 events. Sports included in the 2012 summer games in London, England, will be the same as in 2008 with the exception of baseball and softball, which have been dropped from the competition schedule. Summer Olympic sports are listed in Table 1.5.

The Winter Olympics also take place every four years, halfway between the summer games. The winter games are smaller than the summer games. The International Olympic Committee (IOC) (2009, http://www.olympic.org/uk/games/ past/index_uk.asp?OLGT=2&OLGY=2006) notes that the

TABLE 1.5

Olympic sports

Summer games	Winter games
Aquatics	Alpine skiing
Archery	Biathlon
Athletics	Bobsleigh
Badminton	Cross-country skiing
Basketball	Curling
Boxing	Figure skating
Canoe/kayak	Freestyle skiing
Cycling	Ice hockey
Equestrian	Ice sledge hockey
Fencing	Luge
Football	Nordic combined
Gymnastics	Short track speed skating
Handball	Skeleton
Hockey	Ski jumping
Judo	Snowboard
Modern pentathlon	Speed skating
Rowing	
Sailing	
Shooting	
Table tennis	
Taekwondo	
Tennis	
Triathlon	
Volleyball	
Weightlifting	
Wrestling	

SOURCE: Adapted from "Sports on the Olympic Programme," in *Sports*, International Olympic Committee, 2009, http://www.olympic.org/uk/sports/ index_uk.asp (accessed July 23, 2009)

2006 Winter Olympics in Turin, Italy, featured 2,508 athletes from 80 countries, competing in 84 events. Table 1.5 also lists winter Olympic sports included in the 2010 winter games in Vancouver, British Columbia, Canada.

The founder of the modern Olympics was the French historian and educator Pierre de Coubertin (1862–1937). Coubertin believed that war could be averted if nations participated together in friendly athletic competition. His ideas have not proved true, but the Olympic movement has thrived anyway. The inaugural Olympic Games of the modern era took place in 1896 in Athens, Greece, where 241 athletes from 14 countries competed in what was the largest international sporting event in history at the time.

The winter games arose initially as an outgrowth of the summer games. A handful of winter sports were included in early versions of the Olympics. The Winter Olympics finally became its own event in 1924. Until 1992 the winter games took place the same year as the summer games; beginning in 1994 they have been held in the years halfway between the Summer Olympics.

Politics have frequently disrupted, or even canceled, the Olympics. The 1916 games were canceled because of World War I (1914–1918), and World War II (1939–1945) caused the cancellation of the 1940 and 1944 Olympics. Boycotts have also diminished the scope of the games. In 1972 the militant Palestinian group Black September abducted and murdered 11 members of the Israeli Olympic team during the summer games in Munich, West Germany. The U.S. team, along with 64 other Western nations, boycotted the 1980 Olympics in Moscow in protest of the Soviet invasion of Afghanistan. In 1984 the Soviet Union and 14 of its allies boycotted the Olympics in Los Angeles, ostensibly because of security concerns but more realistically as a response to the Moscow boycott. Scandals related to doping—such as the BALCO affair described in detail in Chapter 9—and bribery—including the implication of the organizing committee for the 2002 winter games in Salt Lake City—have also marred the idealistic image of international cooperation and amateur athleticism on which the Olympics were founded.

The International Olympic Committee (IOC) is the worldwide governing body for the Olympics. Each participating country has its own national Olympic committee (NOC), whose role is to support that nation's Olympic team and to coordinate bids by cities within their country to host the Olympics. The U.S. Olympic Committee, headquartered in Colorado Springs, Colorado, is the NOC in the United States.

Individual sports are governed worldwide by International Federations, which make the rules for the events within their portfolio. On the national level, there are corresponding organizations called national governing bodies (NGBs). Some of the NGBs in the United States include USA Gymnastics, USA Swimming, and USA Track and Field. These organizations are in charge of choosing which athletes will represent the United States in that sport. In the host country the Olympic Games are planned by an Organizing Committee for the Olympic Games, which takes care of the logistical preparations for the Olympics.

The Olympics generates billions of dollars through a handful of marketing programs. The biggest source of money is television broadcast revenue. Other sources include corporate sponsorships, ticket sales, and sales of licensed merchandise. Chapter 7 contains detailed information about Olympic revenue. It also includes descriptions of other Olympic-style meets, such as the Special Olympics, Paralympics, and Deaflympics.

SPORTS AND HEALTH

Participation in sports yields great health benefits. Many health benefits of physical activity have been well documented. Physical activity builds and maintains bones and muscles, reduces fat, reduces blood pressure, and decreases the risk of obesity and heart attacks. There is also substantial evidence that physical activity improves mental health and may help fend off depression. A number of studies, including a massive 2001 survey conducted by researchers at the University of Florida (http://news.ufl.edu/2001/03/07/body-image/), link sports participation with a better self-image and a healthier attitude toward one's own body. A number of studies over the years have shown that sports participation by youth reduces the likelihood of engaging in risky behavior. A January 2008 article in *Medicine and Science in Sports and Exercise* (http://www.medscape.com/viewarticle/568124) asserted that participation in sports and other vigorous physical activity may reduce suicidal thoughts and attempts in young people. The Women's Sports Foundation, in its comprehensive 2008 study "Go Out and Play: Youth Sports in America," (http://www.womenssportsfoundation.org/Content/Research-Reports/Go-Out-and-Play.aspx) extended the benefits of youth sports participation to whole families, suggesting that children's participation in sports improved family communication and trust, in addition to the commonly cited individual benefits related to physical health and self-esteem.

These benefits do not come without risk, however. Every year, millions of people injure themselves participating in sports. The most common sports injuries are muscle sprains and strains, ligament and tendon tears, dislocated joints, and bone fractures. The University of Chicago Medical Center indicates in "Sports Injuries" (2009, http://www.uchospitals.edu/online-library/content=P00725) that soft tissue injuries, such as bruises, sprains, and tendonitis, account for about 95% of all sports injuries. Injuries that happen suddenly during an activity, such as those resulting from a fall, are called acute injuries, whereas injuries that occur through repeated overuse are called chronic injuries.

According to the National Center for Health Statistics' *Monthly Statistical E-Letter* (March 2007, http://www.cdc.gov/nchs/pressroom/data/mnh_0307.htm), there were about 5.4 million sports injuries in the United States serious enough to require medical consultation in 2005. Bjorn Carey notes in "The Most Dangerous Sports in America" (Livescience.com, June 14, 2006) that in 2005 basketball, cycling, and football were the sports responsible for the greatest number of sports injuries requiring a trip to the emergency room.

Sports participation brings special hazards for children and youth. Children who are placed under severe pressure to succeed by parents, coaches, and other adults are at risk of psychological damage. The stress of ultracompetitive sports participation leads to high rates of burnout among young athletes. Pressure to perform also puts children and youth at elevated risk of physical injury, as demands are put on young bodies not yet developed enough to withstand the strain. According to the June 2009 report "Sports Injuries in Children Requiring Hospital Emergency Care, 2006" by the federal Agency for Healthcare Research and Quality (http://www.hcup-us.ahrq.gov/reports/statbriefs/sb75.pdf), sports injuries were responsible for one out of five emergency room visits for children ages 5 to 17. For young people age 15 to 24, sports were the most common activity leading to injury, according to *Injury in the United States: 2007 Chartbook* (http://www.cdc.gov/nchs/data/misc/injury2007.pdf), published by the National Center for Health Statistics in 2008. Chapter 8 in this volume explores both the health benefits and health risks of athletic participation.

Doping

The use of prohibited substances to give an athlete an unfair advantage over other competitors is called doping. Doping has been around almost as long as sports have. Historical writings suggest that athletes were using concoctions made of herbs or psychoactive mushrooms to give themselves a competitive edge as early as the ancient Olympics.

The modern era of doping began in 1935, when injectable testosterone was first developed by scientists in Nazi Germany. Testosterone is a male hormone that occurs naturally in the body. Boosting its levels in the blood is thought to increase strength and aggressiveness.

Several decades later, anabolic steroids—chemical variants of testosterone—were developed. John Ziegler (1917–2000), the team physician for the U.S. weightlifting squad, learned about steroids from his Soviet counterparts, and soon steroids were in wide use in the United States. By the late 1960s the IOC had compiled a list of officially banned substances, but it had no effective way to monitor steroid use.

Steroids soon spread to professional football and other sports requiring extreme strength and bulk. Professional and Olympic sports eventually developed into a kind of cat-and-mouse game between developers of performance-enhancing drugs and the governing bodies of sports that prohibited their use. The latter would invent a way to detect the latest drugs, only to discover that the former had invented a new method for avoiding detection. The issue of doping in elite athletics still remains.

One of the biggest doping scandals to date, the BALCO scandal, has been unfolding since 2003. BALCO, the Bay Area Laboratory Co-Operative, was a California-based drug distributor. The scandal erupted in the summer of 2003, when Trevor Graham (1964–), a disgruntled track coach, provided authorities with a syringe containing a previously unknown steroid called THG. Authorities raided BALCO facilities and uncovered not only large amounts of steroids but also documents implicating a number of high-profile athletes and trainers in football, baseball, and track and field. The scandal continued to follow baseball superstar Barry Bonds (1964–) during the 2007 season as he approached the all-time home-run record long held by Hank Aaron (1934–). Fan reaction to the prospect of Bonds holding the record was decidedly mixed, as suspicion lingered that Bonds had made his way toward this landmark with the aid of illicit substances.

Professional cycling has also been hit hard by steroid scandals. Floyd Landis (1975–), a 2006 Tour de France champion, tested positive for steroids, raising questions about the legitimacy of his victory. Then, just when the Tour needed to display its cleanliness the most, several more top Tour contenders failed drug tests in 2007, throwing the sport into chaos. In September 2007 Landis was stripped of his 2006 Tour title.

Even in the post-BALCO era, baseball continued to reel from revelations of steroid use among top players. Alex Rodriguez (1975–) of the New York Yankees admitted in 2009 to having used steroids in 2003 after reports of positive drug tests surfaced. In addition, Los Angeles Dodgers superstar Manny Ramirez (1972–) served a 50-game suspension in 2009 after officials determined that he had used steroids from 2001 to 2003.

Steroid use has been linked to many potentially serious health problems, including liver and kidney tumors, high blood pressure, elevated cholesterol, severe acne, and in men, shrunken testicles. Steroid use is also associated with emotional disturbances, including violent mood swings commonly known as "'roid rage." In 2007, when pro wrestler Chris Benoit killed his wife and son before committing suicide, a toxicology report revealed that he had 10 times the normal amount of testosterone in his system. Speculation ran rampant that 'roid rage was to blame. However, the medical examiner determined that there was no indication that steroids played a role.

Besides steroids, athletes turned to a number of other substances to gain an advantage before each was banned from sports. These include erythropoietin, a hormone that increases oxygen in the blood, which was at the center of a 1998 doping scandal in cycling; androstenedione, which stimulates testosterone production and was made famous by the home-run leader Mark McGwire (1963–); and ephedra, an herbal stimulant that has been used in Chinese medicine for centuries.

Steroid use in youth sports has tapered off, after a period of explosive growth during the late 1990s and early 2000s. (See Figure 1.1.) Approximately 1.5% of 12th graders in 2008 reported having used steroids in the previous year, according to the National Institute on Drug Abuse reports in "NIDA InfoFacts: Steroids (Anabolic-Androgenic)" (July 2009, http://www.drugabuse.gov/Infofacts/Steroids.html). The number of high school seniors who perceived steroids as being harmful increased from 55% in 2003 to 61% in 2008, according to data from the National Institute on Drug Abuse, as reported in *Monitoring the Future* (http://www.monitoringthefuture.org/pubs/monographs/overview2008.pdf).

FIGURE 1.1

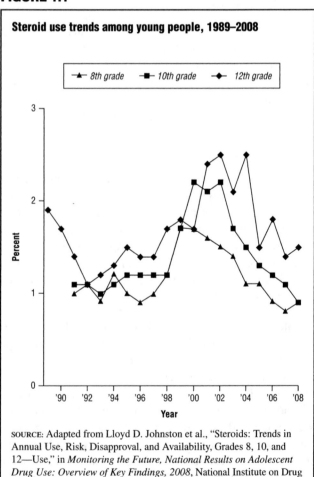

Steroid use trends among young people, 1989–2008

SOURCE: Adapted from Lloyd D. Johnston et al., "Steroids: Trends in Annual Use, Risk, Disapproval, and Availability, Grades 8, 10, and 12—Use," in *Monitoring the Future, National Results on Adolescent Drug Use: Overview of Key Findings, 2008*, National Institute on Drug Abuse, May 2009, http://www.monitoringthefuture.org/pubs/monographs/overview2008.pdf (accessed June 9, 2009)

Chapter 9 includes more detailed information on the variety of anabolic steroids and other performance-enhancing substances that have been used over the years.

SPORTS AND GAMBLING

For millions of sports fans, the pleasure of watching a sporting event is enhanced by betting on its outcome. Even though gambling on sports (not including horse- and greyhound racing) is technically legal only in Nevada, Americans nevertheless find ways to engage in sports wagering in huge numbers, whether through small-scale office pools or via offshore Internet gambling sites of questionable legality.

Legal Sports Betting

In Nevada legal sports betting is practiced through legitimate bookmaking operations, which are often affiliated with and located in a casino. Bookmakers set the line (margin) of victory required to win the bet for each game. Football is the biggest betting draw among the major team sports. The Nevada Gaming Control Board (February 3, 2009, http://www.gaming.nv.gov/documents/pdf/pr_09superbowl.pdf) reports that more than $81.5 million was bet legally on the Super Bowl alone in 2009, a significant decrease from the $92 million wagered the previous year, and well below the record $94.5 million wagered in 2006.

Although most sports gambling remains illegal, polls show that many Americans are perfectly comfortable with sports gambling, even though a relatively small percentage actually participate. According to the Pew Research Center, in *Gambling: As the Take Rises, So Does Public Concern* (May 23, 2006, http://pewresearch.org/assets/social/pdf/Gambling.pdf), in 2006, 42% of respondents approved of legalized gambling on professional sports. However, Gallup's December 2007 Lifestyle poll found that only 14% had actually bet on professional sports in the previous year (February 1, 2008, http://www.gallup.com/poll/104086/onesix-americans-gamble-sports.aspx).

Gambling on horse racing, dog racing, and jai alai (a handball-like sport popular in Florida) uses what is called the pari-mutuel system. In this type of betting, all the wagers go into a single pool, which is then split among the winners, with management taking a small share off the top. In the fact sheet "Gaming Revenue: Current-Year Data" (January 2009, http://www.americangaming.org/Industry/factsheets/statistics_detail.cfv?id=7), the American Gaming Association (AGA) estimates that total revenue from pari-mutuel gambling in the United States was nearly $3.5 billion in 2007. At the prestigious Kentucky Derby in May 2009, winner Mine That Bird reaped one of the best payouts in the history of the annual race. As reported by Billy Reed of the *San Francisco Chronicle* (May 3, 2009, http://www.sfgate.com/cgi-bin/article.cgi?f=/c/a/2009/05/03/SPNM17DLAE.DTL&feed=rss.sports), the gelding came in first place having been given odds of 50 to 1. A $2.00 bet on Mine That Bird paid $103.20 to win, $54.00 to place (second place), and $25.80 to show (third place).

Illegal Sports Betting

In spite of these impressive dollar amounts for both Nevada sports books and pari-mutuel gambling, these sums represent just the tip of the sports betting iceberg. Legal gambling in the United States is utterly dwarfed by illegal gambling. The AGA estimates in the fact sheet "Sports Wagering" (February 4, 2009, http://www.americangaming .org/Industry/factsheets/issues_detail.cfv?id=16) that Nevada sports books account for less than 1% of all sports gambling nationwide in a typical year. It is almost impossible to gauge how much money is bet on sports when illegal bets are included. The AGA fact sheet notes that the National Gambling Impact Study has estimated that illegal sports betting in the United States could total as much as $380 billion per year.

The newest frontier for sports gambling is the Internet. Christiansen Capital Advisors, a gaming and entertainment consulting firm that publishes *Insight: The Journal of the North American Gambling Industry*, estimates that American adults bet $5.8 billion online in 2007 (January 2009, http:// www.cca-i.com/insight/V6i10.htm), while noting that it has become much more difficult to make this estimate since passage of the Unlawful Internet Gambling Enforcement Act of 2006 (UIGEA). UIGEA made it difficult for financial institutions to transfer funds to and from online gambling operations. However, there is still a fair amount of disagreement as to the legal status of online gambling—partly because most operations are not based in the United States—and while the full impact of UIGEA remains to be seen, it has clearly resulted in a reduction in sports wagering taking place over the Internet.

CHAPTER 2

SPORTS PARTICIPATION
AND ATTENDANCE

For when the One Great Scorer comes

to write against your name,

He marks—not that you won or lost—

But how you played the game.

—American sportswriter Grantland Rice (1880–1954)

People have been playing games in one form or another ever since the first time a pair of humans decided to start grappling for fun rather than over food. The number and variety of sports in which people have participated through the ages is impossible to calculate. In North America, Native Americans were playing lacrosse and many other organized sports before Europeans settled permanently on the continent. In addition, one need only think of gladiators doing battle at the Colosseum in ancient Rome to realize that people have been gathering to watch other people play sports for centuries as well. The following is a summary of sports participation and sports attendance in the United States, drawing information from government and industry publications.

SPORTS PARTICIPATION

There is no shortage of data available on sports participation in the United States. Participation is measured by market research firms, coordinating bodies of individual sports, and government agencies, among others. Sports participation is nevertheless a difficult thing to measure, and nobody has yet figured out how to measure it with complete accuracy. People who go for a casual walk or swim at the beach may not think of themselves as engaging in a sport, but those interested in selling walking shoes or studying the health benefits of physical activity might disagree. Then there is the matter of defining the word *participation*—does it mean a person plays the sport once per year, once per month, or only those who play almost every day? Besides determining who qualifies as a sports participant, the

reliability of self-reported data presents additional problems. For example, can an individual accurately report that he played touch football with his friends 12 months ago rather than 15 months ago? Distortion is inevitable, especially with regard to recreational activities that participants tend to engage in less frequently, such as scuba diving. There is also a tendency when responding to this kind of survey to want to receive credit for having participated in a sport, especially a glamorous one such as rock climbing, even if the respondent has not undertaken the activity in several years. Another way to assess participation is through sales of sports equipment. However, this approach also has its perils. As Harvey Lauer, the president of American Sports Data (ASD), observes in "Sports Participation Research: Not Yet a Science" (2006, http://www.americansportsdata.com/pr-participantsportmeth odology.asp), "80% of all athletic/sports shoes are never sweated in."

Sporting Goods Manufacturers Association Survey

Each year, the Sporting Goods Manufacturers Association (SGMA) publishes reports on various aspects of sports participation in the United States based on extensive survey data. The SGMA's annual *Sports Participation Topline Report* (2009, Sporting Goods Manufacturers Association) outlines major trends in every category of sports participation. The 2009 *Topline Report* contains data from 41,500 telephone surveys conducted in January and February 2009.

TEAM SPORTS. Table 2.1 shows the total number of people participating by sport in the years 2000 and 2008. Basketball was the most popular team sport in which to engage. About 26.3 million Americans aged six and over reported that they played basketball at least once in 2008, about the same number as in 2000. Football (25.5 million, including tackle, touch, and flag), baseball (15 million), and outdoor soccer (14.2 million) were the other team sports with the most participants in 2008.

TABLE 2.1

Team sports participation, 2000 vs. 2008

[In thousands]

Team sports	Definition	2000	2008	8 year change
Baseball				
Total participation	1+ times	15,848	15,020	−5.2%
Basketball				
Total participation	1+ times	26,215	26,254	0.1%
Cheerleading				
Total participation	1+ times	2,634	3,104	17.8%
Field hockey				
Total participation	1+ times		1,118	
Football (flag)				
Total participation	1+ times		7,310	
Football (touch)				
Total participation	1+ times		10,493	
Football (tackle)				
Total participation	1+ times	8,229	7,692	−6.5%
Gymnastics				
Total participation	1+ times	4,876	3,883	−20.4%
Ice hockey				
Total participation	1+ times	2,432	1,902	−21.8%
Lacrosse				
Total participation	1+ times	518	1,127	117.6%
Paintball				
Total participation	1+ times	3,615	4,857	34.3%
Roller hockey				
Total participation	1+ times	3,888	1,562	−59.8%
Rugby				
Total participation	1+ times		690	
Soccer (indoor)				
Total participation	1+ times		4,737	
Soccer (outdoor)				
Total participation	1+ times		14,223	
Softball (fast pitch)				
Total participation	1+ times	2,693	2,316	−14.0%
Softball (slow-pitch)				
Total participation	1+ times	13,577	9,835	−27.6%
Track and field				
Total participation	1+ times		4,516	
Ultimate frisbee				
Total participation	1+ times		4,879	
Volleyball (beach)				
Total participation	1+ times	5,248	4,171	−20.5%
Volleyball (court)				
Total participation	1+ times		8,190	
Volleyball (grass)				
Total participation	1+ times		5,086	
Wrestling				
Total participation	1+ times	3,743	3,358	−10.3%

SOURCE: Adapted from "Team Sports," in *2009 SGMA Sports and Fitness Participation Topline Report*, Sporting Goods Manufacturers Association, 2009

Although still among the most popular sports when measured by participation, baseball (−5.2%) and tackle football (−6.5%) have experienced declining participation since 2000. Other sports that experienced decreasing participation, as shown in Table 2.1, include gymnastics (−20.4%), beach volleyball (−20.5%), and slow-pitch softball (−27.6%). More than 1.9 million people played ice hockey in 2008, according to the *Topline Report*, yet that figure is nearly 22% lower than the 2.4 million who played in 2000.

Sports that grew significantly over the eight-year period include lacrosse (117.8%) and cheerleading (17.8%). Lacrosse is still played by relatively few people compared to the sports mentioned earlier, but it has been exploding in popularity. Its 1.1 million participants in 2008 were more than double the 518,000 who played in 2000. (See Table 2.1.)

INDIVIDUAL AND RACQUET SPORTS. Table 2.2 shows data on participation in individual sports. Bowling, pool,

TABLE 2.2

Individual sports participation, 2000 vs. 2008

[In thousands]

Individual sports	Definition	2000	2008	8 year change
Adventure racing				
Total participation	1+ times		781	
Archery				
Total participation	1+ times	6,285	6,409	2.0%
Billiards/pool				
Total participation	1+ times	46,336	49,018	5.8%
Bowling				
Total participation	1+ times	51,938	58,650	12.9%
Boxing				
Total participation	1+ times	4,084	2,358	−42.3%
Darts				
Total participation	1+ times		23,451	
Horseback riding				
Total participation	1+ times		10,816	
Ice skating				
Total participation	1+ times	11,835	10,999	−7.1%
Martial arts				
Total participation	1+ times	6,161	6,770	9.9%
Roller skating (2×2 wheels)				
Total participation	1+ times	7,746	7,855	1.4%
Roller skating (inline wheels)				
Total participation	1+ times	21,912	9,608	−56.2%
Scooter riding (non-motorized)				
Total participation	1+ times	9,968	6,394	−35.9%
Skateboarding				
Total participation	1+ times	9,859	7,807	−20.8%
Trail running				
Total participation	1+ times	4,167	4,857	16.6%
Triathlon (non-traditional/off road)				
Total participation	1+ times		422	
Triathlon (traditional/road)				
Total participation	1+ times		815	

SOURCE: Adapted from "Individual Sports," in *2009 SGMA Sports and Fitness Participation Topline Report*, Sporting Goods Manufacturers Association, 2009

golf, and tennis remain quite popular pastimes among the American public. According to the *Topline Report*, nearly 58.7 million Americans bowled in 2008—an impressive 12.9% increase since 2000—making it the most popular of all competitive sports in the United States. Bowling has been undergoing a transformation in the form that participation takes. In the past a large percentage of bowlers played on a team affiliated with a bowling league. The SGMA estimates that during the 1980s about two-thirds of all bowling was done by league bowlers; since the turn of the 21st century, about one-third of all bowling takes place under the auspices of a league. The decline in the number of league bowlers has been compensated for by the addition of a great number of young, individual bowlers. However, these bowlers are less serious about the sport than league players. Only 23% of bowlers in 2008 were "core" bowlers, meaning they bowled at least 13 times during the year. As a result of this shift, sales of bowling equipment have stagnated in spite of strong numbers of people who can be counted as participants.

The U.S. Bowling Congress notes that another challenge facing bowling is that the number of places to bowl has been decreasing for several years. This trend is partly the result of consolidation, as older, smaller bowling centers are replaced by larger, state-of-the-art facilities, many of which feature upscale decor and good food service, in contrast to the stereotypical grimy, beer-splashed dens of the mid-20th century. Newer bowling centers usually offer modern, automated scoring, as well as better in-house balls and shoes. Some are mega-centers offering other activities as well, including golf driving ranges, skating, or even basketball. Efforts to lure a younger crowd back to bowling alleys also include special events such as "Rock 'n' Bowl," or "Cosmic Bowling," which features glow-in-the-dark pins and discotheque or ultraviolet lighting.

As in the bowling industry, proprietors of billiards halls are attempting to shed the game's rough image in an effort to attract to the sport new players who may have previously been put off by pool's unsavory reputation. According to the *Topline Report*, 49 million people shot pool or billiards in 2008, down slightly from the previous year but still 5.8% higher than in 2000. (See Table 2.2.) The SGMA states that the profile of the typical billiards player has changed over the past few decades. Pool halls were once frequented primarily by older men, but in the 21st century pool is becoming a sport played increasingly by women and young people. Since the 1980s many facilities have upgraded their traditional low-budget style, and most no longer resemble the no-nonsense rooms immortalized in such movies as *The Hustler* (1961). New and refurbished billiards rooms, similar to contemporary bowling centers, are well lit, clean, and frequently part of multi-activity facilities offering many recreation options.

TABLE 2.3

Racquet sports participation, 2000 vs. 2008

[In thousands]

Racquet sports	Definition	2000	2008	8 year change
Badminton				
Total participation	1+ times	8,769	7,239	−17.5%
Cardio tennis				
Total participation	1+ times		830	
Racquetball				
Total participation	1+ times	4,475	4,993	11.6%
Squash				
Total participation	1+ times		706	
Table tennis				
Total participation	1+ times	12,712	17,201	35.3%
Tennis				
Total participation	1+ times	12,974	18,558	43.0%

SOURCE: Adapted from "Racquet Sports," in *2009 SGMA Sports and Fitness Participation Topline Report*, Sporting Goods Manufacturers Association, 2009

The 2009 *Topline Report* does not include data for golf, but in the article "Golf Participation Falls to 1995 Level" (May 2009, http://www.golfincmagazine.com/news/top-news/golf-participation-falls-1995-level), *Golf Inc.* reports that the National Golf Foundation estimates the total number of golfers in 2008 at 28.6 million, well below the peak of 30 million reached in 2005. Tennis has been enjoying an upswing in popularity in recent years, according to SGMA data. In 2000 about 13 million tennis enthusiasts hoisted a racket. By 2008 the total had grown by 43%, to 18.6 million. (See Table 2.3.) One factor in the resurgence of tennis is a conscious effort to democratize the sport. Once played primarily by the wealthy at country clubs, tennis is now available to people at all socioeconomic levels. The U.S. Tennis Association (USTA; 2008, http://www.usta.com) has helped this trend along by investing heavily in programs aimed at growing the sport, including a $50-million initiative launched in 1997 called the USA Tennis Plan for Growth, which offered free lessons around the country. The USTA also has a Diversity Plan aimed at encouraging multicultural participation in a sport that has long been dominated by white players, coaches, and officials. Gains in minority participation have received a boost from the success and popularity of such African-American stars as Serena Williams (1981–), Venus Williams (1980–), and James Blake (1979–). As shown in Table 2.3, the *Topline Report* indicates that in 2008 other widely played racquet sports included table tennis (17.2 million participants), badminton (7.2 million), and racquetball (5 million).

Outdoor and Water Sports

Millions of Americans who refrain from competitive sports—individual or team—enjoy engaging in outdoor sports and water sports. Over 38.1 million people bicycled on roads or other paved surfaces in 2008, according to the *Topline Report* (see Table 2.4), and another 7.6 million went mountain biking, or other off-road riding. Fishing is another immensely popular outdoor sport. According to the *Topline Report*, a combined total of some 60 million people went

fishing in 2008, when the totals for freshwater, saltwater, and fly-fishing are combined.

Many water sports have declined significantly in popularity since 2000, according to the SGMA in its 2009 *Topline Report*. Table 2.5 shows that waterskiing, scuba diving,

TABLE 2.4

Outdoor sports participation, 2000 vs. 2008

[In thousands]

Outdoor sports	Definition	2000	2008	8 year change
Backpacking overnight—more than 1/4 mile from vehicle/home				
Total participation	1+ times		7,867	
Bicycling—BMX				
Total participation	1+ times	3,213	1,904	−40.7%
Bicycling (mountain/non-paved surface)				
Total participation	1+ times		7,592	
Bicycling (road/paved surface)				
Total participation	1+ times		38,114	
Birdwatching more than 1/4 mile from home/vehicle				
Total participation	1+ times		12,417	
Camping (recreational vehicle)				
Total participation	1+ times	17,893	16,517	−7.7%
Camping within 1/4 mile of vehicle/home				
Total participation	1+ times		33,686	
Climbing (sport/indoor/boulder)				
Total participation	1+ times		4,769	
Climbing (traditional/ice/mountaineering)				
Total participation	1+ times		2,288	
Fishing (fly)				
Total participation	1+ times	6,717	5,941	−11.5%
Fishing (freshwater—other)				
Total participation	1+ times	43,696	40,331	−7.7%
Fishing (saltwater)				
Total participation	1+ times	14,739	13,804	−6.3%
Hiking (day)				
Total participation	1+ times	30,051	32,511	8.2%
Hunting (bow)				
Total participation	1+ times	4,633	3,722	−19.7%
Hunting (handgun)				
Total participation	1+ times		2,873	
Hunting (rifle)				
Total participation	1+ times		10,344	
Hunting (shotgun)				
Total participation	1+ times		8,731	
Shooting (sport clays)				
Total participation	1+ times	4,437	4,282	−3.5%
Shooting (trap/skeet)				
Total participation	1+ times	3,416	3,669	7.4%
Target shooting (handgun)				
Total participation	1+ times		13,365	
Target shooting (rifle)				
Total participation	1+ times	10,022	13,102	30.7%
Wildlife viewing more than 1/4 mile from home/vehicle				
Total participation	1+ times		24,113	

SOURCE: Adapted from "Outdoor Sports," in *2009 SGMA Sports and Fitness Participation Topline Report*, Sporting Goods Manufacturers Association, 2009

TABLE 2.5

Water sports participation, 2000 vs. 2008

[In thousands]

Water sports	Definition	2000	2008	8 year change
Boardsailing/windsurfing				
Total participation	1+ times	1,739	1,307	−24.8%
Canoeing				
Total participation	1+ times	10,880	9,935	−8.7%
Jet skiing				
Total participation	1+ times	9,475	7,815	−17.5%
Kayaking (recreational)				
Total participation	1+ times		5,025	
Kayaking (sea/touring)				
Total participation	1+ times		1,467	
Kayaking (white water)				
Total participation	1+ times		1,086	
Rafting				
Total participation	1+ times	5,259	4,651	−11.6%
Sailing				
Total participation	1+ times	4,405	4,226	−4.1%
Scuba diving				
Total participation	1+ times	4,305	3,216	−25.3%
Snorkeling				
Total participation	1+ times	10,302	10,296	−0.1%
Surfing				
Total participation	1+ times	2,191	2,607	19.0%
Wakeboarding				
Total participation	1+ times	4,558	3,544	−22.3%
Water skiing				
Total participation	1+ times	8,765	5,593	−36.2%

SOURCE: Adapted from "Water Sports," in *2009 SGMA Sports and Fitness Participation Topline Report*, Sporting Goods Manufacturers Association, 2009

windsurfing, and jet skiing all experienced significant decreases in participation between 2000 and 2008. In contrast, participation in surfing grew by 19% during that span. Snorkeling and canoeing were the top water sports in 2008, with 10.3 million and 9.9 million participants, respectively.

National Sporting Goods Association Survey

The NSGA also conducts a broad nationwide survey on sports participation. The following are a few highlights from the 2008 NSGA survey.

Table 1.2 in Chapter 1 ranks sports and other physical activities by total participation and provides a useful snapshot of what Americans choose to do when they want to move their bodies, as reported by the NSGA in 2009. Table 2.6 provides a sport-by-sport glance at trends in participation since 1998. According to NSGA data, basketball and baseball participation have remained relatively stable over the past ten years, while soccer and tackle football have enjoyed recent growth. It is interesting to note that as participation in skiing has tapered off over the past ten years, that decline has been offset by growth in snowboarding.

YOUTH SPORTS. According to the NSGA, youth participation in many team sports is on the decline. (See Table 2.7.) According to NSGA data, youth baseball participation shrank by 12% between 1998 and 2007. Basketball participation shrank by 17.9% during this period. Even soccer, which is generally perceived as an emerging sport, saw participation growth among youth of only 4.6%; however, that percentage increase is less than the percentage increase of the nation's total youth population, meaning the percentage of youth playing soccer actually decreased even as the number of youth who played grew. Football, skateboarding, and snowboarding all saw strong increases in youth participation between 1998 and 2007.

SPORTS PARTICIPATION AND GENDER. According to NSGA survey data, the sports that drew the greatest number of female participants in 2007 (excluding exercise and recreational activities such as walking, aerobics, and camping) were swimming (28.4 million), bowling (21.9 million), and bicycling (17.5 million). (See Table 2.8.) Basketball, at 7.5 million participants, topped the list among team sports, with volleyball (6.9 million participants) not far behind. Tennis, soccer, and golf were also high on the list. Women represent a greater share of participants in some sports than in others. For example, 57.5% of the nation's volleyball players and 46.8% of tennis players in 2007 were women, whereas women represented only 22.6% of golfers. Table 2.9 shows changes in participation among women between 2002 and 2007. Few sports experienced dramatic shifts in participation among women between these two years. One sport that increased in percentage of female participants was skateboarding; in 2002 fewer than one in five skateboarders (19.5%) were female, compared with more than one in four (26.6%) in 2007.

Extreme Sports

As participation in traditional team sports such as baseball and basketball stagnates, especially among youth and young adults, a generation of sports participants is turning instead to a class of activities collectively known as "extreme" or "action" sports. Even though there is no consensus on exactly which sports qualify as extreme, their binding characteristic can be loosely identified as pointing to sports that result in a so-called adrenaline rush, or a degree of risk-taking not associated with old-school sports. Most lists include skateboarding, rock climbing, snowboarding, mountain biking, BMX bicycling, and windsurfing. The boldest of extreme sportspeople will engage in such daredevilry as riding a motorcycle off of a ski jump. Many of these sports saw rapid growth in participation during the first years of the 21st century.

TABLE 2.6

Ten-year history of selected sports participation, selected years 1998–2008

[In millions]

	2008	2006	2004	2002	2000	1998
Aerobic exercising	36.2	33.7	29.5	29.0	26.7	25.8
Archery (target)	na	na	5.3	4.2	4.5	4.8
Backpack/wilderness camp	13.0	13.3	15.3	14.8	15.4	14.6
Baseball	15.2	14.6	15.9	15.6	15.6	15.9
Basketball	29.7	26.7	27.8	28.9	27.1	29.4
Bicycle riding	44.7	35.6	40.3	39.7	43.1	43.5
Billiards/pool	31.7	31.8	34.2	33.1	32.5	32.3
Boating, motor/power	27.8	29.3	22.8	26.6	24.2	25.7
Bowling	49.5	44.8	43.8	42.4	43.1	40.1
Camping (vacation/overnite)	49.4	48.6	55.3	55.4	49.9	46.5
Canoeing	10.3	7.1	7.5	7.6	6.2	7.1
Cheerleading	2.9	3.8	3.8	na	na	3.1
Dart throwing	na	na	na	18.5	17.4	20.8
Exercise walking	96.6	87.5	84.7	82.2	81.3	77.6
Exercising with equipment	63.0	52.4	52.2	46.8	44.8	46.1
Fishing	42.2	40.6	41.2	44.2	47.2	43.6
Football (tackle)	10.5	10.1	8.6	7.8	8.0	8.1
Football (touch)	na	na	9.6	10.3	9.8	10.8
Golf	25.6	24.4	24.5	27.1	26.4	27.5
Hiking	38.0	31.0	28.3	27.2	24.3	27.2
Hockey (ice)	1.9	2.3	2.4	2.1	1.9	2.1
Hunting with firearms	18.8	19.9	19.5	17.8	18.4	19.2
Hunting w/bow & arrow	6.2	5.9	5.8	4.6	4.7	5.6
In-line roller skating	9.3	10.5	11.7	18.8	21.8	27.0
Martial arts	na	na	4.7	4.2	5.4	4.6
Mountain biking (off road)	10.2	8.5	8.0	7.8	7.1	8.6
Mountain/rock climbing	na	na	3.8	na	3.3	2.7
Muzzleloading	3.4	3.7	3.8	3.6	2.9	3.1
Paintball games	6.7	8.0	9.4	6.9	5.3	na
Racquetball	na	4.0	na	na	3.2	4.0
Running/jogging	35.9	28.8	26.7	24.7	22.8	22.5
Sailing	na	na	2.6	na	2.5	3.6
Scooter riding	10.1	9.5	12.9	13.4	11.6	na
Skateboarding	9.8	9.7	10.3	9.7	9.1	5.8
Skiing (alpine)	6.5	6.4	6.3	7.4	7.4	7.7
Skiing (cross country)	1.6	2.6	2.4	2.2	2.3	2.6
Snowboarding	5.9	5.2	6.6	5.6	4.3	3.6
Soccer	15.5	14.0	13.3	13.7	12.9	13.2
Softball	12.8	12.4	12.5	13.6	14.0	15.6
Swimming	63.5	56.5	53.4	53.1	58.8	58.2
Target shooting	20.3	19.1	19.2	18.9	16.9	18.9
Target shooting—airgun	5.0	6.1	5.1	4.1	3.0	3.3
Tennis	12.6	10.4	9.6	11.0	10.0	11.2
Volleyball	12.2	11.1	11.8	11.5	12.3	14.8
Water skiing	5.6	6.3	5.3	6.9	5.9	7.2
Weightlifting	37.5	32.9	26.2	25.1	22.8	na
Workout at club	39.3	34.9	31.8	28.9	24.1	26.5
Wrestling	na	3.2	na	na	na	na
Yoga	16.0	na	na	na	na	na

Notes: Participated more than once. Seven (7) years of age and older.

SOURCE: "Ten-Year History of Sports Participation," in *Information Center and Research: Sports Participation*, National Sporting Goods Association, Mount Prospect, IL © 2009, http://www.nsga.org/files/public/10YearHistory_4web_090327.pdf (accessed June 10, 2009).

INLINE SKATING AND SKATEBOARDING. Inline skating is by far the most popular extreme sport. (See Table 2.10.) In 2007, 10.8 million people aged six and over donned inline skates, according to the SGMA. Skateboarding was second, with 8.4 million participants. Although skateboarders tend to be a youthful group, the sheer number of people participating suggests that skateboarding and other extreme sports are not just the domain of the young. The numbers suggest that as this youthful core group ages, these sports may continue to outgrow their "alternative" status and become more mainstream.

Skateboarding developed in the mid-20th century in California, where surfers attached small wooden platforms to roller-skate wheels and began riding on sidewalks as a pastime when the surf was low. By the mid-1960s skateboards were being commercially manufactured, and by the 1970s improvements had been made in the design and materials enough that riders gained increased speed and control over their maneuvers. During a severe drought in California in 1976, some skaters began practicing skateboard tricks in empty swimming pools, thus originating the vertical skating style that would eventually catapult the sport

TABLE 2.7

Youth sports participation, 2007 vs. 1998

[In thousands]

	Year	Total	Change vs 1998	Total 7–11	Change vs 1998	Total 12–17	Change vs 1998
Total U.S.	1998	242,884		19,876		23,241	
Total U.S.	2007	265,381	9.3%	19,410	−2.3%	25,341	9.0%
Baseball	1998	15,856		4,714		4,307	
Baseball	2007	13,951	−12.0%	3,975	−15.7%	2,909	−32.5%
Basketball	1998	29,417		6,273		8,246	
Basketball	2007	24,145	−17.9%	4,923	−21.5%	6,952	−15.7%
Bicycle riding	1998	43,535		10,055		7,844	
Bicycle riding	2007	37,405	−14.1%	7,046	−29.9%	6,518	−16.9%
Bowling	1998	40,063		4,865		6,055	
Bowling	2007	43,466	8.5%	5,091	4.6%	6,813	12.5%
Fishing (fresh water)	1998	38,640		4,627		4,086	
Fishing (fresh water)	2007	30,825	−20.2%	2,894	−37.5%	3,107	−24.0%
Football (tackle)	1998	7,448		1,211		3,014	
Football (tackle)	2007	9,195	23.5%	1,442	19.1%	3,906	29.6%
Golf	1998	27,496		1,264		2,432	
Golf	2007	22,729	−17.3%	654	−48.3%	1,441	−40.7%
Hockey (ice)	1998	2,131		365		593	
Hockey (ice)	2007	2,071	−2.8%	252	−31.0%	419	−29.3%
Mountain biking (off road)	1998	8,610		1,040		1,224	
Mountain biking (off road)	2007	7,425	−13.8%	640	−38.5%	942	−23.0%
Roller skating (in-line)	1998	27,033		9,052		6,892	
Roller skating (in-line)	2007	10,713	−60.4%	3,013	−66.7%	3,384	−50.9%
Skateboarding	1998	5,782		2,309		2,253	
Skateboarding	2007	10,137	75.3%	3,156	36.7%	4,171	85.1%
Skiing (alpine)	1998	7,680		548		1,262	
Skiing (alpine)	2007	5,494	−28.5%	533	−2.7%	821	−34.9%
Snowboarding	1998	3,635		487		1,477	
Snowboarding	2007	5,063	39.3%	782	60.6%	1,352	−8.5%
Soccer	1998	13,167		5,489		3,936	
Soccer	2007	13,770	4.6%	5,041	−8.2%	3,332	−15.3%
Softball	1998	15,595		3,040		3,263	
Softball	2007	9,958	−36.1%	1,155	−62.0%	1,795	−45.0%
Tennis	1998	11,227		1,204		2,011	
Tennis	2007	12,290	9.5%	1,446	20.1%	1,883	−6.4%
Volleyball	1998	14,788		1,551		3,807	
Volleyball	2007	12,029	−18.7%	1,189	−23.3%	3,041	−20.1%

Notes: Participated more than once. Seven (7) years of age and older.

SOURCE: "2007 Youth Participation in Selected Sports with Comparisons to 1998," in *Information Center and Research: Sports Participation*, National Sporting Goods Association, Mount Prospect, IL © 2008, http://www.nsga.org/files/public/2006YouthParticipationInSelectedSportsWithComparisons.pdf (accessed June 10, 2009)

into international significance. Skate teams representing board companies performed and competed in order to promote their sponsors' products, and stars such as Tony Hawk (1968–) rose to fame in the late 1980s and early 1990s. Hawk leveraged his fame on wheels into a fortune from merchandise and video games bearing his name and image.

SNOWBOARDING. Like skateboarding, snowboarding developed in the United States during the mid-20th century and grew rapidly as technology improved and young enthusiasts adopted the sport. Nearly three-quarters of all snowboarders are under the age of 24, according to the SGMA. The first snowboards were crudely fashioned wood items made by high school shop students and home hobbyists, all inspired by the idea of surfing or skateboarding on snow. One such creation, the Snurfer, by Sherman Poppen (1930–) of Muskegon, Michigan, gained national distribution through a manufacturing deal with Brunswick in the mid-1960s. Snurf competitions were

held, and other innovators, such as Jake Burton Carpenter (1954–), improved on the design and incorporated boot bindings and laminate materials. In 1982 Suicide Six in Woodstock, Vermont, was the first ski area to open itself to snowboarders when it held the first national competition.

Other ski resorts barred snowboarders due to concerns about safety and insurance coverage. With many younger participants preferring snowboarding to the more expensive downhill skiing, slopes eventually welcomed snowboarders, and the sport increased in popularity. By 2009 nearly all ski areas in the United States allowed snowboarding; exceptions included Alta and Deer Valley in Utah and Mad River Glen in Vermont. Snowboarding became an Olympic sport in 1998, with giant slalom and half-pipe events during the winter games in Nagano, Japan. One of the biggest names in extreme sports involving boards has been Olympic gold-medalist Shaun White (1986–). Instantly recognizable to fans by his wild shock

TABLE 2.8

Sports participation among women, by total participation, 2007

[In millions]

Sport	Total female	Percent female
Exercise walking	56.1	62.5%
Swimming	28.4	54.2%
Exercising with equipment	27.0	51.1%
Camping (vacation/overnite)	23.3	49.0%
Bowling	21.9	50.4%
Aerobic exercising	21.5	70.8%
Workout at club	18.6	55.0%
Bicycle riding	17.5	46.8%
Running/jogging	14.5	47.8%
Hiking	13.9	48.5%
Boating, motor/power	13.6	42.6%
Weightlifting	11.8	35.7%
Billiards/pool	11.7	39.6%
Fishing	11.4	32.3%
Yoga	9.1	85.3%
Basketball	7.5	31.0%
Volleyball	6.9	57.5%
In-line roller skating	5.8	54.3%
Tennis	5.7	46.8%
Backpack/wilderness camp	5.4	41.3%
Soccer	5.3	38.7%
Golf	5.1	22.6%
Dart throwing	5.0	41.2%
Softball	4.8	48.4%
Scooter riding	4.8	45.2%
Target shooting	4.7	23.1%
Baseball	3.2	23.4%
Kayaking	2.9	49.3%
Skateboarding	2.7	26.6%
Hunting with firearms	2.5	13.0%
Mountain biking (off road)	2.5	33.5%
Skiing (alpine)	2.2	39.3%
Water skiing	2.2	41.0%
Mountain/rock climbing	1.9	41.2%
Snowboarding	1.3	26.5%
Football (tackle)	1.3	13.8%
Archery (target)	1.2	18.3%
Scuba diving (open water)	1.0	41.3%
Paintball games	0.8	11.1%
Skiing (cross country)	0.8	47.1%
Lacrosse	0.6	53.0%
Hunting w/bow & arrow	0.4	7.7%
Hockey (ice)	0.4	18.1%
Wrestling	0.3	16.5%
Muzzleloading	0.3	7.8%

Notes: Participated more than once. Seven (7) years of age and older.

SOURCE: "2007 Women's Participation Ranked by Total Female Participation," in *Information Center and Research: Sports Participation*, National Sporting Goods Association, Mount Prospect, IL © 2008, http://www.nsga.org/files/public/2007Women%27sParticipation-byTotalFemaleParticipation_4Web_080512.pdf (accessed June 10, 2009)

players. Players use netted sticks to throw and catch a small rubber ball and, ultimately, to propel the ball into the opponents' goal, which resembles a hockey goal. Lacrosse may be the oldest sport in North America. It originated among Native Americans and has been played in one form or another for at least 500 years.

U.S. Lacrosse, the organization that coordinates lacrosse activity nationwide, estimates that there were 524,230 active lacrosse players in the United States in 2008, up from 253,931 in 2001. (See Table 2.11.) According to U.S. Lacrosse's most recent nationwide survey, about half of current players are in the youth category (265,214 in 2008). (See Table 2.12.) Another 218,823 played high school lacrosse, and 29,822 played at the collegiate level. Lacrosse has long been popular in the Northeast and in the mid-Atlantic states, but in the 2000s it has been surging in popularity in many parts of the country, including the Pacific Northwest and the Rocky Mountain states.

SOCCER. Soccer is the only well-established team sport that does not appear to be losing players, largely because of its growing popularity among children and adolescents. The organization U.S. Youth Soccer (2009, http://www.usyouthsoccer.org/) reports the registration of 3.2 million players between the ages of five and 19—an impressive number when compared with the 100,000 registered members the organization had in 1974, the year it was founded. Moreover, two other smaller nationwide youth soccer agencies—the American Youth Soccer Organization (2009, http://soccer.org/) and the Soccer Association for Youth (2009, http://www.saysoccer.org/)—have a combined 900,000 registered players. The presence of these young soccer players on U.S. soccer fields, as well as the growing populations of people from places such as Latin America, where soccer has long reigned supreme among sports, is likely to lift soccer into prominence among adults in the coming years.

CONSUMER PURCHASES OF SPORTING GOODS

Besides asking individuals about their sports participation, the NSGA also tracks nationwide retail sales of sporting goods. Americans spent $90.8 billion on sports-related items in 2007, though they were projected to spend a little less in 2008 because of the recession. (See Table 2.13.) Of this total, $37.3 billion was spent in 2007 on what the NSGA calls "recreational transport," a category that includes bicycles, pleasure boats, recreational vehicles, and snowmobiles. The other $53.5 billion was spent on what most people consider "sporting goods," including specialized equipment, footwear, and clothing. Footwear accounted for $17.4 billion of this spending and clothing for $10.8 billion.

Excluding apparel, footwear, and exercise equipment, hunting and firearms and golf equipment accounted for

of flame-red hair, White is unique for having developed into a world-class performer in both skateboarding and snowboarding. Popular female snowboarders include Hannah Teter (1987–) and Gretchen Bleiler (1981–), who won gold and silver medals, respectively for the United States at the 2006 Olympic Games in Italy.

Emerging Sports

LACROSSE. Among the fastest-growing team sports in the United States is lacrosse. Lacrosse is similar in form to hockey or soccer. It is played on a field by two teams of ten

TABLE 2.9

Female sports participation, 2007 vs. 2002

[In millions]

Sport	2007 total female	2007 percent female	2002 total female	2002 percent female	Percent difference
Aerobic exercising	21.5	70.8%	21.3	73.2%	−2.4%
Archery (target)	1.2	18.3%	1.0	23.1%	−4.8%
Backpack/wilderness camp	5.4	41.3%	6.0	38.8%	2.5%
Baseball	3.2	23.4%	4.1	26.2%	−2.8%
Basketball	7.5	31.0%	9.6	33.0%	−2.0%
Bicycle riding	17.5	46.8%	18.9	45.7%	1.1%
Billiards/pool	11.7	39.6%	13.7	39.0%	0.6%
Boating, motor/power	13.6	42.6%	11.6	43.6%	−1.0%
Bowling	21.9	50.4%	21.5	48.9%	1.5%
Camping (vacation/overnite)	23.3	49.0%	26.7	48.1%	0.9%
Dart throwing	5.0	41.2%	6.9	37.1%	4.1%
Exercise walking	56.1	62.5%	51.6	62.8%	−0.3%
Exercising with equipment	27.0	51.1%	27.1	54.0%	−2.9%
Fishing	11.4	32.3%	15.0	33.8%	−1.5%
Football (tackle)	1.3	13.8%	0.7	9.7%	4.1%
Golf	5.1	22.6%	5.8	20.7%	1.9%
Hiking	13.9	48.5%	15.2	49.6%	−1.1%
Hockey (ice)	0.4	18.1%	0.5	21.7%	−3.6%
Hunting w/bow & arrow	0.4	7.7%	0.4	9.6%	−1.9%
Hunting with firearms	2.5	13.0%	2.6	13.4%	−0.4%
In-line roller skating	5.8	54.3%	9.8	52.0%	2.3%
Mountain biking (off road)	2.5	33.5%	2.9	37.5%	−4.0%
Muzzleloading	0.3	7.8%	0.3	7.6%	0.2%
Paintball games	0.8	11.1%	1.4	20.7%	−9.6%
Running/jogging	14.5	47.8%	11.4	46.0%	1.8%
Scooter riding	4.8	45.2%	5.6	41.6%	3.6%
Skateboarding	2.7	26.6%	1.9	19.5%	7.1%
Skiing (alpine)	2.2	39.3%	2.9	39.3%	0.0%
Skiing (cross country)	0.8	47.1%	1.0	46.5%	0.6%
Snowboarding	1.3	26.5%	1.3	23.0%	3.5%
Soccer	5.3	38.7%	5.5	37.8%	0.9%
Softball	4.8	48.4%	6.7	49.4%	−1.0%
Swimming	28.4	54.2%	29.2	53.4%	0.8%
Target shooting	4.7	23.1%	4.6	24.3%	−1.2%
Tennis	5.7	46.8%	4.8	43.5%	3.3%
Volleyball	6.9	57.5%	6.2	54.5%	3.0%
Water skiing	2.2	41.0%	2.8	41.2%	−0.2%
Weightlifting	11.8	35.7%	9.7	34.6%	1.1%
Workout at club	18.6	55.0%	15.6	54.0%	1.0%

Notes: Participated more than once. Seven (7) years of age and older.

SOURCE: "Female Sports Participation—2007 vs. 2002," in *Information Center and Research: Sports Participation*, National Sporting Goods Association, Mount Prospect, IL © 2008, http://www.nsga.org/files/public/2007-2002Women%27sParticipation_080919.pdf (accessed June 10, 2009)

the largest shares of sports equipment purchased by Americans in 2007. (See Table 1.3 in Chapter 1.) Consumer purchases of golf gear tallied more than $3.8 billion. According to the National Golf Foundation (2009, http://www.ngf.org/cgi/home.asp), avid golfers (those who play at least 25 times per year) account for nearly two-thirds of the spending, even though they make up less than a quarter of the nation's golfers. Hunting and firearms, one of the fastest-growing categories of consumer purchases, has now eclipsed golf, registering just under $4 billion in equipment sales in 2007.

SPORTS FANS

Since 2000 the Gallup Organization has been asking Americans whether or not they are sports fans. A majority has said yes each year, and the 63% answering positively in February 2009 was one of the highest percentages yet

recorded. It should be noted, however, that the figure fluctuates seasonally and from year to year, so this does not necessarily represent a long-term trend (2009, http://www.gallup.com/poll/4735/Sports.aspx). Table 1.1 in Chapter 1 ranks each sport according to the percentage of people who say it is their favorite sport to watch. Football, at 41%, towers over all the other sports in the survey. Gallup data show that there are gender and generational differences in sports preference. Football was the top choice of both men and women based on aggregate data from 2005 through 2008, but it was the favorite of a much greater percentage of men (49%) than women (32%). (See Table 2.14.) Younger people were also more likely to name football as their favorite sport than were older adults, though football was the top choice among all age groups. Table 2.15 takes a longer view of the question. It shows the gradual rise of football and decline of baseball as a favorite sport to watch over several decades.

TABLE 2.10

Extreme sports participation, 2007

Extreme sport	# of participants (participated at least once in 2007)
1. Inline skating	10,814,000
2. Skateboarding	8,429,000
3. Mountain biking	6,892,000
4. Snowboarding	6,841,000
5. Paintball	5,476,000
6. Cardio kickboxing	4,812,000
7. Climbing (indoor, sport, boulder)	4,514,000
8. Trail running	4,216,000
9. Ultimate frisbee	4,038,000
10. Wakeboarding	3,521,000
11. Mountain/rock climbing	2,062,000
12. BMX bicycling	1,887,000
13. Roller hockey	1,847,000
14. Boardsailing/windsurfing	1,118,000

SOURCE: "Most Popular Extreme Sports in the USA," in *Extreme Sports: An Ever-Popular Attraction*, Sporting Goods Manufacturers Association, July 7, 2008, http://www.sgma.com/press/2_Extreme-Sports:-An-Ever-Popular-Attraction (accessed June 10, 2009)

TABLE 2.11

Lacrosse participation, 2001–08

Year	Players
2001	253,931
2002	288,104
2003	301,560
2004	351,852
2005	381,568
2006	426,022
2007	480,627
2008	524,230

SOURCE: Adapted from "Lacrosse Growth since 2001," in *US Lacrosse Participation Survey 2008*, US Lacrosse, 2009, http://www.uslacrosse.org/pdf/08participation.pdf (accessed June 10, 2009)

TABLE 2.12

Lacrosse participation at various levels, 2008

Level	Male players	Female players	Total players
Youth	168,768	96,446	265,214
High school	131,092	87,731	218,823
College	18,148	11,674	29,822
Professional	300	0	300
Post-collegiate	7,933	2,138	10,071
Total	**326,241**	**197,989**	**524,230**

SOURCE: Adapted from "Lacrosse Participation in 2008," in *US Lacrosse Participation Survey 2008*, US Lacrosse, 2009, http://www.uslacrosse.org/pdf/08participation.pdf (accessed June 10, 2009)

Even though baseball has long been called the national pastime, as of February 2008 only 35% of the population considered themselves fans of the professional version of the sport, with another 8% calling themselves "somewhat of a fan." As shown in Figure 2.1, the percentage of people identifying themselves as baseball fans has been declining steadily over the past decade. In contrast, both professional and college football fan bases (see Figure 2.2 and Table 2.16) have held steady during that period. As of December 2007, 54% of respondents reported to Gallup that they were pro football fans, and another 6% said they were somewhat of a fan (http://www.gallup.com/poll/1705/Football.aspx). Over the long term, it is clear that football and baseball have been moving in opposite directions in terms of favorite sport for decades. (See Figure 2.3.) While basketball had surpassed baseball as a favorite sport for Americans to watch for several recent years, its fan base has declined. As of December 2008, basketball had slipped back below baseball as a favorite sport to watch, at just 9%. (See Figure 2.4.)

Data from another well-established polling company, Harris Interactive, echoes the Gallup findings. As shown in Table 2.17, the percentage calling pro football their favorite sport has increased by the same amount between 1985 and 2008, 7%, as the decrease in the percentage naming baseball as their favorite sport.

Race

Gallup polls have shown over the years a general shift among American sports fans away from baseball and toward basketball and football, but the pace of this shift has been even more pronounced among African-Americans. In "The Disappearing Black Baseball Fan" (July 15, 2003, http://www.gallup.com/poll/8854/Disappearing-Black-Baseball-Fan.aspx), Jeffrey M. Jones of the Gallup Organization states that 43% of African-Americans named baseball as their favorite sport in 1960, compared with 33% of the overall American public. This strong preference among African-Americans may have been the result of the integration of professional baseball over the previous decade, beginning with Jackie Robinson (1919–1972) crossing baseball's "color line" in 1947, followed by the emergence of such African-American stars as Hank Aaron (1934–), Ernie Banks (1931–), Willie Mays (1931–), and Frank Robinson (1935–).

Jones notes that a Gallup analysis found that by 1985 the percentage of African-Americans calling baseball their favorite sport had fallen to just 17%, a drop that far outpaced the decline among white fans, from 32% to 19%. Combined polls from 2000 to 2002 demonstrate a continuation of the decline of baseball's popularity among African-Americans. By this time, only 5% said baseball was their favorite sport. Meanwhile, both basketball and football had gained substantial popularity among African-American sports fans: Football was the favorite of 31%, and basketball was the favorite of 37%.

TABLE 2.13

Sales of sporting goods, by category, 2001–08

[In millions of dollars]

	2001	2002	2003	2004	2005	2006	2007	2008[b]	Change 07 vs 06
Equipment	21,599	21,699	22,394	23,328	23,688	24,497	25,267	24,884	3%
Footwear	13,814	14,144	14,446	14,752	15,719	16,910	17,366	17,715	3%
Clothing	10,217	9,801	10,543	11,201	10,898	10,580	10,834	10,770	2%
Subtotal	45,630	45,644	47,382	49,280	50,305	51,987	53,468	53,369	3%
Recreational transport[a]	28,712	32,106	32,396	36,531	38,082	38,485	37,334	33,979	−3%
Total	74,342	77,750	79,778	85,811	88,387	90,472	90,802	87,348	−%

[a]Bicycles, pleasure boats, recreational vehicles and snowmobiles; projections provided by other associations.
[b]Projected

SOURCE: "Consumer Purchases of Sporting Goods by Category," in *Information Center and Research: Consumer Purchases/Sporting Goods Market*, National Sporting Goods Association, Mount Prospect, IL © 2009, http://www.nsga.org/files/public/ConsumerPurchasesofSptGdsbyCategory2.pdf (accessed June 17, 2009)

TABLE 2.14

Poll respondents' rating of their favorite sport to watch, by gender and age, 2005–08 aggregate

	Football	Baseball	Basketball
	%	%	%
Men	49	11	9
Women	32	13	13
18 to 29 years old	46	6	16
30 to 49 years old	43	11	10
50 to 64 years old	37	14	10
65 years and older	33	17	11

SOURCE: Jeffrey M. Jones, "Favorite Sport, by Gender and Age," in *Football Remains Runaway Leader As Favorite Sport*, The Gallup Organization, December 29, 2008, http://www.gallup.com/poll/113503/Football-Remains-Runaway-Leader-Favorite-Sport.aspx (accessed June 3, 2009). Copyright © 2008 by The Gallup Organization. Reproduced by permission of The Gallup Organization.

TABLE 2.15

Poll respondents' favorite sport to watch, long-term trend, selected years, 1937–2008

WHAT IS YOUR FAVORITE SPORT TO WATCH?

	Football	Baseball	Basketball	Ice hockey	Auto racing	Ice/figure skating
	%	%	%	%	%	%
2008 Dec 4–7	41	10	9	4	3	1
2007 Dec 6–9	43	13	11	4	3	2
2006 Dec 11–14	43	11	12	2	4	3
2005 Dec 5–8	34	12	12	4	5	3
2004 Dec 5–8	37	10	13	3	5	4
2003 Dec 11–14	37	10	14	5	5	6
2002 Dec 5–8	37	12	13	3	5	4
2001 Mar 26–28	28	12	16	3	6	4
2000 Mar 30–Apr 2	33	13	15	5	5	4
1998 Nov 20–22	36	16	12	3	3	2
1997 Apr 18–20[a]	30	14	17	3	7	2
1995 Apr 17–19	32	16	15	3	2	2
1994 Sep 16–20	37	16	13	1	2	3
1994 Aug 8–9	35	21	11	3	2	3
1992 Sept	38	16	12	4	2	2
1990 Feb	35	16	15	3	1	2
1981 Jan	38	16	9	2	1	2
1972 Oct	32	24	9	4	2	1
1960 Dec	21	34	9	3	[b]	1
1948 Apr 9–14	17	39	10	3	1	[b]
1937 Mar 24–29	23	34	8	2	1	1

[a]Wording: What is your favorite sport to follow?
[b]Less than 0.5%

SOURCE: "What Is Your Favorite Sport to Watch?" in *Football*, The Gallup Organization, 2007, http://www.gallup.com/poll/1705/Football.aspx (accessed June 8, 2009). Copyright © 2007 by The Gallup Organization. Reproduced by permission of The Gallup Organization.

The contrast between the sports preferences of white and African-American fans is striking. Jones combines the Gallup data from 2002 and 2003 and shows that when asked simply whether they are baseball fans and whether they are basketball fans, white respondents gave baseball an edge over basketball, 39% to 28%. Nearly twice as many African-American respondents said they were basketball fans (60%) as said they were baseball fans (33%). Jones's analysis of these results suggests two possible reasons for the differences:

- The dominance of professional basketball by African-American players

- The relative lack of baseball facilities and programs in urban areas with predominantly African-American populations

More recent data from Harris confirmed the presence of significant racial differences. Their December 2008 poll found that only 8% of African-Americans considered baseball their favorite sport, and only 1% of African-Americans said their favorite sport was auto racing. (See Table 2.18.)

Geography

The Harris Poll found significant differences in favorite sport by region as well. As Table 2.18 shows,

FIGURE 2.1

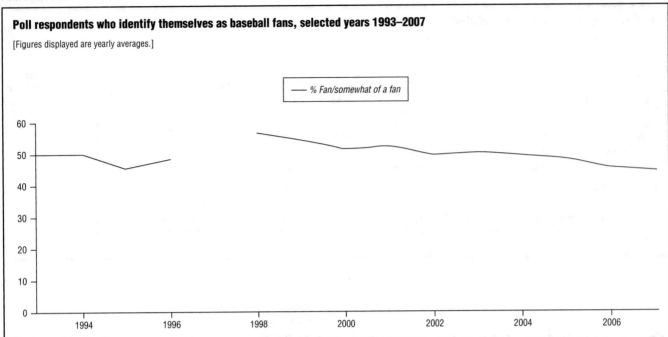

Poll respondents who identify themselves as baseball fans, selected years 1993–2007

[Figures displayed are yearly averages.]

SOURCE: Jeffrey M. Jones, "Percentage of Americans Identifying As Baseball Fans, 1993–2007 Gallup Polls," in *Less Than Half of Americans Are Baseball Fans*, The Gallup Organization, October 24, 2007, http://www.gallup.com/poll/102343/Less-Than-Half-Americans-Baseball-Fans.aspx (accessed June 3, 2009). Copyright © 2008 by The Gallup Organization. Reproduced by permission of The Gallup Organization.

FIGURE 2.2

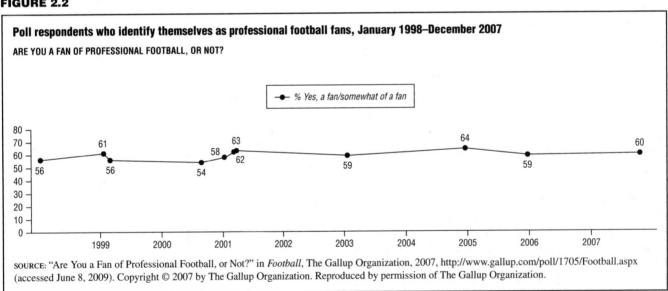

Poll respondents who identify themselves as professional football fans, January 1998–December 2007

ARE YOU A FAN OF PROFESSIONAL FOOTBALL, OR NOT?

SOURCE: "Are You a Fan of Professional Football, or Not?" in *Football*, The Gallup Organization, 2007, http://www.gallup.com/poll/1705/Football.aspx (accessed June 8, 2009). Copyright © 2007 by The Gallup Organization. Reproduced by permission of The Gallup Organization.

professional football was most popular in the East with 38% naming it as their favorite sport, and least popular in the West (23%). Baseball's strongest region was the West, at 21%. College football was the favorite sport of 20% of Southerners, but only 3% of Easterners.

SPORTS ATTENDANCE

Attendance trends vary considerably from one sport to another, and in general one sport's loss, whether because of

scandal or declining interest, translates into another sport's gain. Professional sports teams rely on revenue from ticket sales to cover much of the cost of the huge salaries they pay their players. At the college level, ticket sales are a big part of what keeps university athletic programs solvent.

Major Sports

BASEBALL. Even though the national pastime seems to have lost some of its luster in terms of participation

Poll respondents who are or are not college football fans, 1999–2007

ARE YOU A FAN OF COLLEGE FOOTBALL, OR NOT?

	Yes, a fan	Somewhat of a fan (vol.)	No, not a fan	No opinion
	%	%	%	%
2007 Nov 2–4	39	6	54	*
2006 Jul 28–30	39	6	54	*
2006 Jul 6–9	37	7	56	*
2006 Jun 23–25	42	8	50	—
2006 Jun 9–11	47	7	46	*
2005 Jul 22–24	37	6	57	—
2004 Dec 5–8	47	7	46	*
2001 Dec 14–16	39	8	53	*
2001 Mar 26–28	44	9	46	1
2000 Nov 13–15	41	6	53	*
2000 Aug 24–27	32	10	58	*
1999 Oct 21–24	36	10	54	*

*Less than 0.5%
(vol.) = Volunteered response

SOURCE: "Are You a Fan of College Football, or Not?" in *Football*, The Gallup Organization, 2007, http://www.gallup.com/poll/1705/Football.aspx (accessed June 8, 2009). Copyright © 2007 by The Gallup Organization. Reproduced by permission of The Gallup Organization.

MLB games for the year was 32,529, also the second highest ever, according to the press release "National League, Seven Clubs Set All-Time Attendance Records" (October 1, 2008, http://mlb.mlb.com/news/press_releases/press_release.jsp?ymd=20081001&content_id=3578727&vkey=pr_mlb&fext=.jsp&c_id=mlb). Ten different teams had attendance figures that exceeded 3 million for home games. Seven teams—the Boston Red Sox, Chicago Cubs, Detroit Tigers, Milwaukee Brewers, New York Mets, New York Yankees, and Philadelphia Phillies—set attendance records for their regular season home games.

BASKETBALL. Professional basketball has been enjoying strong ticket sales since the turn of the 21st century. According to the press release "Regular Season Closes with Third-Highest Attendance All Time" (April 17, 2009, http://www.nba.com/2009/playoffs2009/04/17/attendance/index.html), the National Basketball Association (NBA) drew 21.5 million spectators to its arenas during the 2008–09 regular season, falling just short of its attendance record, set during the 2006–07 regular season. That total represented an average of 17,520 spectators per game. The Detroit Pistons led the league in attendance, drawing an average of 21,877 fans to each of its home games. The Chicago Bulls, Portland Trail Blazers, Dallas Mavericks, and Cleveland Cavaliers also drew more than 20,000 spectators per game on average. The Sacramento Kings were the league's poorest-drawing squad, averaging a crowd of just 12,571 per game.

and self-identified fan base over the decades, the public is still taking itself out to the ball game. Over 78.6 million fans attended Major League Baseball (MLB) games during the 2008 regular season, about one million fewer than the record set a year earlier. Average attendance at

Poll respondents' preference for football vs. baseball as favorite sport to watch, 1937–2008

WHAT IS YOUR FAVORITE SPORT TO WATCH?

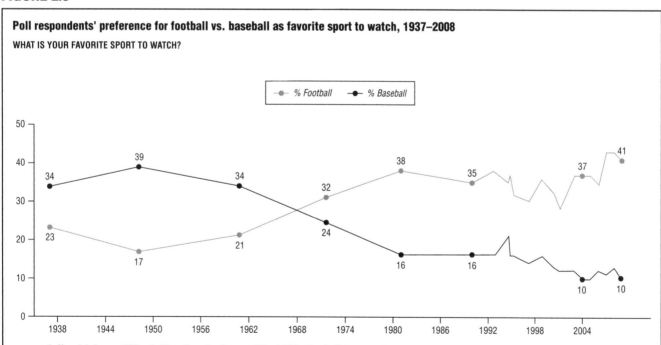

SOURCE: Jeffrey M. Jones, "What Is Your Favorite Sport to Watch?" in *Football Remains Runaway Leader As Favorite Sport*, The Gallup Organization, December 29, 2008, http://www.gallup.com/poll/113503/Football-Remains-Runaway-Leader-Favorite-Sport.aspx (accessed June 3, 2009). Copyright © 2008 by The Gallup Organization. Reproduced by permission of The Gallup Organization.

FIGURE 2.4

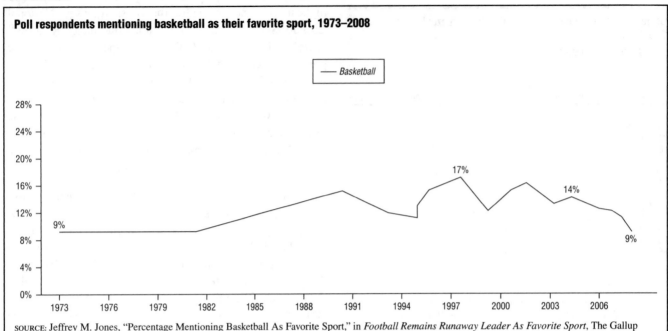

Poll respondents mentioning basketball as their favorite sport, 1973–2008

SOURCE: Jeffrey M. Jones, "Percentage Mentioning Basketball As Favorite Sport," in *Football Remains Runaway Leader As Favorite Sport*, The Gallup Organization, December 29, 2008, http://www.gallup.com/poll/113503/Football-Remains-Runaway-Leader-Favorite-Sport.aspx (accessed June 3, 2009). Copyright © 2008 by The Gallup Organization. Reproduced by permission of The Gallup Organization.

TABLE 2.17

Americans' favorite sport, selected years 1985–2008

[Base: All adults who follow one or more sport]

"IF YOU HAD TO CHOOSE, WHICH ONE OF THESE SPORTS WOULD YOU SAY IS YOUR FAVORITE?"

	1985	1989	1992	1993	1994	1997	1998	2002	2003	2004	2005	2006	2008	2008	Change 1985–2008
	%	%	%	%	%	%	%	%	%	%	%	%	%	%	%
Pro football	24	26	28	24	24	28	26	27	29	30	33	29	30	31	+7
Baseball	23	19	21	18	17	17	18	14	13	15	14	14	15	16	−7
College football	10	6	7	8	7	10	9	9	9	11	13	13	12	12	+2
Auto racing	5	4	5	6	5	5	7	10	9	7	11	9	10	8	+3
Men's pro basketball	6	7	8	12	11	13	13	11	10	7	4	7	4	6	0
Hockey	2	3	3	3	5	4	3	3	3	4	5	4	5	5	+3
Men's college basketball	6	10	8	8	8	6	4	4	6	6	5	5	4	5	−1
Men's golf	3	4	4	6	5	6	4	4	5	4	4	4	4	4	+1
Men's soccer	3	2	2	1	3	3	4	3	3	3	2	2	2	3	0
Swimming	NA	NA	NA	NA	NA	NA	NA	NA	NA	NA	NA	NA	NA	2	NA
Boxing	NA	NA	NA	NA	NA	NA	NA	NA	2	2	1	1	2	NA
Women's tennis	NA	NA	NA	NA	NA	NA	NA	3	2	2	1	1	*	1	NA
Horse racing	4	3	3	2	2	2	2	1	2	1	2	1	2	1	−3
Bowling	3	5	2	2	1	1	2	2	1	1	1	1	2	1	−2
Track & field	2	2	1	1	2	2	3	1	3	1	*	2	1	1	−1
Men's tennis	5	4	4	4	3	3	4	1	2	1	1	2	1	1	−4
Women's pro basketball	NA	NA	NA	NA	NA	NA	*	1	1	*	*	*	*	*	NA
Women's soccer	NA	NA	NA	NA	NA	NA	NA	NA	NA	1	*	*	*	*	NA
Women's college basketball	NA	NA	NA	NA	NA	NA	1	1	*	1	*	1	1	*	NA
Women's golf	NA	NA	NA	NA	NA	NA	NA	NA	1	*	*	1	*	*	NA
Not sure	*	1	4	1	2	2	1	3	1	2	2	3	2	1	—
Pro football's lead over baseball	**1**	**7**	**7**	**6**	**7**	**11**	**8**	**13**	**16**	**15**	**19**	**15**	**15**	**15**	**+14**

Notes: NA = Not asked in that year. Men and women's sports were not always distinguished.
Percentages may not add up to 100% due to rounding.
*Indicates less than 0.5%

SOURCE: "Table 1. Favorite Sports," in *Professional Football Continues Dominance over Baseball As America's Favorite Sport*, Harris Interactive, Inc., January 27, 2009, http://www.harrisinteractive.com/harris_poll/pubs/Harris_Poll_2009_01_27.pdf (accessed June 17, 2009)

TABLE 2.18

Demographic variations in favorite sports, 2008

[Base: All adults who follow more than one sport]

"IF YOU HAD TO CHOOSE, WHICH ONE OF THESE SPORTS WOULD YOU SAY IS YOUR FAVORITE?"

Sport	All adults %	Highest	%	Lowest	%
Pro football	31	Income $50,000–$74,999	43	Post-graduates	20
		African Americans	42	Westerners	23
		Those aged 30–39	39	Those 65 and older	26
		Easterners	38	Hispanics	27
Baseball	16	Westerners	21	Those aged 30–39	8
		Those 65 and older	21	African Americans	8
		Hispanics	20	Income $50,000–$74,999	10
College football	12	College graduates	21	Easterners	3
		Southerners	20	African Americans	4
		Those aged 25–29	20	Hispanics	6
Auto racing	8	Those aged 50–64	14	African Americans	1
		HS or less education	11	Post-graduates	2
		Midwesterners	10	Those aged 18–24	2

SOURCE: "Table 2. Demographic Variations in Favorite Sports," in *Professional Football Continues Dominance over Baseball As America's Favorite Sport*, Harris Interactive, Inc., January 27, 2009, http://www.harrisinteractive.com/harris_poll/pubs/Harris_Poll_2009_01_27.pdf (accessed June 17, 2009)

On a team-by-team basis, attendance in the NBA has a lot to do with the success of the team and the size of the city. It is not difficult to predict that a winning team in a large city is likely to sell more tickets than a lousy team in a small market. Perhaps more than any other sport, however, professional basketball attendance is influenced by personalities. The acquisition of a truly high-profile player—such as Shaquille O'Neal (1972–) or LeBron James (1984–)—can lead to a spike in ticket sales for the star's new team. Periodically, a player or set of players emerges with such charisma that the entire league's attendance numbers benefit. This was the case during the 1980s, when the ongoing rivalry between the team of Magic Johnson (1959–)—the Los Angeles Lakers—and that of Larry Bird (1956–)—the Boston Celtics—spurred a surge of interest throughout the league. Michael Jordan (1963–) had a similar impact during the 1990s. In 2009 it looked as if the burgeoning rivalry between James and the Lakers' Kobe Bryant (1978–) had the potential to boost the entire league's popularity.

FOOTBALL. Professional football also saw a slight decline in attendance for the 2008 regular season. The official league tally showed total paid attendance for the National Football League (NFL) to be 17.5 million—down from a record 17.6 million in 2007—with an average paid attendance of 68,241 per game. Team-by-team attendance figures gathered by ESPN (2009, http://sports.espn.go.com/nfl/attendance?year=2008) show that the Washington Redskins led the league in attendance in 2008. The pride of the nation's capital attracted 708,835 paying customers over the course of its eight home games in 2008, for an average of 88,604 fans per game. New York City is a big enough market not only to have two NFL squads—the Jets and the Giants—but also to have these two teams place second (Giants) and third (Jets) in attendance. (Both the Jets and the Giants play their home games at Giants Stadium in East Rutherford, New Jersey, just across the Hudson River from New York City. A new facility, the New Meadowlands Stadium, was scheduled to be completed in time for the 2010 season.)

As with all spectator sports, one of the most important factors in an NFL team's attendance—along with market size and personalities—is team performance. However, in 2008 market size clearly trumped performance: The Pittsburgh Steelers, the eventual champs of the 2009 Super Bowl, finished 26th on the attendance list, drawing average paid attendance of 62,890 per game, for a regular-season total of 503,125 fans. In general, attendance at both college and professional football games has shown significant growth over the long term. Table 2.19 shows attendance figures, along with other relevant data, for college and pro football for selected years since 1990.

The Super Bowl, which determines the NFL champion from between the champions of its two conferences, is much more about television viewing than about live attendance. Its paid attendees are limited by the size of the venue, which changes each year. For example, the St. Louis Web site stltoday.com, reporting attendance figures from Stats.com, indicated that 70,774 fans watched Super Bowl XLIII live at Raymond James Stadium in Tampa, Florida (2009, http://stltoday.stats.com/fb/boxscore.asp?gamecode—20090201022&home=22&vis=23), where the Pittsburgh Steelers defeated the Arizona Cardinals in dramatic fashion. This was nowhere near record attendance for a Super Bowl; according to the NFL, in 1980, 103,985 spectators packed the Rose Bowl in Pasadena, California, to watch the Steelers beat the Los Angeles Rams in Super Bowl XIV.

TABLE 2.19

College and professional football attendance, selected years, 1990–2007

[35,330 represents 35,330,000.]

Sport	Unit	1990	1995	2000	2003	2004	2005	2006	2007
NCAA college									
Teams	Number	533	565	606	617	612	615	615	619
Attendance	1,000	35,330	35,638	39,059	46,145	43,106	43,487	47,909	48,752
National Football League									
Teams	Number	28	30	31	32	32	32	32	32
Attendance, total[a]	1,000	17,666	19,203	20,954	21,639	21,709	21,792	22,200	22,256
Regular season	1,000	13,960	15,044	16,387	16,914	17,001	17,012	17,341	17,345
Average per game	Number	62,321	62,682	66,078	66,328	66,409	66,455	67,738	67,755
Postseason games[b]	1,000	848	(NA)	809	806	789	802	776	792

NA = Not available
[a]Preseason attendance data are not shown.
[b]Includes Pro Bowl (a nonchampionship game) and Super Bowl.

SOURCE: Adapted from "Table 1204. College and Professional Football Summary: 1990 to 2007," in *Statistical Abstract of the United States: 2009*, 128th ed., U.S. Census Bureau, 2008, http://www.census.gov/compendia/statab/tables/09s1204.pdf (accessed June 17, 2009). Data from NCAA and NFL.

HOCKEY. National Hockey League (NHL) attendance for the 2008–09 season was nearly 21.5 million, setting a new record for the fourth consecutive year (April 12, 2009, http://www.nhl.com/ice/news.htm?id=417969). The NHL continues to regain the fans it lost during the 2004–05 season, which was canceled in its entirety because of labor turmoil. According to ESPN (http://sports.espn.go.com/nhl/attendance?sort=home_pct&year=2009), the top draw in 2008–09 was the Chicago Blackhawks, with 912,155 spectators over the course of the season, for an average of 22,247 per home game. Only one other team, the Montreal Canadiens, drew more than 20,000 fans per game. The New York Islanders had the poorest turnout for the season, with total attendance of 564,697.

SOCCER. Even as soccer emerges as a major sport in the United States, attendance at Major League Soccer (MLS) games has not grown all that much. According to Tripp Mickle in *SportsBusiness Journal* (November 3, 2008, http://www.sportsbusinessjournal.com/article/60481), MLS games drew an average of 16,459 fans during the 2008 regular season. This figure was slightly lower than the previous year, when the arrival of British superstar David Beckham (1975–) as a member of the Los Angeles Galaxy provided a boost to both attendance and television ratings. According to ESPN (http://soccernet.espn.go.com/stats/attendance?league=USA.1&year=2008&cc=5901), the Galaxy were by far the best drawing MLS team, with an average home game attendance of 26,050 in 2008. Only one other team, Toronto FC, broke the 20,000 patron-per-game mark. The league's worst-drawing team, the Kansas City Wizards, attracted barely half that many fans per game, at 10,673.

AUTO RACING. Auto racing enjoyed a surge in popularity during the first years of the 21st century. The most prominent auto racing event in the United States is the Indianapolis 500 (Indy 500), a 200-lap, 500-mile (805-km) race that is held on Memorial Day weekend each year at Indianapolis Motor Speedway. The 2009 race was the 93rd Indy 500. The Indy 500 does not release official attendance figures, but CBS Sports reports that estimates are typically in the 400,000 range, and certainly over 250,000 (2009, http://www.cbssports.com/autoracing/story/11776519).

However, the Indy Racing League (IndyCar) is only one faction of the broader auto racing scene. There is also NASCAR, which has become such a phenomenon that its followers (also known as "NASCAR dads") are now viewed by political analysts as a powerful voting bloc alongside so-called soccer moms. The Super Bowl of the NASCAR circuit is the Daytona 500, which is held in February at the Daytona International Speedway in Florida. Like the Indy 500, exact attendance figures for Daytona are not released, but Ben Klayman reports in the Reuters article "NASCAR Expects Lower Attendance in 2009" (February 11, 2009, http://www.reuters.com/article/reutersEdge/idUSTRE51B03J20090212) that attendance at Daytona was expected to be approximately 200,000.

Besides the IndyCar and NASCAR circuits, there are the Formula One Grand Prix series, the National Hot Rod Association, and various smaller racing circuits. Of these races, NASCAR has by far the greatest overall attendance numbers, drawing 4.4 million spectators in 2004, according to John W. Schoen in "Auto Racing Revs Up Revenues, Profits" (May 28, 2005, http://www.msnbc.msn.com/id/8007370). However, by late 2006 the industry was concerned about an apparent dip in attendance at auto racing events, as reported by Nate Ryan, in "NASCAR's Growth Slows after 15 Years in the Fast Lane" (*USA Today*, November 15, 2006), reflecting a possible end to the NASCAR boom. By 2009, with the economy in shambles, NASCAR was expecting a second consecutive year of declining attendance, according to Klayman's February 2009 article.

TABLE 2.20

Adult attendance at sports events, by frequency, 2007

[In thousands (2,343 represents 2,343,000), except percent. For fall 2007. Based on survey and subject to sampling error.]

Event	Attend one or more times a month		Attend less than once a month	
	Number	Percent	Number	Percent
Auto racing—NASCAR*	2,343	1.1	10,209	4.6
Auto racing—other	2,384	1.1	7,443	3.4
Baseball	7,591	3.4	20,664	9.4
Basketball				
College games	3,812	1.7	9,830	4.5
Professional games	3,280	1.5	10,996	5.0
Bowling	1,602	0.7	5,460	2.5
Boxing	990	0.5	5,012	2.3
Equestrian events	475	0.2	5,177	2.3
Figure skating	391	0.2	5,044	2.3
Fishing tournaments	740	0.3	4,933	2.2
Football				
College games	5,759	2.6	12,705	5.8
Monday night professional games	2,165	1.0	6,821	3.1
Weekend professional games	4,007	1.8	11,787	5.3
Golf	1,499	0.7	6,122	2.8
High school sports	10,850	4.9	10,557	4.8
Horse racing				
Flats, runners	1,279	0.6	5,860	2.7
Trotters/harness	629	0.3	4,906	2.2
Ice hockey	1,872	0.9	8,499	3.9
Motorcycle racing	854	0.4	5,127	2.3
Pro beach volleyball	403	0.2	4,729	2.1
Rodeo/bull riding	744	0.3	6,333	2.9
Soccer	3,437	1.6	6,497	2.9
Tennis	901	0.4	5,527	2.5
Truck and tractor pull/mud racing	904	0.4	5,895	2.7
Wrestling—professional	943	0.4	5,562	2.5

*NASCAR = National Assocation for Stock Car Auto Racing

SOURCE: "Table 1206. Adult Attendance at Sports Events by Frequency: 2007," in *Statistical Abstract of the United States: 2009*, 128th ed., U.S. Census Bureau, 2008, http://www.census.gov/compendia/statab/tables/09s1206.pdf (accessed June 17, 2009). Data from Mediamark Research, Inc.

OTHER SPORTS. It can be assumed that what draws these hundreds of thousands of spectators to auto races such as the Indy 500 each year is the speed—the experience of watching people hurtle around a track at well over 200 miles per hour (322 km/h). However, people also jam Boston's streets each year to watch a race in which the fastest entrant averages a mere 12 miles per hour (19 km/h). That race is the Boston Marathon, the most famous marathon in the world. Each year, according to the Boston Athletic Association (2009, http://www.bostonmarathon.org/BostonMarathon/RaceFacts.asp), 500,000 spectators line the streets along the marathon's 26.2-mile (42.2-km) route. Few other sporting events in the world are witnessed live by as many people as is the Boston Marathon.

Table 2.20 presents information on 2007 attendance by adults at various sporting events. Table 2.21 puts attendance patterns for a handful of sports into historical perspective, using statistics dating back to 1990.

TABLE 2.21

Attendance at selected spectator sports, selected years 1990–2007

[55,512 represents 55,512,000]

Sport	Unit	1990	1995	2000	2003	2004	2005	2006	2007
Baseball, major leagues									
Attendance	1,000	55,512	51,288	74,339	69,501	74,822	76,286	77,524	80,803
Regular season	1,000	54,824	50,469	72,748	67,568	73,023	74,926	76,043	79,503
Playoffs[a]	1,000	479	533	1,314	1,568	1,625	1,191	1,218	1,083
World Series	1,000	209	286	277	365	174	168	225	173
Players' salaries									
Average	$1,000	598	1,111	1,896	2,372	2,313	2,476	2,699	2,825
Basketball[b]									
NCAA—men's college									
Teams	Number	767	868	932	967	981	983	984	982
Attendance	1,000	28,741	28,548	29,025	30,124	30,761	30,569	30,940	32,836
NCAA—women's college									
Teams	Number	782	864	956	1,009	1,008	1,036	1,018	1,003
Attendance[c]	1,000	2,777	4,962	8,698	10,164	10,016	9,940	9,903	10,878
National Hockey League[d]									
Regular season attendance	1,000	12,580	9,234	18,800	20,409	20,356	([e])	20,854	20,862
Playoffs attendance	1,000	1,356	1,329	1,525	1,636	1,709	([e])	1,530	1,497
Professional rodeo									
Rodeos	Number	754	739	688	657	671	662	649	592
Performances	Number	2,159	2,217	2,081	1,949	1,982	1,940	1,884	1,733
Members	Number	5,693	6,894	6,255	6,158	6,247	6,127	5,892	5,528
Permit-holders (rookies)	Number	3,290	3,835	3,249	3,121	2,990	2,701	2,468	2,186
Total prize money	Mil. dol.	18.2	24.5	32.3	34.3	35.5	36.6	36.2	40.5

[a]Beginning 1997, two rounds of playoffs were played. Prior years had one round.
[b]Season ending in year shown.
[c]For women's attendance total, excludes double-headers with men's teams.
[d]For season ending in year shown.
[e]In September 2004, franchise owners locked out their players upon the expiration of the collective bargaining agreement. The entire season was cancelled in Feburary 2005.

SOURCE: "Table 1205. Selected Spectator Sports: 1990 to 2007," in *Statistical Abstract of the United States: 2009*, 128th ed., U.S. Census Bureau, 2008, http://www.census.gov/compendia/statab/tables/09s1205.pdf (accessed June 17, 2009). Data compiled from Major League Baseball; The American League of Professional Baseball Clubs; Major League Baseball Players Association; National Collegiate Athletic Association; National Hockey League, Montreal, Quebec; Professional Rodeo Cowboys Association.

CHAPTER 3
SPORTS AND THE MEDIA

Sports and the media are so thoroughly intertwined in the United States that it is difficult to think of them as two distinct industries. The financial relationship is complex and reciprocal. Media enterprises, mostly broadcast and cable television stations but also Web based, pay the sports leagues millions of dollars for the rights to broadcast their games. Leagues distribute this money to their member teams—the distribution formula varies from sport to sport—which then transfer most of this money to their players in the form of salaries. The media outlets try to recoup their huge expenditures by selling advertising time during sports broadcasts to companies that believe their products will appeal to the kinds of people who like to watch sports on television. These consumer product companies also pay large sums to individual athletes to endorse their products, or in some cases to teams to display their company logos on their uniforms or, in the case of auto racing, on their cars. Consumers then purchase these products, providing the money the companies use to buy advertising and pay for celebrity endorsements. The more people who watch a sport, the more the station can charge for advertising. The more the station can charge for advertising, the more it can offer the league for broadcast rights. The more the league gets for broadcast rights, the more the teams can pay their players.

THE HISTORY OF SPORTS ON TELEVISION

In "Sports and Television" (2004, http://www.museum.tv/archives/etv/S/htmlS/sportsandte/sportsandte.htm), Harry Coyle, a pioneering television sports director, states that "television got off the ground because of sports. Today, maybe, sports need television to survive, but it was just the opposite when it first started. When we [NBC] put on the World Series in 1947, heavyweight fights, the Army-Navy football game, the sales of television sets just spurted."

Even though it may be an exaggeration to credit the explosive growth of television in its early days solely to sports, sports certainly played a significant role. The first-ever televised sporting event was a baseball game between Columbia and Princeton universities in 1939. It was covered by one camera that was positioned along the third base line. The first network-wide sports broadcast came five years later with the premier of the National Broadcasting Corporation's (NBC) *Gillette Cavalcade of Sports*, the first installment of which featured a featherweight championship boxing match between Willie Pep (1922–2006) and Chalky Wright (1912–1957). Sports quickly became a staple of primetime network fare, accounting for up to one-third of primetime programming, but other genres began to catch up during the 1950s, perhaps spurred on by an increase in female viewers. The *Gillette Cavalcade of Sports* remained on the air for 20 years, before giving way to a new model in which sports programs were sponsored by multiple buyers of advertising spots rather than by a single corporation, as the cost of sponsorship became prohibitively expensive in the mid-1960s. The number of hours of sports programming on the networks continued to increase dramatically well into the 1980s, when advertising dollars generated by sports began to decline, making them less profitable for the networks to carry.

The amount of money involved in televising sports was growing fast by the 1970s. Stanley J. Baran, writing on the Web site of the Museum of Broadcast Communications (http://www.museum.tv/archives/etv/S/htmlS/sportsandte/sportsandte.htm), notes that in 1970 the networks paid $50 million for the right to broadcast National Football League (NFL) games, $18 million for Major League Baseball (MLB), and $2 million for National Basketball Association (NBA) broadcast rights. By 1985 these numbers reached $450 million for football, $160 million for baseball, and $45 million for basketball. This explosive growth was fueled by a combination of increasing public interest, better—and therefore more expensive—coverage of events by the networks, and an effort on the part of the networks to lock in their position of dominance in sports programming in the face of challenges from emerging cable television networks. These skyrocketing fees did not cause much of a problem during the 1970s, as the networks were able to pass the high cost of producing sports programs along to their advertisers. However, things began to change during the early 1980s. According to Baran, between 1980 and 1984 professional football lost 7% of its viewing audience, and baseball lost 26% of its viewers. Meanwhile, advertisers became hesitant to pay increasing prices for commercials that would be seen by fewer people. The networks responded by airing more hours of sports. By 1985 the three major networks broadcast a total of 1,500 hours of sports, about twice as many hours as in 1960. However, by the mid-1980s the market for sports programming appeared saturated, and the presence of more shows made it harder for the networks to sell ads at top prices.

The first half of the 1980s marked the rise of sports coverage on cable. According to Baran, the all-sports station Entertainment and Sports Programming Network (ESPN), first launched in 1979, was reaching 4 million households by the middle of 1980. National stations such as WTBS and WGN, as well as the premium channel Home Box Office (HBO), were also airing a substantial number of sporting events. By 1986, 37 million households were subscribing to ESPN.

Between the early 1990s and the early 2000s broadcast television ratings for the four major professional sports generally trended downward. There is no real consensus as to why this happened. Jere Longman, in "Pro Leagues' Ratings Drop; Nobody Is Quite Sure Why" (Scott R. Rosner and Kenneth L. Shropshire, eds., *The Business of Sports*, 2004), points to "a growing dislocation between fans and traditional sports, as players, coaches and teams move frequently, as athletes misbehave publicly, as salaries skyrocket, and as ticket prices become prohibitively expensive" as possible contributing factors in the decline of ratings during that period.

The key challenge for all the major sports leagues—beyond the obvious challenge of attracting as many viewers and listeners as possible—is to balance exposure and distribution of their product against consumer demand. In other words, in an era witnessing the emergence of new media such as the Internet, satellite radio, and even live feeds to cell phones, at what point does the coverage of a sport available for consumption outstrip the public's interest in that sport, thereby becoming a losing financial proposition?

BASEBALL AND TELEVISION: THE CONVERGENCE OF OUR TWO NATIONAL PASTIMES

By 1939 baseball was already known as "America's national pastime." Television was still a novelty at the time. The only option for those who could not attend a baseball game in person was to listen to a live broadcast on the radio.

The first televised professional baseball game, between the Brooklyn Dodgers and the Cincinnati Reds, took place on August 26 of that year. The broadcast used two cameras: one positioned high above home plate and a second one along the third base line. Such a broadcast would appear primitive by 21st-century standards. To cover a typical World Series game in the modern era, broadcasters use perhaps a couple dozen cameras, some of them operated electronically, and at least one mounted on an airborne blimp. In addition, early broadcasts offered none of the additional features contemporary viewers take for granted, including color, instant replays, and statistics superimposed on the screen.

NBC was the network that first brought televised baseball to the American public. Because NBC used home-team announcers to call the World Series, and because the New York Yankees were in the World Series nearly every year, the Yankees announcer Mel Allen (1913–1996) became the first coast-to-coast voice of baseball. The Hall of Fame pitcher Dizzy Dean (1911–1974) became the first nationwide television baseball announcer when the network premiered the *Game of the Week* in 1953, thus initiating the long line of former ball players who have transformed themselves into commentators when their playing careers have ended.

By the 1960s baseball had lost a large share of its audience to other sports, particularly football. Baseball nevertheless remains a solid ratings draw, especially when teams with well-known stars located in large markets square off in the postseason. However, the overall ratings for World Series broadcasts have been declining for years. The Associated Press noted in its post-series coverage (October 30, 2008, http://nbcsports.msnbc.com/id/27462511/) that ratings for the 2008 World Series, in which the Philadelphia Phillies triumphed over the Tampa Bay Rays in five games, hit a record low. The series averaged an 8.4 rating (meaning 8.4% of all households were tuned in) and a 14 share (meaning 14% of those watching something were watching the World Series). These numbers were considerably worse than those of the 2006 World Series, the previously lowest-rated World Series. The 2006 series captured an average rating of 10.1 and a 17 share over the five games. These ratings were a far cry from 1980, when the World Series had a 32.8% rating and a 56 share during the entire series. The AP story attributes the 2008 World Series' abysmal television ratings in part to the brevity of the series and the fact that it was played between two fairly small-market teams.

Professional baseball has increased its media income substantially in recent years. MLB is currently operating under a round of television deals signed in 2005 and 2006. Danielle Sessa reported for the Bloomberg News Service in (July 11, 2006, http://www.bloomberg.com/apps/news?pid=20601089&sid=aUWEuWhFjx5M&refer=home) that ESPN agreed to pay $2.4 billion to start a series of Monday night baseball broadcasts as part of an eight-year contract, which runs through 2013. Under the terms of the deal, ESPN may televise up to 80 regular-season games per season. The agreement also affords ESPN substantial flexibility to move some of the games to Sunday nights. MLB also has a deal with Fox for the broadcast rights to the All-Star Game and the World Series through 2013. MLB's other major television partner is TBS, which is slated to air all regular-season tiebreaker games, Division Series games, and a Sunday afternoon regular-season package through 2013.

Baseball has expanded its radio presence in recent years as well. The 2005 season marked the first year of a six-year contract with ESPN radio worth an average of $11 million per year; a six-year Internet deal with ESPN for an annual average of $30 million; and a $60 million-per-year deal with XM satellite radio to transmit baseball games for 11 years.

In "Is MLB Extending Its Reach or Overreaching?" in the *SportsBusiness Journal* (March 28, 2005, http://www.sportsbusinessjournal.com/index.cfm?fuseaction=page.feature&featureId=1561), Russell Adams observes that the 2005 MLB season marked "a critical juncture for MLB officials, who are charged with managing a perfect storm of peaking demand for content, the emergence of new technologies for delivering it, and the growing number of media outlets demanding a larger piece of both." Adams describes a situation in which baseball clubs' local television partners are clamoring for more content from a sport that has more games to offer than any other. Opportunities abound, many of them in new media, for a sport that has long been criticized for "underutilizing its product"; that is, not showing enough games in sophisticated enough ways, and for neglecting the younger portion of its potential audience. This neglect and underutilization no longer seem to be the case. According to Adams, the Internet division of MLB, known as MLB Advanced Media, has built a thriving subscription business by streaming live video of more than 2,300 regular-season games and live audio of all games, and by packaging and selling video on an on-demand basis once the game has ended. Television contracts do not apply to these sales, because broadcast rights revert to the league once the game has taken place. Meanwhile, players, sports journalists, and other sports personalities have short circuited the process of bringing content to fans through the use of social media tools, such as blogging, Facebook, and most recently, Twitter.

FOOTBALL: BIGGEST ATHLETES, BIGGEST AUDIENCE

Professional Football

It is not an exaggeration to say that television put football where it is today. Before the era of televised sports, baseball was much more popular than football. Stirring television moments such as the 1958 NFL Championship, a thrilling overtime victory by the Baltimore Colts over the New York Giants, helped establish professional football as a big-time spectator sport. A few years later, when *Time* put the Green Bay Packers coach Vince Lombardi (1913–1970) on its cover in 1962—accompanied by the pronouncement that football was "The Sport of the '60s"—it was clear that the sport had come of age as a media phenomenon.

In April 2005 the NFL signed a deal for $1.1 billion per year to move *Monday Night Football* from its long-standing home with the American Broadcasting Company (ABC)—which was paying about half that sum under its expiring contract—to ESPN from 2006 through the 2013 season. (See Table 1.4 in Chapter 1.) Under the terms of the deal, ESPN would continue to make its NFL games available on regular broadcast television in the markets of the participating teams each week. However, unlike basketball, which experienced a loss of casual viewers when games were moved to cable in 2002, regular network television would continue to play a large role in bringing football to the viewing public.

The same day it shook hands with ESPN, the league reached an agreement with NBC, which had not broadcast NFL games since 1997. The NBC contract provides $600 million per year for the rights to carry 17 Sunday night games each season through 2011. (See Table 1.4 in Chapter 1.) Meanwhile, the NFL had agreed in November 2004 to extend its existing relationships with CBS and Fox to carry regular-season American Football Conference and National Football Conference games, respectively. The new CBS agreement included two Super Bowls and guaranteed $622.5 million per year through 2011; the new Fox contract called for five years at $712.5 million per year, with two Super Bowls included in the deal. The league received another $700 million from DirectTV in a five-year agreement covering satellite transmission rights.

What do the networks get for all this money? They get plenty because advertisers know how firmly football is entrenched in U.S. households and sports bars. Football is by far the most popular sport to watch on television in the United States. In a December 2008 poll by the Gallup Organization, 41% of Americans named football as their favorite sport to watch. (See Table 1.1 in Chapter 1.) This is nothing new; football has topped polls consistently since the early 1970s, when it overtook baseball as the public's favorite sport to watch. (See Figure 2.3 in Chapter 2.) In the December 2008 survey, baseball was a distant second at 10%, with basketball close behind at 9%. The preference for watching baseball has been on the decline since its peak in 1948, when 39% said it was their favorite sport to watch.

According to data from Nielsen Media Research, as reported in *SportsBusiness Daily* (February 3, 2009, http://www.sportsbusinessdaily.com/article/127428), two of the three top-rated U.S. television shows of all time have been Super Bowls. Nielsen data show that with 98.7 million viewers, Super Bowl XLIII in February 2009 was the most watched Super Bowl in history, and the second most watched television show of any kind ever, trailing only the final episode of the long-running comedy series *M*A*S*H* in 1983. Super Bowl XLII in 2008 was a close third at 97.4 million.

College Football

Televised college sports have nearly as much appeal as professional sports for American audiences, and since the 1980s they have become the subject of large media contracts as well. In the early days of televised sports, the National Collegiate Athletic Association (NCAA) determined which college teams could play on television. Officially, the NCAA's goal in making these decisions was to protect the schools from the loss of ticket-buying fans who were lured by the glowing screen in a warm home. The NCAA's dominance over the right to broadcast football games went virtually unquestioned for years. According to Welch Suggs in "Football, Television, and the Supreme Court" (*Chronicle of Higher Education*, vol. 50, no. 44, July 9, 2004), the only case of a college losing its membership in the NCAA came in 1951, when the University of Pennsylvania was dismissed for attempting to schedule its own broadcasts in defiance of the NCAA. The school quickly repented, and its membership was restored.

The networks, however, aware of the potential audience for games between large universities with esteemed football programs, kept courting college athletic departments. By the 1970s several universities with top football programs had become frustrated with the limits the NCAA was placing on their television exposure. In 1977 five major conferences, along with a handful of high-profile independents, formed their own group, the College Football Association (CFA), to fight for their interests within the NCAA. A few years later the CFA signed its own television agreement with NBC, the second-largest sports television contract ever signed up to that time. Naturally, the NCAA was unhappy about this development and moved to ban the teams involved from all championship events. The University of Georgia and Oklahoma University sued the NCAA, and the case was eventually decided by the U.S. Supreme Court in *NCAA v. Board of Regents of the University of Oklahoma et al.* (468 U.S. 85, 1984). In the end, the NCAA was found to be in violation of antitrust laws. Thus, the NCAA's stranglehold on television broadcast of college football was broken.

In the wake of the Supreme Court decision, the CFA took on the role of coordinating the television coverage of most of the nation's leading football conferences. Still, some teams found the arrangement too restrictive. Following the defection of a handful of teams and conferences, the CFA folded in 1994, and the conferences were on their own to negotiate television contracts with the networks. The dollars began to flow in an ever-greater volume during this period. Suggs notes that the Southeastern Conference (SEC) signed

a contract in 1990 that brought in $16 million to be divided among its members. In 2008 the SEC signed broadcast contracts with CBS and ESPN that extended for 15 years and guaranteed such participating schools as the University of Alabama, University of Florida, and Louisiana State University an estimated $20 million each per year (August 25, 2008, http://blogs.tampabay.com/gators/2008/08/sec-espn-ag ree.html).

With about a thousand universities participating in over 150,000 sporting events each year, competition for the right to put these events on television is fierce. In 2003 a network devoted strictly to collegiate athletics was launched under the name College Sports Television (CSTV). According to CSTV (http://www.cstv.com/online/), in 2009 the network was available in more than 21 million homes via cable and satellite. CSTV also operates a network of 215 official athletic Web sites for top colleges, and streams audio and/ or video for thousands of events per year on high-speed Internet to online subscribers. CSTV was purchased by CBS in January 2006, and is now called CBS College Sports Network. As often happens in the media world, success has bred competition. In March 2005 ESPN launched ESPNU (2009, http://espn.go.com/college-sports/), its own version of a college-only sports station, available through many cable and satellite television systems.

BASKETBALL

NBA regular-season games have never drawn the kind of television audiences that NFL games routinely attract, simply because there are so many of them—the NBA season lasts 82 games, whereas the NFL's lasts just 16. In basketball, viewership increases significantly during the playoffs and is greatly influenced by the specific teams or personalities involved in a game. The NBA's television ratings have generally been sliding since Michael Jordan (1963–) retired in 1999, though there are signs that ratings have begun to rebound in the waning years of the first decade of the 2000s. Ratings for NBA regular-season broadcasts were up sharply in 2008–09 over the previous season, according to Time Warner, with an average rating of 2.3. (April 16, 2009, http://www.espnmediazone.com/ press_releases/2009_04_april/20090416_NBAAudience GrowthAcrossESPNPlatforms.htm). Although this was a significant improvement over the past few years, it paled in comparison to the NBA's best years. A decade earlier, during the peak of the Jordan era, it had a 5.0 rating, according to Kevin Downey, in "'Monday Night Football' Takes a Hit" (*Media Life*, October 9, 2001). A low point came in 2006, when a game between the Cleveland Cavaliers and the Los Angeles Lakers—pitting two of the sport's brightest stars in LeBron James (1984–) and Kobe Bryant (1978–) against each other—recorded lower ratings than a rained-out National Association for Stock Car Auto Racing (NASCAR) race being broadcast simultaneously on another network. Evidence of a rebound showed during the 2009 NBA finals, featuring a battle between the same two dynamic stars. That matchup between the Lakers and Cavaliers set all-time NBA playoff records for ratings and viewership (8.7 million), according to *SportsBusiness Daily* (June 2, 2009, http://www.sportsbusinessdaily.com/article/130613).

A possible rebound notwithstanding, basketball's television ratings have been plummeting for a variety of reasons. Industry analyst David Carter of the Sports Business Group has placed part of the blame on the slower pace of the game compared to the 1980s. Several recent championship teams have featured stifling defenses, which many viewers find more boring to watch. There is also the issue of the widening gulf between players and fans. Peter Roby, the director of the Center for the Study of Sport in Society at Northeastern University, notes in the *Christian Science Monitor* (June 23, 2005, http://www.csmonitor.com/2005/0623/p11s02-alsp.html), "There is a lack of connection between players and fans because the players make so much money now.... Players in the 1960s and 1970s used to live in the same neighborhoods as the fans. Now there is a wedge between fans and players, so there is no empathy."

Table 3.1 shows the history of the NBA's television contracts since 1953. The rate at which the money involved has increased is striking. The set of deals the league signed in 1990 with TNT and NBC were worth

TABLE 3.1

NBA television contracts, by cable channel or broadcast network, 1953–2016

NBA cable television contracts

Seasons	Station	Contracts amount
1979–80 to 1981–82	USA	$1.5 million/3 years
1982–83 to 1983–84	USA/ESPN	$11 million/2 years
1984–85 to 1985–86	TBS	$20 million/2 years
1986–87 to 1987–88	TBS	$25 million/2 years
1988–89 to 1989–90	TBS/TNT	$50 million/2 years
1990–91 to 1993–94	TNT	$275 million/4 years
1994–95 to 1997–98	TNT/TBS	$397 million/4 years
1998–99 to 2001–02	TNT/TBS	$840 million/4 years
2002–03 to 2007–08	TNT	$2.2 billion/6 years
NBA network television contracts		
1953–54	DUMONT	$39,000/13 games
1954–55 to 1961–62	NBC	N/A
1962–63 to 1972–73	ABC	N/A
1973–74 to 1975–76	CBS	$27 million/3 years
1976–77 to 1977–78	CBS	$21 million/2 years
1978–79 to 1981–82	CBS	$74 million/4 years
1982–83 to 1985–86	CBS	$91.9 million/4 years
1986–87 to 1989–90	CBS	$173 million/4 years
1990–91 to 1993–94	NBC	$601 million/4 years
1994–95 to 1997–98	NBC	$892 million/4 years
1998–99 to 2001–02	NBC	$1.616 billion/4 years
2002–03 to 2007–08	ABC/ESPN	$2.4 billion/6 years
Current contracts, combined cable and network		
2008–16	ABC/ESPN and TNT	$7.44 billion/8 years

SOURCE: Adapted from National Basketball Association, http://www.nba.com/ (accessed June 17, 2009)

well under $1 billion for four years. The most recent contracts, signed in 2007 with TNT and ABC/ESPN, cover eight years (from the 2008–09 season through the 2015–16 season) and have a total value of $7.4 billion. Under these contracts ABC airs 15 regular-season games and the entire NBA finals, along with several earlier round playoff games. ESPN broadcasts up to 75 regular-season games and one of the conference finals, as well as some early-round playoff games. TNT airs 52 regular-season games, the All-Star Game, and playoff games, including one of the conference finals (June 27, 2007, http://sports.espn.go.com/espn/wire?sectionnba&id=2918075).

In 2003 Time Warner Cable, Cox Communications, and Cablevision Systems teamed up on a multiyear agreement with the NBA for distribution of NBA TV, the league's own 24-hour network, which as of 2009 was available via cable systems across the United States and in 79 other countries. In January 2008 Turner Sports, part of Time Warner, took over management of all of the NBA's digital assets, including both NBA TV and nba.com, under a deal to run through 2016. Turner Sports launched an ambitious "rebranding" campaign for NBA TV in the fall of 2008 that featured the new slogan "The game happens here."

HOCKEY

The National Hockey League (NHL) has experienced a downturn in television viewership since the 1990s. So apathetic was the viewing public in 2004 that the conference finals of the Stanley Cup Playoffs did not even draw a large enough share of the potential viewing audience to crack the top-15 program list for the week of May 17 through May 23. As with the NBA, however, there are signs that viewers are coming back. In "Revivals in Chicago and Washington Help Hockey Break Attendance Mark" (April 20, 2009, http://www.sportsbusinessjournal.com/article/62238), Tripp Mickle wrote that "average ratings were up at each of the league's national broadcast partners (in 2008–09). In the United States, average viewership on Versus [a Comcast-owned network] increased 14 percent to 310,000 viewers and a 0.3 cable rating, and NBC's ratings rose from a 1.0 to a 1.1 household rating through nine telecasts." Viewership in Canada increased as well.

Given its sketchy performance as a television draw, it is not surprising that the NHL has the least lucrative national television deals among the major sports. NBC currently pays no fee for broadcast rights, and the NHL does not receive any money until NBC recoups all of its costs. Once this happens, the two entities share advertising revenues equally. In July 2009 NBC and the NHL agreed to extend the deal through the 2010–11 season. Since 2005, the NHL has also had a deal with the Versus (formerly called Outdoor Life Network), in which the league received $72.5 million for 2007–08, with inflationary increases since then. That contract has been extended through the 2010–11 season.

AUTO RACING

In "NASCAR TV Deals Done" (December 7, 2005, http://www.multichannel.com/article/CA6289818.html), Mike Reynolds reports that in 2005 NASCAR signed a set of eight-year television rights contracts with ESPN/ABC Sports ($270 million per year) and Turner Broadcasting's TNT network ($80 million per year). Soon after these lucrative deals were signed, NASCAR's television ratings began to sag. According to Nate Ryan, in "NASCAR's Growth Slows after 15 Years in the Fast Lane" (*USA Today*, November 15, 2006), in 30 of the first 34 races of 2006, ratings were lower than they were the previous year. That trend continued into 2009. In "NASCAR's Trouble at the Track" (February 9, 2009, http://www.forbes.com/2009/02/09/nascar-france-advertising-business-sportsmoney_0209_nascar.html), Jack Gage wrote on Forbes.com that NASCAR's television ratings had dropped 21% since their 2005 peak.

EXTREME SPORTS

Even though television ratings for extreme sports still have a long way to go before they are in the same league as professional football and basketball, the audience is growing. More important, at least from the perspective of advertisers, the audience watching extreme sports is youthful and predominantly male, with a lot of buying power. Not many sports can take credit for completely altering the public image of a soft drink, but extreme sports have done just that for Mountain Dew. Once perceived as a "hillbilly" drink, Mountain Dew is now almost universally associated with youth culture as personified by practitioners of extreme sports. In "Going to Extremes" (*American Demographics*, June 1, 2002), Joan Raymond states that the transformation started in 1992 with the appearance of the "Do the Dew" advertising campaign. The campaign, which featured attractive young people engaging in a variety of extreme activities, helped make Mountain Dew the fastest-growing soft drink during the 1990s.

Raymond notes that by the turn of the millennium, while *Monday Night Football*'s ratings were declining—viewership dropped from an average of 12.7% of the nation's households in 2000 to 11.5% in 2001—ratings for the two premier extreme sports events, the X Games and the Gravity Games, were increasing quickly. About 2 million households tuned in to the 2001 Gravity Games, up from 1.6 million the previous year. However, Chris Isidore states in "X-treme Marks the Spot" (August 6, 2004, http://money.cnn.com/2004/08/06/commentary/column_sportsbiz/sportsbiz/index.htm) that while the best ratings for the 2003 Summer X Games on ABC showed 2.2% of the nation's households watching,

that number was still barely half the rating ABC achieved for the final game of NHL's Stanley Cup Finals, which were themselves considered a ratings disappointment. In "Moto X Racing Added for Summer X Games 13" (March 22, 2007, http://sports.espn.go.com/espn/print?id=2808468&type=story), ESPN states that the 2006 X Games averaged a mere 0.9 rating on ESPN. The X Games 15 in 2009 were the most watched of all time, seen by over 1 million viewers, but still managed to garner only a 1.0 rating (August 14, 2009, http://www.vitalmx.com/news/press-release/ESPN-X-Gam es-15-Sets-Records-For-Exposure-Across-Multiple-Platfor ms,5918).

Broadcasters and advertisers are nevertheless optimistic about the future of extreme sports programming. According to Isidore, the sports' median (half are higher and half are lower) viewership age is 27, compared to a median age of 42 for ESPN's NFL football broadcasts. The ages for some other sports are even higher: baseball's median is 48, and golf's is 55. Media companies are scrambling to ride this youthful wave. On July 1, 2003, Fox launched the digital cable channel FuelTV (2009, http://www.fuel.tv/), which is devoted to "skateboarding, snowboarding, surfing, BMX, freestyle motocross (FMX), ... wakeboarding," and other action sports programming that targets the under-40 demographic. Moreover, this young audience tends to be more comfortable with new media than their parents are. The emergence of mixed martial arts as a popular television sport also holds promise for attracting more viewers in this younger demographic group.

ADVERTISING

Plunkett Research, Ltd. (2009, http://www.plunkettresearch.com/Industries/Sports/SportsStatistics/tabid/273/Default.aspx) estimates that sports in the United States are a $410 billion industry. Of this $410 billion, $30 billion falls into the advertising category. However, television does not account for the largest share of this total. SportsBusiness Journal.com estimated in 2007 that the biggest share, $16.4 billion, was spent on billboards and signage at arenas and stadiums. National network television was the second largest expenditure, at $4.7 billion, followed by radio at $2.3 billion. Another $1.8 billion was spent on advertising on national cable television, and sports magazines accounted for $1.5 billion of the sports advertising total. The rest is spent on regional television, both network and cable, and national syndicated television. The *SportsBusiness Journal* estimated that $239 million was spent on Internet advertising.

A significant portion of sports advertising spending is on commercials aired during noteworthy games. The most expensive television advertisements of any kind are those placed during the NFL's Super Bowl. The article "Advertising History: 40 Years of Prices and Audience" (2007, http://adage.com/SuperBowlBuyers/superbowlhistory07.html)

TABLE 3.2

Top Super Bowl advertising categories, 2008

Category	Minutes of exposure
Automotive	5 1/2
Motion pictures	4 1/4
Beer	4

SOURCE: "Top Categories Super Bowl 2008," in *The Nielsen Company's Guide to Super Bowl XLIII*, The Nielsen Company, January 23, 2009, http://www.nielsenmedia.com/nc/portal/site/Public/menuitem.55dc65b4a7d5 adff3f65936147a062a0/?vgnextoid=0c06122c53ffe110VgnVCM100000ac0 a260aRCRD (accessed June 19, 2009). Copyrighted information of The Nielsen Company, licensed for use herein.

indicates that a 30-second spot during the 2007 Super Bowl cost advertisers $2.6 million, whereas in 1967 it cost only $40,000 (or about $245,350 in 2007 dollars). By 2009 the going rate was $3 million according to CNN.com (February 3, 2009, http://money.cnn.com/2009/01/09/news/companies/superbowl_ads/index.htm). As shown in Table 3.2, cars, movies, and beer are the categories most widely advertised during the Super Bowl, with beer maker Anheuser-Busch leading the charge in 2008 (see Table 3.3). Figure 3.1 gives a historical perspective on Super Bowl viewership. Ratings for the Super Bowl have been strong in recent years; the 2009 game was the most watched Super Bowl in history (see Table 3.4).

Given the cost of Super Bowl air time, advertisers want maximum impact, and they create innovative and sometimes controversial ads just for the occasion. Super Bowl commercials have in fact become something of a genre in themselves. Since 2004, however, advertisers appeared to have toned down the shock factor in the wake of that year's infamous halftime incident in which singer Janet Jackson's breast was exposed during the live broadcast. Advertising during baseball's World Series is a bargain in comparison, but it still yields large sums of money for the broadcaster. In *Sports, Inc.* (2004), Phil Schaaf explains that Fox charged $325,000 for a 30-second spot during the 2002 World

TABLE 3.3

Top Super Bowl advertisers, 2008

Top advertisers Super Bowl XLII	Commercial time
Anheuser-Busch Inc.	4 minutes
Coca-Cola USA	2 minutes
Buena Vista Pictures	1 1/2 minutes
Frito-Lay Inc.	1 1/2 minutes
Pepsi-Cola Co.	1 1/2 minutes

SOURCE: "Top Advertisers Super Bowl XLII," in *The Nielsen Company's Guide to Super Bowl XLIII*, The Nielsen Company, January 23, 2009, http://www.nielsenmedia.com/nc/portal/site/Public/menuitem.55dc65b4a7d5 adff3f65936147a062a0/?vgnextoid=0c06122c53ffe110VgnVCM100000ac0 a260aRCRD (accessed June 19, 2009). Copyrighted information of The Nielsen Company, licensed for use herein.

Series and took in nearly $20 million per game over the course of the series. This means that in just five games, Fox was able to recoup about a quarter of its yearly $400 million investment in MLB. It is worth noting that advertising spots during the first five games were sold out even before it was known which two teams would be participating.

The advertising rate for 30-second commercials during the Super Bowl far exceeds rates for other sports championships. According to the Center for Media Research, network television advertising rates for other top-rated sports events in 2006 included $1.1 million for a 30-second spot during the championship game of the NCAA Men's Basketball Tournament, $900–$956 million for a 30-second ad during the AFC and NFC championship games leading up to the Super Bowl, and $400,000 for an ad during the MLB World Series.

Advertising rates for nonchampionship sporting events, however, are usually negotiated in packages rather than for individual time slots. When broken down into 30-second spots for comparison purposes, other estimated advertising rates that Schaaf mentions include ESPN's *SportsCenter*, $11,000; baseball divisional championship series, $90,000; U.S. Open tennis finals, $175,000; and *Monday Night Football*, $325,000.

Sports Advertising and Alcohol

Sports advertising is dominated by products that appeal to young adult males. However, one product in particular, beer, is the undisputed king of the sports advertising jungle. According to the article "A-B Paces Ad Spending, Olympic Sponsors Climb List" (*SportsBusiness Journal*, March 21, 2005), Anheuser-Busch Companies, the top sports advertiser for years, spends about 83% of its total advertising budget on sports advertising each year.

The Center on Alcohol Marketing and Youth (CAMY) has studied the relationship between sports programming and alcohol advertising. In the fact sheet *Alcohol Advertising on Sports Television, 2001 to 2003* (October 2004, http://camy.org/factsheets/pdf/AlcoholAdvertisingSports Television2001-2003.pdf), CAMY indicated that while sports programming accounted for only 16% to 18% of overall television advertising spending and only about 4% of all ads in those years, over 60% of the alcohol industry's advertising spending and around 30% of its ads were on sports programs. (See Figure 3.2.) Overall, the alcohol industry spent $541 million to place 90,817 ads on television sports programming in 2003. CAMY notes that the percentage of commercials on sports shows that are for alcohol products is triple the percentage of ads on all programming that are for alcohol products. Even though beer advertisements have long been omnipresent on sports television, in recent years ads for hard liquor have been appearing with greater frequency. Sports television advertising for distilled spirits increased 350%

FIGURE 3.1

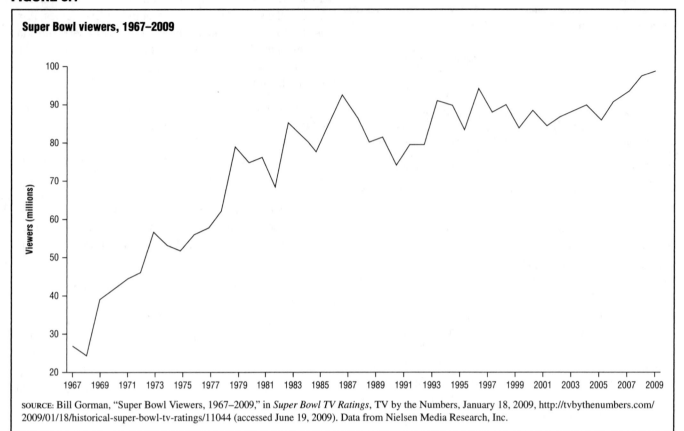

Super Bowl viewers, 1967–2009

Viewers (millions)

SOURCE: Bill Gorman, "Super Bowl Viewers, 1967–2009," in *Super Bowl TV Ratings*, TV by the Numbers, January 18, 2009, http://tvbythenumbers.com/2009/01/18/historical-super-bowl-tv-ratings/11044 (accessed June 19, 2009). Data from Nielsen Media Research, Inc.

TABLE 3.4

Most watched Super Bowls ever

Rank	Super Bowl	Winner	Loser	Avg # of viewers P2+
1	2009	Pittsburgh	Arizona	98,732,000
2	2008	New York	New England	97,448,000
3	1996	Dallas	Pittsburgh	94,080,000
4	2007	Indianapolis	Chicago	93,184,000
5	1986	Chicago	New England	92,570,000
6	1993	Dallas	Buffalo	90,990,000
7	2006	Pittsburgh	Seattle	90,745,000
8	1998	Denver	Green Bay	90,000,000
9	1994	Dallas	Buffalo	90,000,000
10	2004	New England	Carolina	89,795,000

P2+ = age 2 and older

SOURCE: "Super Bowl XLIII Most Watched Game Ever," The Nielsen Company, February 4, 2009, http://blog.nielsen.com/nielsenwire/nielsen-news/super-bowl-xliii-most-watched-game-ever/ (accessed June 19, 2009). Copyrighted information of The Nielsen Company, licensed for use herein.

FIGURE 3.2

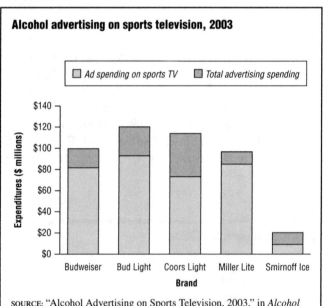

Alcohol advertising on sports television, 2003

☐ Ad spending on sports TV ☐ Total advertising spending

Expenditures ($ millions)

Brand

SOURCE: "Alcohol Advertising on Sports Television, 2003," in *Alcohol Advertising, Televised Sports, and Underage Youth*, Center for Science in the Public Interest, www.cspinet.org, August 2007, http://cspinet.org/booze/FactSheets/0311SportsAdsYouth.pdf (accessed June 19, 2009)

between 2001 and 2003. CAMY also finds that alcohol advertising increased for the Super Bowl, *Monday Night Football*, and other top-rated games.

CAMY states that soccer outranked all other sports in terms of the percentage of its advertising that is for alcohol products; 8.3% of the commercials on televised soccer games were for alcohol. Hockey was second at 7.2%, followed by professional basketball at 6.8%. Overall, 3.2% of all ads shown during televised sporting events in 2003 were for alcohol products. Among professional sports, hockey games had the highest number of alcohol ads per broadcast.

A typical televised hockey game featured 5.3 alcohol ads in 2003. Boxing matches averaged 4.5 alcohol ads, followed closely by professional basketball with 4.4.

According to CAMY, advertising on college sports presentations is at least as alcohol-oriented as on professional sports programming. In 2003 alcohol companies spent $52.2 million to place 4,747 ads on college sports programs. College basketball, at $28.2 million, accounted for more than half of this spending.

SPORTS VIEWING AND GENDER

In "Women Have Turned Chilly to TV Sports" (April 20, 2004, http://www.medialifemagazine.com/news2004/apr04/apr19/2_tues/news4tuesday.html), Toni Fitzgerald suggests that women and men watch sports for different reasons. Women, Fitzgerald proposes, watch sports for the story lines, meaning their primary interest is in the drama and personalities. By contrast, men are interested in the skills and statistics. Fitzgerald points to a report from the media research firm Magna Global USA, which finds that sports viewership by women declined significantly between 1998 and 2003, as measured both by ratings and by total weekly hours spent watching sports. According to the Magna Global data, average broadcast (i.e., non-cable) television ratings among women decreased by 18% during this period. The ratings drop was even more precipitous (44%) for women watching basic cable television sports. The total number of hours women spent watching sports on television—either broadcast or basic cable—dropped by 17%, from 1.5 hours per week in 1998 (with Olympic coverage excluded from the total) to 1.2 hours in 2003. Meanwhile, broadcast ratings for men decreased only 9% during this span, whereas cable ratings fell 36%. Men's viewing hours dropped only 6%, from 2.8 hours per week to 2.6. Fitzgerald argues that these numbers are the result of what is happening in the sports world. When the sports that women like to watch, such as figure skating and tennis, have relatively few appealing story lines in motion, women turn the television off. For example, injuries to Serena Williams (1981–) and Venus Williams (1980–) in tennis were seen to have a measurable effect on viewership among women.

GAMING

Not long ago there were only two options for sports enthusiasts: playing a sport yourself or watching others play it live or onscreen. In recent years, a third way has emerged in the form of sports gaming.

Sports-oriented video games have been around for years, but until the mid-1980s the graphics were mediocre and the action unexciting for a true sports buff. A big change took place during the late 1980s when Electronic Arts (EA), at the time a relatively new company making interactive entertainment software, introduced the first-ever

football video game to offer realistic 11-on-11 action. To make the game as realistic as possible, the company consulted extensively with the former NFL coach and current football commentator John Madden (1936–). They eventually named the game after Madden, and in 1989 the first version of *John Madden Football* was released for Apple II computers. The game was an instant sensation. A version for the Sega Genesis home entertainment system was introduced the following year. Over the next few years the gaming industry grew exponentially, split about evenly between computer games and television-based systems. By the release of the 1995 version of the game, *Madden NFL '95*, EA had hashed out licensing deals with the NFL and the NFL Players Association, allowing it to use likenesses of real players and the official league and team logos and uniforms. *Madden NFL* was eventually made available for every major gaming system. According to Thomas Bassinger in "Madden NFL Is Still Wildly Popular 20 Years Later" (August 11, 2008, http://www.tampabay.com/news/business/article764187.ece), by 2006 *Madden NFL* had sold 70 million units worldwide for various platforms since its 1989 launch; it remains the best-selling video game all-time of any kind, not just sports, finishing in the top ten year after year.

However, *Madden NFL* is just one of a number of highly successful sports games. In "Sports Fans Growing the Video Game Industry, CEA Study Finds" (May 21, 2008, *Business Wire*), the Consumer Electronics Association noted that a much higher percentage of sports fans own gaming systems than do the general public, and it is their game and system purchases that are driving the video game industry's growth. The latest development in sports gaming is the appearance of exclusive licensing contracts between sports leagues and individual game manufacturers. In December 2004 EA—which besides the *Madden NFL* series also makes *NBA Live*—signed a $400 million deal with the NFL, giving it exclusive rights to the likenesses of NFL players, uniforms, and stadiums for five years, effectively freezing out competitors such as Take-Two Interactive Software, which had eroded sales of *Madden NFL* by offering its *ESPN NFL* at sharply reduced prices. The EA-NFL deal has since been extended through 2012. Take-Two's consolation prize was a seven-year, $250 million contract with MLB. EA was also one of five game companies to agree to pay a combined $400 million to the NBA for use of its imagery. In yet another licensing deal, EA is paying ESPN $850 million for 15 years of use of ESPN features, including announcers and scoreboards.

CURRENT ISSUES IN SPORTS AND MEDIA
Native American Mascots

For the last 50 years Native American advocacy groups have expressed opposition to the use of Native American names and mascots by sports teams. Organizations such as the National Coalition on Racism in Sports and Media have embarked on a campaign to convince teams to discard cartoonish Native American mascots and to encourage teams with names such as the Braves, Chiefs, and Redskins to rename themselves. This movement has met with some success. During the 1970s activists convinced Stanford and Dartmouth universities to change their names from Indians to race-neutral names: the Cardinals and the Big Green, respectively. In 1994 Marquette University shed its Warriors nickname and became the Golden Eagles. The St. John's University Redmen became the Red Storm the same year, and in 2007, after a long debate, the University of Illinois finally retired Chief Illiniwek, a school mascot since 1926. However, many more teams have resisted calls to retire their traditional mascots, so the debate continues. In addition, while legislation has been introduced in a number of states that would prohibit the use of Indian-themed team names and mascots, none of these bills had yet been enacted as of the summer of 2009.

Violence and Athlete Role Models

Violence in sports is often a focus of media scrutiny and academic research because the behavior of high-profile athletes can have an impact on fan behavior, according to social scientists. In "Violence in Sports Reflects Society, Says IU Professor" (July 3, 2002, http://newsinfo.iu.edu/news/page/normal/449.html), Lynn Jamieson of Indiana University explains that "sport tends to reflect society, and we live in a violent era. We have a violent society where people use violence to solve problems instead of using other means.... The violence issue is not limited to professional sports. It filters down to the high schools and even to recreational activities.... This is because if it occurs at the professional level, it is likely to be imitated at the lower levels like Little League and city recreational programs."

Some sports include a measure of violence that is held in check by the rules of fair play and by officials who can enforce penalties or regulate the players' behavior to some extent. However, the violence below the surface can often erupt, and violent events involving professional athletes—either on or off the playing field—become major stories covered by news and entertainment organizations in addition to the sports media. The 2004–05 NBA season was marred by a huge brawl during a game between the Detroit Pistons and the Indiana Pacers; the fracas spilled into the stands, resulting in the involvement of both spectators and players. Several players received long suspensions, and the entire season took place under the cloud of the melee. Another large basketball brawl, resulting in the ejection of ten players, took place during a December 2006 NBA game between the Denver Nuggets and the New York Knicks.

However, basketball is not alone in contending with image problems stemming from extended media coverage

of the actions of its players. In October 2005 several members of the NFL's Minnesota Vikings were allegedly involved in a party aboard a chartered boat that erupted into a drunken sex orgy. In August 2007 Michael Vick (1980–) of the Atlanta Falcons was suspended indefinitely by the NFL after he pleaded guilty to felony charges stemming from his involvement in an illegal dog-fighting ring. According to Michael MacCambridge, author of the football history *America's Game* (2004), such incidents result from the unique position athletes are afforded within U.S. society. In the *New York Times* (September 16, 2007, http://www.nytimes.com/2007/09/16/sports/football/16 goodell.html), MacCambridge stated, "There is a tremendous amount of money, free time and scrutiny in the lives of most pro football players, and the combination is more pronounced and more combustible than it was a generation ago." Vick's suspension indicated a no-nonsense response from Roger Goodell (1959–), who in his first year as commissioner of the NFL instituted a strict code of conduct for players and coaches. Goodell reinstated Vick upon completion of his sentence in 2009, and Vick joined the Philadelphia Eagles, returning to play in September 2009.

Additional incidents in both professional and college sports abound. In June 2008 pitcher Shawn Chacón (1977–) of the MLB Houston Astros was suspended indefinitely after allegedly grabbing Astros General Manager Ed Wade (1956–) by the neck and throwing him to the ground. In a Conference USA basketball game in January 2009, the University of Houston's Aubrey Coleman stepped on the face of University of Arizona's Chase Budinger. The video of the incident spread quickly around the Internet. Ultimately, Coleman was suspended for one game. During the first weekend of the 2009 college football season, LeGarrette Blount (1986–) of the University of Oregon punched Boise State defensive end Byron Hout (1987–) and was suspended for the rest of the season. However, a month later, coach Chip Kelly outlined a plan that would allow Blount to be reinstated if and when he met a series of academic, athletic, and behavioral requirements.

ATHLETES AND GUNS. A related issue is the prevalence of professional athletes who carry guns. A large number of pro athletes feel they need to carry a weapon for self-protection given their high profile. The public knows the players are likely to be carrying a lot of money and wearing expensive jewelry, and they are often robbery targets for that reason. The problem is that the athletes sometimes use their guns. In 2006 Stephen Jackson (1978–) of the NBA's Indiana Pacers was charged with felony criminal recklessness after he allegedly fired five shots into the air during an early-morning fight outside an Indianapolis strip club. In August 2009, New York Giants' star wide receiver Plaxico Burress (1977–) was indicted for offenses related to an incident that took place in November 2008, in which he accidentally shot himself in the thigh at a

Manhattan nightclub. Burress pleaded guilty to the weapons charge and was sentenced to two years in prison.

ATHLETES AND DOMESTIC VIOLENCE. Domestic violence is also a cause of concern in professional sports. Numerous examples of violence are reported in the media, and incidents are not limited to athletes who participate in contact sports or whose physical strength sets them apart from mainstream society. In 1992 professional golfer John Daly (1966–) was arrested and charged with third-degree assault on his wife following an argument. NBA guard Ron Artest (1979–), who had previously been suspended for 73 games after taking part in the infamous brawl with Detroit Pistons fans in Auburn Hills, Michigan, in 2004,

was suspended for the first seven games of the 2007 season after he pleaded no contest to domestic violence charges. In the study *Breaking into Baseball: Women and the National Pastime* (2005), Jean Hastings Ardell quoted law professor Phyllis Goldfarb of George Washington University, who noted that domestic violence is the leading cause of arrest among professional athletes. According to Goldfarb, "A celebrity athlete may simply be taught by the culture that he is superior to his wife, that she can ask nothing of him that he doesn't want to give, that if she persists in doing so, she deserves mistreatment, and moreover, is expendable, as there are countless women out there for him."

CHAPTER 4
PROFESSIONAL TEAM SPORTS

For decades baseball, football, basketball, and hockey have been considered the four major professional team sports in the United States. Even though such other sports as auto racing and soccer are gaining ground in terms of popularity, and hockey is struggling to maintain its status, it most likely will be some time before major league sports in the United States means anything other than the four core sports.

Besides being popular spectator events, professional league sports are also major industries that generate huge amounts of money—for team owners and managers, companies that sponsor teams, equipment and athletic gear manufacturers, and the athletes themselves.

MAJOR LEAGUE BASEBALL

Major League Baseball (MLB) is no longer as popular as professional football and is losing ground to other sports, yet it remains firmly ingrained in the American imagination, retaining the title of "national pastime." In 2004, 2005, and 2007 two teams with long histories of futility, the Boston Red Sox and the Chicago White Sox, saw World Series victories. Their success evoked an emotional response in fans across the United States and seemed to spark renewed interest in a sport that has had more than its share of bad publicity since the 1990s, partly because of steroid scandals. Baseball's steroid problem was magnified in 2007, as Barry Bonds (1964–), the player most closely associated with the scandal, approached the all-time home-run record held by Hank Aaron (1934–) since 1974. Bonds broke Aaron's record on August 7, 2007, eliciting an ambivalent response from fans and the national media. It remains to be seen if the renewed interest in baseball will translate into long-term gains in attendance and television viewership in the face of stiff competition from other sports, old and new. The steroid problem flared up again in 2009, when information emerged that in 2003 a number of elite players had tested positive for steroids during a

round of testing the players union had agreed to under a set of conditions that included anonymity. Among the top players revealed to have tested positive were Alex Rodriguez (1975–) of the New York Yankees, Manny Ramirez (1972–) of the Los Angeles Dodgers, and David Ortiz (1975–) of the Boston Red Sox. Ramirez served a 50-game suspension in 2009 as a result of his steroid violations.

MLB Structure and Administration

As of 2009 MLB consisted of 30 teams. (See Table 4.1.) These teams are divided into two leagues: 16 in the National League and 14 in the American League. Each of these leagues is further split into three divisions—East, Central, and West—that are loosely based on geography. The MLB season normally runs from early April through late September and consists of 162 games. This season length was established in 1961, before which teams played a 154-game schedule. Most games are played against teams within each league, though not necessarily within each team's own division.

Following the regular season, the champions of each division (three teams in each league) plus a wild-card team—the team with the best record among those not winning their division—from each league compete in the playoffs. The playoffs consist of three rounds: two best-of-five Division Series in each league; a best-of-seven Championship Series in each league; and finally the World Series, a best-of-seven game series between the champions of each league, to determine the major league champion team.

According to Plunkett Research, in "Sports Industry Overview" (2009, http://www.plunkettresearch.com/Industries/Sports/SportsStatistics/tabid/273/Default.aspx), MLB took in $6.2 billion in revenue in 2009. The average player salary was $3.2 million in 2009, according to ESPN (http://sports.espn.go.com/espn/wire?section=mlb&id=4054745). Table 4.2 shows the latest team values and revenue figures for each MLB team. The *SportsBusiness Journal* estimated

TABLE 4.1

Major League Baseball teams and divisions

American League	National League
East Division	**East Division**
Baltimore Orioles	Atlanta Braves
Boston Red Sox	Florida Marlins
New York Yankees	New York Mets
Tampa Bay Devil Rays	Philadelphia Phillies
Toronto Blue Jays	Washington Nationals
Central Division	**Central Division**
Chicago White Sox	Chicago Cubs
Cleveland Indians	Cincinnati Reds
Detroit Tigers	Houston Astros
Kansas City Royals	Milwaukee Brewers
Minnesota Twins	Pittsburgh Pirates
	St. Louis Cardinals
West Division	**West Division**
Los Angeles Angels of Anaheim	Arizona Diamondbacks
Oakland Athletics	Colorado Rockies
Seattle Mariners	Los Angeles Dodgers
Texas Rangers	San Diego Padres
	San Francisco Giants

SOURCE: Created by Robert Jacobson for Gale, 2009. Data from Major League Baseball, http://www.mlb.com.

TABLE 4.2

Selected baseball team values and revenue, 2008

[In million dollars]

Rank	Team	Current value ($mil)	Revenues ($mil)	Operating income ($mil)
1	New York Yankees	1,500	375	−3.7
2	New York Mets	912	261	23.5
3	Boston Red Sox	833	269	25.7
4	Los Angeles Dodgers	722	241	16.5
5	Chicago Cubs	700	239	29.7
6	Los Angeles Angels of Anaheim	509	212	10.3
7	Philadelphia Phillies	496	216	16.3

SOURCE: Adapted from "Special Report: The Business of Baseball," in *Forbes*, April 22, 2009, http://www.forbes.com/lists/2009/33/baseball-values-09_The-Business-Of-Baseball_Rank.html (accessed June 19, 2009). Reprinted by Permission of Forbes.com © 2009 Forbes LLC.

in 2007 that of the $10.5 billion worth of officially licensed sports merchandise sold annually, from banners to bobble-heads, $2.3 billion is spent on goods licensed by MLB and its member teams, second only to the NFL among the major sport leagues. Technically speaking, "Major League Baseball" refers to the entity that operates the National and American Leagues, the two top professional baseball leagues in North America. MLB operates these two leagues under a joint organizational structure that was established in 1920 with the creation of the Major League Constitution. This constitution has been overhauled many times since then. MLB team owners appoint a commissioner, under whose direction MLB hires and maintains umpiring crews, negotiates market-

ing and television deals, and establishes labor agreements with the MLB Players Association.

MLB maintains a level of control over baseball that is somewhat unique among the major sports. This comes as a result of a 1922 U.S. Supreme Court decision in which baseball was deemed not to be "interstate commerce" and therefore not subject to federal antitrust law. Consequently, MLB is allowed to operate in monopolistic ways that would not be legal in most other industries. This privileged status allowed baseball to stave off player free agency (a professional athlete who is free to sign a contract with any team), and the high salaries that accompanied it, until the mid-1970s.

MLB History

The first professional baseball team was the Cincinnati Red Stockings, founded in 1869. That year the team—which still exists as the Cincinnati Reds—embarked on a 57-game national tour and went undefeated against local amateur teams. Their success led in 1871 to the creation of the first professional baseball league, the nine-team, eight-city National Association of Professional Baseball Players. Various other competing leagues were formed over the next decade, including a precursor to the modern National League. The American League was founded in 1901. The champions of the American and National Leagues faced off in what became the first World Series in 1903. The popularity of professional baseball continued to grow over the next several years. A crisis unfolded in 1919, when several members of the Chicago White Sox were paid by gamblers to throw the World Series, in the so-called Black Sox scandal. In the wake of the scandal, club owners hired baseball's first commissioner, Kenesaw Landis (1866–1944), to clean up the game. As of 2009 the commissioner was Allan H. "Bud" Selig (1934–), a founder of the Milwaukee Brewers. Selig, the ninth commissioner in MLB history, was appointed to the post by the team owners in 1998.

Baseball's golden era took place between the two world wars, marked by the rise of such all-time greats as Babe Ruth (1895–1948), Ty Cobb (1886–1961), and Lou Gehrig (1903–1941). The major leagues survived the Great Depression (1929–1939) by introducing night games, which soon became the norm for games played during the week; weekend games were still played during the day. From its beginnings through World War II (1939–1945), MLB was racially segregated. That changed in 1947, when the African-American player Jackie Robinson (1919–1972) joined the Brooklyn Dodgers. Such legends as Willie Mays (1931–) and Hank Aaron followed over the next decade, and by the middle of the 1950s black players were fairly common on major league rosters. More recently, the number of African-American players in baseball has plummeted, as young African-American athletes have flocked to other sports. The 2005 World Series roster of the

Houston Astros did not include a single black player; it was the first team to compete for the MLB championship without an African-American player in half a century.

After 50 years of stability, the 1950s brought changes to MLB in response to demographic shifts in the United States. The Boston Braves moved to Milwaukee in 1953. Two New York teams moved to the West Coast in 1957: the Brooklyn Dodgers departing for Los Angeles and the New York Giants to San Francisco.

Baseball started losing fans, especially younger ones, in big numbers during the 1960s and 1970s as labor conflicts and other challenges plagued the sport. In 1966 the MLB Players Association was formed. The association's main goal was to end the reserve clause, a contractual provision that essentially gave teams ownership of players, meaning they were bound to a particular team until they were traded or released. The reserve clause was finally overturned in 1975, ushering in the era of free agency in baseball, wherein players were free to negotiate with any team they wanted once their existing contract had expired. Labor squabbles continued over the next 20 years, and parts of several seasons were lost to work stoppages. The worst of these took place in 1994, when the final third of the season, including the World Series, was canceled.

The sport survived in spite of these distractions, however, thanks partly to a handful of individual accomplishments. These included Cal Ripken Jr.'s (1960–) destruction of Gehrig's long-standing record for consecutive games played, and Mark McGwire's (1963–) and Sammy Sosa's (1968–) 1998 competition to break the record for home runs in a season—a record that was broken again by Bonds just three years later. Unfortunately, enthusiasm over these feats has since been muted by ongoing scandals involving performance-enhancing drugs, which call into question the validity of the exploits of Bonds, McGwire, Sosa, and others who just a few years earlier had been credited with reviving public interest in the sport.

The Labor History of MLB: Players versus Owners

MLB's first major strike took place in 1981, as owners sought to blunt the impact of free agency. Team owners wanted to receive compensation when one of their players was signed by another team. The players went on strike in protest, and more than 700 games were canceled before the two sides agreed on a limited form of compensation for free-agent signings.

In 1990 owners proposed a sort of salary cap and the elimination of the arbitration system in place for resolving salary disputes. A 32-day lockout ensued, resulting in the cancellation of spring training that year. The owners finally dropped their demands, and the full regular season took place, though its start was postponed by one week.

In "The Baseball Strike of 1994–95" (*Monthly Labor Review*, March 1997), Paul D. Staudohar reports that in June 1994 the owners proposed a salary cap that would have limited the players to 50% of total industry revenues. This represented a pay cut of about 15% for the players; not surprisingly, they declined the offer and went on strike in August. This strike resulted in the cancellation of the 1994 postseason, including the World Series. A ruling by the federal judge Sonia Sotomayor (1954–) ended the strike in March 1995, as reported by Mark Newman on the MLB Web site (May 26, 2009, http://mlb.mlb.com/news/article .jsp?ymd=20090526&content_id=4961532&vkey=news _mlb&fext=.jsp&c_id=mlb). Sotomayor reinstated the 1990 contract, and the 1995 and 1996 seasons were played under the terms of the expired agreement.

In 2002 MLB appeared to be on the brink of another strike, the causes of which were mainly rooted in imbalances between teams in large and small markets that resulted in some financial disparities. The team owners lobbied for salary caps, but the players were understandably opposed to this. Instead, the owners came up with the idea of a luxury tax, which would be imposed on any team that spent more than a predetermined amount on player salaries. A strike was thus averted. The impact of the luxury tax, however, has been questionable. The New York Yankees, for example, have continued to spend vast sums to lure top players; in 2005 the Yankees became the first team in the history of sports to spend more than $200 million on salaries in a season. According to Barry M. Bloom, in "Yanks, Red Sox Hit with Luxury Tax Bills" (December 21, 2005, http://mlb.mlb.com/ content/printer_friendly/mlb/y2005/m12/d21/c1286225.jsp), this was about $80 million over the luxury tax threshold, triggering a $34 million tax bill for team owner George Steinbrenner. The article "Yankees, Tigers Hit with Luxury Tax" (December 22, 2008, http://mlb.mlb.com/news/article .jsp?ymd=20081222 &content_id=3726222&vkey=news _mlb&fext=.jsp&c_id=mlb) indicates that the Yankees were billed another $26.9 million in December 2008. By contrast, only one other team, the Detroit Tigers, had to pay the luxury tax in 2008, so the tax is generally believed to work as a deterrent to reckless spending for most teams. However, the fines do not seem to have deterred big spending on the part of the Yankees organization. Three of the four highest paid MLB players in 2009—Alex Rodriguez, CC Sabathia (1980–), and Mark Teixeira (1980–)—were members of the Yankees, each earning more than $20 million per year. Another Yankee, Derek Jeter (1974–), was also in the top ten at $18.9 million, according to ESPN (http://sports .espn.go.com/espn/wire?section=mlb&id=3953375).

The other part of the 2002 deal was increased revenue sharing, meaning a greater share of each team's revenue was put into a pot to be divided among the entire major leagues. The biggest difference between baseball's revenue sharing system and football's is that baseball teams earn significant revenue from local television broadcasts, whereas almost all football coverage is national. MLB's 2002 contract brought a sharp increase in the amount of local revenue that teams must share. The 2002 collective bargaining agreement ran through the 2006 season; a new agreement, signed in the fall of 2006 and running through the 2011 season, preserved the luxury tax and revenue sharing systems with only minor alterations.

Current Issues in Baseball

One of the most critical issues facing baseball is how to respond to recent revelations of the rampant use of performance-enhancing drugs among top players (see Chapter 9 for more detailed information). As news has come to light about the use of steroids and other substances by some of the players credited with reviving the sport during the 1990s, professional baseball's credibility has come under fire. Important questions inevitably arise, such as how to account for records broken by players who were probably using banned substances. Bonds's establishment in 2007 of a new all-time home-run record (762), one of the sport's most venerable milestones, has brought this question to the fore. The ability of the league to handle such questions in a way that satisfies disgruntled fans will have a huge impact on the future of professional baseball in the United States.

NATIONAL FOOTBALL LEAGUE

The National Football League (NFL) is the premier U.S. professional football league. North America is the only place where the term *football* refers to the game played by NFL teams; in most other parts of the world, this term refers to soccer. In "Sports Industry Overview," Plunkett Research estimates the NFL's total league-wide revenue to be about $6 billion for 2009. The average NFL salary for 2009 is about $1.8 million, but that figure is a bit misleading. The large majority of players earn less than $1 million per year, but the high salaries of star players bring the average much higher. NFL players typically have a base salary—just under $1 million on average—but can earn much more based on bonuses they earn with their performance over the course of the season. According to *SportsBusiness Journal*, sales of merchandise licensed by the NFL or its teams total $2.5 billion per year, the highest among the major sports. Table 4.3 shows current team values and revenue.

Figure 2.2 in Chapter 2 shows the gradual growth between 1998 and 2007 in the percentage of Americans who identify themselves as fans of professional football. The NFL's success can be credited in part to breakthroughs in the 1960s and 1970s in packaging the sport for television. No other sport has managed to capture the kind of spectacle that NFL broadcasts generate. The league has also benefited from labor relations that have been relatively stable, compared to those of the other major sports (a state some

TABLE 4.3

Selected football team values and revenue, 2007 season

Rank	Team	Current value ($mil)	Revenue ($mil)	Operating income ($mil)
1	Dallas Cowboys	1,612	269	30.6
2	Washington Redskins	1,538	327	58.1
3	New England Patriots	1,324	282	39.2
4	New York Giants	1,178	214	41.2
5	New York Jets	1,170	213	25.9
6	Houston Texans	1,125	239	43.9
7	Philadelphia Eagles	1,116	237	33.5

SOURCE: Adapted from "Special Report: NFL Team Valuations," in *Forbes*, http://www.forbes.com/lists/2008/30/sportsmoney_nfl08_NFL-Team-Valuations_Rank.html (accessed June 22, 2009). Reprinted by Permission of Forbes.com © 2009 Forbes LLC.

TABLE 4.4

National Football League teams and divisions

American Football Conference (AFC)	National Football Conference (NFC)
East Division	**East Division**
Buffalo Bills	Dallas Cowboys
Miami Dolphins	New York Giants
New England Patriots	Philadelphia Eagles
New York Jets	Washington Redskins
North Division	**North Division**
Baltimore Ravens	Chicago Bears
Cincinnati Bengals	Detroit Lions
Cleveland Browns	Green Bay Packers
Pittsburgh Steelers	Minnesota Vikings
South Division	**South Division**
Houston Texans	Atlanta Falcons
Indianapolis Colts	Carolina Panthers
Jacksonville Jaguars	New Orleans Saints
Tennessee Titans	Tampa Bay Buccaneers
West Division	**West Division**
Denver Broncos	Arizona Cardinals
Kansas City Chiefs	St. Louis Rams
Oakland Raiders	San Francisco 49ers
San Diego Chargers	Seattle Seahawks

SOURCE: Created by Robert Jacobson for Gale, 2009. Data from the National Football League, http://www.nfl.com.

commentators attribute to the fact that the NFL Players Association is weak and ineffectual when compared to the unions in other sports). The NFL's revenue-sharing system is also generally considered the best among the major sports in terms of keeping small-market teams competitive.

NFL Structure and Administration

As of 2009 there were 32 teams in the NFL, 16 each in the National and American Football Conferences. (See Table 4.4.) Each conference is divided into four divisions: East, North, South, and West, and each division has four teams. NFL teams play a 16-game regular season, which begins the weekend of Labor Day. Each team also has a bye weekend (no games are played) during the season; therefore, the full regular season lasts 17 weeks. Sunday afternoons have long been the traditional time for professional football games. The exceptions have been one game per week on Sunday night and one on Monday night, although in recent years the league has begun scheduling occasional games on Thursday nights as well.

At the end of the regular season, six teams from each conference qualify for the playoffs: the four division champions and two wild-card teams (those with the best record that did not win their division). The champions of the two conferences square off in the Super Bowl. For much of its history, the Super Bowl has taken place in January; however, since 2002 it has been played in early February.

In the NFL revenue from television contracts and product licensing is shared equally among the teams. The idea behind this approach is to create parity, in contrast to MLB, where teams located in larger markets generally have a lot more money to spend than their rivals in smaller markets. Football teams also split money from ticket sales. Generally, the home team gets 60% of the money from the gate, and the visiting team gets 40%. The exception is luxury boxes; the home team gets to keep all the money from selling its luxury box seating to corporations and other wealthy customers. This is one of the main reasons so many teams have been campaigning for new stadiums containing fewer regular seats and more premium boxes. Owners of teams that generate more money find the NFL's revenue-sharing system unfair, arguing that teams that draw more fans and sell more merchandise should benefit the most. Others contend that if revenue sharing is abolished, the NFL as a whole will suffer as team records begin to reflect the disparity between wealthier teams and those that generate less money.

The NFL is administered by the Office of the Commissioner. The first commissioner of the NFL was Elmer Layden (1903–1973), who had been a star player and later a coach at the University of Notre Dame. Layden held the post from 1941 until 1946, guiding the league through the difficult years of World War II, when most able-bodied American men had either joined or were drafted into the armed services. Layden was succeeded by Bert Bell (1895–1959), the cofounder of the Philadelphia Eagles. Under Bell, whose term as commissioner lasted until his death in 1959, NFL attendance grew every year. Bell is famous for his oft-quoted statement, "On any given Sunday, any team can beat any other team."

However, it was Bell's successor, Pete Rozelle (1926–1996), who led the league through its period of dramatic growth in the 1960s and 1970s. Rozelle introduced the concept of long-term network broadcast contracts and applied sophisticated marketing techniques to sell the NFL brand to the American public. Rozelle oversaw the merger between the American Football League (AFL) and the NFL and guided the league to what is generally considered a

victory over the players' union during the 1987 labor strike. Rozelle retired in 1989 and was replaced by Paul Tagliabue (1940–). Under Tagliabue the NFL was marked by a great deal of team movement between cities, as owners sought to maximize the revenue they could generate from the sale of stadium naming rights and luxury skybox seating. Under Tagliabue the NFL largely avoided the labor disputes that have plagued the other major sports. Tagliabue retired after the 2005 season and was replaced by Roger Goodell (1959–). One of the key issues the commissioner must deal with is the future of the NFL's revenue-sharing system, a debate that may pit owners of big-market teams against owners of teams who play in less populous cities. The revenue-sharing system is inextricably tied to the team owners' contract with the NFL Players Union. In 2008 the owners voted unanimously to end the players' contract two years early, largely due to their dissatisfaction with the cut of league revenue that was going to players. This move set the stage for a possible lockout in 2011 that could potentially result in a disrupted season.

NFL History

The National Football League came to life in 1920 as the American Professional Football Association (APFA). The league adopted its current name two years later, but professional football actually dates back to 1892, when a Pittsburgh club paid Pudge Heffelfinger (1867–1954) $500 to play in a game.

The APFA—which was based in a Canton, Ohio, automobile dealership—consisted of 11 teams, all but one of them located in the Midwest. In its original form, the APFA was not really a league in the modern sense; it was essentially an agreement among member teams not to steal players from each other. Even though professional football remained secondary to the college version in its early years, it gradually gained in popularity when former college stars such as Red Grange (1903–1991) and Benny Friedman (1906–1982) turned professional. An annual championship game was established in 1933. By this time, most of the league's teams, with the notable exception of the Green Bay Packers, had left the small towns of their birth for bigger cities.

Professional football began to challenge college football's dominance in the years following World War II, as a faster-paced, higher-scoring style drew new fans. The NFL expanded to the West Coast in 1945, when the Cleveland Rams relocated to Los Angeles. By the 1950s professional football was firmly entrenched as a major sport in the United States, as television effectively captured the heroics of such glamorous stars as Bobby Layne (1926–1986), Paul Hornung (1935–), and Johnny Unitas (1933–2002). The explosive growth of professional football led to the creation of a rival league, the AFL, in 1960, resulting in a costly bidding war for the services of top players. By the mid-1960s professional football had eclipsed baseball as the nation's favorite sport. In 1970 the two football leagues merged. The AFL's ten teams plus three NFL teams became the American Football Conference; the remaining 13 NFL teams became the National Football Conference. The champions of the two conferences would meet in the newly created Super Bowl to determine the world champion of professional football.

The NFL was the biggest spectator sport in the United States during the 1970s and 1980s. In most years the Super Bowl was the most watched television show of any kind, and *Monday Night Football* set a new standard for sports broadcasting with its innovative mixture of sports and entertainment. Since the 1990s the popularity of football has spread internationally. In 1993 the NFL launched the World League of American Football, whose name was changed to NFL Europe in 1997. NFL Europe, with teams in Germany and the Netherlands, served as a sort of development league in which a player's skills could be honed to reach NFL standards. In June 2007 the NFL abruptly announced that it was shutting down NFL Europe. Its final game, the World Bowl Championship match in which the Hamburg Sea Devils defeated the Frankfurt Galaxy by a score of 37–28, drew a crowd of more than 48,000.

Labor Disputes in the NFL

The NFL Players Union was formed in 1956, when players on the Green Bay Packers and Cleveland Browns utilized a collective approach to demand minimum salaries, team-paid uniforms and equipment, and other benefits from owners. The owners refused to respond to any of these demands. The union threatened to sue, a threat strengthened by *Radovich v. National Football League* (352 U.S. 445, 1957), in which the Supreme Court ruled that the NFL did not enjoy the same special status as MLB did with regard to antitrust laws. The owners eventually gave in to most of the players' demands but did not formally recognize the union for collective bargaining purposes. The NFL Players Association (NFLPA), as it was by then named, did not become the official bargaining agent for players until 1968, following a brief lockout and strike.

After the merger of the NFL and AFL, the NFLPA focused on antitrust litigation that challenged the so-called Rozelle Rule, which required a team signing a free agent to compensate the team losing the player, thereby severely limiting players' ability to benefit from free agency. The union succeeded in getting the Rozelle Rule eliminated in 1977.

When the NFLPA went on strike for a month in 1987, the owners responded by carrying on with the schedule using replacement players and a handful of veterans who chose to cross the picket line. With support weakening, the

union ended its strike in October 1987. Free agency finally came to the NFL in 1992, and this was balanced by the introduction of salary caps during the mid-1990s. The NFL has experienced relatively smooth labor relations since then. The most recent collective bargaining agreement, which was renewed in March 2006, was supposed to be active through the 2011 season; however, the owners abruptly cancelled the agreement in 2008, possibly setting the stage for the NFL's first genuine labor strife since the mid-1990s. As of 2009, plans were for the 2009 and 2010 seasons to go on as scheduled under the previous contract. The 2011 season was in question.

Unlike MLB and the National Basketball Association (NBA), the NFL has a hard salary cap, meaning teams cannot spend more than a specified amount on salaries under any circumstances. For the players and their union, free agency is considered an acceptable trade-off for the introduction of salary caps. With each new contract, the size of the salary cap is a subject of intense negotiation, but to date there have not been any work stoppages over it. Salary caps are considered an important way to ensure competition across the league: They stop the large-market teams from buying their way to the Super Bowl, and they give smaller-market teams such as Kansas City, Cincinnati, and Green Bay the ability to afford high-performing players.

Studies in sports economics show a strong correlation between total team salary and winning percentage. In "Buying Success: Relationships between Team Performance and Wage Bills in the U.S. and European Sports Leagues" (Rodney Fort and John Fizel, eds., *International Sports Economics Comparisons*, 2004), Robert Simmons and David Forrest analyze salary expenditures and percentages of wins in seven professional sports leagues during the 1980s and 1990s—three European soccer leagues, MLB, the National Hockey League (NHL), NBA, and the NFL. The results showed that, in general, a higher overall team salary was associated with a greater likelihood of higher point scoring (in the European leagues) and of entering playoffs (in the North American leagues). Salary caps were invented precisely to mitigate this effect, and by and large they have been effective at balancing the wealth within leagues. The NFL's cap is the "hardest" (it has the fewest loopholes), and as such has had the biggest balancing effect. Of course, wealth parity does not always translate into winning percentage parity, since there are so many other variables involved, such as whether management makes good decisions about how to distribute its limited payroll.

Issues Surrounding Retired Players

In recent years greater attention has been focused on the well-being of former players suffering from physical problems resulting from the pounding their bodies took during their active playing careers. Many players with disabilities severe enough to prevent them from working have faced financial hardships besides physical pain. One story that received a great deal of media attention is the case of Mike Webster (1952–2002), a Hall of Fame–caliber player for the Pittsburgh Steelers. Webster died homeless and destitute at the age of 50 after years of drug addiction and dementia that he believed was caused by the many concussions he suffered during his 17-year career. The NFL denied that Webster's injuries were football-related and withheld assistance. A court later ordered the league to pay Webster's estate more than $1 million.

In June 2007 congressional hearings revealed an NFL disability compensation system that had performed poorly, providing assistance to a shockingly low number of former players who had suffered debilitating injuries, ranging from multiple concussions to severe arthritis necessitating joint replacement. In 2007, in response to this problem, a number of former players—led by Jerry Kramer (1936–) and Mike Ditka (1939–)—formed the Gridiron Greats Assistance Fund, a nonprofit foundation that provides financial assistance to former players who need help with medical or domestic issues. As of 2009 the charity reported that in its first three years of operation it had distributed more than $1.5 million in direct assistance and medical aid to needy former NFL players (2009, http://gridirongreats.org/stories/).

NATIONAL BASKETBALL ASSOCIATION

Professional basketball has changed drastically since its early days; in fact, its evolution has perhaps been more pronounced than that of any other major sport—in dress, style of play, and, most noticeably, the racial composition of teams. Once a sport that featured white men in close-fitting uniforms hoisting up set shots from chest level, by the late 20th century basketball was largely an African-American phenomenon, featuring loose-fitting fashions, a hip-hop sensibility, and an emphasis on the shortest-range shot of all: the slam dunk. Even though a sport such as hockey, for example, has always been dominated by white fans and players, basketball's racial shift has led to an identity crisis of sorts, with the issue of race becoming a major feature of discussion about the game.

NBA Structure and Administration

The 30-team NBA is divided into two conferences: the Eastern Conference, which consists of the Atlantic, Central, and Southeast Divisions; and the Western Conference, which consists of the Northwest, Pacific, and Southwest Divisions. (See Table 4.5.) Each division contains five teams.

The NBA regular season begins in early November. A season consists of 82 games for each team, divided evenly between home and away games. Teams play each

TABLE 4.5

National Basketball Association teams and divisions

Eastern conference	Western conference
Atlantic division	**Southwest division**
Boston Celtics	Dallas Mavericks
New Jersey Nets	Houston Rockets
New York Knicks	Memphis Grizzlies
Philadelphia 76ers	New Orleans Hornets
Toronto Raptors	San Antonio Spurs
Central division	**Northwest division**
Chicago Bulls	Denver Nuggets
Cleveland Cavaliers	Minnesota Timberwolves
Detroit Pistons	Oklahoma City Thunder
Indiana Pacers	Portland Trail Blazers
Milwaukee Bucks	Utah Jazz
Southeast division	**Pacific division**
Atlanta Hawks	Golden State Warriors
Charlotte Bobcats	Los Angeles Clippers
Miami Heat	Los Angeles Lakers
Orlando Magic	Phoenix Suns
Washington Wizards	Sacramento Kings

SOURCE: Created by Robert Jacobson for Gale, 2009

of the other teams in their own division four times per season; they play teams in the other divisions of their own conference three or four times, and they play teams in the other conference twice each. The NBA is currently the only one of the major sports leagues in which all teams play each other over the course of the regular season.

The NBA Playoffs begin in late April. Eight teams from each conference qualify: the winners of each of the three divisions plus the five teams with the next best records. Each round of the playoffs is a best-of-seven series. The third round of the playoffs is for the Conference Championship, and the winners of these two series compete against each other in the NBA Finals, the winner receiving the Larry O'Brien Trophy.

Plunkett Research reports in "Sports Industry Overview" that the NBA generated a total of $3.2 billion in revenue during the 2008–09 season. *SportsBusiness Journal* estimates that sales of NBA-licensed merchandise brings in approximately $1 billion per year. With such revenue teams can afford to pay high salaries. The average player salary was $5.35 million during the 2008–09 season, the highest among the major sports in the United States. Eight NBA players were paid at least $20 million in 2008–09, according to the *USA Today Salaries Databases* (http://content.usatoday.com/sports/basketball/nba/salaries/top25.aspx?year=2008-09). Table 4.6 shows the current values of NBA teams and their most recent revenue figures.

NBA History

Basketball was invented in 1891 by James Naismith (1861–1939), a Canadian physical education instructor and physician. Working at a Young Men's Christian Association

TABLE 4.6

Selected basketball team values and revenue, 2007–08 season

Rank	Team	Current value[a] ($mil)	Revenue[b] ($mil)	Operating income[c] ($mil)
1	New York Knicks	613	208	29.6
2	Los Angeles Lakers	584	191	47.9
3	Chicago Bulls	504	165	55.4
4	Detroit Pistons	480	160	40.4
5	Cleveland Cavaliers	477	159	13.1
6	Houston Rockets	469	156	31.2
7	Dallas Mavericks	466	153	−13.6

Note: Revenues and operating income are for 07–08 season and are net of revenue sharing.
[a]Value of team based on current arena deal (unless new arena is pending) without deduction for debt (other than arena debt).
[b]Net of arena revenues used for debt payments.
[c]Earnings before interest, taxes, depreciation and amortization.

SOURCE: Adapted from "NBA Team Valuations," *Forbes*, December 3, 2008, http://www.forbes.com/lists/2008/32/nba08_NBA-Team-Valuations_Rank .html (accessed June 19, 2009). Reprinted by Permission of Forbes.com © 2009 Forbes LLC.

(YMCA) in Springfield, Massachusetts, Naismith was directed by the head of the physical education department to create an indoor athletic game that would keep a class of young men occupied during the winter months. In two weeks Naismith had developed the game, including the original 13 rules of basketball. Among them: "A player cannot run with the ball" and "The referee shall be judge of the ball and shall decide when the ball is in play, in bounds, to which side it belongs, and shall keep the time." Even though he never sought recognition for his invention, Naismith was present at the 1936 Olympic Games in Berlin, Germany, basketball's first appearance as an Olympic event.

Basketball was first played professionally in 1896, when members of a YMCA team in Trenton, New Jersey, left to form a squad that would play for money. Two years later a group of New Jersey sports journalists founded the National Basketball League (NBL), which consisted of six teams based in Pennsylvania and New Jersey. The NBL petered out after several years, but in the mid-1930s a new league with the same name was founded. A second professional league, the Basketball Association of America (BAA), was formed by a group of New York entrepreneurs. The BAA, which was in direct competition against the NBL, had teams in New York, Boston, Philadelphia, Chicago, and Detroit. Right before the start of the 1948–49 season, four NBL teams—Minneapolis, Rochester, Fort Wayne, and Indianapolis—joined the BAA, and the following year the NBL's six surviving teams followed suit. The BAA was then divided into three divisions and renamed the National Basketball Association. One division was eliminated the following year, leaving the two that became the forerunners of the modern Eastern and Western Conferences of the NBA.

The NBA had no competition for the next two decades. That changed in 1967 with the formation of the American Basketball Association (ABA). The ABA lured fans, and quite a few players, away from the NBA with a flashier style of play that featured a red, white, and blue ball. The ABA disbanded in 1976, and several of its teams became part of the NBA. However, by the late 1970s professional basketball's popularity was sagging. Revenue and television ratings were down, and the game had become dull. The league received a huge boost with the emergence of two new stars: Magic Johnson (1959–) of the Los Angeles Lakers and Larry Bird (1956–) of the Boston Celtics, who together are credited with ushering in a new era of popularity and prosperity to the NBA. Behind Johnson and Bird, the Lakers and Celtics completely dominated the NBA through the 1980s. During the 1990s the game was dominated by Michael Jordan (1963–) and the Chicago Bulls. With the charismatic Jordan leading the way, the NBA continued to thrive through most of the decade.

After the 1997–98 season, tensions between players and owners began to heighten, as the salary cap and other issues came to a head. The owners instituted a player lockout, and the two sides did not reach an agreement until January 1999, by which time more than a third of the regular season had been canceled.

At the turn of the 21st century there was a dramatic increase in the number of foreign-born players in the NBA. The U.S. Olympic basketball team's mediocre performance in 2004 demonstrated that the rest of the world was starting to catch up with the United States in terms of basketball talent. Players from Europe appeared to have a better grounding in basketball fundamentals such as passing and long-range shooting. In "Solving USA Basketball's Long List of Problems" (September 8, 2002, http://sports.espn.go .com/nba/columns/story?columnist=aldridge_david&id= 1427992), David Aldridge noted that top NBA coaches George Karl (1951–) and Larry Brown (1940–) had complained for years that there is less emphasis on skill development and fundamentals on U.S. teams than on teams in other countries. Bringing foreign-born players into the NBA is believed to be one possible solution to the problem. The *Philadelphia Daily News* noted in "NBA's International Lineup" (June 23, 2009, http://www.philly.com/ dailynews/sports/20090623_NBA_s_international_lineup .html?viewAll=y) that there were 77 foreign players on NBA rosters at the end of the 2008–09 season. Some of them, including German-born Dirk Nowitzki (1978–) of the Dallas Mavericks, French-born Tony Parker (1982–) of the San Antonio Spurs, and Chinese-born Yao Ming (1980–) of the Houston Rockets, are among the best players in the league. In fact, the league's Most Valuable Player award was won by an individual born outside the United States for three straight years from 2005 to 2007—one by Nowitzki and two by the Canadian Steve Nash (1974–) of the Phoenix Suns. That streak was ended by Kobe Bryant (1978–), who is American-born but was raised largely in Italy to age 13, in 2008 and LeBron James (1984–) in 2009.

The flow of players across national borders has become a two-way street in recent years. In August 2008 the biggest-name American-born player to defect to Europe to date, Atlanta Hawks forward Josh Childress (1983–), signed a three-year, $32.5 million deal with the Greek club Olympiakos. Childress's decision to play in Europe came shortly after the July 2008 announcement by California high school star Brandon Jennings (1989–) that he would play Italian league basketball after he failed to qualify academically to play at the University of Arizona. Jennings signed with the Milwaukee Bucks after just a year in Europe. European teams have become more aggressive in their bids to lure top players abroad, offering big paydays to top stars. As of 2009, Childress remained the only star player to accept such an offer.

Current Issues in the NBA

SALARY CAPS. Basketball has a soft salary cap, meaning the amount a team can spend on salaries is limited, but there are loopholes and complications. As a result, there are still great disparities in how much the teams spend. According to *USA Today*'s salary database (http://content.usatoday.com/sports/basketball/nba/salaries/totalpayroll.aspx?year=2008-09), the New York Knicks had a total payroll of $97 million for the 2008–09 season, while the Miami Heat paid its players a total of $50 million. Only two teams, the Heat and the Portland Trail Blazers, were below the $58.7 million salary cap for that season. Table 4.7 shows the history of the NBA salary cap since 1984.

TABLE 4.7

NBA salary cap history, 1984–2009

NBA season	NBA salary cap
1984–85	$3.6 million
1985–86	$4.233 million
1986–87	$4.945 million
1987–88	$6.164 million
1988–89	$7.232 million
1989–90	$9.802 million
1990–91	$11.871 million
1991–92	$12.5 million
1992–93	$14.0 million
1993–94	$15.175 million
1994–95	$15.964 million
1995–96	$23.0 million
1996–97	$24.363 million
1997–98	$26.9 million
1998–99	$30.0 million
1999–2000	$34.0 million
2000–01	$35.5 million
2001–02	$42.5 million
2002–03	$40.271 million
2003–04	$43.84 million
2004–05	$43.87 million
2005–06	$49.5 million
2006–07	$53.135 million
2007–08	$55.630 million
2008–09	$58.680 million

SOURCE: Adapted from National Basketball Association, http://www.nba.com/ (accessed June 17, 2009)

Beginning in the late 1980s it became increasingly common for top college players to leave school before graduating and enter the NBA draft. By the mid-1990s the best high school players were foregoing college altogether and moving straight into the professional ranks. The NBA has long sought to discourage players from making the jump from high school to the pros. Toward that end, in 1995 the league enacted a salary limit for rookies, in the hopes of making the move less enticing.

In June 2005, as another labor dispute seemed possible, the league and the players union reached a new collective bargaining agreement. In "The NBA's New Labor Deal: What It Means, Who It Impacts" (*SportsBusiness Journal*, June 27, 2005), Liz Mullen and John Lombardo explained that the agreement's key provisions included a new rule preventing players from entering the NBA straight out of high school, increased drug testing, a 3% increase in the salary cap, and a reduction in the maximum length of free-agent contracts from seven to six years. This agreement remains in effect through the 2010–11 season.

MINIMUM AGE. Among the issues addressed in the NBA's contract, the minimum age requirement generated the most public attention. This provision requires that a player be at least 19 years old and be out of high school for at least one year. Proponents of age restrictions argue that allowing teens in the NBA does them a disservice and that they are much better off playing college basketball—even if it is just for a year—or playing in the NBA Developmental League than they are sitting on the end of an NBA team's bench rarely seeing significant playing time. They also say the NBA's skill level can become diluted with players who have not yet mastered the fundamentals of the game. According to the article "David Stern Media Conference" (April 12, 2004, http://www.insidehoops.com/stern-interview-041104.shtml), the NBA commissioner David Stern (1942–) was the most vocal advocate of age limits, arguing that the presence of NBA recruiters in high school gyms has an overall negative influence on young players, that teens lack the maturity to handle the rigors of NBA life without getting into trouble, and that too many young urban Americans are unrealistically looking to basketball as a pathway out of poverty.

Opponents of the minimum age requirement point out that practicing every day against the best players in the world is not such a bad way to learn the game and wonder what young men can gain from waiting just one extra year before entering the professional league. In "Hunter Still Opposed to Raising NBA Age Limit" (*USA Today*, May 12, 2005), Chris Sheridan noted that Billy Hunter (1943–), the director of the NBA players' union, also questions the possible racial motivations behind the move toward age limits: "I'm still strongly philosophically opposed to it, and I can't understand why people think one is needed except for the fact that the NBA is viewed as a predominantly black sport. You don't see that outcry in other sports, and the arguments that have been in support of an age limit have been defeated." Brandon Jennings's decision to play in Europe rather than sit out what would have been his freshman year in college could represent an approach taken by other young players if the age limit remains in place after 2011.

RACE AND THE NBA. The debate over teens in the NBA and its possible relation to race is connected to the broader issue of public image. Because it is dominated by young African-American males, the NBA struggles with the image the league projects to a predominantly white American public. Some basketball executives, particularly Stern, express concern about the message sent by the appearance and behavior of certain players. The arrests of high-profile players on sexual assault, drugs, and weapons charges have not helped matters. According to Jeff Benedict in *Out of Bounds: Inside the NBA's Culture of Rape, Violence, and Crime* (2004), a startling 40% of NBA players have police records, although, not surprisingly, the NBA disputes this claim. Interestingly, it is not the younger players who are getting in trouble the most. In "Illegal Defense: The Irrational Economics of Banning High School Players from the NBA Draft" (*Virginia Sports and Entertainment Law Journal*, vol. 3, 2004), Michael A. McCann of the Mississippi College School of Law analyzes arrests of NBA players from 1995 to 2004 and finds that 57.1% of the NBA players arrested actually went to college for four years. Another 17.9% of the arrested players went to college for three years. Only 4.8% of those arrested did not go to college at all.

Nonetheless, the question of public image persists. As one way of addressing the image problem, Stern announced in October 2005 a new dress code that would apply to all players when they are participating in NBA-related activities, including arriving at and leaving games, participating in interviews, and making promotional appearances. The new rules banned sleeveless shirts, shorts, T-shirts, chains or medallions worn over the clothes, sunglasses while indoors, and headphones (except on a team bus or plane or in the locker room). The code also required players to wear a sport coat when on the bench but not in uniform. Reactions to the code among players were at best mixed. Some players applauded the league's effort to clean up the game's image. Others were outraged. According to the article "Spurs Superstar Tim Duncan Is Known to Be Understated and Shy, But Not about the NBA's New Dress Code" (FoxSports.com, October 20, 2005), Tim Duncan (1976–) of the San Antonio Spurs, a player often touted by the league as a model citizen, described the dress code as "basically retarded." The article "Pacers' Jackson: Dress Code Is 'Racist': Forward Wears Jewelry to Protest Rules, Which He Says Attacks Culture" (October 20, 2005, http://www.msnbc.msn.com/id/9730334/) reports that Stephen Jackson (1978–) of the Indiana Pacers openly accused the

league of targeting black players. Jackson was particularly critical of the ban on wearing chains, noting that chains are associated with hip-hop culture and are a common fashion choice among young black men. As of 2009, it was unclear whether anybody had yet been punished for violating the dress code. What was clear was that it was not being rigorously enforced; there are many public media images of players in violation of the policy for such practices as wearing sunglasses indoors.

A new image problem for the NBA emerged in July 2007, when it was revealed that the veteran referee Tim Donaghy (1967–) was under investigation for allegedly betting on the outcome of NBA games, including games in which he had officiated. The following month he pleaded guilty to two felony charges, admitting that he personally bet on NBA games and that he provided inside information to associates about likely game outcomes. In 2008 Donaghy was sentenced to 15 months in prison. After serving 11 months in a federal prison camp in Florida, Donaghy was released to a halfway house in June 2009 to serve out the rest of his sentence.

WOMEN'S NATIONAL BASKETBALL ASSOCIATION

The Women's National Basketball Association (WNBA) started play in June 1997 following the celebrated gold medal run of the U.S. women's basketball team in the 1996 Olympics. There had been other professional women's basketball leagues before, but the WNBA was launched with the full support of the NBA, making it much more viable than other upstart leagues. At its inception, the WNBA already had television deals in place with the National Broadcasting Corporation, the Entertainment and Sports Programming Network (ESPN), and Lifetime network.

In its first season, the WNBA had eight teams. By 1999 four more teams had joined the league. That year, players and the league signed the first collective bargaining agreement in the history of women's professional sports. Four more teams were added in 2000. Following the 2002 season, the league's ownership structure was changed. Before that, the NBA owned all the teams in the WNBA. In 2002, however, the NBA sold the women's teams either to their NBA counterparts in the same city or to outside parties. As a result of this restructuring, two teams moved to other cities, and two teams folded. Another team dropped out after the 2003 season.

As of 2009, there were 13 teams in the WNBA: seven in the Eastern Conference and six in the Western Conference. (See Table 4.8.) Each team plays a 34-game regular-season schedule, with the top four teams in each conference competing in the playoffs. The first and second rounds of the playoffs are best-of-three series. The WNBA Finals are best of five. The WNBA season starts in the summer, when the NBA season ends.

TABLE 4.8

WNBA teams and divisions

Eastern Conference	Western Conference
Atlanta Dream	Los Angeles Sparks
Chicago Sky	Minnesota Lynx
Connecticut Sun	Phoenix Mercury
Detroit Shock	Sacramento Monarchs
Indiana Fever	San Antonio Silver Stars
New York Liberty	Seattle Storm
Washington Mystics	

WNBA = Women's National Basketball Association

SOURCE: Created by Robert Jacobson for Gale, 2009

TABLE 4.9

Selected hockey team values and revenue, 2007–08 season

Rank	Team	Current value^a ($mil)	Revenue ($mil)	Operating income^b ($mil)
1	Toronto Maple Leafs	448	160	66.4
2	New York Rangers	411	137	30.7
3	Montreal Canadiens	334	139	39.6
4	Detroit Red Wings	303	110	13.4
5	Philadelphia Flyers	275	102	−1.8
6	Dallas Stars	273	105	14.2
7	Boston Bruins	263	97	−3.0

Note: Revenues and operating income are for 2007–2008 season.
[a]Value of team based on current arena deal (unless new arena is pending), without deduction for debt (other than arena debt).
[b]Earnings before interest, taxes, depreciation and amortization.

SOURCE: Adapted from "Special Report: NHL Team Valuations," in *Forbes*, October 29, 2008, http://www.forbes.com/lists/2008/31/nhl08_NHL-Team-Valuations_Rank.html (accessed June 22, 2009). Reprinted by Permission of Forbes.com © 2009 Forbes LLC.

Even though the WNBA has gained in popularity, it has not been a big financial success. Through 2008, the league had not yet turned a profit in any year, although league officials expressed optimism that 2009 would be the season in which the league finished in the black. Average attendance at WNBA games is only about half that of NBA games. Player salaries are much lower as well. The WNBA collective bargaining agreement (http://www.womensbasketballonline.com/wnba/wnbacba08.pdf), a six-year deal signed in 2008, calls for a maximum player salary of $99,500 for 2009. This salary, available only to veterans with at least six years in the league, is less than one-fourth the minimum salary for an NBA rookie.

NATIONAL HOCKEY LEAGUE

Even though professional hockey has a long and storied history in the United States, it is currently at a crossroads. Its popularity in the United States is declining, whereas other sports such as soccer and auto racing are eagerly courting disenchanted hockey fans. The cancellation of the 2004–05 NHL season because of a bitter labor dispute certainly did not help matters. Regardless, hockey is still big business. Plunkett Research notes in "Sports Industry Overview" that league-wide revenue in the NHL was about $2.4 billion during the 2008–09 season, less than half that of the NFL or MLB, and nearly a billion dollars less than the NBA, which has the same number of teams and games in a season. NHL players earn an average annual salary of about $2 million, according to *SportsBusiness Daily*, which also estimates that sales of merchandise licensed by the NHL and member teams generate about $900 million annually, the lowest among the major sports. The values and recent revenue figures for NHL teams are shown in Table 4.9.

NHL Structure and Administration

The NHL is divided into the Eastern and Western Conferences. (See Table 4.10.) Each conference consists of three divisions, and each division has five teams. The Eastern Conference is split into the Northeast, Atlantic, and Southeast Divisions. The divisions that make up the West-

TABLE 4.10

National Hockey League teams and divisions

Eastern Conference	Western Conference
Atlantic Division	**Central Division**
New Jersey Devils	Chicago Blackhawks
New York Islanders	Columbus Blue Jackets
New York Rangers	Detroit Red Wings
Philadelphia Flyers	Nashville Predators
Pittsburgh Penguins	St. Louis Blues
Northeast Division	**Northwest Division**
Boston Bruins	Calgary Flames
Buffalo Sabres	Colorado Avalanche
Montreal Canadiens	Edmonton Oilers
Ottawa Senators	Minnesota Wild
Toronto Maple Leafs	Vancouver Canucks
Southeast Division	**Pacific Division**
Atlanta Thrashers	Anaheim Ducks
Carolina Hurricanes	Dallas Stars
Florida Panthers	Los Angeles Kings
Tampa Bay Lightning	Phoenix Coyotes
Washington Capitals	San Jose Sharks

SOURCE: Created by Robert Jacobson for Gale, 2009. Data from the National Hockey League, http://www.nhl.com.

ern Conference are the Northwest, Central, and Pacific. NHL teams play an 82-game regular season, split evenly between home and away games. Before the 2004–05 lockout each team played all the others at least once during the season, but this is no longer the case. Teams now play 10 games against opponents outside of their own conference, and 40 games against teams in a different division within their own conference.

At the conclusion of the regular season, the champion of each division plus the five teams in each conference with the next best records compete in the Stanley Cup Playoffs. The structure is similar to that of the NBA: a single-elimination tournament consisting of four rounds of best-of-seven series, culminating in the Stanley Cup Finals, usually played in the late spring.

NHL History

Even though hockey in North America started in Canada, the first professional version of the game was launched in the United States. In 1904 the International Pro Hockey League was founded in the iron-mining areas of Michigan's Upper Peninsula. That league lasted only a few years, but in 1910 a new league, the National Hockey Association (NHA), arose. The Pacific Coast League (PCL) was founded soon after the NHA. It was arranged that the champions of the two leagues would play a championship series, the winner gaining possession of the coveted Stanley Cup, a trophy named for Frederick A. Stanley (1841–1908), a former British governor-general of Canada.

World War I (1914–1918) put a temporary halt to the fledgling sport, but when the war ended professional hockey reorganized itself as the National Hockey League. At first the NHL was strictly a Canadian affair. The league initially consisted of five teams: Montreal Canadiens, Montreal Wanderers, Ottawa Senators, Quebec Bulldogs, and Toronto Arenas (later renamed the Maple Leafs). The first game took place in December 1917. The NHL expanded into the United States in the 1920s, adding the Boston Bruins in 1924; the New York Americans and Pittsburgh Pirates in 1925; and the New York Rangers, Chicago Blackhawks, and Detroit Cougars (which later became the Red Wings) in 1926. By the end of the 1930–31 season, there were ten teams in the NHL. The Depression and World War II took their toll on the league, however, and by its 25th birthday the NHL was reduced to six teams. Those six teams—the Canadiens, Maple Leafs, Red Wings, Bruins, Rangers, and Blackhawks—are commonly referred to, though not very accurately, as the "Original Six" of the NHL.

The NHL did not expand again until 1967, when six new teams were added, forming their own division. Two other franchises came on board three years later. In 1972 a new rival league, the World Hockey Association (WHA), was formed. In response, the NHL accelerated its own plans for expansion, adding four new teams over the next three years. This double-barreled expansion of professional hockey in North America diluted the pool of available players, however, and the quality of play suffered as a result. The WHA folded in 1979, and four of its teams joined the NHL. The league continued to expand over the next two decades, as league officials sought to follow demographic trends in the United States. The NHL reached its current total of 30 teams in 2000. Unfortunately, the league's southward and westward expansion has not been entirely successful, as interest is weak in warm-weather regions. Even though many Canadian towns have lost their teams to U.S. cities, and suffered economically as a result, a large percentage of Canadians remain diehard hockey fans. According to the

Canadian Broadcasting Corporation (2009, http://archives .cbc.ca/programs/1284/), *Hockey Night in Canada* is consistently one of the highest-rated programs on Canadian television, and is recognized as the oldest and longest-running weekly sports shows in the world. In the United States, however, hockey is in danger of losing its major sport status.

Labor Issues in the NHL: A Season on Ice

In its long history the NHL has been interrupted only three times by labor strife. The first, a 1992 strike by the NHL Players Association (NHLPA), lasted only ten days, short enough for all missed games to be made up. A lockout at the start of the 1994–95 season was more disruptive. It lasted three months and resulted in the cancellation of 36 games, nearly half of the regular season.

With the 1995 deal moving toward its 2004 expiration date, negotiations between players and owners turned bitter. Unlike the 1994 lockout, which came at a time when the NHL was enjoying strong fan support and rising popularity, interest in the league had been waning for several years by 2004. As in other major sports, one of the biggest points of contention was proposed limits on the amount teams could spend on player salaries. The league proposed what it called cost certainty, which the players' union argued was just a fancy term for a salary cap. The union rejected the idea and instead proposed a luxury tax. Not surprisingly, the owners were opposed. The two sides failed to reach an agreement, and the entire 2004–05 season, from preseason training through the Stanley Cup Finals, was canceled—the first time a major sport had lost a whole season to labor unrest.

In July 2005 the NHLPA and the league finally agreed to the terms of a new collective bargaining agreement, which was published as the *Collective Bargaining Agreement, 2005* (http://www.nhlpa.com/CBA/2005CBA.asp). The deal, which runs through the 2010–11 season, gives players 54% to 57% of league-wide revenues, depending on the total. The agreement includes a salary cap—which according to ESPN is $56.8 million for the 2009–10 season—and enhances revenue sharing to help the smaller market teams remain competitive. It does not include a luxury tax.

Naturally, hockey fans across North America were greatly disappointed by the loss of an entire season. In response, the NHL took measures to try to lure back fans—both those who had wandered away from the sport before the lockout and those who lost interest directly because of it. These measures included a handful of rule changes designed to speed up the pace of the game and increase scoring.

A bigger challenge to the NHL remains: making hockey popular in parts of the United States that do not have long-standing hockey traditions. The expansion that the league undertook during the last two decades of the

20th century was focused primarily in the southern and southwestern regions of the United States, the very parts of the country experiencing rapid population growth. Even though this expansion strategy made sense at the time, to date it has not produced the expected new generation of hockey fans in these regions.

MAJOR LEAGUE SOCCER

Major League Soccer (MLS), the premier professional soccer league in the United States, was launched in April 1996. MLS has a unique ownership and operating structure that is unlike those of other major U.S. sports leagues. Even though the other leagues are confederations of independent franchise owners, MLS has a single-entity structure, which allows investors to own a share of the league as well as individual teams.

As of the 2007 season, MLS consisted of 15 teams that were divided into two conferences: Eastern and Western. (See Table 4.11.) Teams compete through a season that runs from April through the MLS Cup championship in November. Each team plays 30 regular-season games, evenly divided between home and away matches. Each team plays against every other team in its conference twice, once at home and once away, for a total of 28 games. The remaining two games are against nonconference opponents. Eight teams advance to the MLS Cup Playoffs, which begin in mid-October and culminate in the crowning of a new MLS Cup champion.

Plans to start up MLS were first announced in December 1993. Twenty-two cities submitted bids to secure teams, of which ten were selected. A player draft was conducted in February 1996, and the league's first game took place a few months later on April 6, 1996. The new league was launched before a full stadium of 31,683 spectators and a national ESPN viewing audience, with the San Jose Clash defeating D.C. United by a score of 1–0 (2009, http://ww2.mlsnet.com/about/).

Two additional teams were added in 1998. The following year the Columbus Crew built the first major league stadium ever constructed specifically for soccer in the United States. The Crew ended up leading the league in attendance for the year. In 2002 the league was forced to cut two teams for financial reasons, returning MLS to its original ten-team size. Two new teams were added in 2005, bringing the league to 12 teams once again. The addition of Toronto FC before the 2007 season made the league 13 strong. The San Jose Earthquakes morphed into the expansion Houston Dynamo in 2006, but a new version of the Earthquakes was formed in San Jose in 2008. The Seattle Sounders FC joined the league in 2009. Further expansion was planned for 2010 and 2011, with teams planned to go into action in Philadelphia, Vancouver, and Portland.

MLS is far more ethnically diverse than any of the traditional four major sports in the United States. As of March 31, 2009, there were 128 players born outside the United States on MLS rosters, representing 47 different countries, from Argentina to Zimbabwe. MLS has also played a huge role in preparing American players for greater impact on the international soccer scene.

Women's Professional Soccer

Women's professional soccer in the United States has not met with great success, but players and fans are hopeful that its most recent incarnation, Women's Professional Soccer (WPS), will catch on. The first women's professional outdoor league to be sanctioned by U.S. Soccer, the Women's United Soccer Association, was launched in 2001. It featured stars from the popular 2000 U.S. Olympic team, including Mia Hamm (1972–), Brandi Chastain (1968–), and Julie Foudy (1971–). Faced with financial struggles, the association suspended operations in September 2003.

In 2004 a new nonprofit organization, the Women's Soccer Initiative, was established with the goal of reviving women's professional soccer in the United States. In September 2007 the Women's Soccer Initiative announced plans to relaunch a professional women's league in 2009. As scheduled, Women's Professional Soccer (WPS, http://www.womensprosoccer.com) opened its inaugural season in March 2009, with seven teams each playing 20 regular season games. Teams in the league were located in Boston, Chicago, Los Angeles, New Jersey/New York, San Francisco, St. Louis, and Washington, D.C.; teams in Atlanta and Philadelphia were joining the league in 2010. The New Jersey–based Sky Blue FC defeated the Los Angeles Sol in the first league championship game in August 2009.

DIVERSITY IN THE MAJOR SPORTS

Diversity has long been an issue in major league sports in the United States. MLB was all white until Jackie Robinson crossed the color line in 1947. Over the next few decades the number of prominent black ballplayers grew, and baseball took on the appearance of an inclusive sport (at least on the field; managerial jobs for African-Americans

TABLE 4.11

Major League Soccer teams and divisions

Eastern Conference	Western Conference
Chicago Fire	Chivas USA
Columbus Crew	Colorado Rapids
D.C. United	FC Dallas
Kansas City Wizards	Houston Dynamo
New England Revolution	Los Angeles Galaxy
New York Red Bulls	Real Salt Lake
Toronto FC	San Jose Earthquakes
	Seattle Sounders FC

SOURCE: Created by Robert Jacobson for Gale, 2009

remained scarce). However, the trend has reversed itself. Once again, MLB teams have few African-Americans on their rosters, although the number of Hispanic players has increased dramatically. The percentage of foreign-born players was 19% on opening day in 1997, according to the Associated Press in "More Foreigners in Majors for Sixth Straight Year" (April 2, 2003). Mike Bauman reports in "MLB Must Preserve Civil Rights Legacy" (June 21, 2009) that in 2009 the share of MLB players from Latin America was 27 percent. According to *Baseball Almanac* (http://www .baseball-almanac.com/players/birthplace.php?y=2008), the country that has produced the greatest number of players born outside the United States is the Dominican Republic, with 137 players in 2008. Venezuela was second with 89.

Concerns about diversity in professional sports extend beyond the playing field. Coaching and management opportunities have traditionally been limited for minorities, though this trend may be shifting. The University of Central Florida's Institute for Diversity and Ethics in Sport issues annual racial and gender report cards that examine the front office, support staff, playing, and coaching opportunities for women and minorities in football, basketball, baseball, and soccer at the professional and college levels. The most recent report, *The 2009 Racial and Gender Report Card* (http://web.bus.ucf.edu/ sportbusiness/?page=1445), gives top marks for racial diversity to the WNBA for the second straight year, noting that five of the league's 13 teams began the 2008 season with African-American head coaches. In addition, one-third of WNBA general managers are African-American. The WNBA was also the leader in gender diversity, according to the *Report Card*. Forty-six percent of head coaches and 58% of general managers in the league are women.

THE STADIUM SCRAMBLE

Since the early 1990s there has been an unprecedented boom in the construction of new stadiums for U.S. sports teams. The main reason is that team owners believe that they can make more money selling skyboxes to wealthy corporate customers than they can by selling cheaper seats to the masses, and many older stadiums lack luxury accommodations. A skybox can sell for upward of $200,000 per season. Table 4.12 shows the typical cost of a luxury skybox at venues that host each of the major sports. An additional incentive is that the revenue from sales of these luxury skyboxes is exempt from the revenue-sharing formulas of both MLB and the NFL, meaning that teams get to keep all the money generated by skybox sales.

Public Funding for Stadiums

Owners have been further encouraged by the success of their peers in obtaining public funding for the construction of their new stadiums. A number of team owners have succeeded in securing public dollars for new stadiums by

TABLE 4.12

Average prices for luxury suites within major sports leagues, 2009

Sport/league	Averages		
	Quantity	Low	High
Major League Baseball	76	$100,397	$200,072
National Football League	142	$64,061	$196,578
National Basketball Association	88	$137,418	$281,053
National Hockey League	96	$124,933	$261,933

SOURCE: "Luxury Suites," in *Free Venue Information*, Revenues from Sports Venues, 2009, http://www.sportsvenues.com/info.htm (accessed June 22, 2009)

threatening to move to a different city if the taxpayers did not foot the bill. Owners usually argue that a new stadium will generate additional tax revenue, as fans flock to the new facility and, so they claim, spend vast sums of money at nearby businesses.

However, opponents of public funding for stadiums have challenged the view that stadiums provide economic benefits to the surrounding region. In "Do Economists Reach a Conclusion on Subsidies for Sports Franchises, Stadiums, and Mega-Events?" (September 2008, http://www.aier.org/ejw/ archive/doc_view/3626-ejw-200809), Dennis Coates of the University of Maryland and Brad R. Humphreys of the University of Alberta report on survey data and economic research measuring the benefits of subsidies for sports facilities and conclude that from an economic standpoint, most research does not support subsidies. They write, "The large and growing peer-reviewed economics literature on the economic impacts of stadiums, arenas, sports franchises, and sport mega-events has consistently found no substantial evidence of increased jobs, incomes, or tax revenues for a community associated with any of these things. . . . If professional sports franchises and facilities do not have any important positive economic impact in the local economy, then subsidies for the construction and operation of these facilities are even more difficult to justify."

In addition, critics such as Representative Dennis Kucinich (D-OH; 1946–) note that public funds being used for stadium construction are sorely needed for regional infrastructure improvements, including bridge and road repair. In 2007 the Domestic Policy subcommittee of the U.S. House of Representatives Committee on Oversight and Government Reform conducted a series of hearings on the topic "Public Infrastructure and Professional Sports Stadiums" (October 10, 2007, http://domesticpolicy.oversight .house.gov/story.asp?ID=1526). Kucinich, the chairman of the subcommittee, cited the case of Minnesota, in which a freeway bridge collapse claimed the lives of 13 motorists in August 2007. Kucinich pointed out that tax increases to fund infrastructure improvements were consistently vetoed in Minnesota, yet in the year preceding the deadly bridge collapse the Minnesota Twins professional baseball team was awarded public funding for a new baseball stadium. He reported similar cases in New York City, where the Yankees received funding for a $1 billion stadium although the American Society of Civil Engineers had identified 50 structurally deficient bridges in the city, as well as Chicago (2 new stadiums, 82 structurally deficient bridges), Philadelphia (3 new stadiums, 42 structurally deficient bridges), Cleveland (3 new stadiums, 5 structurally deficient bridges, and Baltimore (2 new stadiums, 8 deficient bridges).

In response to research that disputes the economic benefits of public funding for sports facilities, taxpayer backlash has begun to make some state legislatures skittish. In Seattle, lawmakers' refusal in 2008 to cave in to the demands for public funding to expand KeyArena—a refusal encouraged by outspoken taxpayer protests—resulted in Seattle's NBA team, the SuperSonics, pulling up stakes and moving to Oklahoma City.

CORPORATE SPONSORSHIP OF STADIUMS

Another source of revenue from stadiums comes from the sale of naming rights. Where in the past most stadiums had straightforward names such as Tiger Stadium or the Houston Astrodome, in the 21st century an increasing number of facilities bear the name of a corporate sponsor that has paid millions of dollars for the privilege. The following are only three out of several examples that Revenues from Sports Venues cites in *Free Venue Information* (February 26, 2009, http://www.sportsvenues.com/pdf/names.pdf):

- Comerica Park in Detroit, home of MLB's Detroit Tigers ($66 million for 30 years)
- Citi Field in Flushing, New York, home of baseball's New York Mets ($400 million for 20 years)
- American Airlines Center in Dallas, home of both basketball's Mavericks and hockey's Stars ($195 million for 30 years)

Sometimes these deals backfire. Darren Rovell reported in "Astros Stuck with Enron Name—For Now" (January 25, 2002, http://espn.go.com/sportsbusiness/s/2002/0124/1316712.html) that in 1999 Enron, a U.S. energy company, signed a 30-year, $100 million deal with the Houston Astros. In 2001 Enron filed for bankruptcy following an accounting scandal. The collapse of the company forced the Astros to buy their way out of the deal to get Enron's name off their stadium. In 2002 a new sponsor was found, and the field was rechristened Minute Maid Park.

CHAPTER 5
OTHER PROFESSIONAL SPORTS

As important as professional team sports are in the United States, Americans' sports obsession extends well beyond them. Not every sports enthusiast is engrossed by the hoopla of *Monday Night Football* or the high-flying acrobatics of the National Basketball Association. Some fans prefer the quiet beauty of a perfect putt or the battle of wills that takes place across the Centre Court net at Wimbledon. Others are attracted to the blunt truth of boxing or the raw speed of the National Association for Stock Car Auto Racing (NASCAR). This chapter considers several sports that fall below the top tier of U.S. sports in terms of audience or revenue but are nevertheless important components of the nation's professional sports culture.

GOLF

Professional golf in the United States is coordinated by the Professional Golfers' Association (PGA) of America, a nonprofit organization that promotes the sport while enhancing golf's professional standards. The PGA of America (2009, http://www.pga.com/pgaofamerica) states that in 2009 there were more than 28,000 PGA professionals in the United States, both men and women, making it the largest working sports organization in the world. However, most of these members were primarily golf instructors; only a small fraction compete in high-profile tournaments.

The PGA of America traces its roots to 1916, when a group of golf professionals and serious amateurs in the New York area got together at a luncheon sponsored by the department store magnate Rodman Wanamaker (1863–1928). The point of the meeting was to discuss forming a national organization to promote golf and elevate the occupation of golf professionals. The meeting led to the organization of the first PGA Championship tournament, which was played later that year. The PGA Championship has grown to become one of professional golf's four major championships, along with the British Open, the Masters, and the U.S. Open. Together, these four tournaments make up the unofficial Grand Slam of golf. (See Table 5.1.) Besides the PGA Championship, the PGA of America sponsors three other top golf events: the Senior PGA Championship; the Ryder Cup, which every two years pits a team of top American golfers against their European counterparts; and the PGA Grand Slam of Golf, an annual event in which the winners of the four major championships compete head to head. Besides these championships, the PGA of America also conducts about 40 tournaments for PGA professionals.

However, while professional golfers in the United States are members of the PGA of America, most of the actual golf they play is under the auspices of other organizations. Worldwide, professional golf is organized into several regional tours, each of which usually holds a series of tournaments over the course of a season. There are approximately 20 of these tours around the world, each run by a national or regional PGA or by an independent tour organization. Each tour has members who may compete in as many of its events as they want. Joining a tour usually requires that a golfer achieve some specified level of success, often by performing well in a qualifying tournament. A player can be a member of multiple tours.

The world's top tour by far, in terms of money and prestige, is the PGA Tour, which since 1968 has been a completely separate organizational entity from the PGA of America. In 2009 the PGA Tour (http://www.pgatour.com/r/schedule/) consisted of 57 events offering more than $307 million in total prize money. The PGA Tour organization also runs two other tours: the Champions Tour for golfers over age 50; and the Nationwide Tour, a sort of minor league of professional golf.

The History of the PGA

According to the PGA Tour (2009, http://www.pgatour.com/company/pgatour_history.html), the first U.S.

TABLE 5.1

Golf Grand Slam events

Event	Location	Scheduled time
The Masters	Augusta, Georgia	April
U.S. Open	Location varies	June
British Open	Location varies	July
PGA Championship	Location varies	August

SOURCE: Created by Robert Jacobson for Gale, 2009

Open took place in 1895 in Newport, Rhode Island. Ten professionals and one amateur competed in the event. The Western Open made its debut in Chicago, Illinois, four years later. Tournaments were initiated throughout the country at about this time, although there was no coordination or continuity among them. English players dominated the competition in U.S. tournaments. As interest in golf continued to grow, American players improved. Enthusiasm for the sport began to increase after John McDermott (1891–1971) became the first U.S.-born player to win the U.S. Open in 1911. By the 1920s professional golf had spread to the West Coast and southward to Florida, and the prize money was becoming substantial.

The PGA Tour was formally launched in late 1968, when the Tournament Players Division of the PGA broke away from the parent organization. The tour grew during the 1970s and 1980s, with its total annual revenue increasing from $3.9 million in 1974 to $229 million in 1993. Assessing 2008 PGA revenue, Jon Show in *Sports-Business Journal* (September 7, 2009, http://www.sports businessjournal.com/article/63454) reports that "combined revenue from tournaments and supporting business ... is creeping closer to the $1 billion mark."

The Champions Tour

The Champions Tour, which is run by the PGA Tour organization, hosts 30 events each year in the United States and Canada for golfers at least 50 years old. Many of the most successful players on the PGA Tour go on to play on the Champions Tour when they reach age 50. The tour grew out of a highly successful 1978 event called the Legends of Golf, which featured two-member teams composed of some of the game's best-known former champions. Following the success of the Legends event, the Senior PGA Tour was established in 1980, with two tournaments and $250,000 in prize money. The Senior Tour proved remarkably popular, as fans flocked to golf courses and tuned in on television to see legendary competitors such as Arnold Palmer (1929–) and Sam Snead (1912–2002) in action. Even though their playing skills may have diminished somewhat from the level of their prime playing years, the former champions proved popular with golf lovers across the country. At the start of the 2003 season the Senior Tour changed its name to

the Champions Tour. The 2009 Champions Tour (2009, http://ww.pgatour.com/s/schedule/) offered total prize money of $51.4 million over 26 tournaments.

Most tournaments on the Champions Tour are played over three rounds (54 holes) rather than the customary four rounds (72 holes) typical of PGA tournaments. The five majors of the senior circuit are exceptions; they are played over four rounds. The major tournaments of the Champions Tour are the Senior PGA Championship, the Senior Players Championship, the Senior British Open, the U.S. Senior Open, and The Tradition. Since 2003 The Tradition has been called the JELD-WEN Tradition because of its ongoing sponsorship by JELD-WEN Windows and Doors. Also due to corporate sponsorship, the Senior Players Championship has been known as the Constellation Energy Senior Players Championship since 2007.

The Nationwide Tour

The Nationwide Tour is the developmental tour for the PGA Tour. Its players are professionals who have missed the criteria to get into the main tour by failing to score well enough in the PGA Tour's qualifying tournament, known as Qualifying School, or who have made it into the main tour but failed to win enough money to stay there. The Nationwide Tour gets its name from the company that bought the naming rights in 2003, the Nationwide Mutual Insurance Company of Columbus, Ohio. It was called the Nike Tour and the Buy.com Tour before that. When the tour was first launched in its original form in 1990, it was known as the Ben Hogan Tour.

In 2009 the Nationwide Tour (http://www.pgatour .com/h/schedule/) consisted of 29 events in 18 states and 5 countries outside the United States. The prize money for Nationwide Tour events is typically about one-tenth that of a PGA Tour tournament; the total prize winnings for the 2009 tour stood at $19 million.

The Nationwide Tour has proven to be an excellent feeder system for the PGA Tour. The PGA Tour reports in "NBC Sports to Air Special on PGA Tour Graduates" (January 8, 2009, http://www.pgatour.com/2009/h/01/08/ nbc_special/index.html) that through 2008, Nationwide Tour alumni had won 237 PGA Tour titles. A number of top players, including Ernie Els (1969–), David Duval (1971–), Jim Furyk (1970–), David Toms (1967–), and Stuart Appleby (1971–), played the Nationwide circuit before achieving success on the PGA Tour.

Other Men's Tours

As noted earlier, the PGA Tour is merely the biggest and richest of the world's many professional golf tours. There are many others around the world, some of which—such as the Nationwide Tour—prepare players for entry into the PGA Tour. In 1996 the International

Federation of PGA Tours was formed by golf's five chief governing bodies around the world. As of 2009 the International Federation (http://www.worldgolfchampion ships.com/wgc/internationalfederation/index.html) had six members: the PGA Tour (United States), the Asian Tour (Singapore), the Japan Golf Tour Organization, the PGA European Tour, the PGA Tour of Australasia, and the Sunshine Tour (South Africa). Together, these tours sanction the Official World Golf Rankings. The Federation also had two associate members: the Canadian Tour and the Tour de las Americas.

The PGA European Tour, headquartered in England, is the premier professional golf tour in Europe and is second only to the PGA Tour in money and international prestige. The European Tour was established by the British PGA, but in 1984 it became a separate entity, just as the PGA Tour became independent from the PGA of America in 1968. In 2009 the European Tour (2009, http://www.europeantour.com/) consisted of 53 official money tournaments. Most of the top players on the European Tour, including Els, Retief Goosen (1969–), Sergio Garcia (1980–), and Padraig Harrington (1971–), are also members of the PGA Tour. Like the PGA Tour, the European Tour has a developmental tour, called the Challenge Tour, and a senior tour, called the European Seniors Tour. In 2008 the European Tour introduced the Race to Dubai, a season-long competition over 51 tournaments in 26 destinations featuring players from at least 40 countries, culminating in the extremely lucrative Dubai World Championship.

The Japan Golf Tour, founded in 1973 (2009, http://www.jgto.org/jgto/WG01000000Init.do) is the third-biggest professional men's tour (not counting senior tours) in terms of prize money available. However, prize money in the Japanese Tour has not kept pace with the growth of money in the PGA and European tours in recent years.

Performance in all the previously mentioned tours—the International Federation members, plus the Nationwide and Challenge Tours—earns Official World Golf Ranking points. Other regional tours worth noting are the Indian Golf Tour; and the NGA/Hooters Tour, which is the third-tier U.S.-based professional tour, below the Nationwide Tour in money and prestige.

Women's Tours

Women's professional golf, like men's golf, is organized into several regional tours. The top tour for female professional golfers is the Ladies Professional Golf Association (LPGA), which operates the LPGA Tour. Unlike the PGA Tour, the LPGA Tour and the LPGA are not distinct organizations. Both of these terms generally refer to the LPGA that is based in the United States. Internationally, there are other regional LPGAs and tours, including the LPGA of Japan, the LPGA of Korea, the Australian Ladies Professional Golf Tour, and the Ladies European Tour.

Founded in 1950 by a group of 13 golfers, the LPGA is the oldest continuing women's professional sports organization in the United States. It features the best female golfers from all over the world. The 2009 LPGA Tour (2009, http://www.lpga.com/tournaments_index .aspx) consisted of 29 events—down from 34 in 2008—offering total prize money of nearly $50 million. Most LPGA Tour events take place in the United States. In 2009 three tournaments were scheduled for Mexico and one each in Singapore, Canada, France, England, China, South Korea, Thailand, and Japan. Four of the tournaments held outside North America were co-sanctioned with other professional tours. Four LPGA tournaments are considered the tour's majors: the Kraft Nabisco Championship, McDonald's U.S. LPGA Championship Presented by Coca-Cola, the U.S. Women's Open, and the Ricoh Women's British Open (held jointly with the Ladies European Tour).

Besides the main tour, the LPGA also coordinates a developmental tour called the Duramed Futures Tour. The Futures Tour began in Florida in 1981 as the Tampa Bay Mini Tour but is now a national tour that functions as a feeder system for the LPGA, filling the same role as the Nationwide Tour does for the men. In 2009 the Duramed Futures Tour (2009, http://www.duramedfutures tour.com/AboutUs.asp) featured a 17-tournament national schedule and a total purse of about $1.8 million.

In 2001 the LPGA created the Women's Senior Golf Tour for players over age 45. Its name was changed to the Legends Tour before the 2006 season. In 2009 the Legends Tour was scheduled to showcase five events (2009, http://www.thelegendstour.com/tournaments.htm).

Women in the PGA

Ever since the outstanding female athlete Babe Didrikson Zaharias (1914–1956) played in the 1938 Los Angeles Open, there have been women who sought to achieve crossover success competing against men in PGA events. Only a few women tried to play against the men in the remainder of the 20th century following Zaharias's PGA participation, but since 2000 the issue of LPGA players competing against men has come to the fore. Most of the attention has focused on Annika Sorenstam (1970–) and Michelle Wie (1989–). In 2003 Sorenstam was dominating women's golf almost as thoroughly as Tiger Woods (1975–) was towering over the other male competitors. That year, she accepted a sponsor's invitation to compete in the Bank of America Colonial tournament. She missed the cut (failed to achieve a good enough score to continue in the second portion of the tournament) by four strokes. Wie has played against men in eight PGA events since 2006. She has failed to make the cut each time. Some fellow LPGA members have criticized Wie for continuing to enter men's tournaments in light of her performance, especially given the fact that as of late summer 2009 she was still winless in her professional LPGA career playing against women.

One reason a women golfer might want to compete in PGA events is because the potential payday is much greater. The top prize for an LPGA victory is typically a fraction of what a PGA winner makes. In Scotland's *Sunday Herald* ("Sponsors Snub Golf's Supermum," August 9, 2009, http://www.heraldscotland.com/news/home-news/sponsors-snub-golf-s-supermum-1.822070#), writer Ed Masterton reported that the prize money received by Catriona Matthew, winner of the 2009 Women's British Open, was only 23% the prize claimed by Stewart Cink for winning the men's Open two weeks earlier.

TENNIS

The modern sport of tennis developed out of various games that involved hitting a ball with a racket or the hand dating back to ancient times. Lawn tennis was developed in 1873 in Wales by Walter C. Wingfield (1833–1912). It is based on the older sport of Real tennis (French for Royal tennis), which was itself based on earlier forms of racket sports. Tennis gained popularity across Great Britain, and the first world tennis championship was held just four years later at the All England Croquet Club at Wimbledon. This tournament evolved into the famous Wimbledon Championships, which remain the most prestigious tennis titles to this day. A women's championship was added at Wimbledon in 1884. Over the next several years, tennis spread across many parts of the British Empire, becoming especially popular in Australia.

Tennis arrived in the United States early on in this process. A tennis court was set up in Staten Island, New York, in about 1874. The first National Championship in the United States—for men only—was held in 1881 in Newport, Rhode Island. A women's championship was added six years later. The National Championship moved to Forest Hills, New York, in 1915, where it remained under various names for more than 60 years. Now known as the U.S. Open, the event has been held at the National Tennis Center in Flushing, New York, since 1978.

The Development of Professional Tennis

As tennis spread around the British Empire early in the 20th century, national federations were formed in countries where the sport caught on. These federations eventually joined forces to form the International Tennis Federation (ITF), which was the worldwide sanctioning authority for tennis. International competitions between national teams soon arose, the most important being the Davis Cup tournament, founded in 1900, and the Wightman Cup, an annual competition between women's teams from England and the United States, founded in 1923.

Most sports turned professional during the first half of the 20th century, but tennis remained primarily an amateur endeavor, largely a pastime for wealthy country club members. By the late 1920s it became economically feasible for a top player to make a decent living on the professional tour, but it meant giving up the sport's most prestigious, amateur-only events, such as those at Wimbledon and Forest Hills. The move toward professionalism accelerated after Will T. Tilden II (1893–1953), the best player of his time and a winner of seven U.S. singles championships and three Wimbledon titles as an amateur, turned professional in 1931. Over the next few decades more and more top players trickled into the professional ranks, but the professional tour was not glamorous and the money was mediocre. The ITF fought hard against the professionalization of tennis. In 1968 the All England Lawn Tennis and Croquet Club decided to open Wimbledon to professional players, thus ushering in the "open era" of tennis in which professional players are allowed to compete in the sport's biggest tournaments.

About this time, women players became frustrated at the gender disparity in tennis prize money. Women winning a tournament often received a mere fraction of what the men's champion in the same tournament took home. In 1971 a women-only professional tour was formed to address these inequities. This new Virginia Slims Tour was an instant hit. It made Billie Jean King (1943–) the first woman athlete in any sport to earn more than $100,000 in a single year.

Men's Professional Tennis

Men's professional tennis is coordinated by the Association of Tennis Professionals (ATP), which organizes the ATP Tour (the principal worldwide tennis tour), and the ITF, which coordinates international play including the Davis Cup and the Grand Slam tournaments. The ATP was originally formed in 1972 as a sort of trade union to protect the interests of male professional tennis players. The organization assumed its role as the chief coordinating body of the professional tour in 1990. The most important professional tennis tournaments are those that make up tennis's Grand Slam: the Australian Open, the French Open, the U.S. Open, and Wimbledon. (See Table 5.2.) Only two men have ever won the Grand Slam of tennis: Don Budge (1915–2000) in 1938 and Rod Laver (1938–) in both 1962 and 1969. Total prize money for Wimbledon in 2009 was approximately $20.7 million, with the men's and ladies' singles champions each receiving a prize of about $1.4 million (based on 2009 exchange rates; http://www.wimbledon.org/en_GB/about/guide/prizemoney.html). According to the U.S. Open (2009, http://2009

TABLE 5.2

Tennis Grand Slam events

Event	Location	Scheduled time
Australian Open	Melbourne	Last fortnight of January
French Open	Paris	May/June
Wimbledon	Wimbledon, England	June/July
U.S. Open	Flushing Meadows, Queens, New York	August/September

SOURCE: Created by Robert Jacobson for Gale, 2009

.usopen.org/en_US/about/history/prizemoney.html), the 2009 tournament offered a payout of $21.6 million, with the men's and women's singles champions taking home $1.6 million each. The ATP also operates the Challenger Series, a second-tier professional circuit in which many top players have started their professional careers.

Women's Professional Tennis

Women's professional tennis is coordinated by the Women's Tennis Association (WTA, which is to the women's game what the ATP is to the men's game). The WTA runs the premier professional women's tour, which in 2005 became known as the Sony Ericsson WTA Tour. In 2009 the Sony Ericsson Tour (2009, http://www.sonyericssonwta tour.com/page/AboutTheTour/0,,12781,00.html) involved more than 2,200 players representing 96 nations competing for $86 million in prize money at 51 events in 31 countries. Women also compete in the same four Grand Slam events, governed by the ITF, as do the men.

The WTA was born in 1973, initially, like the ATP, as a professional organization to protect the interests of the players. The tour itself, which started out as the Virginia Slims Tour, was originally formed out of protest at the disparity between the prize money for men and women. At the dawn of the open era (1968), when professionals were first allowed to compete in Grand Slam tournaments, the male singles winner sometimes received as much as ten times what the female champion was paid. By 1980 more than 250 women were playing professionally all over the world in a tour consisting of 47 global events, offering a total $7.2 million in prize money. The tour remained under the governance of the Women's Tennis Council, an umbrella agency run by representatives from the ITF, the tournament promoters, and the players, into the 1990s. The WTA Tour in its current form was created in 1995 through the merger of the WTA Players Association and the Women's Tennis Council. Several sponsors have funded the tour over the years, including Colgate, Avon, Toyota, Kraft General Foods, and Sony Ericsson.

AUTO RACING

There are several different top-level auto-racing circuits in the United States, in which different kinds of cars

race. The two most popular types of race cars are stock cars and open-wheeled racers. From the outside, stock cars essentially look like the regular cars that populate U.S. highways, only covered with corporate logos. Stock car racing is dominated by the National Association for Stock Car Auto Racing (NASCAR). Open-wheel cars are single-seat vehicles with special aerodynamic features that allow them to travel at speeds well over 200 miles per hour without flying off the track. Open-wheel racing was in a state of civil war between two chief circuits, the Indy Racing League (IRL) and the Champ Car Series, for several years until Champ Car was merged into IRL in 2008. Another open-wheel circuit, Formula One Grand Prix, is dominant in Europe.

NASCAR

The largest sanctioning body of motor sports in the United States is NASCAR, which oversees a number of racing series, the largest among them being the NASCAR Sprint Cup, the NASCAR Nationwide Series, and the Craftsman Truck Series. In all, NASCAR (2009, http:// www.nascar.com/guides/about/nascar/) sanctions some 1,200 races at 100 tracks in more than 30 U.S. states, Canada, and Mexico. The article "NASCAR Evolution: Survival of the Fastest" (*Sports Illustrated*, February 19, 2007) noted that 13 million NASCAR fans regularly filled 22 tracks in 19 states. Discussing the total number of fans and their purchases, Reuters in 2008 ("HMSHost Corporation and NASCAR Debut the NASCAR Shop," January 18, 2008, http://www.reuters.com/article/pressRelease/idUS 193876+18-Jan-2008+BW20080118) declared, "More than 75 million brand-loyal NASCAR followers purchase an estimated $2 billion worth of licensed products annually." Once merely a regional diversion in the South, NASCAR has exploded into a nationwide phenomenon, rivaling baseball for the number-two spot behind football for the hearts and viewing hours of American sports fans, though both attendance and television viewership have slumped since 2005 after a decade of impressive growth.

Stock car racing evolved out of bootlegging in the rural South. Alcohol runners would modify their cars to make them faster and more maneuverable. It was natural for these drivers to start racing their souped-up autos against one another.

NASCAR was founded in 1948 by William France Sr. (1909–1992) and Ed Otto (1908–1986) as a way to organize, standardize, and promote racing of unmodified, or stock, cars for entertainment. The first NASCAR Strictly Stock race took place at North Carolina's Charlotte Speedway in June 1949. Over time, modifications were allowed into the sport, and by the mid-1960s only the bodies of the cars looked stock; the innards were specially built for speed.

NASCAR's rapid growth began in the 1970s, when R. J. Reynolds Tobacco Company began to sponsor racing as a way to promote its products after they had been banned from television advertising. The top series, formerly known as the Grand National Series, became the Winston Cup. At about this time, television networks began to occasionally cover stock car racing. The Columbia Broadcasting System (CBS) broadcast of the 1979 Daytona 500 was the first time a stock car race had been aired nationwide from start to finish.

In 2004 Nextel assumed sponsorship of the series formerly known as the Winston Cup. That year, NASCAR established a new 10-race playoff system called the Chase for the Cup, in which the top 10 drivers (according to NASCAR's point system) after 26 races compete for the series championship. In 2008 the Nextel Cup became the Sprint Cup Series to reflect the merger of Nextel Communications with the phone company Sprint. As of 2009 the Sprint Cup remained the most prominent and lucrative NASCAR racing series.

Open-Wheel Cars

As millions of fans flocked to stock car racing, the two major open-wheel series, the IRL and the Champ Car Series, struggled beginning around 2000. The reasons for this are complex, but it is reasonable to attribute the situation in part to the acrimonious relationship between the IRL and Champ Car. Neither was doing well financially, although the success of the rookie Danica Patrick (1982–) breathed some life into IRL in 2005. When Champ Car was merged into IRL in 2008, open-wheel aficionados were hopeful that the merger would help restore the stature of their sport. The Associated Press reported in "After 12 Years of Conflict, IRL and Champ Car Merge" (February 22, 2008, http://sports.espn.go .com/rpm/news/story?id=3259364), "After 12 years of bitter rivalry that confused fans, promoted apathy and nearly buried the sport, Champ Car agreed to cease operations, giving the surviving IRL the opportunity to rebuild open-wheel's lost prestige."

Indy Racing League

The IRL was formed in 1994 by a group of drivers breaking away from the Championship Auto Racing Teams (CART; later known as the Champ Car Series), which had coordinated Indy car racing since breaking away from the U.S. Auto Club (USAC) in 1979. The IRL consists of two series: the premier IndyCar Series, which is virtually synonymous with the IRL, and the Firestone Indy Lights Series (formerly known as the Indy Pro Series), which functions as a developmental series for drivers aspiring to join the IndyCar circuit.

Before 1979 the term *IndyCar* was generically used to refer to cars racing in USAC events. By the 1980s IndyCar was a term commonly used to refer to CART, which by that time was the preeminent sanctioning body

for open-wheel racing in the United States. The name "IndyCar" became the subject of fierce legal battles in the 1990s. The Indianapolis Motor Speedway, home of the Indianapolis 500, trademarked the name in 1992 and licensed it to CART, which in turn renamed its championship the IndyCar World Series. Two years later Tony George (1959–), the president of the speedway, started his own racing series called the Indy Racing League. In 1996 CART sued to protect its right to continue using the IndyCar name. The speedway countered with its own suit. The two groups eventually reached a settlement in which CART agreed to stop using the IndyCar name after the 1996 season, and the IRL could start using it after the 2002 season. The IRL's premier series has been called the IRL IndyCar Series since the beginning of the 2003 season. The 2009 IndyCar Series (2009, http://www.indycar.com/ schedule/) featured 18 races from April to October.

Champ Car Series

The USAC was formed in 1956 to take over coordination of the national driving championship from the American Automobile Association, which had launched the championship in 1909. The USAC controlled the championship until 1979, when a group of car owners formed the Championship Auto Racing Teams that they hoped would give them power in negotiations with the USAC over media contracts, race purses, promotion, and other issues. The two entities immediately clashed, and CART soon separated from the USAC to establish its own racing series. Most of the top teams defected from the USAC, and CART quickly became the dominant open-wheel racing circuit. The USAC held its last National Championship in 1979, before reluctantly handing the reins over to CART.

The IRL's split from CART threw open-wheel racing into a tailspin. The rivalry may have helped pave the way for NASCAR's rise, as both competing organizations struggled for control over the sport's available pot of money. In 2003 CART declared bankruptcy, and its assets were liquidated and put up for sale. A group of CART car owners bought the company and opened the 2004 season under the new name Champ Car Series. Beginning in 2005 Champ Car ran both the Champ Car World Series and the Champ Car Atlantic Championship, which functioned as a developmental circuit for drivers trying to get into Champ Car. In February 2008 George and owners of the Champ Car World Series reached an agreement that unified the sport. As a result of the agreement, the Champ Car World Series was suspended except for one race, the Long Beach Grand Prix, and many former Champ Car teams moved over to the IndyCar Series.

BOXING

Boxing is unique among professional sports in that there is no nationwide commission that oversees it, no regular schedules, no seasons, and few universal rules. Every set of matches (called a card) is set up separately, usually by one of a handful of top-level boxing promoters. Each state has its own boxing commission with its own set of rules. Some state boxing commissions regulate the sport more rigorously than others, and the different governing organizations establish their own regulations. For example, variations exist regarding whether a boxer who has been knocked down can be "saved by the bell," whether a referee or a ringside physician has the authority to stop a match, and whether a match should automatically be stopped if a fighter is knocked down three times within one round.

Boxing matches in the United States consist of a maximum of 12 three-minute rounds with one minute of rest between rounds. Opponents in a fight must belong to the same weight class, with competitors being weighed before the fight to ensure that neither holds an unfair weight advantage. The three judges at ringside score the fight according to a 10-point must system; that is, each judge must award 10 points to the winner of the round and fewer points to the loser of the round. Matches end in one of five ways:

- Knockout—one fighter is unable to return to his feet within 10 seconds of a knockdown

- Technical knockout—a decision is made to stop the fight because one fighter is clearly losing

- Decision—the fight ends without a knockout or technical knockout and is won based on the scoring of the three judges at ringside

- Draw—the fight ends without a knockout or technical knockout, and the scorecards award each fighter the same number of points

- Disqualification—the fight is stopped because of a rule infraction on the part of one of the fighters

Unlike other professional sports, boxing does not use a playoff series or point system to name a champion. In fact, there is not necessarily even a consensus about who is the champion of any given weight class. Different champions are recognized by several competing boxing organizations. The most prominent boxing organizations are the World Boxing Association, the World Boxing Council, the World Boxing Organization, and the International Boxing Federation. A fighter may be recognized as champion in his weight class by more than one of these organizations at a time, or each may have a different champion at any given time. Some of the biggest boxing matches are unification bouts between champions recognized by two different sanctioning organizations, the winner walking away with both titles.

Because boxing competitions are often international in nature, it is difficult to gauge the size of the boxing industry in the United States. Much of the money comes from cable television, where championship fights are usually broadcast on a pay-per-view basis.

Boxing has a long history of both glamour and corruption. It has inspired famous writers such as Norman Mailer (1923–2007), Albert Camus (1913–1960), Ernest Hemingway (1899–1961), and Joyce Carol Oates (1938–), and landmark films such as *The Champ* (1931), *Body and Soul* (1947), *On the Waterfront* (1954), *Requiem for a Heavyweight* (1962), *Raging Bull* (1980), *Million Dollar Baby* (2004), and the *Rocky* series (1976–2006). However, because the scoring system is complex and because the overall rankings often appear somewhat arbitrary, the sport has long been a tempting target for organized crime and others seeking illicit financial gain. Even in the 21st century bribery is thought to be rampant. Mysterious judging decisions and bizarre rankings are not at all rare. Boxing's reputation also suffers because of the sheer brutality of the sport. Fighters have sometimes died or suffered disabling brain trauma as a result of a particularly violent bout. Mike Tyson (1966–), a former heavyweight champ and convict, once bit off part of an opponent's ear in the ring. Onlookers over the years, including writer Jack Newfield in the *Nation* ("The Shame of Boxing," November 12, 2001), have cited several cases of fixed fights, rigged rankings, cronyism, and instances of money being prioritized over safety in the sport.

Attempts have been made over the years to clean up boxing. Congress has been involved in trying to regulate the sport, and in 1996 it established minimum health and safety standards for professional boxing, later expanded by the Muhammad Ali Boxing Reform Act of 2000. In 2004 former boxer Muhammad Ali (1942–) testified in favor of a bill proposed by Senator John McCain (1936–) to create a boxing commission. The bill failed—it was approved in the Senate but not the House—and McCain introduced the legislation again in early 2009. According to Frederic J. Frommer writing for the Associated Press (February 4, 2009, http://www.house.gov/apps/list/speech/ny03_king/AP_020409.html), "The proposed legislation would establish a U.S. Boxing Commission under the Commerce Department, charged with protecting the health, safety and general interests of boxers. The commission would oversee all professional boxing matches and license boxers, promoters, managers and sanctioning organizations." The bill, according to McCain as quoted by Frommer, would "better protect professional boxing from the fraud, corruption and ineffective regulation that have plagued the sport for far too many years and that have devastated physically and financially many of our nation's professional boxers." As of fall 2009 the House and Senate had yet to vote on the legislation.

World Boxing Association

The World Boxing Association (WBA; 2009, http://www.wbaonline.com/) was the first sanctioning body of professional boxing. It was formed as the National Boxing Association (NBA) in 1921. The first NBA-sanctioned match was a heavyweight championship fight between Jack Dempsey (1895–1983) and Georges Carpentier (1894–1975). Brilliant and colorful champions such as Joe Louis (1914–1981) carried the WBA through the World War II (1939–1945) era. The dawn of television boosted the popularity of professional boxing in the 1950s. The sport's globalization during this period led the organization to change its name in 1962 to the World Boxing Association, an entity that would usher through future legends such as Ali.

World Boxing Council

The World Boxing Council (WBC; 2009, http://www.wbcboxing.com) was formed in 1963 by representatives of 11 countries (United States, Mexico, Venezuela, Panama, Peru, Brazil, Japan, Argentina, Spain, Great Britain, and the Philippines) and Puerto Rico. Its purpose, according to WBC founders, was to improve the standards of professional boxing, including the safety of fighters. Among the WBC's innovations was the 1983 shortening of world championship fights from 15 to 12 rounds, a move that was eventually adopted by the other sanctioning organizations. In 2003 the WBC filed for bankruptcy in an attempt to avoid paying $30 million in damages from a lawsuit over questionable handling of title fight eligibility. The following year the lawsuit was settled for a lesser amount, allowing the WBC to avoid having to disband and liquidate its assets.

International Boxing Federation

Boxing historian Herb Goldman, in "Boxing Bodies: A Brief Chronology and Rundown" (*International Boxing Digest,* January 1998), explains that the International Boxing Federation (IBF) was formed in 1983 by a group of WBA representatives upset with political machinations within that agency. Its creation was spearheaded by Robert W. Lee, the president of a smaller regional organization called the U.S. Boxing Association (USBA). The new group was originally called the IBF-USBA. In its first year of operation, the IBF remained fairly obscure. In 1984, however, the IBF decided to recognize as champions a number of high-profile fighters who were already established as other organizations' title holders, including Larry Holmes (1949–) and Marvin Hagler (1952–). When Holmes opted to relinquish his WBC title to accept the IBF's, it instantly gave the IBF the credibility it had previously lacked. The IBF's reputation took a major hit in 1999, when Lee was convicted on racketeering and other charges. By 2009 it nevertheless remained one of professional boxing's major sanctioning bodies.

World Boxing Organization

The World Boxing Organization (WBO; 2009, http://www.wbo-int.com/) was formed in 1988 by a group of

Puerto Rican and Dominican businessmen disenchanted with what they perceived as illegitimate rules and rating systems within the WBA. The WBO's first championship fight was a junior welterweight championship match between Héctor Camacho (1962–) and Ray Mancini (1961–). The WBO achieved a level of legitimacy comparable to that of the WBA, the WBC, and the IBF, largely thanks to its recognition as champions of many of the sport's best-known competitors. The WBO has also tended at times to provide more opportunities for non-U.S.-based fighters than the other organizations. Even though the WBO was formed out of protest against allegedly corrupt practices, it has certainly exhibited its share of inexplicable decisions that raise questions about the organization's integrity. In "New WBO Division: Dead Weight" (February 20, 2001, http://assets.espn.go.com/boxing/columns/graham/1097210.html), Tim Graham notes that a particularly embarrassing example took place in 2001, when the WBO twice moved Darrin Morris (1966–2000) up in its super-middleweight rankings, even though he had fought only once in the past three years, and, more important, he was dead.

Women's Boxing

Women's professional boxing began to gain in popularity in the 1990s. As in men's boxing, there are several sanctioning bodies that govern women's professional fighting: the International Women's Boxing Federation, the Women's International Boxing Association, and the Women's International Boxing Federation. Part of the sport's popularity can be attributed to the participation of Laila Ali (1977–), daughter of boxing great Muhammad Ali. Another daughter of a legendary boxer, Jacqui Frazier (1961–)—daughter of Joe Frazier (1944–)—has also been prominent in the sport. Ali made her professional boxing debut in 1999. In 2001 she and Frazier squared off, with Ali emerging victorious. In another of the biggest matches in women's boxing history, Ali knocked out Christy Martin in 2003.

The 2004 film *Million Dollar Baby* brought greater attention to the sport of women's boxing, not all of it positive, because the movie highlighted some of the more brutal aspects of the sport. Although the absence of charismatic new boxers has been an obstacle to the continued growth of professional women's boxing, the amateur version of the sport has been gaining participants. In August 2009 the International Olympic Committee voted unanimously to include women's boxing in the 2012 Olympic Games.

Challenges to Boxing's Future

By 2009 boxing had been declining in popularity for years. A major part of the problem has been the lack of big-name, attention-drawing stars, particularly in the heavyweight division. The sport thrives when it is dominated by colorful heavyweights, like when Ali and Tyson took center stage. Ali was the public face of boxing for decades and was arguably the most recognized athlete in the world. Fans have not been as enthusiastic about plodding champions and contenders with unfamiliar names, such as the Klitschko brothers, Vitali (1971–) and Wladimir (1976–), who were at the top of the heavyweight ranks in the first decade of the 21st century.

The biggest name in boxing since the 1990s has been Oscar De La Hoya (1973–). Nicknamed the "Golden Boy," De La Hoya won an Olympic gold medal in 1992 and went on to capture 10 professional titles in 6 different weight classes. De la Hoya's 2007 match against Floyd Mayweather Jr. (1977–), which he lost in a split decision, was the biggest pay-per-view boxing match ever. Robert Cassidy, writing in *Newsday* ("Boxing Facing Challenge from Mixed Martial Arts" August 4, 2007, http://www.newsday.com/sports/boxing-facing-challenge-from-mixed-martial-arts-1.876394), reported that the De La Hoya–Mayweather bout generated a record 2.15 million pay-per-view purchases worth $120 million. Another $19.3 million was collected from live spectators. De La Hoya, however, was already past his prime by that time. He announced his retirement in April 2009, a few months after he was badly beaten in a much-hyped match against rising star Manny Pacquiao (1978–).

For most of the 1990s and 2000s, De La Hoya was boxing's only guaranteed big draw. The sport's health moving forward depended to a large extent on the emergence of a new "golden boy."

As boxing struggled to regain the allegiance of fight fans, the sport found itself competing to an increasing degree with the emerging sport of mixed martial arts (MMA), a more brutal sport that allows not only punching but also kicking, wrestling, elbowing, and choking one's opponent into submission. The top MMA circuit, Ultimate Fighting Championship (UFC), has emerged as a serious challenger to boxing for domination of the fight game. As of 2009 its pay-per-view events did not yet attract as many viewers as those of boxing, but viewership was increasing quickly, and the sport had a large and growing base of loyal, mostly young, fans. It has been suggested that there may also be a racial element to the rise of MMA. Profiled by Steve Cotfield in Yahoo! Sports ("Mayweather: Whites Needed a Fight Sport, So They Invented MMA," July 20, 2009, http://sports.yahoo.com/mma/blog/cagewriter/post/Mayweather-Whites-needed-a-fight-sport-so-they?urn=mma,177541), boxer Mayweather opined that white fans have embraced the sport—many top UFC contenders are white—in response to the dominance of boxing by African-American and Hispanic athletes.

CHAPTER 6
COLLEGE, HIGH SCHOOL, AND YOUTH SPORTS

College athletics function as a minor, or preparatory, league for some professional sports, particularly football and basketball, but there is nothing minor about Americans' passion for them or about the sums of money intercollegiate sports generate. Just as college sports serve as a feeder system for professional leagues, high schools fill the same role for colleges, and schools often compete for the services of elite teenage athletes. For the most part, high school and college athletes participate in sports for their own rewards. Most of them understand that the chances of striking it rich as a professional athlete are remote. For example, out of 156,096 boys who play on high school basketball teams during their senior year, only 44 (0.03%) will become professional basketball players. (See Table 6.1.) Regardless, the money that flows through the sports industry—an industry of which intercollegiate sports are an integral part—is so abundant that its influence can be felt even in U.S. high schools. Even youth sports, such as Little League baseball and youth basketball leagues, have become big business, as industry insiders seek to identify the next generation of superstars at ever-younger ages.

COLLEGE SPORTS

In contrast to professional sports, where turning a profit is the motivating force behind most decisions, college sports must reconcile commercial interests, educational priorities, and a jumble of other influences ranging from alumni pride to institutional prestige. Even though it may make high-minded university officials uncomfortable to admit it, college sports have become big business in the United States.

The most important governing organization of college sports in the United States is the National Collegiate Athletic Association (NCAA), although there are other governing bodies as well.

National Collegiate Athletic Association

The NCAA is a voluntary association whose members comprised 1,288 institutions, conferences, organizations, and individuals in 2009; 1,051 of them were active member schools. (See Table 6.2.) The NCAA's main purpose, according to its constitution, is to "maintain intercollegiate athletics as an integral part of the educational program and the athlete as an integral part of the study body and, by so doing, retain a clear line of demarcation between intercollegiate athletics and professional sports." In other words, college sports are supposed to be strictly amateur and are supposed to fulfill an educational role.

Organizationally, the NCAA's structure consists of more than 125 committees, which, since a new governance structure was adopted in 1997, have enjoyed a fair amount of autonomy. Several of these committees are association-wide, including the Executive Committee and committees having to do with ethics, women's opportunities, and minority opportunities. The rest are specific to one of the NCAA's three divisions—Divisions I, II, and III—which classify the schools by the number of sports they sponsor and other factors. NCAA member schools and organizations vote on the rules they will have to follow. It is then up to the NCAA National Office staff of about 300 to implement and enforce the rules and bylaws dictated by the members.

The NCAA's divisions are based on factors such as the number of sports sponsored, attendance at the school's sporting events, and financial support to athletes. Division I is further divided into the Football Bowl Subdivision (FBS, formerly Division 1-A) and the Football Championship Subdivision (FCS, formerly Division I-AA). There are also schools that do not offer football, which are sometimes referred to as Division I-AAA, though they may compete against FBS or FCS colleges

TABLE 6.1

Estimated probability of competing in athletics beyond high school

Student-athletes	Men's basketball	Women's basketball	Football	Baseball	Men's ice hockey	Men's soccer
High school student athletes	546,335	452,929	1,071,775	470,671	36,263	358,935
High school senior student athletes	156,096	129,408	306,221	134,477	10,361	102,553
NCAA student athletes	16,571	15,096	61,252	28,767	3,973	19,793
NCAA freshman roster positions	4,735	4,313	17,501	8,219	1,135	5,655
NCAA senior student athletes	3,682	3,355	13,612	6,393	883	4,398
NCAA student athletes drafted	44	32	250	600	33	76
Percent high school to NCAA	**3.0%**	**3.3%**	**5.7%**	**6.1%**	**11.0%**	**5.5%**
Percent NCAA to professional	**1.2%**	**1.0%**	**1.8%**	**9.4%**	**3.7%**	**1.7%**
Percent high school to professional	**0.03%**	**0.02%**	**0.08%**	**0.45%**	**0.32%**	**0.07%**

Note: These percentages are based on estimated data and should be considered approximations of the actual percentages.

SOURCE: "Estimated Probability of Competing in Athletics beyond the High School Interscholastic Level," in *Academics and Athletes: Education and Research*, National Collegiate Athletic Association, 2007, http://www.ncaa.org/wps/ncaa?key=/ncaa/NCAA/Academics%20and%20Athletes/Education%20and%20 Research/ Probability%20of%20Competing/ (accessed June 23, 2009)

TABLE 6.2

Composition of NCAA membership

	Division I				Division II	Division III	Total
	I-FBS	I-FCS	I	Total			
Active	119	119	93	331	291	429	1,051
Provisional	0	0	2	2	1	15	18
Voting conference	11	10	10	31	22	42	95
Nonvoting conference	0	3	20	23	1	17	41
Corresponding							12
Affiliated							71
Total							**1,288**

NCAA = National Collegiate Athletic Association
I-FBS = Division I Football Bowl Subdivision
I-FCS = Division I Football Championship Subdivision

Notes:
Active member

An active member is a four-year college or university or a two-year upper-level collegiate institution accredited by the appropriate regional accrediting agency and duly elected to active membership under the provisions of the Association bylaws. Active members have the right to compete in NCAA championships, to vote on legislation and other issues before the Association, and to enjoy other privileges of membership designated in the constitution and bylaws of the Association.

Provisional member

A provisional member is a four-year college or university or a two-year upper-level collegiate institution accredited by the appropriate regional accrediting agency and that has applied for active membership in the Association. Provisional membership is a prerequisite for active membership in the Association. The institution shall be elected to provisional membership under the bylaws of the Association. Provisional members shall receive all publications and mailings received by active members in addition to other privileges designated in the constitution and bylaws of the Association.

Member conference

A member conference is a group of colleges and/or universities that conducts competition among its members and determines a conference champion in one or more sports (in which the NCAA conducts championships or for which it is responsible for providing playing rules for intercollegiate competition), duly elected to conference membership under the provisions of the bylaws of the Association. A member conference is entitled to all of the privileges of active members except the right to compete in NCAA championships. Only those conferences that meet specific criteria as competitive and legislative bodies and minimum standards related to size and division status are permitted to vote on legislation or other issues before the Association.

Affiliated member

An affiliated member is a nonprofit group or association whose function and purpose are directly related to one or more sports in which the NCAA conducts championships, duly elected to affiliated membership under the provisions of the Association bylaws. An affiliated member is entitled to be represented by one nonvoting delegate at any NCAA Convention and enjoys other privileges as designated by the bylaws of the Association.

Corresponding member

A corresponding member is an institution, a nonprofit organization or a conference that is not eligible for active, provisional, conference or affiliated membership and desires to receive membership publications and mailings. A corresponding member duly elected under the provision of the Association bylaws receives all publications and mailings received by the general NCAA membership and is not otherwise entitled to any membership privileges.

SOURCE: "Current Composition," in *Composition and Sport Sponsorship of the NCAA*, National Collegiate Athletic Association, 2009, http://www.ncaa.org/ wps/ncaa?key=/ncaa/NCAA/About The NCAA/Membership/Our Members/membership_breakdown.html (accessed June 23, 2009)

---

in other sports. Intercollegiate sports under the auspices of the NCAA are also divided into conferences, which function like the leagues and divisions in professional sports. The most prominent conferences, often referred to collectively as the Big Six, are shown in Table 6.3. The colleges in these conferences sponsor many sports,

TABLE 6.3

NCAA "Big 6" conferences, 2009

Atlantic Coast conference (ACC)

Boston College
Clemson University
Duke University
Florida State University
George Tech
University of Maryland
University of Miami
University of North Carolina
North Carolina State University
University of Virginia
Virginia Tech
Wake Forest University

Big East conference

University of Cincinnati
University of Connecticut
DePaul University
Georgetown University
University of Louisville
Marquette University
University of Notre Dame
University of Pittsburgh
Providence College
Rutgers University
St. John's University
Seton Hall University
University of South Florida
Syracuse University
Villanova University
West Virginia University

Big Ten conference

University of Illinois
Indiana University
University of Iowa
University of Michigan
Michigan State University
University of Minnesota
Northwestern University
Ohio State University
Pennsylvania State University
Purdue University
University of Wisconsin

Big 12 conference

Baylor University
University of Colorado
Iowa State University
University of Kansas
Kansas State University
University of Missouri
University of Nebraska
University of Oklahoma
Oklahoma State University
University of Texas
Texas A&M University
Texas Tech

Pacific-10 conference (Pac-10)

University of Arizona
Arizona State University
University of California, Berkeley (Cal)
University of Oregon
Oregon State University
Stanford University
University of California, Los Angeles (UCLA)
University of Southern California
University of Washington
Washington State University

TABLE 6.3

NCAA "Big 6" conferences, 2009 [CONTINUED]

Southeastern conference (SEC)

University of Alabama
University of Arkansas
Auburn University
University of Florida
University of Georgia
University of Kentucky
Louisiana State University
University of Mississippi (Ole Miss)
Mississippi State University
University of South Carolina
University of Tennessee
Vanderbilt University

SOURCE: Created by Robert Jacobson for Gale, 2009

History of the NCAA

Up until the middle of the 19th century, there was no governing body that oversaw intercollegiate athletics. Typically, it was students rather than faculty or administrators who ran the programs. Even so, there was already a fair amount of commercialization and illicit professionalism in college sports. For example, James Hogan (1876–1910), the captain of the Yale football team in 1904, was compensated with, among other things, a suite of rooms in the dorm, free University Club meals, profits from the sale of programs, and a ten-day vacation to Cuba. However, what finally led administrators to the conclusion that formal oversight was necessary was the sheer brutality of college sports, particularly football. According to *The Business of Sports* (2004), edited by Scott R. Rosner and Kenneth L. Shropshire, there were at least 18 deaths and more than 100 major injuries in intercollegiate football in 1905 alone. In response to the growing violence of college football, President Theodore Roosevelt (1858–1919) convened a White House conference of representatives from Harvard, Princeton, and Yale universities to review the rules of the game. When the deaths and serious injuries continued, Henry M. MacCracken (1840–1918), the chancellor of the University of the City of New York (now New York University), called for a national gathering of representatives from the major football schools. In early December 1905 representatives of 13 schools, including West Point, Columbia, and the University of Kansas, met with Mac-Cracken and formed a Rules Committee. This group held another meeting on December 28 that was attended by representatives of more than 60 college football programs, during which the Intercollegiate Athletic Association (IAA) was formed. The IAA was a national organization with 62 founding members, including schools in Minnesota, Nebraska, New Hampshire, New York, Ohio, Pennsylvania, and Texas. The IAA became the NCAA in 1910.

have big athletic budgets, and draw many fans. Table 6.4 shows that among both men and women, basketball is the sport sponsored by the greatest number of colleges and universities.

TABLE 6.4

NCAA sports sponsorship, by sport and division, 2009

	Men's				Women's				Mixed			
	I	II	III	T	I	II	III	T	I	II	III	T
Baseball	291	242	373	**906**								
Basketball	333	288	412	**1033**	331	289	436	**1056**				
Bowling	1	1	0	**2**	29	18	9	**56**				
Cross country	301	241	372	**914**	327	270	393	**990**				
Fencing	18	3	12	**33**	23	4	15	**42**	0	0	0	**0**
Field hockey					77	26	158	**261**				
Football												
(I-FBS 119)												
(I-FCS 119)	238	154	239	**631**								
Golf	291	210	284	**785**	243	134	164	**541**				
Gymnastics	16	0	2	**18**	63	5	16	**84**				
Ice hockey	58	7	73	**138**	35	2	46	**83**				
Lacrosse	57	35	151	**243**	85	48	180	**313**				
Rifle	2	0	2	**4**	8	1	2	**11**	17	3	5	**25**
Rowing	28	4	31	**63**	86	16	43	**145**				
Skiing	13	6	18	**37**	14	7	19	**40**				
Soccer	198	179	401	**778**	310	225	424	**959**				
Softball					276	268	408	**952**				
Swimming	139	56	197	**392**	193	72	242	**507**				
Tennis	258	168	325	**751**	311	220	371	**902**				
Track, indoor	243	113	225	**581**	294	128	231	**653**				
Track, outdoor	269	162	267	**698**	307	174	274	**755**				
Volleyball	22	13	47	**82**	317	276	423	**1016**				
Water polo	22	5	15	**42**	32	7	20	**59**				
Wrestling	86	45	92	**223**								

I-FBS = Division I Football Bowl Subdivision.
I-FCS = Division I Football Championship Subdivision.
NCAA = National Collegiate Athletic Association.
Note: These totals include sport sponsorship data provided by active and provisional members.

SOURCE: "Current Sport Sponsorship," in *Composition and Sport Sponsorship of the NCAA*, National Collegiate Athletic Association, 2009, http://www.ncaa.org/wps/ncaa?key=/ncaa/NCAA/About The NCAA/ Membership/Our Members/membership_breakdown.html (accessed June 23, 2009)

Initially, the NCAA did not really govern college sports. Its chief role was simply to make rules to keep the sports safe and fair. It also served as a forum for discussion of any other issues that happened to arise in the world of intercollegiate athletics, such as the formation of conferences and the transition of oversight responsibilities from students to faculty. In 1921 the NCAA organized its first national championship, the National Collegiate Track and Field Championships. More championships in other sports followed, as did an increasingly complex bureaucracy featuring additional rules committees.

By the 1920s college athletics were firmly entrenched both as an integral part of college life and as a subject of intense public interest. Along with this interest came creeping commercialism. In 1929 the Carnegie Foundation for the Advancement of Education issued a major report on college sports, which stated that "a change of values is needed in a field that is sodden with the commercial and the material and the vested interests that these forces have created. Commercialism in college athletics must be diminished and college sport must rise to a point where it is esteemed primarily and sincerely for the opportunities it affords to mature youth."

In response to the Carnegie report, token attempts were made to reduce commercial influences on college sports, but the trend continued. A dramatic increase in access to higher education following World War II (1939–1945) further accelerated both interest in and commercialization of college athletics. A series of gambling scandals and questionable recruiting incidents finally moved the NCAA to act. In 1948 the NCAA adopted the Sanity Code, which established guidelines for recruiting and limited financial aid. In addition, the code set academic standards for players and defined the status of college athletes as amateurs—that is, those "to whom athletics is an avocation." The NCAA also created a Constitutional Compliance Committee to enforce the Sanity Code and investigate possible violations. The Sanity Code did not have much of an impact and was repealed in 1951. The Constitutional Compliance Committee was replaced by the Committee on Infractions, which was given broader authority to sanction institutions that broke the rules. The NCAA also hired its first full-time executive director, Walter Byers (1922–), that same year. A national headquarters was established in Kansas City, Missouri, the following year. The 1950s also brought the first lucrative television broadcast contracts, which provided the NCAA with the revenue it needed to become more active. Its capacity to enforce rules expanded throughout the 1950s and 1960s. Nevertheless, the influence of money on college sports continued to grow. In 1956 the NCAA moved to regulate athletic scholarships, but the eight schools of the Ivy League—Brown, Columbia, Cornell, Dartmouth, Harvard, Penn, Princeton, and Yale—refused to comply.

In 1973 the NCAA divided its membership into three divisions to group schools by their competitive firepower. Three years later, the NCAA acquired the authority to penalize colleges directly for violating rules, opening itself up to criticisms of unfair enforcement practices. In 1978, in response to the rapid growth in the number of football programs relative to other sports, Division I members voted to break the division solely for football purposes into two subdivisions, I-A and I-AA.

During the 1970s and 1980s major football colleges began to see that they could make more money from broadcast revenue by negotiating their own deals. A group of schools, led by the University of Georgia and Oklahoma University, began to challenge the NCAA's monopoly on negotiation of lucrative television contracts. In 1984 the U.S. Supreme Court ruled in *NCAA v. Board of Regents of the University of Oklahoma et al.* (468 U.S. 85) that the NCAA had violated antitrust laws. This ruling allowed colleges to start negotiating broadcast deals directly. Meanwhile, the relationship between sports and academics remained a matter of intense debate, as reports of student-athletes ignoring the first half of this role proliferated. In 1986 the NCAA implemented Proposition 48, later modified by Proposition 16 (1995), which set down minimum academic standards for athletes entering college. Among the requirements, student-athletes needed to maintain a 2.0 grade point average (GPA) in academic courses and have a Scholastic Assessment Test (SAT) score of 1010 or a combined American College Text (ACT) score of 86.

SCANDALS AND SANCTIONS IN NCAA SPORTS PROGRAMS. More than a century after Hogan's royal treatment at Yale, payments and other special perks for student-athletes remain prevalent in college sports, in spite of the NCAA's enforcement efforts. There have been several cases of institutions and their boosters making illicit payments to players. In the early 1980s Southern Methodist University (SMU) was a football powerhouse. Its ability to attract top football players was enhanced by a highly organized system of player payments in blatant violation of NCAA rules. According to Chris DuFresne, in "Life after Death" (*Newsday*, December 28, 2005), the payoff system, which had been in place for decades, began to unravel in November 1986, when SMU linebacker David Stanley admitted to reporters that he had accepted $25,000 from boosters. Within days another player, Albert Reese, told the *Dallas Morning News* that he had been living in a rent-free apartment provided by a booster. After an investigation that turned up widespread corruption and cover-ups that went as high as the Texas governor's office, the NCAA hit the university with what became known in

college sports as the "death penalty." The sanctions included cancellation of SMU's entire 1987 football season and restriction of the following season to eight games.

The NCAA has not wielded the death penalty again since then. Moreover, its threat has not halted these practices on the part of boosters elsewhere. Another high-profile case involved the National Basketball Association star Chris Webber (1973–). On July 14, 2003, Webber pleaded guilty to criminal contempt related to charges that he had received tens of thousands of dollars from the booster Ed Martin (1933?–2003) while a member of the University of Michigan basketball team in 1994. Martin pleaded guilty to money laundering in May 2002. Webber's sentence, a fine of $100,000, was announced in August 2005.

Special treatment of student-athletes does not always involve money. Sometimes it comes in the form of academic breaks. In 1998 Texas Tech was penalized by the NCAA for, among other things, allowing a star running back to play despite maintaining a 0.0 grade point average. David Lagesse reports in "Troubleshooting" (*U.S. News & World Report*, March 18, 2002) that nine Texas Tech sports departments were sanctioned after the resulting investigation, and the football team's ban from postseason bowl games cost the school an estimated $1.7 million. In 1999 a University of Minnesota employee told the *St. Paul Pioneer Press* that she had completed course work for at least 20 members of the school's basketball program. Four top sports officials at Minnesota lost their jobs in the resulting scandal. Academics also figured prominently in a scandal that resulted in the NCAA stripping the University of Memphis of its entire 2007–08 season, which included an impressive 38 victories and a trip to the Final Four. Memphis's star player, Derrick Rose (1988–), now a star for the NBA's Chicago Bulls, allegedly paid another student to take the SAT exams for him, after he failed the ACT three times.

One highly charged college sports scandal that developed in 2006 turned out to be manufactured. The Associated Press notes in "North Carolina State Bar Issues Formal Disbarment Order for Nifong" (July 12, 2007, http://sports.espn.go.com/ncaa/news/story?id=2933841) that in March 2006 a stripper accused three members of the Duke University men's lacrosse team of sexually assaulting her at a party. The three students were indicted, the remainder of the lacrosse team's 2006 season was canceled, and the team coach was forced to resign. However, all charges against the players were dropped in April 2007 after many inconsistencies in the alleged victim's story were revealed, and deoxyribonucleic acid (DNA) evidence came to light that did not support the allegations. It also became clear that the prosecutor in the case, Mike Nifong (1950–), had employed

TABLE 6.5

NCAA participation in women's sports, by division, 2007–08

Sport	Division I			Division II			Division III			Overall		
	Teams	Athletes	Avg. squad	Teams	Athletes	Avg. squad	Teams	Athletes	Avg. squad	Teams	Athletes	Avg. squad
Championship sports												
Basketball	328	4,765	14.5	294	4,291	14.6	435	6,251	14.4	1,057	15,307	14.5
Bowling	28	245	8.8	17	146	8.6	7	71	10.1	52	462	8.9
Cross country	325	5,311	16.3	275	3,054	11.1	388	5,126	13.2	988	13,491	13.7
Fencing*	24	373	15.5	4	46	11.5	15	236	15.7	43	655	15.2
Field hockey	78	1,791	23.0	25	564	22.6	155	3,278	21.1	258	5,633	21.8
Golf	234	2,047	8.7	130	973	7.5	152	1,076	7.1	516	4,096	7.9
Gymnastics	64	1,070	16.7	5	92	18.4	16	268	16.8	85	1,430	16.8
Ice hockey	34	837	24.6	2	52	26.0	45	1,007	22.4	81	1,896	23.4
Lacrosse	84	2,317	27.6	42	919	21.9	175	3,594	20.5	301	6,830	22.7
Rifle*	25	136	5.4	3	17	5.7	8	29	3.6	36	182	5.1
Rowing	86	5,239	60.9	15	465	31.0	43	1,320	30.7	144	7,024	48.8
Skiing*	14	236	16.9	8	87	10.9	20	224	11.2	42	547	13.0
Soccer	307	7,955	25.9	227	5,344	23.5	422	9,383	22.2	956	22,682	23.7
Softball	272	5,285	19.4	272	4,905	18.0	406	6,964	17.2	950	17,154	18.1
Swimming/diving	192	5,155	26.8	76	1,392	18.3	241	4,691	19.5	509	11,238	22.1
Tennis	308	2,891	9.4	224	2,004	8.9	366	3,826	10.5	898	8,721	9.7
Track, indoor	292	10,944	37.5	127	3,504	27.6	226	5,965	26.4	645	20,413	31.6
Track, outdoor	304	11,230	36.9	175	4,451	25.4	266	6,682	25.1	745	22,363	30.0
Volleyball	316	4,650	14.7	278	4,020	14.5	420	6,045	14.4	1,014	14,715	14.5
Water polo	32	670	20.9	9	184	20.4	19	301	15.8	60	1,155	19.3
Subtotal	**3,347**	**73,147**		**2,208**	**36,510**		**3,825**	**66,337**		**9,380**	**175,994**	
Emerging Sports												
Archery	1	12	12.0	0	0	N/A	0	0	N/A	1	12	12.0
Badminton	0	0	N/A	0	0	N/A	2	22	11.0	2	22	11.0
Equestrian	18	684	38.0	6	184	30.7	21	520	24.8	45	1,388	30.8
Rugby	1	26	26.0	1	45	30.0	3	110	36.7	5	181	36.2
Squash	9	121	13.4	0	0	N/A	19	262	13.8	28	383	13.7
Synchronized swimming	4	62	15.5	1	12	12.0	3	30	10.0	8	104	13.0
Team handball	0	0	N/A	0	0	N/A			N/A	0	0	N/A
Subtotal	**33**	**905**		**8**	**241**		**48**	**944**		**89**	**2,090**	
Total	**3,380**	**74,052**		**2,216**	**36,751**		**3,873**	**67,281**		**9,469**	**178,084**	

*Coed Championship Sport

NCAA = National Collegiate Athletic Association.

Notes: Participation totals are adjusted to reflect all institutions sponsoring each sport. Provisional members are included in these numbers.

Coed sport teams from the sports sponsorship database were added to both the men's and women's team data. The following sports had coed teams: a) cross country, b) equestrian, c) fencing, d) golf, e) rifle, f) skiing, g) swimming & diving, h) indoor track & field and i) outdoor track & field.

The total row contains data from the emerging sports subtotal row added to the championship sports subtotal row.

N/A = not applicable

SOURCE: Denise M. DeHass, "2007–08 Participation Study—Women's Sports," in *1981–82–2007–08 NCAA Sports Sponsorship and Participation Rates Report*, National Collegiate Athletic Association, 2009, http://www.ncaapublications.com/Uploads/PDF/ParticipationRates2009c2f40573–60aa-4a08–874d-1aff4192c5e4.pdf (accessed June 23, 2009)

a number of illegal and unethical tactics in his handling of the case; he was disbarred in June 2007 for fraud, misrepresentation, and withholding exculpatory DNA evidence.

College Sports Participation

The *1981–82—2007–08 NCAA Sports Sponsorship and Participation Rates Report* (April 2009, http://www.ncaapublications.com/Uploads/PDF/ParticipationRates 2009c2f40573-60aa-4a08-874d-1aff4192c5e4.pdf) by Denise DeHass, contains detailed information on participation across the full range of college sports. As of 2007–08, there were 412,768 student-athletes participating in championship sports at NCAA schools. Even though women's teams outnumbered men's teams, there were more men—57.4% of the total—than women actually playing on those teams. The average NCAA institution had about 400 student-athletes in 2007–08, 232 of them men and 168 women.

Even though the gender gap has widened some since 2004, until then it had actually been closing since the 1980s.

Table 6.5 shows participation in women's sports at NCAA schools in 2007–08. According to DeHass, 11,230 women participated on NCAA Division I outdoor track and field teams that year, the highest total of any women's sport. Nearly as many participated during the indoor track season. (These are essentially the same athletes; a few schools offer only outdoor track and field.) NCAA women's Division I soccer teams had 7,955 total participants in 2007–08. Including all sports, both championship and emerging, 74,052 women participated in Division I sports that year. Another 36,751 women played at the Division II level; Division III had 67,281 female athletes.

Table 6.6 shows participation in men's collegiate sports in 2007–08. DeHass indicates that 90,304 student-athletes

TABLE 6.6

NCAA participation in men's sports, by division, 2007–08

Sport	Division I			Division II			Division III			Overall		
	Teams	Athletes	Avg. squad	Teams	Athletes	Avg. squad	Teams	Athletes	Avg. squad	Teams	Athletes	Avg. squad
Championship sports												
Baseball	287	10,195	35.5	250	8,603	34.4	369	11,588	31.4	906	30,386	33.5
Basketball	329	5,119	15.6	293	4,768	16.3	409	7,194	17.6	1,031	17,081	16.6
Cross country	299	4,453	14.9	245	2,901	11.8	368	5,124	13.9	912	12,478	13.7
Fencing*	20	352	17.6	3	42	14.0	12	231	19.3	35	625	17.9
Football	236	25,658	108.7	156	15,764	101.1	237	22,813	96.3	629	64,235	102.1
FBS	119	14,131	118.7			N/A			N/A	N/A	N/A	N/A
FCS	117	11,527	98.5			N/A			N/A	N/A	N/A	N/A
Golf	289	2,960	10.2	216	2,280	10.6	290	3,075	10.6	795	8,315	10.5
Gymnastics	16	319	19.9	0	0	0.0	2	34	17.0	18	353	19.6
Ice hockey	59	1,632	27.7	7	218	31.1	72	2,156	29.9	138	4,006	29.0
Lacrosse	56	2,507	44.8	34	1,258	37.0	149	5,135	34.5	239	8,900	37.2
Rifle*	20	138	6.9	2	19	9.5	7	56	8.0	29	213	7.3
Skiing*	13	210	16.2	7	100	14.3	19	257	13.5	39	567	14.5
Soccer	198	5,556	28.1	178	4,801	27.0	399	10,674	26.8	775	21,031	27.1
Swimming/diving	135	3,670	27.2	58	1,080	18.6	196	3,632	18.5	389	8,382	21.5
Tennis	260	2,680	10.3	170	1,619	9.5	324	3,551	11.0	754	7,850	10.4
Track, indoor	240	9,231	38.5	114	3,772	33.1	221	7,343	33.2	575	20,346	35.4
Track, outdoor	265	10,266	38.7	165	5,052	30.6	257	8,161	31.8	687	23,479	34.2
Volleyball	22	456	20.7	13	238	18.3	47	604	12.9	82	1,298	15.8
Water polo	22	575	26.1	5	75	15.0	15	269	17.9	42	919	21.9
Wrestling	89	2,648	29.8	46	1,318	28.7	92	2,344	25.5	227	6,310	27.8
Subtotal	**2,855**	**88,625**		**1,962**	**53,908**		**3,485**	**94,241**		**8,302**	**236,774**	
Non-championship sports												
Archery	0	0	N/A	0		N/A	0	0	N/A	0	0	N/A
Badminton	0	0	N/A	0		N/A	0	0	N/A	0	0	N/A
Bowling	0	0	N/A	0		N/A	0	0	N/A	0	0	N/A
Equestrian	0	0	N/A	0		N/A	2	4	2.0	2	4	2.0
Rowing	38	1,307	34.4	6	101	16.8	43	1,004	23.3	87	2,412	27.7
Rugby	0	0	N/A	0	0	N/A	2	79	39.5	2	79	39.5
Sailing	10	210	21.0	1	18	18.0	13	300	23.1	24	528	22.0
Squash	11	162	14.7	0	0	N/A	20	302	15.1	31	464	15.0
Subtotal	**59**	**1,679**		**7**	**119**		**80**	**1,689**		**146**	**3,487**	
Total	**2,914**	**90,304**		**1,969**	**54,027**		**3,565**	**95,930**		**8,448**	**240,261**	

*Coed championship sport.
NCAA = National Collegiate Athletic Association.
FBS = Football Bowl Subdivision.
FCS = Football Championship Subdivision.
N/A = Not Applicable.
Notes: Participation totals are adjusted to reflect all institutions sponsoring each sport. Provisional members are included in these numbers.
Coed sport teams from the sports sponsorship database were added to both the men's and women's team data. The following sports had coed teams: a) cross country, b) equestrian, c) fencing, d) golf, e) rifle, f) sailing, g) skiing, h) swimming & diving, i) indoor track & field and j) outdoor track & field.
The total row contains data from the non-championship sports subtotal row added to the championship sports subtotal row.

SOURCE: Denise M. DeHass, "2007–08 Participation Study—Men's Sports," in *1981–82–2007–08 NCAA Sports Sponsorship and Participation Rates Report*, National Collegiate Athletic Association, 2009, http://www.ncaapublications.com/Uploads/PDF/ParticipationRates2009c2f40573-60aa-4a08-874d-1aff4192c5e4.pdf (accessed June 23, 2009)

participated on 2,914 Division I men's teams that year. The sport with the greatest number of Division I teams was basketball, with 329. However, basketball squads are relatively small, averaging 15.6 members per school in Division I. Therefore, several other sports actually have more participants. Over 25,000 men played football at the Division I level in 2007–08. Outdoor track was second, with 10,266 participants, followed closely by baseball with 10,195. Division II sports included 54,027 men participants in 2007–08 and Division III had 95,930. Football had the most participants at both of these levels as well.

Figure 6.1 and Figure 6.2 put college sports participation in historical perspective. In 1981–82 there were 231,445 athletes competing in NCAA championship sports in all divisions; 167,055 of them were men. By 1994–95 the total number of athletes had grown to 294,212. About twice as much of this growth was on the women's side as on the men's. The total number of athletes had grown to 412,768 by 2007–08. However, it is important to note a change in the way the total is calculated: provisional NCAA members were included in the count beginning in 1995–96. In addition, the numbers for 1995–96 and 1996–97 were adjusted to comply with the Equity in Athletics Disclosure Act, making it difficult to compare current participation numbers with data from before 1995.

Figure 6.3 and Figure 6.4 show the number of championship sports sponsored by NCAA member schools

FIGURE 6.1

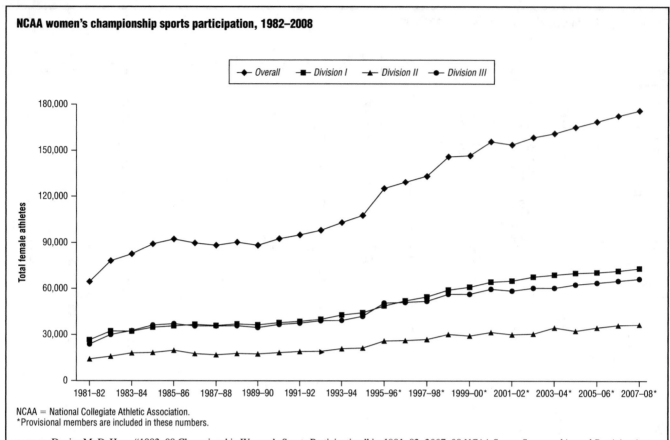

NCAA women's championship sports participation, 1982–2008

NCAA = National Collegiate Athletic Association.
*Provisional members are included in these numbers.

SOURCE: Denise M. DeHass, "1982–08 Championship Women's Sports Participation," in *1981–82–2007–08 NCAA Sports Sponsorship and Participation Rates Report*, National Collegiate Athletic Association, 2009, http://www.ncaapublications.com/Uploads/PDF/ParticipationRates2009c2f40573-60aa-4a08-874d-1aff4192c5e4.pdf (accessed June 23, 2009)

over the same period. There were 11,025 teams in NCAA championship sports in 1981–82, 6,746 of them men's teams. By 1994–95 there were 13,799. Much more of this growth was in women's sports than in men's. The number of women's teams surpassed the men's total in 1996–97 and has remained higher since then. The total number of teams was 17,682 in 2007–08, though the same caveat pertaining to comparisons of older and newer participation data apply.

Figure 6.5 and Figure 6.6 vividly illustrate the trends in the number of sports offered per school since the early 1980s. Even though the overall average number of teams per college, across all divisions, has increased slightly during this period, the gender balance has shifted. For example, in 1981–82 the average number of teams across all divisions was 9.1 for men and 6.4 for women; by 2007–08 the average number of men's teams declined to 8.1, whereas the women's teams increased to 9.0. As shown in Figure 6.7 and Figure 6.8, the average number of male student-athletes per college across all divisions has remained fairly stable; from 225.8 in 1981–82 compared to 232.3 in 2007–08, whereas the average number of female student-athletes per college has risen from 98.7 in 1981–82 to 167.6 in 2007–08.

Women's Sports and Gender Equity

Figure 6.9 graphically illustrates what has happened to the gender gap since 1991 at the Division I level. In 1991–92 the average number of female and male athletes per institution were 112 and 250, respectively; by 2005–06 this average increased to 218 for women and 269 for men. Overall, the average number of women athletes per institution grew by more than 100 between 1991 and 2004, whereas the average number of male athletes grew by only 19. In terms of average expenses, however, the gender gap has not narrowed significantly in Division I. In 1995–96 the average athletic expense per institution for men's sports was $3.4 million, whereas for women it was $1.5 million—a difference of a little under $2 million. By 2005–06 this difference had increased, rather than decreased, to over $4 million; $8.7 million was expended on men's sports and $4.4 million on women's sports on average. (See Figure 6.10.) In spite of this, considerable progress has been made in equalizing scholarship spending. In 1991–92 an average of $505,246 in scholarships was awarded to women in Division I-A, whereas nearly $1.3 million was given to men. This average increased to $2.5 million for women and $3.4 million for men in Division I-FBS in 2005–06. (See Figure 6.11.)

FIGURE 6.2

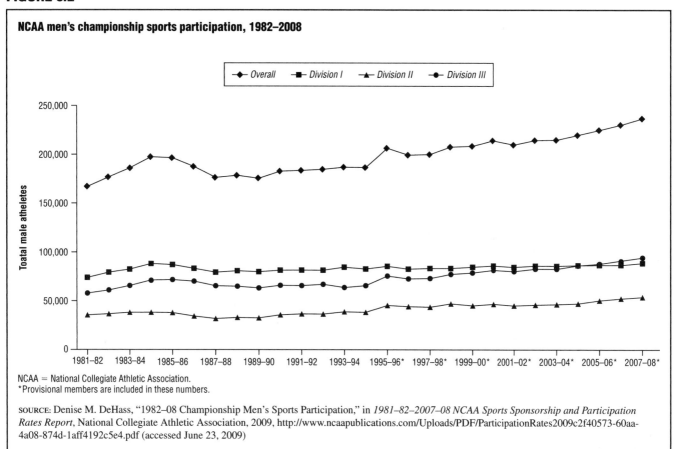

NCAA men's championship sports participation, 1982–2008

Legend: ◆ Overall   ■ Division I   ▲ Division II   ● Division III

NCAA = National Collegiate Athletic Association.
*Provisional members are included in these numbers.

SOURCE: Denise M. DeHass, "1982–08 Championship Men's Sports Participation," in *1981–82–2007–08 NCAA Sports Sponsorship and Participation Rates Report*, National Collegiate Athletic Association, 2009, http://www.ncaapublications.com/Uploads/PDF/ParticipationRates2009c2f40573-60aa-4a08-874d-1aff4192c5e4.pdf (accessed June 23, 2009)

In *Women in Intercollegiate Sport: A Longitudinal, National Study—Thirty-One Year Update, 1977–2008* (2008, http://www.acostacarpenter.org/2008%20Summary%20Final.pdf), Linda Jean Carpenter and R. Vivian Acosta, emeritus professors at Brooklyn College, examine the status of women's college athletics between 1977 and 2008. Carpenter and Acosta find that nationwide, college women have more athletic teams available to them than ever before. Since 1978 (the mandatory compliance date for Title IX, explained below) the number of women's athletic teams per school rose from 5.6 to 8.7 in 2008. There were a total of 9,101 varsity women's intercollegiate teams in the NCAA in 2008.

According to Carpenter and Acosta, the sport most frequently found in women's intercollegiate athletic programs was basketball, which was offered by 98.8% of NCAA schools in 2008. (See Table 6.7.) Basketball was the most popular sport throughout the period covered in the study. It ranked number one in 1977, when it was offered at 90.4% of colleges. Three other sports—volleyball, soccer, and cross-country—were offered for women at more than 90% of colleges in 2008. Like basketball, volleyball has maintained its ranking since 1977, when it was offered at 80.1% of schools.

Title IX

No piece of legislation has had a greater impact on gender equity in sports participation than Title IX of the Education Amendments of 1972 of the Civil Rights Act of 1964, usually referred to simply as Title IX. In 1971 the gender disparity in sports participation was overwhelming. According to the Women's Sports Foundation, in "Playing Fair: A Title IX Playbook for Victory" (April 2009, http://www.womenssportsfoundation.org/~/media/Files/PDFs%20and%20other%20files%20by%20Topic/Issues/Title%20IX/P/Play%20Fair/Play%20Fair_Final.pdf), 294,015 girls were participating in interscholastic sports programs that year, compared with 3.5 million boys. Title IX was based on the notion that unequal federal funding between genders was an illegal form of discrimination. Title IX requires institutions receiving federal funding—including both secondary schools and colleges—to provide resources equally to male and female students. In practice, this has meant that schools must attempt to maintain equal facilities, equal coaching staffs, and a gender ratio among athletes similar to the ratio among the student body as a whole. Critics of Title IX have been dismayed by the fact that compliance has sometimes meant cuts in men's sports programs, but the biggest impact has been an explosion in the prevalence and popularity of women's sports. In 2002 President George W. Bush (1946–) officially renamed Title IX the Patsy T. Mink Equal Opportunity in Education Act, after the legislation's author, a congresswoman from Hawaii. However, it is still generally referred to as Title IX.

FIGURE 6.3

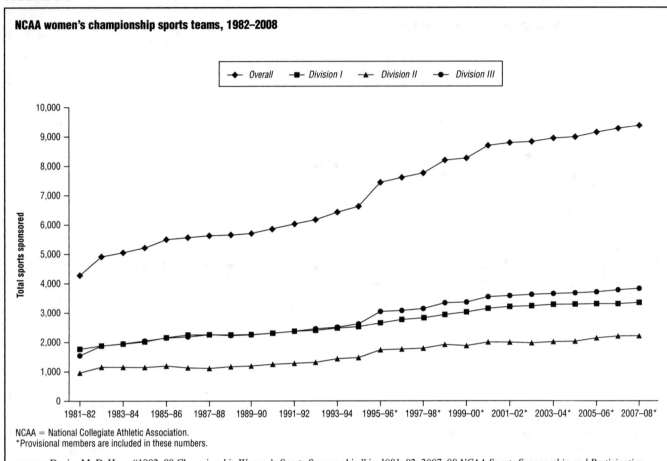

NCAA women's championship sports teams, 1982–2008

NCAA = National Collegiate Athletic Association.
*Provisional members are included in these numbers.

SOURCE: Denise M. DeHass, "1982–08 Championship Women's Sports Sponsorship," in *1981–82–2007–08 NCAA Sports Sponsorship and Participation Rates Report*, National Collegiate Athletic Association, 2009, http://www.ncaapublications.com/Uploads/PDF/ParticipationRates2009c2f40573-60aa-4a08-874d-1aff4192c5e4.pdf (accessed June 23, 2009)

The Women's Sports Foundation notes that there is both good and bad news regarding gender equity in high school and college sports in the Title IX era. Female high school sports participation increased by 904% between 1972, when Title IX went into effect, and 2007, and female college sports participation increased by 456% during this same period. By contrast, women athletes in college received only 38% of sports operating dollars, 45% of athletic scholarship dollars, and 33% of recruitment spending in 2007. In high school, where girls represented 49% of all students, they received only 41% of the opportunities to participate in school athletics.

Women Coaches in College

One ironic consequence of the increase in the number of women's sports offered in college is a decrease in the percentage of teams that are coached by women. In 1972 women coached more than 90% of women's college sports teams. (See Table 6.8.) By 1978 the percentage had dropped to 58.2%. Acosta and Carpenter suggest that this drop was because of the rapid increase in the number of women's sports teams, which was not accompanied by a comparable growth in the number of qualified female coaches. However, the percentage has continued to fall

since 1978, and in 2006 it stood at 42.4%, an all-time low, before seeing a slight uptick to 42.8% in 2008. Acosta and Carpenter argue that this decline in women's representation in college coaching is due in part to discrimination and differences in the way male and female coaches are recruited. The percentage varies substantially from sport to sport. Table 6.9 shows that 59.1% of women's college basketball teams had female coaches in 2008, and 55% of volleyball coaches were female. However, men dominated the coaching ranks of women's track and field (18% were female), cross-country (19.2%), and soccer (33.1%).

Acosta and Carpenter note that the percentage of female coaches is higher among schools at which the athletic director is also a woman. However, they also note that only 21.3% of NCAA schools had female athletic directors in 2008.

College Sports and Ethnicity

According to Denise DeHass in *1999–00—2006–07 NCAA Student-Athlete Race and Ethnicity Report* (August 2008, http://www.ncaapublications.com/Uploads/PDF/Race-Ethnicity_2008bc054067-3afd-4d76-b1cc-c1e9422eca18.pdf), the percentage of African-American

FIGURE 6.4

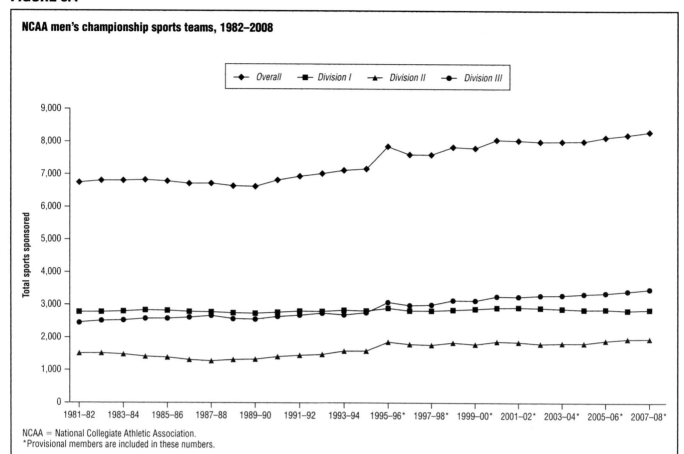

NCAA men's championship sports teams, 1982–2008

NCAA = National Collegiate Athletic Association.
*Provisional members are included in these numbers.

SOURCE: Denise M. DeHass, "1982–08 Championship Men's Sports Sponsorship," in *1981–82–2007–08 NCAA Sports Sponsorship and Participation Rates Report*, National Collegiate Athletic Association, 2009, http://www.ncaapublications.com/Uploads/PDF/ParticipationRates2009c2f40573-60aa-4a08-874d-1aff4192c5e4.pdf (accessed June 23, 2009)

male student-athletes increased from 16.3% in 1999–2000 to 18.3% in 2006–07. During this same period the percentage of African-American female athletes increased from 9.4% to 11.2%.

Table 6.10 breaks down sports participation ethnic percentages (all divisions combined) by ethnicity and sport. Some sports, such as lacrosse at a little over 90% for each gender, are overwhelmingly white. In contrast, a substantial portion of college basketball players—44.1% of men and 30.6% of women—are non-Hispanic black. The overall ethnic balance across all divisions has remained fairly stable over the last several years, among both male and female athletes. This stability is represented visually in Figure 6.12 and Figure 6.13, which trace the ethnicity percentages of student-athletes between 1999 and 2007. In these two graphs, the line representing non-Hispanic white male athletes hovers at just over 70% across the entire time span; the line representing non-Hispanic white women similarly hovers at a little under 80%.

Spending on College Sports

In "Athletic Spending Grows as Academic Funds Dry Up" (February 18, 2004, http://www.usatoday.com/

sports/college/2004-02-18-athletic-spending-cover_x.htm), MaryJo Sylwester and Tom Witosky indicate that in 2004 spending on Division I sports increased at more than twice the rate of overall average university spending between 1995 and 2001. Spending on athletics, adjusted for inflation, grew an average of about 25% during this period, whereas university spending increased only 10% on average. According to Sylwester and Witosky, part of this disparity is due to increases in basic costs, such as scholarships and travel; however, a bigger factor is simply the desire by schools to have winning teams, which translates into higher attendance at sports events, better television ratings, and increased alumni support.

The trend has continued in the years since then. Steve Wieberg and Steve Berkowitz write in "NCAA Report: College Sports Spending Keeps Skyrocketing" (April 30, 2009, http://www.usatoday.com/sports/college/2009-04-29-college-athletic-spending-report_N.htm) that average spending on sports by Division I-FBS schools grew from $31 million in 2004 to $42.2 million in 2007. As a share of overall university spending, spending on sports grew from 3.8% to 6% during that span.

FIGURE 6.5

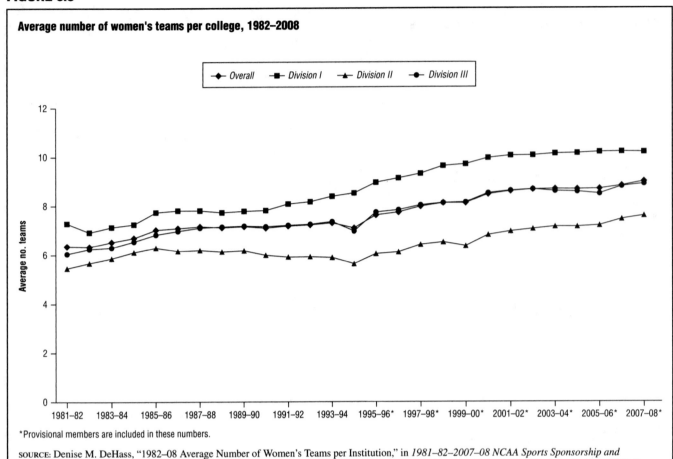

Average number of women's teams per college, 1982–2008

*Provisional members are included in these numbers.

SOURCE: Denise M. DeHass, "1982–08 Average Number of Women's Teams per Institution," in *1981–82–2007–08 NCAA Sports Sponsorship and Participation Rates Report*, National Collegiate Athletic Association, 2009, http://www.ncaapublications.com/Uploads/PDF/ParticipationRates2009c2 f40573-60aa-4a08-874d-1aff4192c5e4.pdf (accessed June 23, 2009)

Revenue generated by university sports does not typically cover the costs of running the programs. Sylwester and Witosky state that only about 40 schools had self-sustaining athletic departments in 2004. Therefore, most departments were reliant on the school for financial support. About 60% of Division I schools used student fees to help fund their athletic department.

The trend toward university-subsidized sports appears to be accelerating, leading to growing tensions between athletics and academics on the campuses of many top schools. The debate has gotten more fierce as substantial cuts in higher education funding by state governments have led many schools to eliminate jobs, downsize academic programs, increase class sizes, and raise tuition.

The NCAA actively rebuts the argument that college sports have become "big business." In "Is College Sports Big Business?" (*NCAA News Online*, August 29, 2005), Gary T. Brown asserts that the money that flows through college athletic programs pales in comparison to the dollars that professional sports and the corporate world overall generate. Brown notes that Myles Brand (1942–2009), the president of the NCAA at the time,

placed the blame on the media for creating the impression that college sports are all about money. For example, Brand argued that media coverage of college sports reports the NCAA's $6.2 billion television contract, but rarely mentions the fact that the $6.2 billion is spread over 11 years. Brad Wolverton, in "College Presidents Call for Increased Disclosure of Athletics Spending" (*Chronicle of Higher Education*, November 10, 2006), quotes Brand as saying that the revenue generated by college sports is well spent in educationally valid ways, including the $1.2 billion spent by Division I schools on athletic scholarships in 2005–06 and $150 million on academic support programs for student-athletes.

In *2002–03 NCAA Revenues and Expenses of Divisions I and II Intercollegiate Athletics Programs Report* (February 2005), Daniel L. Fulks of the NCAA states that in 1985 the average Division I-A athletic program had total revenues of $6.8 million ($6.7 million of it from men's sports) and expenses of $6.9 million ($6.2 million on the men's side). By 2006, according to Fulks in *2004–06 NCAA Revenues and Expenses of Division I Intercollegiate Athletics Programs Report* (March 2008, http://www.ncaapublications.com/Uploads/PDF/NCAA_Revenues

FIGURE 6.6

Average number of men's teams per college, 1982–2008

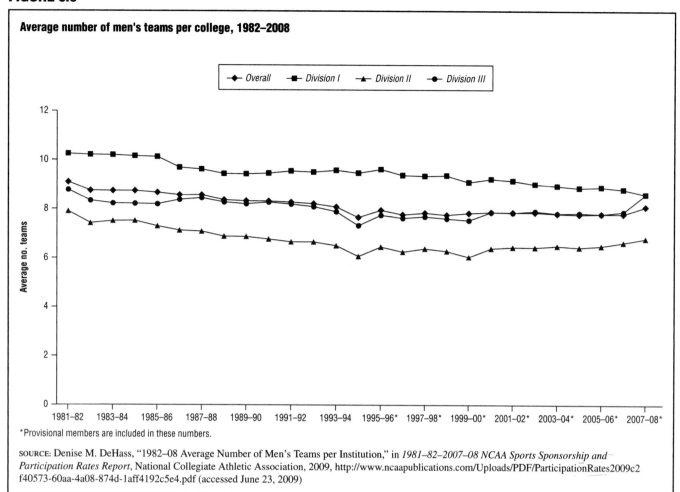

*Provisional members are included in these numbers.

SOURCE: Denise M. DeHass, "1982–08 Average Number of Men's Teams per Institution," in *1981–82–2007–08 NCAA Sports Sponsorship and Participation Rates Report*, National Collegiate Athletic Association, 2009, http://www.ncaapublications.com/Uploads/PDF/ParticipationRates2009c2 f40573-60aa-4a08-874d-1aff4192c5e4.pdf (accessed June 23, 2009)

_Expenses.pdf798f201d-c82a-4cb3-9b05-e845a3cf24ec.pdf), the median sports revenue for Division I-FBS schools had grown to $35.4 million, with $18.8 million of this total coming from men's sports. These schools were nearly breaking even as average expenses were $35.8 million, just a few hundred thousand dollars over their average revenue.

In 2006 football ($10.6 million in revenue and $8.5 million in expenses) and men's basketball ($4 million in revenue and $3.1 million in expenses) accounted for a huge share of both the median spending and median revenue in Division 1-FBS college sports, and both produced sizable net financial gains. (See Table 6.11.) Table 6.12 details where Division I-FBS schools' athletics revenue came from in 2006. Ticket sales were the biggest source, accounting for a median of $7.4 million of the total revenue.

Academic Eligibility

Incoming student-athletes must meet a set of academic standards to participate in NCAA-sanctioned sports programs. These standards vary according to the division in which a school competes. According to the

NCAA, in *2008–09 Guide for the College-Bound Student-Athlete* (2008, http://www.ncaapublications.com/Uploads/PDF/2008-09%20CBSA9c29e699-00f6-48ba-98a9-6456c9b98957.pdf), Division I academic eligibility rules for 2008–09 require that the student:

- Graduates from high school

- Completes 14 core courses: four years of English; three of math; two of science; one extra year of English, math, or science; two years of social science; and four extra core courses of English, math, or science, or foreign language, nondoctrinal religion, or philosophy

- Achieves a minimum required GPA in core courses

- Achieves a combined SAT or ACT score that matches the student's GPA on a special NCAA chart

The requirements for Divisions II and III are similar to those of Division I, though less stringent.

The *Guide for the College-Bound Student-Athlete* also outlines the rules for recruiting high school athletes, which vary somewhat by sport as well as by division. The recruiting rules for Division I are summarized in

FIGURE 6.7

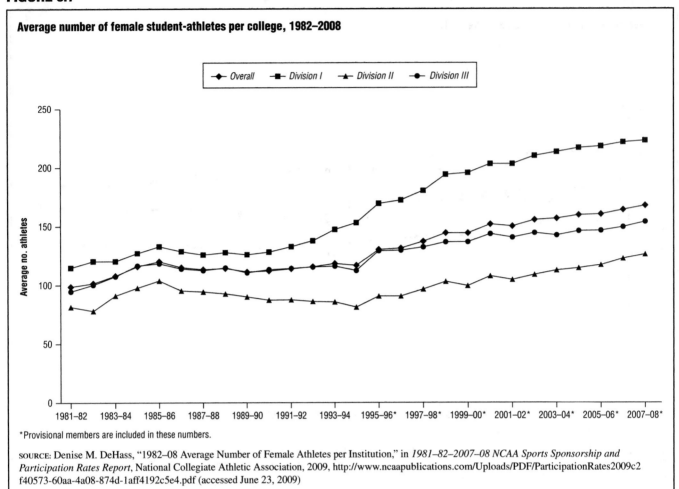

Average number of female student-athletes per college, 1982–2008

*Provisional members are included in these numbers.

SOURCE: Denise M. DeHass, "1982–08 Average Number of Female Athletes per Institution," in *1981–82–2007–08 NCAA Sports Sponsorship and Participation Rates Report*, National Collegiate Athletic Association, 2009, http://www.ncaapublications.com/Uploads/PDF/ParticipationRates2009c2 f40573-60aa-4a08-874d-1aff4192c5e4.pdf (accessed June 23, 2009)

Table 6.13 and include regulations pertaining to phone contact, campus visits, and other forms of communication between coaches and prospective college athletes.

HIGH SCHOOL SPORTS
Participation

According to the U.S. Centers for Disease Control and Prevention, 56% of U.S. high school students played on a sports team in 2005. (See Table 6.14.) The percentage was higher among boys (61.8% of all boys in high school) than girls (50.2%). Nearly 58% of white students played on a sports team. Minority students played sports in lesser proportions: 53.7% of non-Hispanic African-American students and 53% of Hispanic students played on sports teams.

Since 1971 the National Federation of State High School Associations (NFHS) has compiled data on sports participation from its member associations. The most recent data are published in the *2008–09 High School Athletics Participation Survey* (2009, http://www.nfhs.org/WorkArea/linkit.aspx?LinkIdentifier=id&ItemID=3506). Table 6.15 summarizes this NFHS data for 1971 through 2009. In 2008–09 the number of participants in high school sports reached 7.5 million. At more than 3.1

million, participation among girls reached an all-time high in 2008–09. The total for boys, more than 4.4 million, was also a new high.

Table 6.16 shows the most popular high school sports for boys. About 1.1 million boys participated in football in 2008–09. Boys' track and field had 558,007 participants, about half as many participants as football. Basketball (545,145), baseball (473,184), and soccer (383,824) were the third-, fourth-, and fifth-most popular boys' sports, respectively. Among high school girls, outdoor track and field was the most popular sport, with 457,732 participants, followed by basketball (444,809), volleyball (404,243), fast-pitch softball (368,921), and soccer (344,534). (See Table 6.17.)

According to the NFHS, the state with the largest number of high school athletes in 2008–09 was Texas, with 781,000. Other leading states included California (771,465), New York (380,870), Illinois (341,763), and Ohio (330,056).

Data from Lloyd D. Johnston et al. in *Monitoring the Future, National Results on Adolescent Drug Use: Overview of Key Findings, 2008* (May 2009, http://www.moni

FIGURE 6.8

Average number of male student-athletes per college, 1982–2008

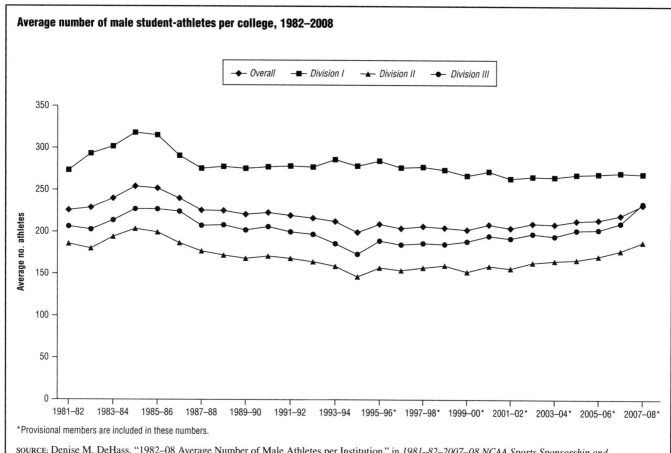

*Provisional members are included in these numbers.

SOURCE: Denise M. DeHass, "1982–08 Average Number of Male Athletes per Institution," in *1981–82–2007–08 NCAA Sports Sponsorship and Participation Rates Report*, National Collegiate Athletic Association, 2009, http://www.ncaapublications.com/Uploads/PDF/ParticipationRates2009c2 f40573-60aa-4a08-874d-1aff4192c5e4.pdf (accessed June 23, 2009)

toringthefuture.org/pubs/monographs/overview2008.pdf), an ongoing nationwide study of youth behavior and attitudes, suggest that the percentage of middle and high school students participating in school sports has generally declined over the past decade, although girls' participation has held fairly steady. A greater percentage of boys than girls have participated in school sports throughout this span. The national advocacy group Child Trends analyzed data on school sports participation from *Monitoring the Future* over several years, and its findings are summarized in Table 6.18. The analysis by Child Trends shows that participation in athletics among 10th-grade boys decreased from 68.7% in 1991 to 67.4% in 2006, whereas participation among 10th-grade girls increased slightly, from 51.9% in 1991 to 58.3% in 2006. The pattern was similar among 12th graders. Child Trends finds that since 1991 the gender gap in high school sports participation has decreased substantially. Among 10th graders, the difference between boys and girls declined from 17 percentage points in 1991 (boys, 69%, and girls, 52%) to nine percentage points in 2006 (boys, 67%, and girls, 58%). (See Figure 6.14.) Likewise, the gap for 12th graders declined from 18 percentage points in 1991 (boys, 65%, and girls, 47%) to nine percentage points in 2006 (boys, 59%, and girls, 50%).

Child Trends also finds a correlation between parents' education and students' participation in school athletics. Youth whose parents were better educated were more likely to participate than their peers whose parents had fewer years of education. In 2006, 74% of 10th graders with a parent who had attended graduate school participated in school sports, whereas participation among 10th graders whose parents did not finish high school was only 43%. (See Figure 6.15.)

Benefits of High School Sports Participation

In September 2005 the National Center for Education Statistics (NCES) published the report *What Is the Status of High School Athletes 8 Years after Their Senior Year?* (http://nces.ed.gov/pubs2005/2005303.pdf), which analyzes the status of former high school athletes in their mid-20s. The report was part of the National Education Longitudinal Study of 1988, which tracked a large sample of students who were seniors in 1992. This report examined their educational achievement, employment success, and health status as of 2000. The NCES finds that elite (those who were team captains or most valuable players) and varsity-level athletes were more likely than nonathletes to have received some postsecondary education

FIGURE 6.9

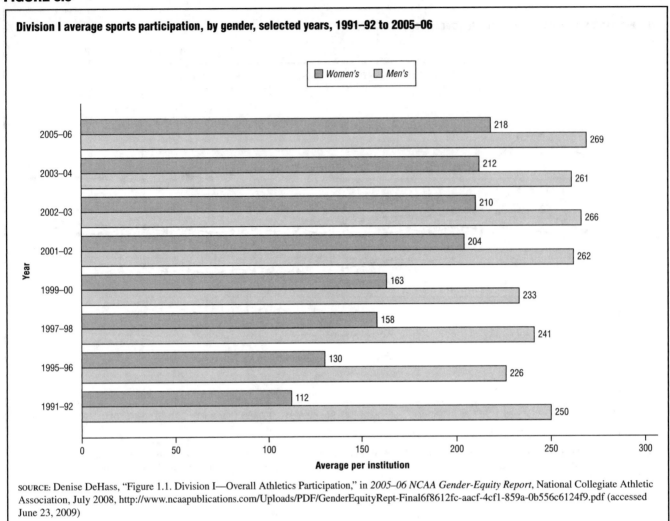

Division I average sports participation, by gender, selected years, 1991–92 to 2005–06

Women's   Men's

SOURCE: Denise DeHass, "Figure 1.1. Division I—Overall Athletics Participation," in *2005–06 NCAA Gender-Equity Report*, National Collegiate Athletic Association, July 2008, http://www.ncaapublications.com/Uploads/PDF/GenderEquityRept-Final6f8612fc-aacf-4cf1-859a-0b556c6124f9.pdf (accessed June 23, 2009)

and more likely to have earned a bachelor's degree. It also finds that elite athletes were more likely than nonathletes to be employed, and employed full time, in 2000. Elite and varsity athletes had higher incomes on average than those who did not participate in high school sports. In addition, the NCES finds that high school athletes were more likely than nonathletes to participate in fitness activities and group sports eight years after their senior year. Elite and varsity athletes were less likely to be daily smokers than their nonathletic peers. The only negative impact the NCES notes is that elite and varsity athletes were more likely than nonathletes to binge drink (i.e., these survey respondents reported having five or more alcoholic drinks on at least one occasion during the two weeks before the survey).

Money and High School Athletics

The perceived corruption of college sports by money appears to have seeped down to the high school level. A series of *New York Times* articles by Duff Wilson and Pete Thamel in November and December 2005, including "The Quick Fix" (November 27) and "NCAA Calls for

Investigation into Correspondence School" (December 2), reported on a Florida high school that was basically functioning as a diploma mill for elite athletes whose poor school performance threatened their chances to play at top-level universities. The school, the University High School in Miami, had no accreditation from the state, offered no classes for students to attend, and provided no real instruction. Students "attended" University High via correspondence courses, which essentially consisted of a series of open-book tests. Wilson and Thamel identified 28 athletes who raised their sagging GPAs, often just enough to qualify for intercollegiate athletics, by enrolling in University High. Fourteen of them had already committed to attend NCAA Division I schools. Students paid about $400 to boost their grades in this way.

The vast sums of money involved in college sports have also led to extremely aggressive recruiting practices. According to Mark Schlabach in "NCAA Cracks Down on Recruiting Practices" (*Washington Post*, August 6, 2004), high-profile recruiting scandals at two major colleges, the University of Colorado and the University of

FIGURE 6.10

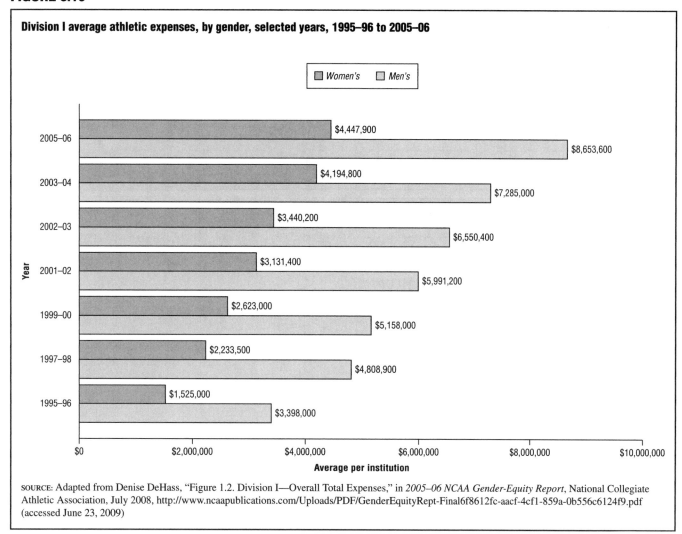

Division I average athletic expenses, by gender, selected years, 1995–96 to 2005–06

SOURCE: Adapted from Denise DeHass, "Figure 1.2. Division I—Overall Total Expenses," in *2005–06 NCAA Gender-Equity Report*, National Collegiate Athletic Association, July 2008, http://www.ncaapublications.com/Uploads/PDF/GenderEquityRept-Final6f8612fc-aacf-4cf1-859a-0b556c6124f9.pdf (accessed June 23, 2009)

Miami, led to the creation of a special NCAA task force. The work of the task force culminated in new rules, approved by the NCAA Division I Board of Directors in August 2004, aimed at eliminating what Brand called a "culture of entitlement." Previously, colleges were wooing prospects with high-priced meals and stays in luxury hotels, often transporting them to campus in expensive chartered planes and limousines. Schlabach also mentions widely reported earlier charges that colleges were plying top high-school athletes with sex and alcohol. The revised rules prohibit schools from employing any of these practices, requiring that prospects be transported from airports in standard vehicles and fed "standard meals similar to those offered on campus." They also require schools to establish policies explicitly forbidding illegal actions during recruiting, such as underage drinking and sex for hire.

YOUTH SPORTS

As noted in Chapter 2, participation in youth sports has generally been declining in the United States over the last several years. However, that trend has been accompanied by another phenomenon: a growing intensity as youth leagues are increasingly seen as a feeder system for the big money college and professional systems. The well-documented benefits of participation in youth sports are outlined in Chapter 9. However, the adult-driven pressure on young athletes has drawbacks. It has resulted in greater pressure on young athletes to perform, specialization on a single sport at earlier ages, year-round play, and more travel in top-level youth leagues.

Citizenship Through Sports Alliance (CTSA), a national coalition of professional and amateur sports organizations, including the NCAA, MLB, NBA and WNBA, and NHL, issued a Youth Sports National Report Card in 2005 (http://www.sportsmanship.org/News/1105%20Report%20 Card-Fgrade.pdf). The report card gave the nation's youth sports system poor grades for failing to exhibit a child-centered philosophy and for fostering negative behavior by coaches and parents due to a "win at all costs" mentality that too often ignores the best interests of the child.

In his book *Until It Hurts: America's Obsession with Youth Sports and How It Harms Our Kids* (2009), author

FIGURE 6.11

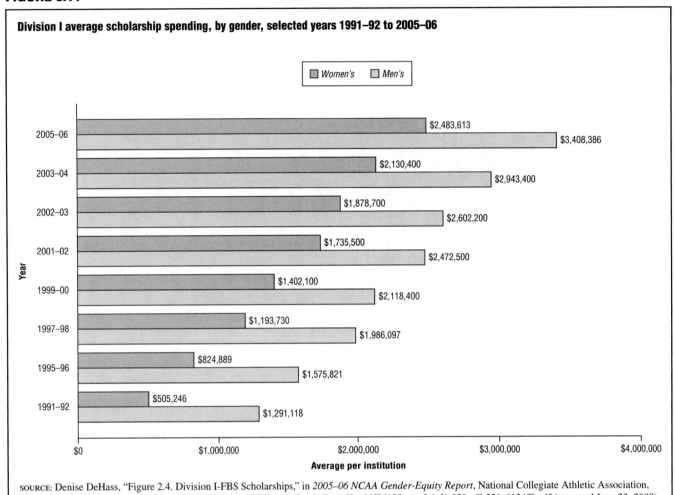

Division I average scholarship spending, by gender, selected years 1991–92 to 2005–06

SOURCE: Denise DeHass, "Figure 2.4. Division I-FBS Scholarships," in *2005–06 NCAA Gender-Equity Report*, National Collegiate Athletic Association, July 2008, http://www.ncaapublications.com/Uploads/PDF/GenderEquityRept-Final6f8612fc-aacf-4cf1-859a-0b556c6124f9.pdf (accessed June 23, 2009)

TABLE 6.7

Most popular intercollegiate women's sports, selected years 1977–2008

Rank in 2008	% offering sport	Rank in 2006		Rank in 2004		Rank in 2002		Rank in 1977	
1. Basketball	98.8	1	98.4	1	98.3	1	98.8	1	90.4
2. Volleyball	95.7	2	95.2	2	94.6	2	95.4	2	80.1
3. Soccer	92.0	3	89.4	4	88.6	3	87.9	20	2.8
4. Cross country	90.8	4	89.2	3	88.8	5	86.5	8	29.4
5. Softball	89.2	5	87.1	5	86.4	6	86.2	4	48.4
6. Tennis	84.7	6	85.1	6	85.2	4	87.7	3	80.0
7. Track & field	70.9	7	67.4	7	67.4	7	67.5	5	46.1
8. Golf	54.4	8	52.2	8 tie	48.7	9	48.4	10	19.9
9. Swimming	52.3	9	50.9	9 tie	48.7	8	52.0	6	41.0
10. Lacrosse	32.6	10	30.6	10	28.5	11	26.7	11	13.0
11. Field hockey	27.9	11	28.0	11	28.2	10	27.0	7	36.3
12. Crew/rowing	17.4	12	15.2	12	14.0	12	16.2	13	6.9
13. Gymnastics	10.7	14	9.5	13	11.0	13	12.0	9	25.9
14. Ice hockey	9.4	13	9.7	14	8.8	14	8.5	24	1.3
15. Water polo	6.7	16 tie	5.9	15	6.5	15	6.0	—	—
16. Fencing	5.2 tie	15 tie	5.9	17	4.6	16	5.8	12	9.8
17. Riding/equest.	5.2 tie	19	3.6	19	3.6	19	3.6	23	2.0
18. Skiing	4.3	17	5.7	16	5.8	17	5.0	16	3.6
19. Squash	4.2	20 tie	3.4	18	3.8	21	3.1	21 tie	2.3
20. Sailing	3.2 tie	18	3.8	21	3.2	20	3.1	21 tie	2.3
21. Bowling	3.2 tie	22	3.2	20	3.3	22	2.6	17	3.4
22. Riflery	2.8	21 tie	3.4	22	2.8	18	3.8	15	3.8
23. Synchro swim	1.2	23	1.3	23	0.5	23	1.0	18	3.3
24. Badminton	0.2	24	0.4	24	0.3	25	0.1	14	5.9
25. Archery	0.1	25	0.2	25	0.2	24	0.5	19	3.0

SOURCE: R. Vivian Acosta and Linda Jean Carpenter, "Most Popular Sports in 2008 (Most Frequently Found Sports in Women's Intercollegiate Programs)," in *Women in Intercollegiate Sport: A Longitudinal, National Study—Thirty-One Year Update, 1977–2008*, Acosta/Carpenter, 2009, http://www.acostacarpenter.org/2008%20Summary%20Final.pdf (accessed June 23, 2009)

TABLE 6.8

Percentage of female coaches in women's intercollegiate sports, selected years 1972–2008

2008	42.8%
2006	42.4%
2004	44.1%
2003	44.0%
2002	44.0%
2001	44.7%
2000	45.6%
1999	46.3%
1998	47.4%
1997	47.4%
1996	47.7%
1995	48.3%
1994	49.4%
1993	48.1%
1992	48.3%
1991	47.7%
1990	47.3%
1989	47.7%
1988	48.3%
1987	48.8%
1986	50.6%
1985	50.7%
1984	53.8%
1983	56.2%
1982	52.4%
1981	54.6%
1980	54.2%
1979	56.1%
1978	58.2%
1972	90.0% + Women coaching women's teams.

SOURCE: R. Vivian Acosta and Linda Jean Carpenter, "Percentage of Female Head Coaches, All Division, All Sports, 2008," in *Women in Intercollegiate Sport: A Longitudinal, National Study—Thirty-One Year Update, 1977–2008*, Acosta/Carpenter, 2009, http://www.acostacarpenter.org/2008%20Summary%20Final.pdf (accessed June 23, 2009)

TABLE 6.9

Percentage of female coaches, by sport, 1977 and 2008

	2008	1977
Archery	0.0%	83.4%
Badminton	0.0%	75.0%
Basketball	59.1%	79.4%
Bowling	36.8%	42.9%
Crew/rowing	42.3%	11.9%
Cross country	19.2%	35.2%
Fencing	16.1%	51.7%
Field hockey	95.2%	99.1%
Golf	38.8%	54.6%
Gymnastics	57.8%	69.7%
Ice hockey	30.4%	37.5%
Lacrosse	84.6%	90.7%
Riding	80.0%	75.0%
Riflery	17.6%	17.4%
Sailing	10.5%	7.1%
Skiing	7.7%	22.7%
Soccer	33.1%	29.4%
Softball	64.7%	83.5%
Squash	36.0%	71.4%
Swim/diving	24.3%	53.6%
Synch. swim	100.0%	85.0%
Tennis	29.8%	72.9%
Track and field	18.0%	52.3%
Volleyball	55.0%	86.6%
Water polo	15.0%	—

SOURCE: R. Vivian Acosta and Linda Jean Carpenter, "Percentage and Number of Female Coaches, All Divisions, 2008 and 1977," in *Women in Intercollegiate Sport: A Longitudinal, National Study—Thirty-One Year Update, 1977–2008*, Acosta/Carpenter, 2009, http://www.acostacarpenter.org/2008%20Summary%20Final.pdf (accessed June 23, 2009)

Mark Hyman cites numerous examples of children being injured because coaches, eager to win at all costs, ignored clear warning signs that their star players were damaging their bodies. In particular, Hyman notes that young baseball pitchers risk serious, permanent arm injuries from overuse, as evidenced by the sharp rise in the number of adolescents needing elbow surgery. Hyman points to, among other things, a growing reliance on the curveball, which exerts a great deal of strain on still-developing arms.

Brooke DeLench, in "Early Travel Team Play Fosters Elitism" (2008, http://www.youthsportsparents.com/successful-parenting/parenting-elite-athletes/specialization/early-travel-team-play-fosters-elitism), argues that the rise of top-level teams that travel long distances to play other elite squads has harmed less-talented kids by excluding them, while offering little benefit to those highly-skilled children forced into a demanding travel schedule that resembles professional play more than the recreational, community-based play shown to yield the most beneficial effects. Travel teams also disadvantage players from lower-income families because of the high financial cost of participation.

In this article and a series of others on the Web site YouthSportsParents (http://www.youthsportsparents.com), DeLench and others make a compelling case against early specialization in a single sport, including debunking the myth that a strenuous travel schedule and specialization—pushed mostly by adults looking for scholarships and professional careers—contribute to the development of top-notch professional sports talent. Hyman concurs, noting that there is a surprising lack of former Little League superstar pitchers performing in Major League Baseball.

TABLE 6.10

College athletes and ethnicity, 2006–07

Sport	American Indian/ Alaskan Native		Asian/ Pacific Islander		Black, non-Hispanic		Hispanic		Other		White, non-Hispanic	
	Men	Women	Men	Women	Men	Women	Men	Women	Men	Women	Men	Women
Archery	0.0	0.0	0.0	0.0	0.0	0.0	0.0	0.0	11.1	26.1	88.9	73.9
Badminton	0.0	0.0	0.0	34.6	0.0	3.8	0.0	0.0	0.0	23.1	0.0	38.5
Baseball	0.3	N/A	0.9	N/A	4.5	N/A	5.4	N/A	1.8	N/A	87.1	N/A
Basketball	0.2	0.6	0.7	1.1	44.1	30.6	2.5	2.8	3.2	2.7	49.3	62.1
Bowling	0.0	0.0	0.0	0.9	3.4	51.9	0.0	2.1	0.0	2.1	96.6	43.1
Cross country	0.5	0.4	1.5	1.6	9.4	9.6	5.2	4.6	3.7	3.4	79.8	80.4
Equestrian	0.0	0.4	0.0	1.0	0.0	0.6	0.0	1.5	0.0	2.1	100.0	94.5
Fencing	0.3	0.4	10.8	14.1	3.5	4.9	4.3	6.2	9.1	10.8	72.0	63.5
Field hockey	N/A	0.1	N/A	1.5	N/A	1.5	N/A	1.2	N/A	3.4	N/A	92.3
Football	0.4	N/A	1.0	N/A	33.5	N/A	2.5	N/A	2.4	N/A	60.2	N/A
Golf	0.3	0.4	2.2	4.8	2.1	2.7	1.8	3.6	4.1	5.6	89.5	83.0
Gymnastics	0.9	0.5	7.1	6.0	4.0	4.3	2.8	2.7	4.6	4.4	80.6	82.1
Ice hockey	0.4	0.6	0.8	1.4	0.7	0.4	0.5	0.6	6.9	8.6	90.7	88.5
Lacrosse	0.2	0.2	0.7	1.4	2.0	2.0	1.3	1.7	3.5	3.3	92.3	91.5
Rifle	0.5	0.4	2.2	6.2	1.6	0.9	0.5	4.0	3.2	2.7	91.9	85.8
Rowing	0.4	0.7	3.5	3.8	1.2	1.7	3.2	3.2	10.0	7.4	81.6	83.1
Rugby	0.0	1.4	1.0	4.2	3.1	8.4	6.2	9.8	0.0	0.7	89.7	75.5
Sailing	0.0	N/A	3.4	N/A	0.2	N/A	1.1	N/A	5.3	N/A	90.0	N/A
Skiing	0.4	0.0	1.3	0.9	0.6	0.6	0.4	0.4	8.4	5.9	88.9	92.2
Soccer	0.2	0.2	2.2	1.8	7.2	4.0	7.2	4.1	5.2	3.1	78.0	86.8
Softball	N/A	0.5	N/A	1.5	N/A	6.4	N/A	5.2	N/A	2.0	N/A	84.3
Squash	0.4	0.0	8.3	6.1	0.7	1.4	1.6	1.7	13.0	13.6	76.0	77.2
Swimming/diving	0.1	0.3	3.1	2.7	1.7	1.2	3.7	3.1	5.9	4.3	85.6	88.5
Sync. swimming	N/A	1.0	N/A	6.0	N/A	0.0	N/A	3.0	N/A	13.0	N/A	77.0
Team handball	N/A	0.0	N/A	0.0	N/A	0.0	N/A	0.0	N/A	0.0	N/A	0.0
Tennis	0.2	0.2	5.7	4.7	4.8	7.0	6.5	4.6	11.6	8.5	71.3	75.1
Track, indoor	0.4	0.4	1.5	1.3	20.9	21.1	3.5	2.9	3.8	3.9	70.0	70.4
Track, outdoor	0.4	0.4	1.6	1.5	21.7	21.1	4.3	3.7	3.6	3.9	68.4	69.5
Volleyball	0.4	0.4	5.6	2.2	7.4	9.4	13.3	3.9	5.2	3.3	68.0	80.9
Water polo	0.6	0.7	3.5	4.8	1.3	0.9	6.4	7.6	9.5	6.2	78.7	79.9
Wrestling	0.5	N/A	1.5	N/A	5.3	N/A	4.7	N/A	3.2	N/A	84.7	N/A
All sports	0.3	0.4	1.6	2.1	18.3	11.2	3.9	3.6	3.7	3.9	72.2	78.8

Note: Beginning in 2006–07 resident alien status is collected separate from ethnicity (following Division III).
N/A = Not Applicable.

SOURCE: Denise DeHass, "2006–07 Student-Athlete Race/Ethnicity Percentages for Divisions I, II and III Overall," in *1999–00–2006–07 NCAA® Student-Athlete Race and Ethnicity Report*, National Collegiate Athletic Association, August 2008, http://www.ncaapublications.com/Uploads/PDF/Race-Ethnicity_2008bc054067-3afd-4d76-b1cc-c1e9422eca18.pdf (accessed June 23, 2009)

FIGURE 6.12

Ethnicity of male collegiate athletes, by percentage, 1999–2000 to 2006–07

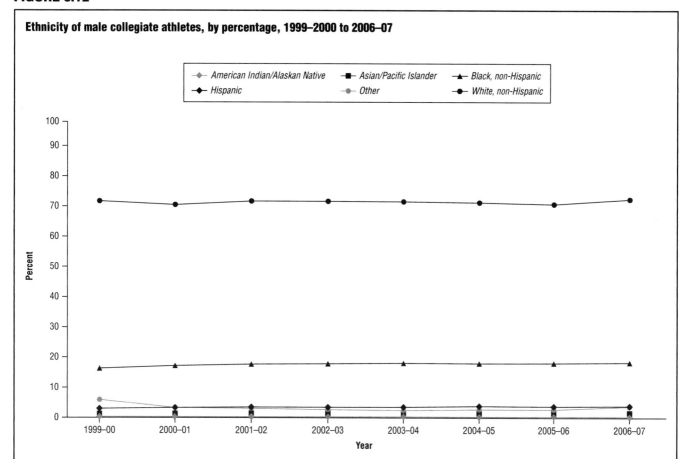

SOURCE: Denise DeHass, "Male Student-Athlete Race/Ethnicity Percentages for Divisions I, II and III Overall," in *1999–00–2006–07 NCAA® Student-Athlete Race and Ethnicity Report*, National Collegiate Athletic Association, August 2008, http://www.ncaapublications.com/Uploads/PDF/Race-Ethnicity_2008bc054067-3afd-4d76-b1cc-c1e9422eca18.pdf (accessed June 23, 2009)

FIGURE 6.13

Ethnicity of female collegiate athletes, by percentage, 1999–2000 to 2006–07

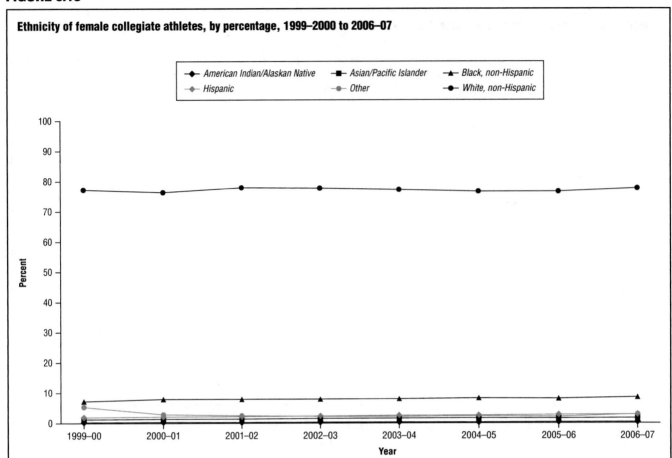

SOURCE: Denise DeHass, "Female Student-Athlete Race/Ethnicity Percentages for Divisions I, II and III Overall," in *1999–00–2006–07 NCAA® Student-Athlete Race and Ethnicity Report*, National Collegiate Athletic Association, August 2008, http://www.ncaapublications.com/Uploads/PDF/Race-Ethnicity_2008bc054067-3afd-4d76-b1cc-c1e9422eca18.pdf (accessed June 23, 2009)

TABLE 6.11

Division I–FBS (Football Bowl Subdivision) revenue and expenses, by sport, fiscal year 2006

Sport	Men's programs			Women's programs		
	Generated revenues	Expenses	Net revenue	Generated revenues	Expenses	Net revenue
Baseball	214,000	924,700	(694,900)	N/A	N/A	N/A
Basketball	3,980,800	3,058,500	1,576,200	182,600	1,495,900	(1,276,100)
Crew	N/A	N/A	N/A	50,900	884,500	(785,400)
Equestrian	N/A	N/A	N/A	29,300	607,400	(523,800)
Fencing	21,800	121,300	(148,700)	30,105	188,900	(180,600)
Field hockey	N/A	N/A	N/A	48,780	670,800	(600,700)
Football	10,616,700	8,535,300	5,347,800	N/A	N/A	N/A
Golf	57,400	300,600	(222,500)	38,500	340,000	(270,400)
Gymnastics	42,000	472,400	(385,400)	58,100	667,200	(606,500)
Ice hockey	689,700	1,672,700	(90,200)	51,700	937,500	(942,100)
Lacrosse	332,400	902,700	(571,000)	66,000	703,000	(610,900)
Rifle	0	25,600	(25,300)	0	33,400	(78,200)
Skiing	19,400	247,700	(220,700)	3,600	190,800	(213,500)
Soccer	86,000	569,600	(490,200)	42,700	669,500	(578,300)
Softball	N/A	N/A	N/A	40,900	654,800	(622,500)
Swimming	54,800	546,300	(498,800)	37,400	620,300	(581,600)
Synchronized swimming	N/A	N/A	N/A	17,000	431,600	(575,300)
Tennis	28,300	368,300	(317,500)	21,200	394,600	(372,200)
Track & field/cross country	33,300	584,500	(558,300)	24,600	761,000	(692,200)
Volleyball	172,200	521,400	(357,200)	55,500	728,800	(633,200)
Water polo	121,700	447,200	(291,500)	15,200	482,000	(446,300)
Wrestling	131,000	595,200	(405,800)	N/A	N/A	N/A
Other	193,000	428,100	(352,900)	7,000	78,400	(184,800)

Notes: Revenues are reported excluding all allocated revenues. Expenses are reported excluding third party support. Medians shown represent only those institutions reporting some amount for revenues or expenses.

SOURCE: Daniel L. Fulks, "Table 3.32. Total Generated Revenues and Expenses by Sport, Football Bowl Subdivision, Median Values, Fiscal Year 2006," in *2004–06 NCAA Revenues and Expenses of Division I Intercollegiate Athletics Programs Report*, National Collegiate Athletic Association, March 2008, http://www.ncaapublications.com/Uploads/PDF/NCAA_Revenues_Expenses.pdf798f201d-c82a-4cb3-9b05-e845a3cf24ec.pdf (accessed June 30, 2009)

TABLE 6.12

Sources of revenue, NCAA Division I-FBS, fiscal year 2006

	Public	Private	Total
Total ticket sales	**7,786,000**	**6,587,000**	**7,442,000**
NCAA and conference distributions	4,800,000	5,232,000	4,863,000
Guarantees and options	736,000	920,000	738,000
Cash contributions from alumni and others	6,331,000	5,428,000	5,826,000
Third party support	0	0	0
Other			
Concessions/programs/novelties	668,000	306,000	604,000
Broadcast rights	184,000	91,000	168,000
Royalties/advertising/sponsorship	1,347,000	1,312,000	1,334,000
Sports camps	106,000	35,000	77,000
Endowment/investment income	261,000	1,260,000	387,000
Miscellaneous	594,000	588,000	592,000
Total generated revenues	**23,910,000**	**26,668,000**	**26,432,000**
Allocated revenues			
Direct institutional support	1,883,000	8,305,000	2,118,000
Indirect institutional support	0	2,112,000	0
Student fees	1,743,000	0	1,418,000
Direct government support	0	0	0
Total allocated revenues	**6,538,000**	**12,265,000**	**7,202,000**
Total all revenues	**32,004,000**	**38,715,000**	**35,400,000**

Notes: Generated revenues represent revenues earned by the athletics department and do not include allocated revenues. Allocated revenues include direct institutional support, indirect support, student fees, and governmental support. Total public schools reporting =102; total private schools reporting = 17.
NCAA = National Collegiate Athletic Association.
I-FBS = Division I Football Bowl Subdivision.

SOURCE: Daniel L. Fulks, "Table 3.29. Sources of Revenues, Football Bowl Subdivision, Fiscal Year 2006, Median Values," in *2004–06 NCAA Revenues and Expenses of Division I Intercollegiate Athletics Programs Report*, National Collegiate Athletic Association, March 2008, http://www .ncaapublications.com/Uploads/PDF/NCAA_Revenues_Expenses .pdf798f201d-c82a-4cb3-9b05-e845a3cf24ec.pdf (accessed June 30, 2009)

TABLE 6.13

Summary of NCAA Division I recruiting rules, 2008–09

Recruiting method	Men's basketball	Women's basketball	Football	Other sports
Sophomore year				
Recruiting materials	You may receive brochures for camps and questionnaires. You may begin receiving recruiting materials June 15 after your sophomore year.	You may receive brochures for camps and questionnaires.	You may receive brochures for camps and questionnaires.	You may receive brochures for camps and questionnaires.
Telephone calls	You may make calls to coach at your expense. College may accept collect calls from you at end of your sophomore year. College coach cannot call you.	You may make calls to coach at your expense only. College coach cannot call you.	You may make calls to coach at your expense only. College coach cannot call you.	You may make calls to coach at your expense only. College coach cannot call you. Women's ice hockey—If you are an international prospect, a college coach may call you once in July after sophomore year.
Off-campus contact	None allowed.	None allowed.	None allowed.	None allowed.
Official visit	None allowed.	None allowed.	None allowed.	None allowed.
Unofficial visit	You may make an unlimited number of unofficial visits.	You may make an unlimited number of unofficial visits.	You may make an unlimited number of unofficial visits.	You may make an unlimited number of unofficial visits.
Junior year				
Recruiting materials	Allowed. You may begin receiving recruiting materials June 15 after your sophomore year.	You may begin receiving September 1 of a junior year.	You may begin receiving September 1 of junior year.	You may begin receiving September 1 of junior year. Men's ice hockey—You may begin receiving recruiting materials June 15 after your sophomore year.
Telephone calls	You may make calls to the coach at your expense.	You may make calls to the coach at your expense.	You may make calls to the coach at your expense.	You may make calls to the coach at your expense.
College coaches may call you	Once per month beginning June 15, before your junior year, through July 31 after your junior year.	Once per month in April, May and June 1–20. Once between June 21 and June 30 after your junior year. Three times in July after your junior year (max. of one call per week).	Once from April 15 to May 31 of your junior year.	Once per week starting July 1 after your junior year. Men's ice hockey—Once per month beginning June 15, before your junior year, through July 31 after your junior year.
Off-campus contact	None allowed.	None allowed.	None allowed.	Allowed starting July 1 after your junior year. For gymnastics—allowed after July 15 after your junior year.
Official visit	None allowed.	None allowed.	None allowed.	None allowed.
Unofficial visit	You may make an unlimited number of unofficial visits.	You may make an unlimited number of unofficial visits.	You may make an unlimited number of unofficial visits.	You may make an unlimited number of unofficial visits.

TABLE 6.13

Summary of NCAA Division I recruiting rules, 2008–09 [CONTINUED]

Recruiting method	Men's basketball	Women's basketball	Football	Other sports
Senior year				
Recruiting materials	Allowed.	Allowed.	Allowed.	Allowed.
Telephone calls	You may make calls to the coach at your expense.	You may make calls to the coach at your expense.	You may make calls to the coach at your expense.	You may make calls to the coach at your expense.
College coaches may call you	Twice per week beginning August 1.	Once per week beginning August 1.	Once per week beginning September 1.	Once per week beginning July 1. Men's ice hockey—Once per week beginning August 1.
Off-campus contact	Allowed beginning September 9.	Allowed beginning September 16.	Allowed beginning November 30.	Allowed.
Official visit	Allowed beginning opening day of classes your senior year. You are limited to one official visit per college up to a maximum of five official visits to Divisions I and II colleges.	Allowed beginning opening day of classes your senior year. You are limited to one official visit per college up to a maximum of five official visits to Divisions I and II colleges.	Allowed beginning opening day of classes your senior year. You are limited to one official visit per college up to a maximum of five official visits to Divisions I and II colleges.	Allowed beginning opening day of classes your senior year. You are limited to one official visit per college up to a maximum of five official visits to Divisions I and II colleges.
Unofficial visit	You may make an unlimited number of unofficial visits.	You may make an unlimited number of unofficial visits.	You may make an unlimited number of unofficial visits.	You may make an unlimited number of unofficial visits.
Evaluation and contacts	Up to seven times during your senior year.	Up to five times during your senior year.	Up to six times during your senior year.	Up to seven times during your senior year.
How often can a coach see me or talk to me off the college's campus?	A college coach may contact you or your parents/legal guardians not more than three times during your senior year.	A college coach may contact you or your parents/legal guardians not more than three times during your senior year.	A college coach may contact you or your parents/legal guardians (including evaluating you off the college's campus), six times. One evaluation during September, October and November.	A college coach may contact you or your parents/legal guardians not more than three times during your senior year.

SOURCE: "Summary of Recruiting Rules for Each Sport—Division I," in *2008–09 Guide for the College-Bound Student–Athlete*, National Collegiate Athletic Association, 2008, http://www.ncaapublications.com/Uploads/PDF/2008-09%20CBSA9c29e699-00f6-48ba-98a9-6456c9b98957.pdf (accessed June 30, 2009).

TABLE 6.14

High school students engaged in organized physical activity, by sex, race, and Hispanic origin, 2005

[In percent. For students in grades 9 to 12. Based on the Youth Risk Behavior Survey, a school-based survey and subject to sampling error.]

	Met currently recommended levels of physical activity[a]	Met previously recommended levels of physical activity[b]	No vigorous or moderate physical activity[c]	Enrolled in physical education class			Played on a sports team	Watched three or more hours/day of TV
				Total	Attended daily	Exercised 20 minutes or more per class[d]		
Characteristic	Percent	Percent	Percent	Percent	Percent	Percent	Percent	Percent
All students	**35.8**	**68.7**	**9.6**	**54.2**	**33.0**	**84.0**	**56.0**	**37.2**
Male	43.8	75.8	7.9	60.0	37.1	87.2	61.8	38.0
Grade 9	42.8	78.4	7.2	72.8	46.5	86.3	64.7	42.4
Grade 10	46.8	77.8	7.5	65.4	39.0	88.0	63.4	42.7
Grade 11	43.8	74.2	8.4	51.1	33.5	87.5	61.0	34.1
Grade 12	41.9	71.9	8.4	45.9	26.1	87.3	57.3	30.3
Female	27.8	61.5	11.3	48.3	29.0	80.3	50.2	36.3
Grade 9	30.8	68.4	8.2	70.3	43.1	80.3	56.1	42.4
Grade 10	30.0	63.0	10.3	53.0	31.5	81.0	52.3	37.4
Grade 11	25.1	60.7	12.4	32.9	19.4	79.5	48.9	31.7
Grade 12	24.0	51.7	15.2	32.0	18.8	79.7	41.3	32.4
White, non-Hispanic	38.7	70.2	8.1	52.1	31.7	86.3	57.8	29.2
Male	46.9	77.0	6.9	58.1	36.7	89.3	61.5	30.2
Female	30.2	63.3	9.3	46.1	26.6	82.5	53.9	28.1
Black, non-Hispanic	29.5	62.0	14.4	55.8	34.4	78.7	53.7	64.1
Male	38.2	71.7	10.2	61.7	37.5	83.8	64.6	63.5
Female	21.3	53.1	18.2	50.5	31.6	73.1	43.6	64.5
Hispanic	32.9	69.4	10.6	61.5	38.3	81.6	53.0	45.8
Male	39.0	76.0	8.9	65.9	38.1	85.0	62.0	45.8
Female	26.5	62.6	12.3	57.1	38.6	77.5	43.8	45.8

[a]Were physically active doing any kind of physical activity that increased their heart rate and made them breathe hard some of the time for a total of at least 60 minutes/day for at least 5 or more days out of the 7 days preceding the survey.
[b]Participated in at least 20 minutes of vigorous physical activity on at least 3 or more days of the 7 days preceding the survey and/or at least 30 minutes of moderate physical activity (physical activity that did not make them sweat or breathe hard) on at least 5 or more days of the 7 days preceding the survey.
[c]During the 7 days preceding the survey.
[d]For students enrolled in physical education classes.

SOURCE: "Table 205. High School Students Engaged in Organized Physical Activity by Sex, Race, and Hispanic Origin: 2005," in *Statistical Abstract of the United States: 2009*, 128th ed., U.S. Census Bureau, 2008, http://www.census.gov/compendia/statab/cats/health_nutrition.html (accessed June 30, 2009)

TABLE 6.15

Participation in high school athletic programs, by sex, 1971–72 to 2008–09

Year	Boys participants	Girls participants	Total
1971–72	3,666,917	294,015	3,960,932
1972–73	3,770,621	817,073	4,587,694
1973–74	4,070,125	1,300,169	5,370,294
1975–76	4,109,021	1,645,039	5,754,060
1977–78	4,367,442	2,083,040	6,450,482
1978–79	3,709,512	1,854,400	5,563,912
1979–80	3,517,829	1,750,264	5,268,093
1980–81	3,503,124	1,853,789	5,356,913
1981–82	3,409,081	1,810,671	5,219,752
1982–83	3,355,558	1,779,972	5,135,530
1983–84	3,303,599	1,747,346	5,050,945
1984–85	3,354,284	1,757,884	5,112,168
1985–86	3,344,275	1,807,121	5,151,396
1986–87	3,364,082	1,836,356	5,200,438
1987–88	3,425,777	1,849,684	5,275,461
1988–89	3,416,844	1,839,352	5,256,196
1989–90	3,398,192	1,858,659	5,256,851
1990–91	3,406,355	1,892,316	5,298,671
1991–92	3,429,853	1,940,801	5,370,654
1992–93	3,416,389	1,997,489	5,413,878
1993–94	3,472,967	2,130,315	5,603,282
1994–95	3,536,359	2,240,461	5,776,820
1995–96	3,634,052	2,367,936	6,001,988
1996–97	3,706,225	2,474,043	6,180,268
1997–98	3,763,120	2,570,333	6,333,453
1998–99	3,832,352	2,652,726	6,485,078
1999–00	3,861,749	2,675,874	6,537,623
2000–01	3,921,069	2,784,154	6,705,223
2001–02	3,960,517	2,806,998	6,767,515
2002–03	3,988,738	2,856,358	6,845,096
2003–04	4,038,253	2,865,299	6,903,552
2004–05	4,110,319	2,908,390	7,018,709
2005–06	4,206,549	2,953,355	7,159,904
2006–07	4,321,103	3,021,807	7,342,910
2007–08	4,372,115	3,057,266	7,429,381
2008–09	4,422,662	3,114,091	7,536,753

SOURCE: "Athletic Participation Survey Totals," in *2007–08 High School Athletics Participation Survey*, National Federation of State High School Associations, 2008, http://www.nfhs.org/WorkArea/linkit.aspx?Link Identifier=id&ItemID=3506 (accessed September 17, 2009)

TABLE 6.16

Most popular high school sports for boys, by number of schools and number of participants, 2008–09

Ten most popular boys programs

	Schools			Participants	
1.	Basketball	17,869	1.	Football—11-player	1,112,303
2.	Track and field—outdoor	15,936	2.	Track and field—outdoor	558,007
3.	Baseball	15,699	3.	Basketball	545,145
4.	Football—11-player	14,105	4.	Baseball	473,184
5.	Cross country	13,647	5.	Soccer	383,824
6.	Golf	13,543	6.	Wrestling	267,378
7.	Soccer	11,139	7.	Cross country	231,452
8.	Wrestling	10,254	8.	Tennis	157,165
9.	Tennis	9,499	9.	Golf	157,062
10.	Swimming and diving	6,556	10.	Swimming and diving	130,182

SOURCE: "Ten Most Popular Boys Programs," in *2008–09 High School Athletics Participation Survey*, National Federation of State High School Associations, 2009, http://www.nfhs.org/WorkArea/linkit.aspx?LinkIdentifier =id&ItemID=3506 (accessed September 17, 2009)

TABLE 6.17

Most popular high school sports for girls, by number of schools and number of participants, 2008–09

Ten most popular girls programs

	Schools			Participants	
1.	Basketball	17,582	1.	Track and field—outdoor	457,732
2.	Track and field—outdoor	15,864	2.	Basketball	444,809
3.	Softball—fast pitch	15,172	3.	Volleyball	404,243
4.	Volleyball	15,069	4.	Softball—fast pitch	368,921
5.	Cross country	13,457	5.	Soccer	344,534
6.	Soccer	10,548	6.	Cross country	198,199
7.	Tennis	9,693	7.	Tennis	177,593
8.	Golf	9,344	8.	Swimming and diving	158,878
9.	Swimming and diving	6,902	9.	Competitive spirit squads	117,793
10.	Competitive spirit squads	4,748	10.	Golf	69,223

SOURCE: "Ten Most Popular Girls Programs," in *2008–09 High School Athletics Participation Survey*, National Federation of State High School Associations, 2009, http://www.nfhs.org/WorkArea/linkit.aspx?LinkIdentifier =id&ItemID=3506 (accessed September 17, 2009)

TABLE 6.18

Participation in school athletics, 1991–2006

	1991	1992	1993	1994	1995	1996	1997	1998	1999	2000	2001	2002	2003	2004	2005	2006
Eighth grade	**69.6**	**67.3**	**66.6**	**66.5**	**68.1**	**67.4**	**66.7**	**68.7**	**67.7**	**67.3**	**69.1**	**67.2**	**65.3**	**65.7**	**64.1**	**63.4**
Gender																
Male	73.4	71.0	71.1	70.2	72.5	69.8	68.0	71.7	69.0	69.2	70.8	68.3	68.0	66.6	66.0	65.4
Female	66.2	64.0	62.7	63.2	64.3	65.6	65.5	65.8	66.6	65.8	67.5	66.1	62.9	64.9	62.6	62.0
Race																
White	71.1	68.7	70.0	69.8	69.5	70.7	70.1	71.2	70.0	70.2	72.6	71.9	67.5	68.0	67.4	66.1
Black	73.8	68.4	61.8	62.4	69.7	64.5	63.0	64.9	69.5	63.4	67.3	65.9	67.2	64.5	60.6	60.5
Parental education*																
Less than high school	54.3	47.7	49.9	51.0	50.5	53.4	52.3	53.0	55.0	47.5	53.3	55.5	51.3	48.8	45.3	46.7
Completed high school	66.1	63.7	62.5	63.9	64.8	64.2	61.5	63.0	63.3	64.3	64.1	63.0	64.4	58.1	57.9	58.8
Some college	73.3	67.6	69.7	69.5	73.8	69.4	70.5	70.2	69.6	69.8	69.1	66.8	65.0	67.0	63.8	66.0
Completed college	73.6	75.5	72.7	72.3	71.3	75.3	71.6	74.0	74.1	74.0	77.0	72.5	69.7	74.0	72.9	69.8
Graduate school	76.6	76.7	76.3	74.4	74.9	77.7	74.8	76.6	75.4	75.8	78.7	76.9	76.2	74.8	76.5	73.2
College plans																
None or under 4 years	49.9	46.9	47.9	51.0	51.3	50.5	50.2	49.4	46.8	46.8	46.5	49.0	41.4	45.7	39.3	43.8
Complete four years	72.7	70.4	69.0	68.7	70.3	70.0	68.9	70.9	70.2	69.5	71.6	68.7	67.8	67.9	66.8	65.4
Tenth grade	**60.2**	**62.9**	**62.0**	**61.8**	**62.6**	**61.5**	**61.7**	**61.6**	**62.2**	**61.5**	**62.9**	**61.1**	**60.2**	**61.1**	**60.4**	**62.7**
Gender																
Male	68.7	69.8	68.0	69.2	68.2	65.5	66.0	67.8	68.1	65.5	66.3	64.3	63.4	65.5	65.5	67.4
Female	51.9	56.6	56.5	54.9	57.5	57.7	57.5	56.1	57.4	58.3	60.0	57.8	57.0	57.2	55.6	58.3
Race																
White	61.8	64.6	64.1	64.0	63.6	63.5	63.3	63.6	65.4	63.8	65.2	62.8	62.8	64.3	63.3	65.6
Black	55.7	62.8	59.9	57.2	62.3	56.5	62.5	58.8	57.2	55.7	60.9	64.8	58.5	57.0	59.1	56.5
Parental education*																
Less than high school	44.5	40.1	42.5	42.7	40.9	42.7	44.2	46.7	44.0	45.9	48.3	40.2	44.0	42.0	42.9	43.1
Completed high school	54.4	56.8	58.2	53.2	54.3	53.7	56.3	53.6	54.0	51.7	56.5	54.7	50.9	54.2	53.5	52.5
Some college	59.8	63.6	62.9	62.0	62.6	62.4	60.5	64.7	65.2	61.4	63.0	60.9	61.8	60.8	59.6	62.2
Completed college	67.2	72.6	67.3	70.3	71.8	68.3	68.8	68.1	70.0	69.9	68.9	70.6	66.4	67.7	66.8	70.9
Graduate school	70.9	74.6	75.1	74.0	74.9	73.5	72.7	72.9	71.9	75.9	75.5	72.0	74.4	73.0	72.5	74.4
College plans																
None or under 4 years	38.9	42.7	41.3	39.9	39.9	40.3	42.0	45.5	39.0	39.4	41.1	37.5	40.6	38.6	37.6	38.8
Complete four years	64.6	66.9	66.0	66.5	66.2	65.1	64.8	64.4	66.0	65.0	66.4	64.9	63.1	64.0	63.4	65.7
Twelfth grade	**56.2**	**55.6**	**55.7**	**56.3**	**55.1**	**55.1**	**55.5**	**55.9**	**54.3**	**55.0**	**55.0**	**54.0**	**53.3**	**54.8**	**56.3**	**54.3**
Gender																
Male	64.9	63.8	65.5	66.1	62.4	62.7	63.4	63.0	62.3	64.2	61.9	60.2	58.9	59.5	61.7	58.7
Female	47.0	48.0	46.2	47.5	48.1	48.0	48.4	48.7	47.3	46.9	48.6	48.7	48.0	51.3	51.0	50.1
Race																
White	57.0	57.3	56.7	57.7	54.9	56.8	56.3	57.7	56.5	57.4	57.5	56.3	55.4	56.5	56.9	55.4
Black	56.2	50.9	52.9	59.7	56.7	53.1	52.9	54.1	50.1	55.4	57.9	48.4	50.5	53.2	64.1	59.2
Parental education*																
Less than high school	41.3	46.7	44.4	41.7	38.7	35.3	37.2	41.3	43.5	33.2	38.0	39.7	42.6	41.9	45.2	48.4
Completed high school	50.3	49.1	52.8	51.2	48.4	50.1	50.2	52.5	49.5	53.5	50.1	47.0	49.1	48.5	52.7	49.7
Some college	60.3	54.9	55.8	57.1	53.2	54.3	55.5	57.4	54.6	56.8	56.1	53.3	51.5	55.0	55.6	52.3
Completed college	61.7	63.8	60.8	61.8	62.2	62.1	60.6	59.1	57.3	58.6	62.1	62.1	57.8	60.8	59.6	58.9
Graduate school	66.4	67.5	66.4	68.4	68.0	64.6	66.7	66.2	65.8	63.0	63.5	62.6	66.7	63.8	63.4	64.0
College plans																
None or under 4 years	42.6	41.0	40.0	44.0	41.2	41.6	39.8	42.2	43.3	42.0	40.7	41.6	40.9	40.2	43.6	44.0
Complete four years	61.5	60.7	60.4	60.0	58.8	59.0	60.3	59.9	57.8	58.4	58.8	57.7	56.2	58.8	59.0	56.8

*Parental educaton is calcuated by the Institute of Social Research as the average of the mother's and father's education. Child Trends has relabeled these results to reflect the education level of the most educated parent. In those circumstances where the gap between mothers' and fathers' education is more than one level, this results in an underestimate of the most educated parent's education level.

SOURCE: "Table 1. Participation in School Athletics, 1991–2006," in *Participation in School Athletics*, Child Trends, November 2008, http://www .childtrendsdatabank.org/pdf/37_PDF.pdf (accessed June 30, 2009)

FIGURE 6.14

Percentage of students who participated in school athletics, by gender, 1991 and 2006

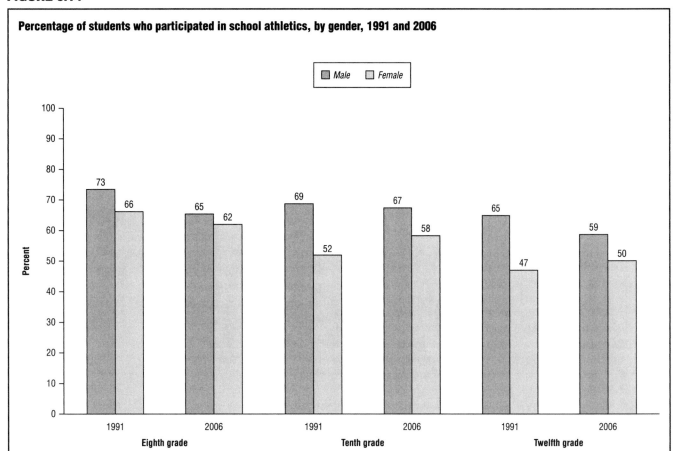

Note: Participation in school athletics includes all students who have participated to any degree in school athletic teams during the current school year.

SOURCE: "Figure 1. Percentage of Students in Grades 8, 10, and 12 Who Participate in School Athletics, by Gender, 1991 and 2006," in *Participation in School Athletics*, Child Trends, November 2008, http://www.childtrendsdatabank.org/pdf/37_PDF.pdf (accessed June 30, 2009)

FIGURE 6.15

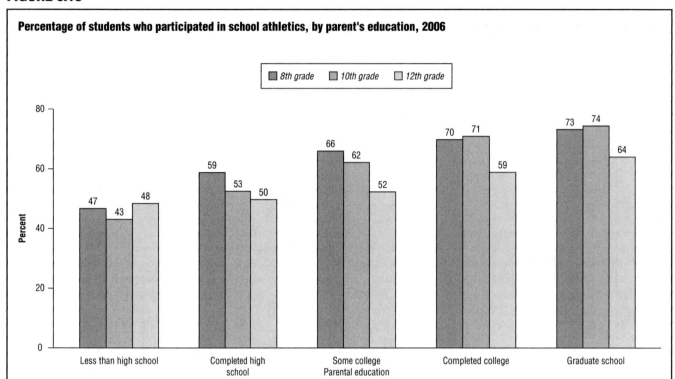

Percentage of students who participated in school athletics, by parent's education, 2006

Notes: Participation in school athletics includes all students who have participated to any degree in school athletic teams during the current school year. Parental education is calculated by the Institute of Social Research as the average of the mother's and father's education. Child Trends has relabeled these results to reflect the education level of the most educated parent. In those circumstances where the gap between mothers' and fathers' education is more than one level, this results in an underestimate of the most educated parent's education level.

SOURCE: "Figure 2. Percentage of Students in Grades 8, 10, and 12 Who Participate in School Athletics, by Parent's Education, 2006," in *Participation in School Athletics*, Child Trends, November 2008, http://www.childtrendsdatabank.org/pdf/37_PDF.pdf (accessed June 30, 2009)

CHAPTER 7

THE OLYMPICS

If professional team sports in the United States epitomize the corporatization of athletics, the Olympics, at least in theory, exemplify the opposite: global goodwill and celebration that surround the pursuit of athletic excellence for its own sake. This does not, however, diminish the fact that vast sums of money change hands via the Olympics. Nor does it prevent the pursuit of these vast sums, or political grandstanding, from sometimes overshadowing the Olympic ideal.

The XXIX Summer Olympiad took place over 17 days in August 2008 in Beijing, China. According to the official Web site of the Beijing 2008 summer games (http://en.beijing2008.cn/live/pressconference/mpc/n214494667.shtml), 11,028 athletes from 204 countries competed in those games, which comprised 28 sports. Medals were awarded in 302 events, one more than at the 2004 Olympics in Athens, Greece. Eight of the gold medals were awarded to American swimmer Michael Phelps—setting an all-time record—who delivered perhaps the greatest Olympic performance ever. The list of sports for the 2012 summer games, to be held in London, England, will be the same as in 2008, with the exception of baseball and softball, which have been dropped from the games. Table 7.1 shows the list of summer Olympic sports, minus baseball and softball, from the 2008 games. In October 2009 the International Olympic Committee (IOC) approved two sports to replace baseball and softball: Golf and rugby will be added starting with the 2016 summer games.

The winter Olympic Games are much smaller than the summer games. The IOC (2007, http://www.olympic.org/uk/games/past/index_uk.asp?OLGT=2&OLGY=2006) notes that the 2006 Winter Olympics in Turin, Italy, featured 2,508 athletes from 80 countries, competing in 7 sports that encompassed 84 events. Table 7.2 shows the list of winter Olympic sports as of the 2010 games.

The IOC regularly reviews which sports are to be included in the Olympic Games. A number of factors are taken into consideration, most prominently popularity and cost. For example, beach volleyball made its Olympic debut in 1996, snowboarding was added to the winter games program in 1998, and, as mentioned previously, baseball and softball have been eliminated, starting with the 2012 games. The Olympic Charter limits the number of sports that can take place at the Olympics; therefore, sports must be cut to accommodate the addition of new ones. In "Olympic Sports of the Past" (2009, http://www.olympic.org/uk/sports/past/index_uk.asp), the IOC notes that sports have come and gone from the lineup over the decades, including tug-of-war (1900–20), golf (1900–04), rugby (1900, 1908, and 1920–24), and polo (1900, 1908, 1920–24, and 1936). For the 2008 summer games, women's boxing was eliminated, while open-water swimming and women's steeplechase were added.

Before the 1996 games the Olympics sometimes included demonstration sports, the purpose of which was to showcase an emerging or locally popular sport before a global audience. Winners in these sports were not officially recognized as Olympic champions. Some of these sports, such as flat-water canoeing and kayaking, were later added as regular Olympic events at subsequent games. Winter sports that have been demonstrated include speed skiing, curling, and freestyle aerial skiing.

HISTORY OF THE OLYMPICS

In "The Ancient Olympic Games, 776 B.C.–393 A.D." (2009, http://www.olympic.org/uk/games/ancient/index_uk.asp), the IOC explains that the roots of the Olympic Games are in ancient Greece. Exactly when the ancient Olympics started is unknown, but the first recorded games took place in the city of Olympia in 776 BC. The games grew in importance over the next few centuries, reaching their peak in the fifth and sixth centuries BC. By that time, they had grown from a single event—a 200-yard foot race called the

TABLE 7.1

Summer Olympic sports

Aquatics	Hockey
Archery	Judo
Athletics	Modern pentathlon
Badminton	Rowing
Basketball	Sailing
Boxing	Shooting
Canoe/kayak	Table tennis
Cycling	Taekwondo
Equestrian	Tennis
Fencing	Triathlon
Football	Volleyball
Gymnastics	Weightlifting
Handball	Wrestling

SOURCE: Created by Robert Jacobson for Gale, 2009

TABLE 7.2

Winter Olympic sports

Biathlon
Bobsleigh
Curling
Ice hockey
Luge
Skating
Skiing

SOURCE: Created by Robert Jacobson for Gale, 2009

TABLE 7.3

Summer Olympic games sites

1896–Athens, Greece
1900–Paris, France
1904–St. Louis, United States
1908–London, United Kingdom
1912–Stockholm, Sweden
1920–Antwerp, Belgium
1924–Paris, France
1928–Amsterdam, Netherlands
1932–Los Angeles, United States
1936–Berlin, Germany
1948–London, United Kingdom
1952–Helsinki, Finland
1956–Melbourne, Australia
1960–Rome, Italy
1964–Tokyo, Japan
1968–Mexico City, Mexico
1972–Munich, West Germany
1976–Montreal, Canada
1980–Moscow, U.S.S.R.
1984–Los Angeles, United States
1988–Seoul, South Korea
1992–Barcelona, Spain
1996–Atlanta, United States
2000–Sydney, Australia
2004–Athens, Greece
2008–Beijing, China
2012–London, United Kingdom

SOURCE: Created by Robert Jacobson for Gale, 2009

stadion—to 20 events spread over several days. Like today, the Greek Olympic games were held every four years.

As the Roman Empire rose to power in the region and subsequently adopted Christianity as its official religion, the Olympic games declined in stature. The games, which had always been a religious as much as an athletic celebration, were eventually outlawed in AD 393 by the emperor Theodosius (c. 346–395).

Interest in the Olympics was revived in the mid-19th century, when modern archaeologists began to unearth the ruins of ancient Olympia. In 1890 the French historian and educator Pierre de Coubertin (1862–1937) developed the idea of holding an international competition of young athletes as a way to promote peace and cooperation among nations. He presented his ideas at the Sorbonne University in Paris in 1894, and two years later the first modern Olympic Games were held in Athens, Greece.

According to the IOC in "Athens 1896" (2009, http://www.olympic.org/uk/games/past/index_uk.asp?OLGT=1&OLGY=1896), the inaugural Olympic Games of 1896 featured 241 athletes from 14 countries competing in 43 events—the largest international sporting event ever held up to that time. The event was repeated in Paris in 1900 and again in St. Louis, Missouri, in 1904. (See Table 7.3.)

Winter Olympics History

By 1908, movement toward establishing a winter version of the Olympics had begun. That year, figure skating was introduced during the summer games in London. A cluster of winter events was scheduled to be added for 1916, but the games were canceled because of the outbreak of World War I (1914–1918). When the Olympics resumed in 1920, they included figure skating and ice hockey as medal events. In "Participation in Winter Olympics: A Sluggish Start" (http://multimedia.olympic.org/pdf/en_report_662.pdf), the IOC indicates that over the objections of Coubertin and the organizers of an Olympic-style Scandinavian winter competition that had been held periodically since 1901, the committee approved an 11-day International Winter Sports Week that featured Nordic skiing, speed skating, figure skating, hockey, and bobsledding in Chamonix, France, in 1924. These games were a success and were retroactively dubbed the first Winter Olympics by the IOC in 1926. The winter games took place during regular Olympic years until 1992. Beginning with the 1994 games in Lillehammer, Norway, the winter games have been held every four years, alternating with the summer games. Table 7.4 shows the sites at which all the Winter Olympics have been held.

Politics and the Olympics

Coubertin's dream of a world made more peaceful through sport did not materialize. Moreover, wars and other political complications crippled the Olympic movement at

TABLE 7.4

Winter Olympic games sites

1924–Chamonix, France
1928–St. Moritz, Switzerland
1932–Lake Placid, New York, United States
1936–Garmisch-Partenkirchen, Germany
1948–St. Moritz, Switzerland
1952–Oslo, Norway
1956–Cortina d'Ampezzo, Italy
1960–Squaw Valley, California, United States
1964–Innsbruck, Austria
1968–Grenoble, France
1972–Sapporo, Japan
1976–Innsbruck, Austria
1980–Lake Placid, New York, United States
1984–Sarajevo, Yugoslavia (now Bosnia and Herzegovina)
1988–Calgary, Alberta, Canada
1992–Albertville, France
1994–Lillehammer, Norway
1998–Nagano, Japan
2002–Salt Lake City, Utah, United States
2006–Torino (Turin), Italy
2010–Vancouver, Canada
2014–Sochi, Russia

SOURCE: Created by Robert Jacobson for Gale, 2009

several points during the 20th century. The 1916 games were a casualty of World War I, and World War II (1939–1945) claimed the 1940 and 1944 Olympics.

Twice the Olympics have been the scene of violent acts of terrorism. At the 1972 summer games in Munich, West Germany, members of the Palestinian terrorist group Black September took members of the Israeli team hostage on September 5. A rescue attempt was unsuccessful, and by the end of the ordeal the militants had killed 11 Israeli athletes and coaches, as well as a West German police officer. Five of the eight terrorists were also killed. During the crisis Mark Spitz, a Jewish American swimmer who had finished his events after winning a then record seven gold medals, was evacuated out of fear he was a target for the terrorists. In the aftermath of the attack, the games were temporarily suspended, and a large memorial ceremony was held in the Olympic stadium. While consideration had been given to halting the games altogether, competition resumed on September 7.

On July 27, 1996, one person was killed, another died of a heart attack running to the scene, and 111 were injured when a bomb exploded on a crowded Centennial Olympic Park at the 1996 summer games in Atlanta, Georgia. The perpetrator, Eric Robert Rudolph (1966–)— a member of a radical Christian group violently opposed to abortion and homosexuality—was not arrested until 2003. In 2005 he pleaded guilty to the Olympic bombing, as well as a string of other bombings occurring from 1996 until 1998, and was sentenced to four consecutive life sentences without parole.

BOYCOTTS. Even when the Olympics have taken place on schedule, they have sometimes been used to make political statements. Boycotts have been a frequent occurrence. The IOC notes in "Olympic Games" on its Web site (2009, http://www.olympic.org/uk/games/index_uk.asp) that the 1956 games in Melbourne, Australia, were the scene of two different boycotts: by the Netherlands, Spain, and Switzerland in response to the Soviet Union's brutal handling of that year's Hungarian uprising; and by Egypt, Lebanon, and Iraq in protest of British and French involvement in the Suez crisis in the Middle East. Several African nations threatened to boycott the Olympics in 1968, 1972, and 1976, in protest of South African and Rhodesian racial policies. The IOC bowed to this pressure and banned South Africa and Rhodesia from participating in the 1968 and 1972 Olympics. In 1980 and 1984 the two major cold war powers traded boycotts: The United States and 64 other Western nations stayed home from the 1980 Olympics in Moscow in protest of the Soviet invasion of Afghanistan; four years later the Soviet Union and 14 of its allied nations retaliated by boycotting the Los Angeles games of 1984, on the grounds that the American hosts could not guarantee their safety. In 1988 North Korea boycotted the Olympics in South Korea, arguing that the two countries should have been named cohosts.

SCANDAL. In 1998 information was uncovered revealing that several members of the IOC had accepted gifts from the 2002 Salt Lake City Winter Olympics organizing committee in exchange for their site selection votes. Ten IOC members were forced off of the committee as a result, and in the aftermath of the scandal changes were made in the process for selecting host cities. Questions remain whether the reforms have really eliminated the possibility of bribery in the Olympic site selection process. An August 2004 BBC documentary, *Panorama: Buying the Games* (http://news.bbc.co.uk/1/hi/programmes/panorama/3937425.stm), used hidden cameras and journalists posing as agents interested in securing the games for London to reveal that the IOC was still ripe for corruption.

More controversy occurred during the competition at those 2002 winter games. In the pairs figure skating competition, Russia's Elena Berezhnaya (1977–) and Anton Sikharulidze (1976–) received very high marks in spite of a noticeable error. Meanwhile, the Canadian pair of skaters gave a seemingly flawless performance, strong enough to convince the event's announcers that they had earned the gold medal. When the scores were revealed, however, the Russians had earned the gold. There was widespread speculation about the integrity of the scoring. NBC commentator Sandra Bezic was quoted by the Associated Press in "NBC Commentators Surprised, Shocked by Judges" (February 12, 2002, http://sports.espn.go.com/oly/winter02/figure/news?id=1330413) as saying, "My heart breaks, and I'm embarrassed for our sport right now." During a subsequent investigation of the scoring, the French judge said she was pressured to vote for the Russians. The scandal resulted in a second gold medal being awarded to the Canadian pair, and the IOC and International Skating Union decided to declare both pairs as Olympic co-champions. The French judge later recanted her story. New scoring rules, including anonymous judging, were adopted afterward.

A different sort of controversy emerged six years later at the 2008 summer games, when questions arose regarding the ages of some members of the Chinese gymnastics squad. Allegations surfaced that some of the Chinese tumblers were younger than 16, the minimum age dictated by Olympic rules for the sport. The suspicions went beyond the obvious fact that some of the girls, particularly stars He Kexin and Jiang Yuyuan, were very small and had youthful features and body shapes. Jeré Longman and Juliet Macur reported in "Records Say Chinese Gymnasts May Be Under Age" (July 27, 2008, http://www.nytimes.com/2008/07/27/sports/olympics/27gymnasts.html) that information on official Chinese media news Web sites contradicted the girls' passports, which indicated they were 16 years old.

Less controversial but still eyebrow-raising to some is the increase in the number of American athletes competing for other countries at the Olympics. The practice gets little notice when, for example, an American citizen of Mexican decent chooses to play baseball for the Mexican team, as has happened in several cases. Basketball player Becky Hammon (1977–), however, drew considerable criticism when she accepted an invitation to play Olympic basketball for Russia, a country where she has played professionally but with which she has no other connection, and she does not even speak Russian.

STRUCTURE OF THE OLYMPIC MOVEMENT

The Olympics are run by a complex array of organizations known primarily by their initials. At the center of the structure is the IOC, based in Lausanne, Switzerland. The IOC (2009, http://www.olympic.org/uk/organisation/ioc/organisation/index_uk.asp) is the "supreme authority of the Olympic Movement." Its role is to "promote top-level sport as well as sport for all in accordance with the Olympic Charter. It ensures the regular celebration of the Olympic Games and strongly encourages, by appropriate means, the promotion of women in sport, that of sports ethics and the protection of athletes."

According to the IOC (2009, http://www.olympic.org/uk/organisation/if/index_uk.asp), the next layer of Olympic oversight, the International Federations (IFs), coordinates international competition within a particular sport. Track and field, for example, is governed by the International Amateur Athletics Federation. In 2009 there were 26 IFs involved in the summer games and another seven that presided over sports in the winter games. These federations make all the rules that pertain to their

sport and run the world championships and other international competitions within their realm. Each country that competes in a sport at the international level has a national governing body (NGB), which coordinates the sport domestically.

International Olympic Committee

The IOC (2009, http://www.olympic.org/uk/organisation/ioc/index_uk.asp) was created by the International Athletic Congress of Paris on June 23, 1894, convened by Coubertin, who is generally considered the father of the modern Olympic movement. The original committee in 1894 consisted of 14 members plus Coubertin. Coubertin remained at the helm of the IOC through the 1924 Olympics. The IOC was charged with the control and development of the modern Olympic Games. Membership in the IOC is limited to one member from most countries, and two members from the largest and most active member countries, or countries that have hosted the Olympics. Members must speak French or English and be citizens and residents of a country with a recognized national Olympic committee (NOC).

The IOC runs the Olympic movement according to the terms of the Olympic Charter (July 7, 2007, http://multimedia.olympic.org/pdf/en_report_122.pdf). The charter outlines the six Fundamental Principles of Olympism. These principles, as written in the charter, are:

1. Olympism is a philosophy of life, exalting and combining in a balanced whole the qualities of body, will and mind. Blending sport with culture and education, Olympism seeks to create a way of life based on the joy of effort, the educational value of good example and respect for universal fundamental ethical principles.

2. The goal of Olympism is to place sport at the service of the harmonious development of man, with a view to promoting a peaceful society concerned with the preservation of human dignity.

3. The Olympic Movement is the concerted, organised, universal and permanent action, carried out under the supreme authority of the IOC, of all individuals and entities who are inspired by the values of Olympism. It covers the five continents. It reaches its peak with the bringing together of the world's athletes at the great sports festival, the Olympic Games. Its symbol is five interlaced rings.

4. The practice of sport is a human right. Every individual must have the possibility of practising sport, without discrimination of any kind and in the Olympic spirit, which requires mutual understanding with a spirit of friendship, solidarity and fair play. The organisation, administration and management of sport must be controlled by independent sports organizations.

5. Any form of discrimination with regard to a country or a person on grounds of race, religion, politics, gender or otherwise is incompatible with belonging to the Olympic Movement.

6. Belonging to the Olympic Movement requires compliance with the Olympic Charter and recognition by the IOC.

The IOC has a maximum of 115 members, who meet at least once per year. During this session the committee elects a president for a term of eight years (renewable for another four), and an executive board, whose members serve for four years. The IOC (2009, http://www.olympic.org/uk/organisat ion/commissions/index_uk.asp) is administered by a director general, with the assistance of the directors of the IOC's various units, which include International Relations; Coordination Commissions for the Olympic Games; Finance; Marketing; Juridical; Radio and Television; and Medical.

U.S. Olympic Committee

In the United States, building a team to represent the nation at the Olympics is the responsibility of the U.S. Olympic Committee (USOC). The USOC comprises 72 member organizations. Thirty-nine of them are NGBs—such as USA Gymnastics and USA Track and Field—each of which supports a particular sport. Other USOC members include community- and education-based multisport organizations, U.S. Armed Forces sports, and organizations involved in sports for people with disabilities. Besides the Olympics, the USOC is the driving force for U.S. sports that are part of the Pan American Games program. The Pan American Games are an international goodwill sports competition featuring athletes from the Americas; they take place every four years in the year preceding the Olympics. In the United States the NGBs are responsible for selecting the athletes who will represent their country in their sport at the Olympics. In most events this is done at national competitions called Olympic Trials.

Besides its role in developing the U.S. Olympic team, the USOC is instrumental in U.S. cities' bids to host the Winter or Summer Olympics or the Pan American Games. The USOC may vote on and endorse a particular city's bid to serve as host. All U.S. Olympic Trial site selections also go through the USOC. The USOC gets much of its money from the IOC. According to Ray Lilley in "IOC, USOC Reach Deal for Fresh Funding 'Tier,'" (Associated Press, March 30, 2009, http://www.usatoday.com/sports/olymp ics/2009-03-29-2279136950_x.htm), the USOC receives "20 percent of the IOC's top sponsorship program and 12.75 percent of its TV revenues." Lilley notes that while other national committees have complained about the huge share of Olympic revenue that ends up in USOC coffers, USOC officials counter that the majority of the money pumped into the Olympic system comes from American

companies, including the $894 million paid by NBC to televise the Beijing games.

In "The United States Olympic Committee History" (2009, http://www.usoc.org/content/index/1155), the USOC explains that the organization was created as a small, informal organization in 1896 by James E. Sullivan (1860–1914), the founder of the Amateur Athletic Union. The first elected president of the USOC was Albert G. Spalding (1850–1915), a well-known sporting goods manufacturer. The committee became a formal entity, called the American Olympic Association, in 1921. The name was changed twice in the 1940s—to the United States of America Sports Federation in 1940 and to the U.S. Olympic Association (USOA) in 1945. The USOA received its federal charter as a private nonprofit corporation in 1950. The USOC took its current name in 1961.

In 1978 the USOC acquired its status as the legal coordinating body for the Olympic and Pan American Games through the passage of the Amateur Sports Act. The act also recognized the authority of the NGBs to oversee development within their own sports. In addition, the act mandated that 20% of membership and voting power within both the USOC and the sport-specific agencies be held by "recent or active" athletes. That year, the USOC moved its headquarters from New York City to Colorado Springs, Colorado.

As of 2009 the USOC operated three training centers, located in Colorado Springs; Lake Placid, New York; and Chula Vista, California. The USOC also maintains an Olympic Education Center in Marquette, Michigan, where athletes can pursue an academic degree without interrupting their training.

The USOC is a nonprofit organization, but it must constantly monitor its flow of dollars. Unlike most NOCs around the world, the USOC does not receive direct financial support from the government, but it nevertheless manages to provide millions of dollars per year in direct support to athletes, as well as assistance to NGBs. According to Tripp Mickle in "Beijing Olympics a Financial Boon for USOC" (*SportsBusiness Journal*, June 1, 2009, http://www.sportsbusinessjournal.com/article/62665), the USOC spent $71.4 million on athletes and NGBs in 2008.

THE FLOW OF OLYMPIC MONEY

All the symbols, images, phrases, and other intellectual property associated with the Olympics belong to the IOC. In *Marketing Fact File: 2008 Edition* (2009, http://multime dia.olympic.org/pdf/en_report_344.pdf), the IOC explains that the Olympic movement generates marketing revenue through five major channels: broadcasting, the Olympic Partners worldwide sponsorship program, domestic sponsorships, ticketing, and licensing. The IOC manages the first two; the others are managed by the Organizing

Committees for the Olympic Games (OCOGs) within the host country, under the IOC's direction.

As with the major professional sports in the United States, the biggest financial driver of the Olympics is television, with a startling growth in revenue generated through television broadcasts of the Olympics. In *IOC Marketing Media Guide: Beijing 2008* (July 10, 2008, http://www.olympic.org/uk/organisation/commissions/marketing/full_story_uk.asp?id=2633), the IOC reports that for the 2005–08 Olympic cycle, $2.57 billion was generated in broadcasting revenue. Most of that total came from the United States; NBC alone paid $893 million for the rights to broadcast the 2008 Beijing Olympics, according to the *Marketing Fact File*. European networks contributed another $443 million to broadcast the 2008 games. For the Olympic cycle running from 2001 to 2004, worldwide broadcast rights netted the IOC $2.2 billion. Broadcast revenue in the previous quadrennium was $1.8 billion, and the 1993–96 total was $1.3 billion.

The *Marketing Fact File* reports that 49% of the broadcast rights fees for each Olympics is distributed to the OCOGs responsible for that particular Olympics. The OCOGs consist of top officials from the NOC of the host nation and other key representatives of the host city and country. The other half of the broadcast revenue goes to the Olympic movement. Nielsen Media Research reports in "Beijing Games Most-Watched Olympics Ever" (August 25, 2008, http://blog.nielsen.com/nielsenwire/media_entertainment/beijing-games-most-watched-olympics-ever/) that the first 10 days of the Beijing games attracted a cumulative television audience of 4.4 billion viewers, nearly two-thirds of the world population. This was about a half billion more than the number who watched the 2004 Olympics. All told, a record of more than 5,000 hours of live broadcast feed of the 2008 Olympics was offered worldwide, according to *Marketing Report: Beijing 2008* (April 24, 2009, http://www.olympic.org/uk/organisation/commissions/marketing/full_story_uk.asp?id=3003). The Beijing games were also the first fully digital Olympics, with comprehensive coverage available via the Internet and other digital media. More than 6 million Americans watched coverage of the games on their mobile phones. The *Marketing Report: Torino 2006* (2006, http://multimedia.olympic.org/pdf/en_report_1142.pdf) states that the total viewer hours for the 2006 winter games were 10.6 billion.

A second key revenue source is the IOC's corporate sponsorship program, known officially as the Olympic Partners (TOP) program. The *Marketing Fact File* notes that for the 2005–08 cycle, the TOP program consisted of 12 international corporations, which in return for their money are ensured exclusive sponsorship in their business category. For example, as long as Coca-Cola remains a TOP sponsor, Pepsi will not be one. As with broadcast rights, the United States dominates the TOP program;

seven of the TOP sponsors are U.S. based. According to the *Marketing Fact File*, the TOP program brought in $866 million during the 2005–08 quadrennium. For the 2006 Winter Olympics, the *Marketing Report: Torino 2006* states that the sponsorship revenue totaled 269.8 million euros ($372 million at the August 2007 exchange rate).

Ticket sales represent another major source of revenue for the IOC. *Marketing Report: Beijing 2008* indicates that 6.5 million tickets—95.6% of all tickets made available—were sold at the games, at an average price of $23 per ticket. That comes out to $149.5 million in ticket sales. The other major revenue source, the sale of licensed merchandise bearing Olympic logos and other trademarks, including Olympic coins and stamps, generated the remainder of the IOC's revenue. According to the *Marketing Report: Torino 2006*, ticket sales for the 2006 winter games generated 66 million euros ($91 million), and another 16.7 million euros ($23 million) came from licensing revenue.

About 92% of IOC revenue is subsequently distributed to the other organizations that collectively make up the Olympic movement, including: OCOGs, which, as noted earlier, are the committees formed to run the Olympics within the country that has been selected to host the games; NOCs, whose main role within each of the approximately 200 countries in the Olympic family is to field their country's Olympic team; and IFs, which coordinate and monitor international competition within their specific sport or family of sports. The IOC retains only about 8% of its overall revenue. These funds are used to cover the organization's operating and administrative costs.

According to the *Marketing Fact File*, the summer and winter OCOGs for each four-year period share about half of the TOP program revenue and in-kind contributions. Before 2004 the IOC contributed 60% of broadcast revenue for each Olympic Games to the OCOGs; since 2004 it has contributed 40%.

In contrast to the IOC, IFs, NOCs, and NGBs, the OCOGs are temporary agencies. They disband once the games they were created to organize are over. The OCOGs are highly dependent on the IOC for their funding, receiving a substantial share of the IOC's revenue from sponsorships and broadcasting. OCOGs also generate revenue of their own through sponsorship, ticket sales, and licensing of merchandise. Even though the IOC turns over most of its revenue to other organizations, the *Marketing Fact File* notes that the OCOGs give only 5% of the revenue they generate to the IOC and retain the other 95%, most of which is spent on facility rentals and the construction and removal of temporary facilities.

The vast commercial activity that fuels the Olympic flame would seem to conflict with the philosophical groundings of the Olympic movement, which value the noble spirit of competition above financial matters. The Olympic Charter acknowledges this apparent contradiction, and the IOC has implemented policies designed to address it. No advertising is allowed in the venues where events take place, or on the uniforms of athletes, coaches, or officials. The TOP program is designed to generate the maximum amount of support with a minimum number of corporate sponsors, and images of Olympic events are not allowed to be used for commercial purposes.

SELECTION OF OLYMPIC SITES

One of the IOC's chief responsibilities is to select the cities that will host the Olympics. Olympic site selection is a two-phase procedure. The first phase is called Applicant Cities. Applicant cities must be proposed to the IOC by their NOC. They must then complete a questionnaire that outlines how they plan to carry out the monumental task of hosting the games. The IOC assesses the applications with regard to the cities' ability to organize the games. Criteria include technical capacity, government support, public opinion, general infrastructure, security, venues, accommodations, and transportation. The IOC then accepts a handful of these applicants for the next phase, called Candidate Cities.

In the second phase, candidate cities must provide the IOC with a candidature file. These files are analyzed by the IOC Evaluation Commission, which consists of IOC members, representatives of the IFs, NOCs, the IOC Athletes' Commission, the International Paralympics Committee, and other experts. The Evaluation Commission also physically inspects the candidate cities. It then issues a report, on whose basis the IOC Executive Board prepares a list of final candidates. This list is submitted to the IOC session for a vote. The IOC vote to determine the location of the 2016 summer games drew widespread media attention in the fall of 2009 when President Barack Obama (1961–) joined the campaign to promote his hometown of Chicago, which was in the running against Madrid, Spain, Tokyo, Japan, and Rio de Janeiro, Brazil, as an Olympic host city. Obama went so far as to make an appearance at the location of the voting in Copenhagen, Denmark, speaking on behalf of Chicago in efforts to sway the votes of IOC members. His efforts, however, were in vain; Chicago lost by a wide margin in the first of the three rounds of voting, receiving only 18 of 94 votes. Rio de Janeiro was chosen to host the 2016 summer games.

OLYMPIC ATHLETES: PROFESSIONALS OR AMATEURS?

Early on, the Olympics were considered an arena for strictly amateur competition. Professional athletes were not allowed to participate. This led to a number of controversies and disqualifications over the years, the most famous being the disqualification of the 1912 Olympic pentathlon and decathlon champion Jim Thorpe (1888–1953), who was stripped of his gold medals when it was discovered that he had played semiprofessional baseball.

Eventually, the rigid rules regarding professionalism became less practical. Many countries were supporting their athletes financially, allowing them to train full time and making a mockery of their "amateur" status. This put athletes in other countries at a competitive disadvantage. The regulations prohibiting professional athletes from participating in the Olympics were relaxed in the 1980s and eliminated entirely in the 1990s. This change allowed, for example, the development of the U.S. basketball "Dream Team," featuring a number of top National Basketball Association players, and the participation of National Hockey League players on winter Olympics hockey teams.

DOPING

Almost from the beginning, the use of performance-enhancing substances, known as doping, has plagued the Olympics. An early example was Thomas J. Hicks (1875–1963), winner of the 1904 marathon, who was given strychnine and brandy. Doping methods improved over time, sometimes with disastrous results. The Danish cyclist Knut Jensen (1936–1960) died after falling from his bicycle during the 1960 games. He was found to have taken amphetamines. The international sports federations and the IOC banned doping in the 1960s, but for most of the time since then officials have lacked the tools to adequately police the use of illicit substances. The highest-profile Olympic athlete to be disqualified for doping in the 20th century was the Canadian sprinter Ben Johnson (1961–), winner of the 100-meter race in 1988. A few years later, it was revealed that East German sports officials had doped female athletes for years without the IOC's knowledge. As the problem of doping grew out of control in the 1990s, the international sports community responded by forming the World Anti-Doping Agency (WADA) in 1999. WADA oversees the monitoring and enforcing of doping regulations at the Olympics.

WADA's creation did not, however, solve the problem entirely. Athletes in every Olympic Games since its formation have been found to be in violation of antidoping rules. For the 2008 games, new methods were put in place allowing blood samples to be stored for up to eight years, in case new tests were developed in that time. In "Backup Samples Positive for 5 Olympians" (July 8, 2009, http://sportsillustrated.cnn.com/2009/olympics/wires/07/08/2090.ap.oly.beijing.doping/index.html), the Associated Press reports that 15 athletes tested positive for drug-related violations at the Beijing Olympics. Six of the cases were detected months after the close of the Olympics, thanks to newly available tests on preserved samples. The only

American athlete on the list did not actually use a substance herself, rather one was given to the horse she rode in an equestrian event. The last U.S. competitors to test positive for banned substances in their own bodies during actual competition at the Olympics were the shot-putter Bonnie Dasse and the hammer thrower Jud Logan, both in 1992.

Since then, however, it was discovered after the fact that several Americans had been doping during the Olympics and were stripped of their medals or barred from the Olympics. Others, who appeared headed for the Olympics, have come under a cloud of suspicion and have also been barred. In the wake of the BALCO scandal (see Chapter 9 for more information), the sprinter Kelli White received a two-year ban that kept her out of the 2004 Olympics. The sprinter Tim Montgomery (1975–), also implicated in the BALCO affair, failed to qualify for the 2004 games, but in 2005 he received a two-year ban from competing and was stripped of a number of his past medals and results, including a former world-record performance in the 100-meter dash. Perhaps the highest-profile Olympic athlete embroiled in BALCO was the sprinter Marion Jones (1975–). Jones proclaimed her innocence through several years of investigation, but in October 2007 she admitted to having used illegal performance-enhancing drugs during the 2000 Olympics in Sydney, Australia, in which she won three gold medals and two bronze. Facing pressure from the U.S. Olympic Committee, she surrendered her Olympic medals and was retroactively disqualified from all events dating back to September 1, 2000. The IOC banned her from the Beijing Olympics. In 2008 sprinter Antonio Pettigrew (1967–) admitted to using performance-enhancing drugs from 1997 to 2003, a span that included the 2000 Sydney Olympics in which he won a gold medal in the 4x400 relay event. At the time of his confession Pettigrew volunteered to return his medal, as subsequently did teammate Michael Johnson (1967–), claiming he felt sullied by Pettigrew's admission. By August of 2008 the IOC had determined to strip all members of the relay team of their medals. Like with Montgomery and Jones, Pettigrew received a ban from competing and was stripped of a number of his past awards and results.

OTHER OLYMPIC GAMES
Special Olympics

Special Olympics is a global nonprofit organization that provides opportunities for athletic training and competition for people with developmental disabilities. According to the Special Olympics, in "The History of the Special Olympics" (2009, http://www.specialolympics.org/history .aspx), the organization served nearly 3 million athletes in more than 180 countries as of July 2008. Participants may train or compete in any of 30 Olympic-style summer and winter sports.

The Special Olympics movement began in the summer of 1968, when the First International Special Olympics were held at Soldier Field in Chicago, Illinois, home of the National Football Leagues's Chicago Bears. The roots of the Special Olympics go back to 1962, when Eunice Mary Kennedy Shriver (1920–2009), the sister of President John F. Kennedy (1917–1963), started a day camp for developmentally disabled children. In June of that year Shriver invited 35 boys and girls to Camp Shriver at Timberlawn, her home in Rockville, Maryland. Her idea was that children who were cognitively impaired were capable of accomplishing much more than was generally believed at the time, if they were given opportunities to do so. Building on Camp Shriver, Shriver began to actively promote the notion of involving people with disabilities in physical activities and competition. Through the Kennedy Foundation, she targeted grants to universities, community centers, and recreation departments that created such opportunities. The foundation helped fund 11 camps similar to Camp Shriver across the country in 1963. By 1969, 32 camps serving 10,000 children were being supported by the foundation.

In 1967 the Kennedy Foundation worked with the Chicago Park District to organize a citywide track meet for mentally disabled people that was modeled on the Olympics. The first Special Olympics at Soldier Field attracted 1,000 athletes from 26 states and Canada, who competed in track and field, floor hockey, and aquatics.

According to "World Games: List of Special Olympics World Games" (2009, http://info.specialolympics .org/Special+Olympics+Public+Website/English/Compete/ World_Games/List+of+World+Games.htm), by the Fourth International Special Olympics Summer Games, which took place at Central Michigan University in Mt. Pleasant, Michigan, in August 1975, the number of participants had more than tripled, to 3,200, representing 10 countries. The games were broadcast to a nationwide audience on the television show *CBS Sports Spectacular*. The Special Olympics Winter Games were launched two years later, with about 500 athletes competing in skating and skiing events at Steamboat Springs, Colorado. The 10th Special Olympics World Summer Games, held from June to July 1999 in Raleigh-Durham and Chapel Hill, North Carolina, attracted 7,000 athletes from 150 countries. The games featured 19 sports by this time. The 2007 Special Olympics World Summer Games in Shanghai, China (October 2–11, 2007), served about 7,500 athletes from 164 countries. The Special Olympics World Winter Games in February 2009 in Boise, Idaho, drew nearly 2,000 athletes from nearly 100 countries, according to "The History of the Special Olympics." In the first decade of the 21st century, the fastest growth in Special Olympics participation was taking place in Africa, East Asia, the Asian Pacific, and the Middle East.

In 1988 the IOC formally recognized the Special Olympics, signing an agreement proclaiming its support. The Special Olympics also has a formal relationship with the USOC and has been designated as the National Governing Body/Disabled Sports Organization for athletes with intellectual disabilities. The Special Olympics has other relationships, some of them formal, others less so, with the NOCs of many other nations. Furthermore, the Special Olympics has links with the IFs and NGBs that govern individual sports. Competition must be in accordance with the rules of these organizations, except in cases where they conflict with the Special Olympics' own rules; in such instances, Special Olympics rules take precedence.

Paralympics

While the Special Olympics serves people with mental disabilities, athletes with physical disabilities, including mobility limitations, amputees, and people with visual disabilities and cerebral palsy, may compete in the Paralympics. The International Paralympic Committee (IPC; 2009, http://www.paralympic.org/Paralympic_Games/) notes that the concept for the Paralympics grew out of a 1948 event in Stoke Mandeville, England, a competition for World War II veterans with spinal cord injuries. The first Olympic-style competition for people with physical disabilities took place in 1960 in Rome. These became the Paralympic games. The Winter Paralympics were added in 1976.

Unlike the Special Olympics, the Paralympics have always been held in the same year as the Olympic Games. Since the 1988 summer games in Seoul, South Korea, and the 1992 winter games in Albertville, France, the Paralympics have been held in the same venues as well. This arrangement has been cemented in place by an agreement reached with the IOC in 2001. Since the 2002 games in Salt Lake City, both the Olympic and Paralympic games have been set up by the same organizing committee as well. Paralympic athletes live in the same Olympic village with the same food and medical facilities as their Olympic counterparts, and the ticketing, technology, and transportation systems are shared. A total of 3,951 athletes representing 146 countries competed in the 2008 Summer Paralympics in Beijing, China. In the 2006 Winter Paralympics in Turin, 474 athletes competed. There were 58 medal events in the sports of alpine skiing, ice sledge hockey, Nordic skiing, and wheelchair curling. The IPC oversees the Paralympics, performing much the same role as the IOC does for the Olympics. The IPC consists of 160 national Paralympic committees and five disability-specific international sports federations, similar to the IFs that oversee specific Olympic sports. The national Paralympics organization for the United States is U.S. Paralympics, which is a division of the USOC.

Deaflympics

Besides the Special Olympics and the Paralympics, the IOC also sanctions the Deaflympics, which have existed since 1924—almost as long as the Olympics themselves. The first Deaflympics, organized by the International Committee of Sports for the Deaf (ICSD; 2009, http://www.deaflympics.com/about/), were held in Paris that year. The winter games were added in 1949.

According to the ICSD (2009, http://www.deaflympics.com/games/index.asp?GamesID=35), 2,045 deaf athletes from 63 countries participated in the 20th Summer Games, held in Melbourne, Australia, in January 2005. The 21st Summer Games took place in September 2009 in Taipei, Taiwan. According to the Web site of the Taipei games (2009, http://english.2009deaflympics.org/files/13-1027-2799.php), 3,959 athletes from 81 nations registered with the ICSD for the competition. The 16th Winter Games, held in Salt Lake City in 2007, hosted 298 athletes from 23 different nations. The 17th Winter Games are expected to take place in High Tatras, Slovakia, in 2011. The ICSD (2009, http://www.deaflympics.com/athletes/?ID=239) explains that athletes must have a hearing loss of at least 55 decibels in their better ear to qualify for the Deaflympics. To ensure a level playing field, hearing aids, cochlear implants, and other devices that augment hearing are not used during the competition.

CHAPTER 8
SPORTS AND HEALTH

Sport is a preserver of health.

—Hippocrates (460?–377? BC)

The truth of Hippocrates' assertion has been nearly universally accepted for centuries, but only since the 20th century have researchers worked to quantify the impact of physical activity, or the lack thereof, on physical and mental well-being. In *Focus Area 22: Physical Activity and Fitness Progress Review* (April 14, 2004, http://www.cdc .gov/nchs/ppt/hpdata2010/focusareas/fa22_progress_review .ppt), the Centers for Disease Control and Prevention (CDC) reports that about 1.2 million, or 48%, of the nation's 2.4 million deaths in 2000 were preventable; and of those preventable deaths, 400,000, or 17%, were due to poor diet and physical activity.

Hippocrates may not have appreciated as fully the other side of the sports-health nexus. As sports become a bigger business and as the pressure to perform becomes increasingly intense, greater attention is being given to the potential negative health impact of sports participation, especially on children and youth.

BENEFITS OF PHYSICAL ACTIVITY

Focus Area 22 is a component of a broader initiative called Healthy People 2010 (http://www.healthypeople.gov/). A presentation associated with a progress report on *Focus Area 22* prepared by Richard J. Klein (June 26, 2008, http:// www.cdc.gov/nchs/about/otheract/hpdata2010/focusareas/fa _22_2_ppt/fa22_paf2_ppt.htm) lists several benefits of physical activity and fitness:

- Decreases the risk of obesity and chronic diseases, including osteoporosis.

- Better control of body weight, blood pressure, blood glucose, and cholesterol

- Improved mood and feelings of well-being

- Enhances independent living among older adults

- Improves quality of life for people of all ages

The specific health benefits of sports participation depend on the sport. Speed walking, jogging, cycling, swimming, and skiing have been shown to build cardiovascular endurance. Sports that involve gentle bending or stretching, including bowling, golf, and tai chi, are identified as promoting flexibility, which in turn may reduce the risk of injury. Other sports, such as those involving weightlifting or throwing, build strength. One important result of building strong muscles and, especially, bones is that it helps stave off osteoporosis by increasing the mineral content of bones. In "Lifestyle Factors and the Development of Bone Mass and Bone Strength in Young Women" (*Journal of Pediatrics*, June 2004), Tom Lloyd et al. of Pennsylvania State University report that exercise is more important than taking calcium supplements in promoting strong bones and that exercise was responsible for between 16% and 22% of the variation in hip bone mineral density in the 80 women they studied over 10 years.

Coronary heart disease, diabetes, colon cancer, and high blood pressure can all be prevented or improved through regular physical activity. The CDC, in *Physical Activity and Good Nutrition: Essential Elements to Prevent Chronic Diseases and Obesity, 2008* (February 2008) and on their Web site (2009, http://www.cdc.gov/ NCCdphp/publications/AAG/obesity.htm), points to an obesity epidemic as the key factor in these chronic health problems. According to the CDC, the prevalence of obesity among adults has approximately doubled since 1976–1980. In 2005–2006, 34% of adults over age 20 were obese. The obesity rate among teenagers more than tripled during this span, increasing from 5% to 17.4% for those in the 12 to 19 age group. Youfa Wang and May A. Beydoun of the Johns Hopkins Bloomberg School of Public Health, in "The Obesity Epidemic in the United States—Gender, Age, Socioeconomic, Racial/Ethnic, and

TABLE 8.1

Calories burned through selected sports and other physical activities

	Approximate calories used by a 154-pound person	
	In 1 hour	In 30 minutes
Moderate physical activities		
Hiking	370	185
Light gardening/yard work	330	165
Dancing	330	165
Bicycling (less than 10 miles per hour)	290	145
Walking (3½ miles per hour)	280	140
Weight lifting (general light workout)	220	110
Stretching	180	90
Vigorous physical activities		
Running/jogging (5 miles per hour)	590	295
Bicycling (greater than 10 miles per hour)	590	295
Swimming (slow freestyle laps)	510	255
Aerobics	480	240
Walking (4½ miles per hour)	460	230
Heavy yard work (chopping wood)	440	220
Weight lifting (vigorous effort)	440	220
Basketball (vigorous)	440	220

SOURCE: "Calorie Burner Chart," in *Tools to Help You*, U.S. Department of Agriculture, undated, http://www.fns.usda.gov/eatsmartplayhardhealthy lifestyle/tools/calorieburnerchart.htm (accessed June 30, 2009)

Geographic Characteristics: A Systematic Review and Meta-regression Analysis" (*Epidemiologic Reviews*, vol. 29, August 2007), project that by 2015, 41% of American adults will be obese.

Sports participation helps control weight by burning calories that would otherwise be stored as fat. The more vigorous the sport and the more frequent the participation, the more calories are burned. The article "How Many Calories Have You Burned?" (*USA Today*, February 26, 2007) reported on the number of calories that are burned in one hour of physical activity for those weighing 120, 154, and 170 pounds. For someone weighing 154 pounds, cross-country skiing for one hour would burn 559 calories; tennis, 489 calories; playing basketball, 440 calories; and bowling, 210 calories. Table 8.1 expands on that information, showing the number of calories a 154-pound individual would burn in various moderate and vigorous physical activities in 30 minutes and in an hour.

Sports Participation and Mental Health

Besides the obvious physical benefits of sports participation, there appear to be psychological benefits as well. The press release "Univ. of Fla. Study: Sports Participation Has Mental Perks for All" (March 7, 2001, http://news .ufl.edu/2001/03/07/body-image/) reports that a 2001 survey conducted by University of Florida researchers found that athletes have a better image of their own body than nonathletes. The effect is visible without regard to sport, gender, or level of expertise. According to the press release, Heather Hausenblas, the study's lead author, posits that the effect is part of a broader improvement in self-esteem that

accompanies sports participation. Based on Hausenblas's review of more than 80 other studies, athletes are 20% more likely than nonathletes to have a positive self-image. Competitive athletes have a better body image than casual athletes, and casual athletes have a better body image than nonathletes. The press release also quotes John Russell, president of the American Fitness Association, as saying that even small doses of exercise can benefit people beyond the well-documented cardiovascular effects. Exercise, he said, can alter one's mood by releasing the brain chemical called endorphins. He speculates that endorphins, by putting the exerciser in a better mood, may indirectly improve an athlete's body image.

The idea that sports participation can help improve one's mood is well supported by other scientific research. For example, Rosemarie Kobau et al. report in "Sad, Blue, or Depressed Days: Health Behaviors and Health-Related Quality of Life, Behavioral Risk Factor Surveillance System, 1995–2000" (*Health and Quality of Life Outcomes*, July 30, 2004) that individuals who do not exercise tend to experience more days in which they feel sad. Another study, "Adolescent Women's Sports Involvement and Sexual Behavior/Health: A Process-Level Investigation" (*Journal of Youth and Adolescence*, 2004) by Stephanie Jacobs Lehman and Susan Silverberg Koerner, finds evidence of a link between girls' involvement in organized sports and positive sexual health and behavior. This study links participation in organized sports with positive behavior related to sexual risk-taking, sexual/reproductive health, and sexual/reproductive health-seeking behavior. This effect is connected to self-empowerment and a positive view of one's own body.

Youth Sports Participation as an Indicator of Adult Behavior

Participating in sports as a child or adolescent also increases the likelihood that a person will participate as an adult. In "Childhood and Adolescent Sports Participation as Predictors of Participation in Sports and Physical Fitness Activities during Young Adulthood" (*Youth and Society*, vol. 35, no. 4, 2004), Daniel F. Perkins et al. analyze data from the Michigan Study of Adolescent Life Transitions longitudinal study to examine the connection between sports participation in childhood and physical fitness into young adulthood. The researchers examine survey responses about sports participation from more than 600 respondents when they were 12, 17, and 25 years old and find that childhood sports participation is an excellent predictor of both fitness and participation years later.

Even though many of the previously cited studies highlight the value of sports participation for young people, the benefits of sports are truly multigenerational. According to the Gerontological Society of America, physical activity yields a number of benefits for the elderly as well as for the young. Exercise has been shown to be the key to maintaining mobility in older adults. This activity could be as simple as walking regularly.

HEALTH RISKS OF SPORTS PARTICIPATION
Injuries

TYPES OF INJURIES. In *Sports Injuries* (April 2009, http://www.niams.nih.gov/Health_Info/Sports_Injuries/default.asp), the National Institute of Arthritis and Musculoskeletal and Skin Diseases (NIAMS) details the kinds of injuries athletes are likely to sustain and the activities in which they sustain them. This handout lists muscle sprains and strains, ligament and tendon tears, dislocated joints, and bone fractures as the most common types of sports injuries. (See Table 8.2.) According to NIAMS, the knee is the most commonly injured joint, largely because of its complexity and its role in bearing weight. Every year, knee problems send over 5.5 million people to orthopedic surgeons. Knee injuries can result from twisting the knee awkwardly, a direct blow, landing badly after a jump, or overuse. Injuries can range in severity from a minor bruise to serious damage to one or more of the four ligaments—the anterior cruciate, posterior cruciate, medial collateral, and lateral collateral—that stabilize the joint.

The Achilles tendon, which connects the calf muscle to the back of the heel, is another common site of sports injuries. Achilles tendon injures are especially common in people who do not exercise regularly and may not bother to stretch adequately before a game or session. This makes middle-aged "weekend warriors" particularly susceptible, according to NIAMS.

A fracture is a break in a bone. It can come from a single event, in which case it is called an acute fracture; or it can be caused by repetitive impact, which is called a stress fracture. Stress fractures usually occur in the feet or legs, the result of the pounding these bones take from long periods of running and jumping. When the bones that come together to form a joint get separated, it is called a dislocation. According to NIAMS, the joints of the hand are the most common points of dislocation, followed by the shoulder.

TABLE 8.2

Common types of sports injuries

- Muscle sprains and strains
- Tears of the ligaments that hold joints together
- Tears of the tendons that support joints and allow them to move
- Dislocated joints
- Fractured bones, including vertebrae

SOURCE: "Common Types of Sports Injuries," in *Handout on Health: Sports Injuries*, U.S. Department of Health and Human Services, National Institutes of Health, National Institute of Arthritis and Musculoskeletal and Skin Diseases, April 2009, http://www.niams.nih.gov/Health_Info/Sports_Injuries/default.asp (accessed June 30, 2009)

NIAMS divides all sports injuries into two broad categories: acute and chronic. Acute injuries are those that occur suddenly during an activity. They are characterized by severe pain, swelling, and inability to use the injured body part. Chronic injuries usually occur through overuse over a long period. They usually result in pain when engaging in the activity, and a dull ache when at rest. There may also be swelling.

According to Maureen Haggerty, Teresa G. Odle, and Rebecca J. Frey in "Sports Injuries" (Jacqueline L. Longe, ed., *Gale Encyclopedia of Medicine*, 2006), the vast majority (95%) of sports injuries are minor soft-tissue traumas. These include bruises (or contusions), which occur when blood collects at the point of the injury, causing a discoloration of the skin. Sprains, which account for about one-third of sports injuries, are partial or complete tears of a ligament. Strains are similar to sprains. The difference is that in a strain the torn tissue is a muscle or tendon rather than a ligament. Other soft-tissue sports injuries include tendonitis (inflammation of a tendon) and bursitis (inflammation of the fluid-filled sacs that allow tendons to glide over bones). These two injuries usually result from repeated stress on the tissue involved rather than from a single event. The kinds of sports injuries that result from overuse appear to be on the rise among young people. Mark Hyman notes in his book *Until It Hurts: America's Obsession with Youth Sports and How It Harms Our Kids* (Beacon Press, 2009) that in 1989 overuse injuries accounted for 20% of patients visiting the sports medicine clinic of Children's Hospital Boston. By 2004 the percentage was 70% and on the rise. Hyman writes that "In 2003 more than 3.5 million children under age 15 suffered a sports injury that required medical treatment—about one attended injury for every 10 players." Hyman blames increased pressure to perform from parents and coaches, who seek to turn every promising young athlete into a scholarship recipient and, eventually, a superstar.

Skeletal injuries from sports are less common than soft-tissue injuries. Haggerty, Odle, and Frey indicate that fractures account for 5% to 6% of sports injuries, with arms and legs being the most common sites of a break. Fractures of the skull or spine are rare in sports. Repeated foot pounding associated with such sports as long-distance running, basketball, and volleyball, and the stress fractures that can result, sometimes cause an injury called shin splints. Shin splints, according to Haggerty, Odle, and Frey, "are characterized by soreness and slight swelling of the front, inside, and back of the lower leg, and by sharp pain that develops while exercising and gradually intensifies."

The most dangerous class of sports injuries are those to the brain. A violent jarring of the brain from a blow to the head is called a concussion. Concussions often cause loss of consciousness and may also affect balance, coordination, hearing, memory, and vision.

STATISTICS ON FREQUENCY AND INJURY RATES. The article "Basketball Tops List of Sports with Most Injuries" (2006, http://www.luhs.org/feature.cfm?featureid=509) analyzes the prevalence of sports injuries using data from the U.S. Consumer Product Safety Commission. It indicates that of all sports injuries that were treated in hospital emergency rooms in 2005, basketball was the leading culprit, causing 512,213 of those injuries. Bicycling (485,669) and football (418,260) were close behind with injuries that required emergency room treatment. Soccer and baseball, the next two sports on the list, were far behind, causing 174,686 and 155,898 injuries, respectively.

Because they are still growing, and because their motor and cognitive skills are still developing, children and adolescents are particularly vulnerable to sports injuries. In the fact sheet "Sports and Recreation Safety" (2007, http://www.usa.safekids.org/content_documents/2007_Fact_Sheet_Sport_Rec.doc), Safe Kids USA, a nonprofit network of organizations devoted to reducing accidental injuries of all kinds among children, reports that 3.5 million American children under the age of 14 receive medical treatment for sports injuries every year. Sports participation accounts for about two out of five traumatic brain injuries among children. Among athletes ages 5 to 14 years, 15% of basketball players, 28% of football players, 22% of soccer players, 25% of baseball players, and 12% of softball players have been injured while playing those sports. Almost 392,000 children in that age range were treated in emergency rooms for either football- or basketball-related injuries in 2004.

FACTORS AFFECTING INJURY RATES. Besides children and adolescents, NIAMS notes that middle-aged people and women of all ages are also particularly vulnerable to sports injuries. Middle-aged people are susceptible to injury because they are not as agile and resilient as when they were younger. Some people expect their bodies to perform as well at the age of 50 as they remember their bodies performing at age 20 or 30. As a result, they put themselves at risk of injury. The risk is highest when an individual tries to make too quick a transition from an inactive lifestyle to an active one. As women's sports become faster paced and more physical, injuries among female athletes are increasing. The American Sports Data (ASD) press release "New National Study Is First since 1970's to Document Full Range of Sports Injuries" (May 15, 2003, http://www.americansportsdata.com/pr-sportsinjuries.asp) notes that in 2002 women were the recipients of 40% of all sports injuries and 37% of emergency room admissions.

It has also been discovered that women are more likely to suffer certain kinds of injuries than men. According to Allison Aubrey for National Public Radio ("Training May Curb Some Sports Injuries in Women," September 4, 2008, http://www.npr.org/templates/story/story.php?storyId=93309486), "Women are more prone than their male counterparts to specific injuries—namely knee injuries like tears of the ACL, or anterior cruciate ligament." Aubrey explains that the muscles in women's legs develop unevenly as women use mostly their front quadriceps; "this means that women's bodies [unlike men's] don't fully activate the muscles on the back side, namely the hamstrings and the glutes," the imbalance thus placing stress on the knee. Strength training techniques have been implemented for women athletes to help them avoid this painful ACL tear, an injury that requires surgery and long rehabilitation.

PSYCHOLOGICAL IMPACT OF YOUTH SPORTS PARTICIPATION. Frank Brady states in "Children's Organized Sports: A Developmental Perspective" (*Journal of Physical Education, Recreation, and Dance*, February 2004) that the "positive effect of sports participation for some youths appears to be offset by the negative experiences of others." He quotes Arthur J. Pearl and Bernard R. Cahill in *Intensive Participation in Children's Sports* (1993), who state that "sports are like a double-edged sword. Swung in the right direction, the sword can have tremendously positive effects, but swung in the wrong direction it can be devastating. Adults who supervise children's sports hold the sword. Whether sport is constructive or destructive in the psychological development of young children greatly depends on the values, education and skills of those adults."

The biggest culprit in the negative psychological impact of youth sports participation is an overemphasis on competition, which Brady attributes to misplaced priorities on the part of the adults in supervisory roles.

As a result, there is a high rate of burnout and subsequent dropout in youth sports. Brady explains that sports participation peaks at age 11 and steadily declines through the teenage years. He singles out a subset of the dropout group under the category of "burnout." Burnout refers to young athletes who have been successful in their sport(s) and have participated intensively over a number of years; concentrated training at the expense of other activities can result in diminished enjoyment, competitive anxiety, and ultimately real psychological and emotional damage.

Brady also points to conflicts between heavy sports participation and cognitive development in young children. Most children are not capable of fully grasping the competitive process until about age 12 and have trouble understanding the complex interrelationships that form a team. Some adult coaches get angry and frustrated when, for example, young soccer players swarm to the ball rather than play their positions properly, when in fact many players at age seven or eight are physically incapable of absorbing the concept of a position.

The American Psychological Association (APA) argues that whether youths benefit from sports participation may depend to a large degree on their environment. The APA news release "Environment May Play a Role in Whether Youth Benefit from Sports Participation, According to Two

Studies" (August 25, 2001, http://www.apa.org/releases/sportinvolvement.html) describes two studies with seemingly contradictory messages. A Clark University study of seventh graders from inner-city neighborhoods in central Massachusetts finds that boys and girls who participated in organized sports had higher self-esteem and were perceived by their teachers as having better social skills. Boys involved in sports were less likely to have experimented with marijuana. These positive traits were not accompanied by measurable negative behavior, such as increased aggression. However, the Clark University researchers explicitly caution against making "sweeping pronouncements about benefits or risks of sports involvement."

A larger study of female African-American students in rural high schools tells a different story. This study by Matthew J. Taylor of the University of Wisconsin–LaCrosse, finds that sports participation may actually increase the likelihood of substance use and other undesirable behaviors. Participation in sports did not appear to have a deterrent effect on gang involvement or other forms of delinquency. Taylor explains that the reason for conflicting results is that there are so many other variables involved, such as peer groups and community attitudes toward sports. A 2009 study by Anna M. Adachi-Mejia et al. of the Hood Center for Children and Families at Dartmouth Medical School ("Influence of Movie Smoking Exposure and Team Sports Participation on Established Smoking," *Archives of Pediatrics & Adolescent Medicine*, vol. 163, no. 7, July 2009) seems to contradict the peer group pressure thesis, finding that participation in team sports reduced the probability that a youth will take up cigarette smoking.

PHYSICAL INJURIES AMONG YOUNG ATHLETES. Even though much of the attention to the hazards of youth sports focuses on the mental and emotional pitfalls, physical injuries are a major concern as well. As noted earlier, children as a group are particularly vulnerable to sports injuries. Bill Hewitt, in "Wearing Out Their Bodies?" (*People*, June 13, 2005), elaborates on the theme of youth sports and their connection to increased injury risks. He cites many examples of young athletes pushed into extremely vigorous regimens at early ages and who end up damaging their bodies. One sports surgeon is quoted as saying that 10 years ago, he had never seen a baseball pitcher under 19 years old who needed the elbow ligament replacement operation known as "Tommy John surgery," whereas in 2004 he performed 51 such operations on teenage pitchers. Jeré Longman notes in "Fit Young Pitchers See Elbow Repair as Cure-All" (*New York Times*, July 20, 2007) that some young athletes are now opting to have this surgery even in the absence of an injury, in hopes that it will enhance their capabilities. Hewitt takes parents to task for pressuring their children into trying to become the next Kobe Bryant (1978–), when the odds of even the most talented young athlete ever making the big leagues, much less excelling there, are

microscopic. He notes that about 9 million boys play in organized baseball leagues, but that there are only about 9,700 players on Division I college teams, 7,500 minor leaguers, and 829 players in Major League Baseball. Hewitt advises parents and coaches that children need at least three months off each year from sports that involve throwing. He also urges them not to ignore discomfort, because pain is an indication of an injury that must be addressed.

"The risks of overuse are more serious in the pediatric/adolescent athlete for several reasons," explains Joel S. Brenner and the Council on Sports Medicine and Fitness in a report published in *Pediatrics* ("Overuse Injuries, Overtraining, and Burnout in Child and Adolescent Athletes," vol. 119, no. 6, June 2007, http://pediatrics.aappublications.org/cgi/content/full/119/6/1242). "The growing bones of the young athlete cannot handle as much stress as the mature bones of adults. For example, a young baseball pitcher who has not yet learned proper throwing mechanics (ie, recruiting the entire kinetic chain—from foot to hand—instead of just the arm) is at risk of traction apophysitis of the medial elbow. A young gymnast who performs repetitive hyperextension activities may develop spondylolysis (ie, a stress fracture of the spine), which is an injury particular to the pediatric age group. In addition, young swimmers may not recognize signs of rotator cuff tendonitis, because they may be unable to cognitively connect vague symptoms, such as fatigue or poor performance, as a sign of injury." Brenner cautions that these injuries are a result of young athletes overtraining in one particular sport, causing both physiologic and psychological burnout.

In addition to encouraging children not to overtrain, parents and coaches can play a big role in helping kids avoid injuries, according to the National Alliance for Youth Sports (NAYS). NAYS points to three overarching strategies for minimizing the risk of sports injuries: wearing appropriate, sport-specific, properly fitting protective gear, including helmets and goggles; protecting the skin from damaging solar rays by wearing hats and sunglasses and applying sun block when playing sports in the sun; and keeping adequately hydrated by consuming sports drinks to replace lost fluids and electrolytes lost through sweat.

SPORTS AND HEALTH: THE OUTLOOK

Are Americans heeding all the advice coming from their doctors and their government about the importance of physical activity? Data from the *Early Release of Selected Estimates Based on Data from the 2008 National Health Interview Survey* (June 24, 2009, http://www.cdc.gov/nchs/nhis/released200906.htm) by the CDC indicate that, in general, the answer seems to be "not really." Figure 8.1 shows that the percentage of adults who engaged in regular leisure-time physical activity between 1997 and

FIGURE 8.1

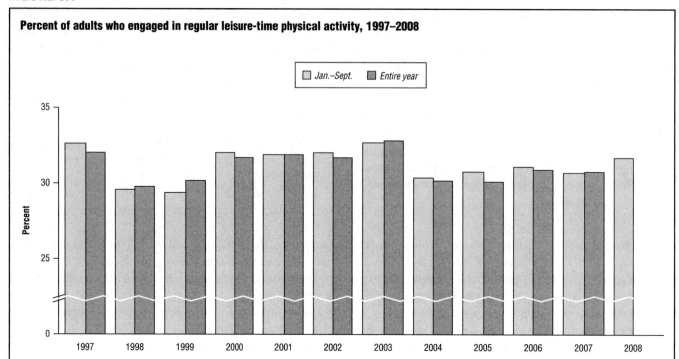

Percent of adults who engaged in regular leisure-time physical activity, 1997–2008

Notes: This measure reflects the definition used for the physical activity Leading Health Indicator (Healthy People 2010, (15)). Regular leisure-time physical activity is defined as engaging in light-moderate leisure-time physical activity for greater than or equal to 30 minutes at a frequency greater than or equal to five times per week or engaging in vigorous leisure-time physical activity for greater than or equal to 20 minutes at a frequency greater than or equal to three times per week. In Early Releases before September 2005 (based on the 2004 National Health Interview Survey (NHIS)), regular physical activity was calculated slightly differently than for Healthy People 2010. The earlier Early Release estimates excluded from the analysis persons with unknown duration of light-moderate or vigorous leisure-time physical activity who were known to have not met the frequency recommendations for light-moderate or vigorous leisure-time physical activity (i.e., partial unknowns). With the current release, persons who were known to have not met the frequency recommendations are classified as "not regular," regardless of duration. All estimates have been rerun using the revised denominator. The impact of the change on the estimates was minimal (typically 0.1 percentage point or less). The analyses excluded persons with unknown physical activity participation (about 3% of respondents each year). Beginning with the 2003 data, NHIS transitioned to weights derived from the 2000 census. In this Early Release, estimates for 2000–2002 were recalculated using weights derived from the 2000 census. Sample Adult Core component of the 1997–September 2008 NHIS. Data are based on household interviews of a sample of the civilian noninstitutionalized population.

SOURCE: "Figure 7.1. Percentage of Adults Aged 18 Years and over Who Engaged in Regular Leisure-Time Physical Activity: United States, 1997–September 2008," in *Early Release of Selected Estimates Based on Data from the January–September 2008 National Health Interview Survey*, U.S. Department of Health and Human Services, Centers for Disease Control and Prevention, National Center for Health Statistics, March 25, 2009, http://www.cdc.gov/nchs/data/nhis/earlyrelease/200903_07.pdf (accessed June 30, 2009)

2008 hovered at around 31%, in spite of the aggressive promotion of exercise by the federal government and others. As shown in Figure 8.2, people tend to exercise less as they age, and this pattern holds true for both genders, with men more likely to be physically active than women in every age category. White adults, at 35%, were more likely to engage in regular leisure-time physical activity than either Hispanics or non-Hispanic African-Americans, both of whom came in at 24%. (See Figure 8.3.)

Another survey, *Physical Activity Survey, 2006* (April 2006, http://assets.aarp.org/rgcenter/health/fitness_06.pdf), by Teresa A. Keenan, finds that in 2006, 49% of adults had been physically active for at least a year and that 36% of adults preferred walking.

By contrast, vigorous physical activity among adolescents seems to be on the rise. The nonprofit research agency Child Trends reports in *Vigorous Physical Activity by Youth* (2008, http://www.childtrendsdatabank.org/pdf/16_PDF.pdf) that 68.7% of students in grades 9 through

12 engaged in vigorous physical activity in 2005, up from 62.6% in 2003. (See Figure 8.4.) Child Trends finds that this increase was evident among both males and females and among white, African-American, and Hispanic subgroups. "Vigorous physical activity" is defined as physical activity for at least 20 minutes that made the person sweat and breathe hard, such as basketball, soccer, running, swimming laps, fast bicycling, fast dancing, or similar aerobic activities, on at least three of the seven days preceding the interview. However, in 2005 the Healthy People 2010 campaign revised its recommendations to 60 minutes of activity—some of which should be vigorous—at least five times a week. Only 35% of high school students met this revised goal in 2007. As shown in Figure 8.5, 44% of ninth-grade boys in 2007 reported engaging in physical activity, whereas 32% of ninth-grade girls reported such activity. Even though the percentages for both genders declined from ninth to 12th grade, boys were consistently more active than girls, with the gap between the genders the widest in 12th grade. African-American and

FIGURE 8.2

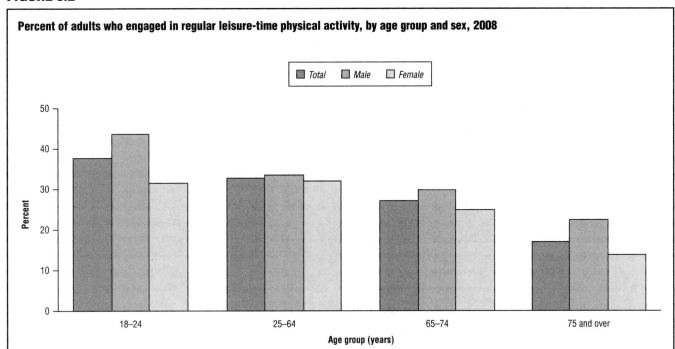

Percent of adults who engaged in regular leisure-time physical activity, by age group and sex, 2008

Notes: This measure reflects the definition used for the physical activity Leading Health Indicator (Healthy People 2010, (15)). Regular leisure-time physical activity is defined as engaging in light-moderate leisure-time physical activity for greater than or equal to 30 minutes at a frequency greater than or equal to five times per week or engaging in vigorous leisure-time physical activity for greater than or equal to 20 minutes at a frequency greater than or equal to three times per week. In Early Releases before September 2005 (based on the 2004 National Health Interview Survey (NHIS)), regular physical activity was calculated slightly differently than for Healthy People 2010. The earlier Early Release estimates excluded from the analysis persons with unknown duration of light-moderate or vigorous leisure-time physical activity who were known to have not met the frequency recommendations for light-moderate or vigorous leisure-time physical activity (i.e., partial unknowns). With the current release, persons who were known to have not met the frequency recommendations are classified as "not regular," regardless of duration. The analyses excluded 514 persons (2.7%) with unknown physical activity participation. Based on data collected from January through September in the Sample Adult Core component of the 2008 NHIS. Data are based on household interviews of a sample of the civilian noninstitutionalized population.

SOURCE: "Figure 7.2. Percentage of Adults Aged 18 Years and over Who Engaged in Regular Leisure-Time Physical Activity, by Age Group and Sex: United States, January–September 2008," in *Early Release of Selected Estimates Based on Data from the January–September 2008 National Health Interview Survey*, U.S. Department of Health and Human Services, Centers for Disease Control and Prevention, National Center for Health Statistics, March 25, 2009, http://www.cdc.gov/nchs/data/nhis/earlyrelease/200903_07.pdf (accessed June 30, 2009)

Hispanic students were about equally likely to have engaged in physical activity, at 31% and 30%, respectively; white students, at 37%, were somewhat more likely to be physically active. (See Figure 8.6.)

In the face of an obesity epidemic in the United States, the federal government has in recent years taken an active role in promoting fitness among Americans. In 1996 the National Center for Chronic Disease Prevention and Health Promotion published *Physical Activity and Health: A Report of the Surgeon General* (http://www.cdc.gov/nccdphp/sgr/pdf/sgrfull.pdf), a blueprint for improving the physical condition of the U.S. population. Among the report's major conclusions were that people of all ages and genders benefit from regular physical activity and that significant health benefits can be obtained by engaging in a moderate amount of physical activity, such as 45 minutes of volleyball, 30 minutes of brisk walking, or 15 minutes of running. The report noted that additional benefits can be gained through more vigorous and greater amounts of activity. Since then, the federal government has continued its efforts to promote physical fitness

through a variety of programs, including Healthy People 2010 and the HealthierUS initiative (http://www.healthierus.gov/), promoted by President George W. Bush (1946–), and the President's Challenge, a fitness initiative of the President's Council on Physical Fitness and Sports. The President's Challenge, a six-week competition to determine the nation's most active state, was renewed in May 2009 by President Barack Obama (1961–), who also declared that month National Physical Fitness and Sports Month.

Television has taken on the obesity epidemic as well. Cable television, a longtime source of fitness programming, features FitTV. Launched in 1993 and owned by Discovery Communications, FitTV as of 2009 continued to draw millions of subscribers. In recent years network television has also gotten in the fitness game. The National Broadcasting Corporation's *The Biggest Loser* is a reality show in which obese contestants compete in various contests designed to help them slim down. The contestant who sheds the most weight (the "biggest loser") is the winner at the end of the season. The show's eighth season launched on September 15, 2009.

FIGURE 8.3

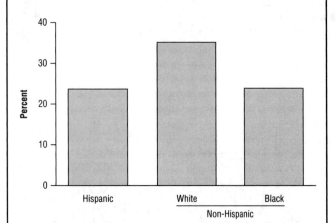

Percent of adults who engaged in regular leisure-time physical activity, by race/ethnicity, 2008

Notes: This measure reflects the definition used for the physical activity Leading Health Indicator (Healthy People 2010, (15)). Regular leisure-time physical activity is defined as engaging in light-moderate leisure-time physical activity for greater than or equal to 30 minutes at a frequency greater than or equal to five times per week or engaging in vigorous leisure-time physical activity for greater than or equal to 20 minutes at a frequency greater than or equal to three times per week. In Early Releases before September 2005 (based on the 2004 National Health Interview Survey (NHIS)), regular physical activity was calculated slightly differently than for Healthy People 2010. The earlier Early Release estimates excluded from the analysis persons with unknown duration of light-moderate or vigorous leisure-time physical activity who were known to have not met the frequency recommendations for light-moderate or vigorous leisure-time physical activity (i.e., partial unknowns). With the current release, persons who were known to have not met the frequency recommendations are classified as "not regular," regardless of duration. The analyses excluded 514 persons (2.7%) with unknown physical activity participation. Estimates are age-sex adjusted using the projected 2000 U.S. population as the standard population and using five age groups: 18–24 years, 25–34 years, 35–44 years, 45–64 years, and 65 years and over.
Based on data collected from January through September in the Sample Adult Core component of the 2008 NHIS.
Data are based on household interviews of a sample of the civilian noninstitutionalized population.

SOURCE: "Figure 7.3. Age-Sex-Adjusted Percentage of Adults Aged 18 Years and over Who Engaged in Regular Leisure-Time Physical Activity, by Race/Ethnicity: United States, January–September 2008," in *Early Release of Selected Estimates Based on Data from the January–September 2008 National Health Interview Survey*, U.S. Department of Health and Human Services, Centers for Disease Control and Prevention, National Center for Health Statistics, March 25, 2009, http://www.cdc.gov/nchs/data/nhis/earlyrelease/200903_07.pdf (accessed June 30, 2009)

FIGURE 8.4

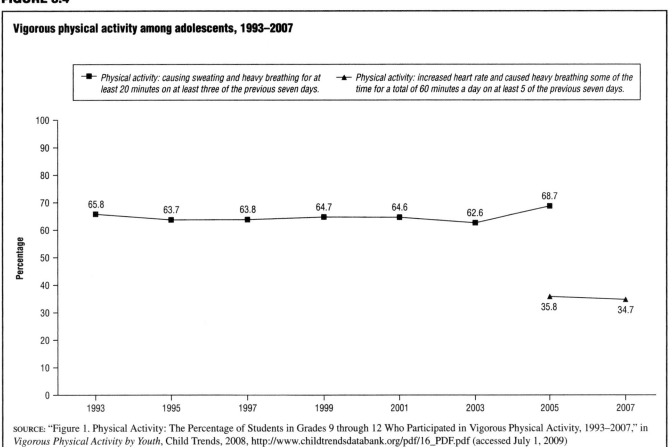

Vigorous physical activity among adolescents, 1993–2007

■— Physical activity: causing sweating and heavy breathing for at least 20 minutes on at least three of the previous seven days.

▲— Physical activity: increased heart rate and caused heavy breathing some of the time for a total of 60 minutes a day on at least 5 of the previous seven days.

SOURCE: "Figure 1. Physical Activity: The Percentage of Students in Grades 9 through 12 Who Participated in Vigorous Physical Activity, 1993–2007," in *Vigorous Physical Activity by Youth*, Child Trends, 2008, http://www.childtrendsdatabank.org/pdf/16_PDF.pdf (accessed July 1, 2009)

FIGURE 8.5

Vigorous physical activity among adolescents, by grade and gender, 2007

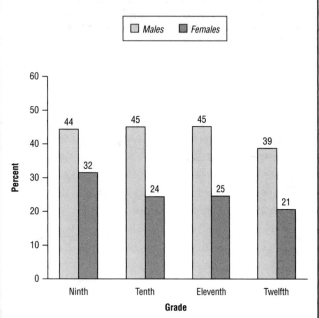

Note: Activities that increased heart rate and caused heavy breathing some of the time for a total of 60 minutes a day on at least 5 of the previous seven days preceding the survey

SOURCE: "Figure 2. Physical Activity: The Percentage of Students in Grades 9 through 12 Who Participated in Regular Vigorous Physical Activity, by Grade and Gender, 2007," in *Vigorous Physical Activity by Youth*, Child Trends, 2008, http://www.childtrendsdatabank.org/pdf/16_PDF.pdf (accessed July 1, 2009)

FIGURE 8.6

Vigorous physical activity among adolescents, by race/ethnicity, 2007

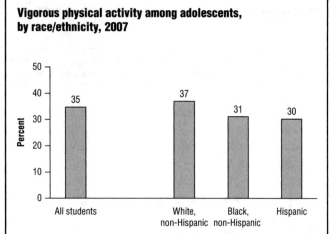

Note: Activities that increased heart rate and caused heavy breathing some of the time for a total of 60 minutes a day on at least 5 of the previous seven days preceding the survey

SOURCE: "Figure 3. Physical Activity: The Percentage of Students in Grades 9 through 12 Who Participated in Vigorous Physical Activity, by Race and Hispanic Origin, 2007," in *Vigorous Physical Activity by Youth*, Child Trends, 2008, http://www.childtrendsdatabank.org/pdf/16_PDF.pdf (accessed July 1, 2009)

CHAPTER 9
PERFORMANCE-ENHANCING DRUGS

The spirit of sport is the celebration of the human spirit, the body and the mind. Doping is contrary to the spirit of sport, erodes public confidence and jeopardises the health and well-being of athletes.

—World Anti-Doping Agency

The word *doping* is often used to refer to any practice involving prohibited substances or other methods to give an athlete an unfair advantage over other competitors. The article "Doping in Sports: Steroids and Supplements" (*World Almanac and Book of Facts*, 2007) notes that the word *dope* probably comes from the Dutch word *dop*, an alcoholic beverage made from grape skins that traditional Zulu warriors believed enhanced their fighting ability.

A BRIEF HISTORY OF DOPING

For as long as people have been engaging in athletic competition, they have been seeking ways to gain an edge on their opponents. There is evidence that doping took place in the ancient Olympics, whose competitions were held from 776 BC until AD 393. For example, Will Carroll notes in *The Juice: The Real Story of Baseball's Drug Problems* (2005) that Greece's Spartan coaches fed their athletes special herb and mushroom concoctions—during a period in which they were supposed to be consuming nothing but cheese and water—believed to render them oblivious to pain.

The first known case of an athlete dying as a result of doping occurred in 1886, when the Welsh cyclist Andrew Linton died during a race from Paris to Bordeaux. The substance he ingested was thought to be trimethyl, an alcohol-based product used by distance racers to ease pain and increase stamina.

According to Carroll, the modern era of doping began with the development of injectable testosterone in 1935. Testosterone is a male hormone produced naturally by the body. Injecting additional testosterone into the system increases muscle mass and strength. Originally introduced by Nazi doctors to make soldiers more aggressive, laboratory-produced testosterone did not take long to make its way from the battlefield to the athletic field. German athletes dominated the medals in the 1936 Olympics, probably with the assistance of these newly developed synthetic drugs.

The father of anabolic steroids—chemical variants of testosterone—in the United States was John Ziegler (1917–2000), a physician for the U.S. weightlifting team in the mid-20th century. Ziegler learned from his Russian counterparts that the Soviet weightlifting team's success was in part attributable to their use of performance-enhancing drugs, the formulas for which had been brought east by German scientists defecting to the Soviet Union after World War II (1939–1945). Deciding that U.S. athletes needed chemical assistance to remain competitive, Ziegler worked with the CIBA Pharmaceutical Company to develop an oral anabolic steroid. These efforts resulted in the creation of methandrostenolone, which appeared on the market in 1960. During the Olympics that year, the Danish cyclist Knut Jensen (1936–1960) collapsed and died while competing in the 100-kilometer (62-mile) race. An autopsy revealed the presence of amphetamines and a drug called nicotinyl tartrade in his system.

Drug testing was introduced at the Olympics in 1968. By this time the International Olympic Committee (IOC) had developed a list of officially banned substances; however, because no test had yet been invented that could distinguish between anabolic steroids and naturally occurring testosterone in the body, the testing was largely ineffective. Only one athlete was found to be in violation of the new drug policy in 1968: the Swedish pentathlete Hans-Gunnar Liljenwall (1941–), who was found to have too much alcohol in his blood after drinking a few beers before the shooting portion of his event.

Steroids found their way into professional football in the late 1960s, as teams began hiring strength and conditioning coaches, who were charged with the task of growing a new breed of bigger, bulkier players. Taking their cue from the weightlifting world, these coaches turned to steroids as the fastest way of accomplishing this goal. During the 1970s performance-enhancing supplements were still way ahead of the dope detectors in the scientific arena. The East Germans showed up at the 1976 Olympics in Montreal with a team of women swimmers sporting man-sized muscles and deep voices. They won most of the medals. However, even though there was much talk about the likelihood that they were using banned substances, not a single one of these athletes tested positive. It later became clear that the athletes themselves were the victims of a mandatory doping program overseen by East German Olympic officials, who injected the swimmers with steroids without their informed consent. Several East German swimmers of that era, as reported by CBC Sports (January 19, 2003, http://www.cbc.ca/sports/in depth/drugs/stories/top10.html#1), have reported that they began receiving steroid injections at age 13 and have suffered serious long-term health consequences—ranging from liver damage to infertility—as a result of doping.

Doping in sports has increased dramatically since then. As the practice has grown, so have the methods for detecting it and for keeping it from being detected. By the 1970s the use of performance-enhancing drugs had reached epidemic proportions among elite athletes. It was widely known that there were whole national sports programs whose success was based largely on sophisticated doping techniques, but scientists lacked the tools to prove what was going on. A breakthrough took place in 1983, when newly developed technology for analyzing blood for the presence of banned substances was deployed at the Pan Am Games in Caracas, Venezuela. The Associated Press reported at that time in "Inquiry Set on Pan Am" (*New York Times*, September 14, 1983) that 16 athletes from several countries were caught with performance-enhancing drugs in their system. Many other athletes, including 12 members of the U.S. track and field squad, withdrew from the event rather than risk the embarrassment of being caught cheating.

The first major Olympic disqualification due to steroids occurred in 1988, when the Canadian sprinter Ben Johnson (1961–) was stripped of both his gold medal and his world record in the 100-meter sprint after testing positive for the banned steroid stanozolol. Years later, it was revealed that a number of U.S. track competitors had tested positive for illicit drugs before the 1988 Olympics in Seoul, South Korea.

WHAT ARE PERFORMANCE-ENHANCING DRUGS?

Anabolic Steroids

When people speak of performance-enhancing drugs, more often than not they are referring to anabolic steroids. In *Steroid Abuse in Today's Society* (March 2004, http://www.deadiversion.usdoj.gov/pubs/brochures/steroids/pro

fessionals/), the U.S. Drug Enforcement Administration (DEA) defines anabolic steroids as "synthetically produced variants of the naturally occurring male hormone testosterone." The full name of this class of drugs is androgenic anabolic steroids. The word *androgenic* means that the drugs promote masculine physical characteristics, and *anabolic* means tissue building. According to the DEA, the list of commonly abused steroids commercially available in the United States includes:

• Fluxoymesterone

• Methyltestosterone

• Nandrolone

• Oxandrolone

• Oxymetholone

• Stanozolol

• Boldenone

Others that are not approved for use in the United States include ethylestrenol, methandriol, methenolone, and methandrostenolone.

The main users of anabolic steroids are athletes seeking to add bulk and strength to their bodies. Besides building lean body mass, another way steroids are purported to help athletes get stronger is by reducing the amount of recovery time needed between workouts, allowing them to train harder. Anabolic steroids are currently banned by most sports organizations, including the IOC, the National Football League (NFL), the National Basketball Association (NBA), the National Collegiate Athletic Association (NCAA), the National Hockey League (NHL), and Major League Baseball (MLB).

The only way to get steroids legally is through a doctor's prescription, and there are many legitimate medical uses for which a doctor might recommend them, including growth deficiencies, muscle-wasting diseases, loss of testicular function, breast cancer, low red blood cell count, or debilitated states resulting from surgery or illness. Steroids are also widely used in veterinary medicine to promote weight gain, to treat anemia, or to counteract tissue breakdown from illness or trauma.

Most illicit steroids come from one of two sources. Some are diverted from the legitimate U.S. market, often through stolen or fraudulent prescriptions. The largest share, however, has been smuggled into the United States from other countries, largely from Mexico, from European countries where a prescription is not required to obtain steroids, or, more recently, from China. Sean Assael reports in "'Raw Deal' Busts Labs across U.S., Many Supplied by China" (*ESPN Magazine*, September 24, 2007, http://sports.espn.go.com/espn/news/story?id=3033532) that in 2007 DEA agents concluded an 18-month crackdown on the illegal manufacturing and selling of steroids, closing down

56 labs and making 124 arrests in 27 states in what DEA officials called "the largest performance-enhancing drug crackdown in U.S. history." Thirty-seven Chinese factories were identified as reported suppliers of the labs. "The crackdown . . . grew out of a 2005 operation targeting eight Mexican labs that were responsible for 80 percent of America's underground steroid trade," explained Assael. "Several large Chinese factories had been supplying the Mexican labs. When the Mexican labs were closed . . . , those Chinese factories redirected their pipeline to the U.S." With China quickly becoming a major player in the underground market for steroids, "the World Anti-Doping [Agency] estimates," Assael concluded, "that Chinese factories are responsible for as much as 70–80 percent, or up to $480 million worldwide, of an annual $600 million black market in human growth hormone."

Steroids are available in several different forms, including tablets, liquids, gels, and creams. Typically, users ingest the drugs orally, inject them into muscle, or rub them on their skin. The doses taken by people who abuse steroids can be 10 to 100 times stronger than those recommended for medical conditions. Many steroid abusers engage in what is called stacking, which means mixing oral steroids with injectable ones, often taking multiple forms of the drug. Another common practice among steroid abusers is pyramiding, which means administering doses in cycles of six to twelve weeks where the dose is slowly increased to a peak midway through the cycle, then tapered back down toward the end. There is a widespread belief among steroid users that stacking and pyramiding maximize the benefits of the drugs while reducing their harmful effects, though there is no scientific evidence to support these contentions.

Other Substances and Supplements

There are a number of performance-enhancing substances besides anabolic steroids, some of which have until recently escaped the scrutiny of those in the business of regulating sports. As a result, these substances, often billed as dietary supplements, have been readily available, usually as nearby as the nutrition and vitamin store in a local mall.

ERYTHROPOIETIN. Erythropoietin (EPO) is a hormone produced naturally by the kidneys. It plays a role in regulating the number of red blood cells in the blood stream. A synthetic version of EPO was developed in the 1980s, and it quickly became popular as a performance-enhancing drug, particularly among athletes involved in endurance sports such as cycling. When used excessively, EPO can increase the number of red blood cells to such a degree that the blood becomes too thick to flow properly, potentially leading to heart attacks and strokes. According to the 2007 *World Almanac and Book of Facts*, in the late 1980s, shortly after the appearance of synthetic EPO, 30 top endurance athletes, mainly cyclists, in Belgium, the

Netherlands, Denmark, and Sweden died; the likely cause of their deaths was EPO. A variant of EPO known as continuous erythropoietin receptor activator (CERA) began to appear in 2008. CERA was the substance for which many of the athletes ejected from the 2008 Tour de France and 2008 Beijing Olympics tested positive.

CREATINE. One of the most popular supplements used by athletes at all levels is creatine. Creatine is available over the counter (without a prescription) and is reputed to help improve performance in sports that involve short bursts of power, such as weightlifting, wrestling, and sprinting. Even though reliable research has not yet established a connection between creatine and serious health problems, there is some evidence that heavy use may cause kidney, liver, and heart problems. Known side effects of creatine include muscle cramps and digestive problems such as stomach pain, diarrhea, and nausea. In "Taking Performance-Enhancing Drugs: Are You Risking Your Health?" (December 26, 2006, http://www.mayoclinic.com/health/performance-enhancing-drugs/HQ01105), the Mayo Clinic explains that what actually happens when people take creatine is that their muscles draw water away from the rest of the body, creating the illusion of added muscle mass. The increased bulk is really just extra water stored in the muscles.

ANDROSTENEDIONE. Androstenedione (or andro) enjoyed a huge burst of popularity in the late 1990s, when MLB player Mark McGwire (1963–) chased, and eventually shattered, the old record for number of home runs in a single season. McGwire admittedly used andro, which was perfectly legal and within the rules of MLB at the time. Countless young aspiring power hitters followed his lead. Whether andro really helped McGwire hit 70 home runs in 1998 is not known.

Andro is a direct precursor to testosterone—meaning it turns into testosterone in the body—and is found naturally in humans. It is also found naturally in Scotch pine trees, which is why manufacturers were allowed to sell it as a dietary supplement. Andro was discovered in the 1930s, but it was not until the 1950s that scientists became aware that it turned into testosterone in the body. Andro is widely believed to boost testosterone production, which in turn increases muscle mass, energy, and strength. The Mayo Clinic disputes these claims, though proponents of andro—including companies that make money selling it—cite research supporting andro's effectiveness as a performance enhancer. Andro is now classified as a controlled substance. The Anabolic Steroid Control Act of 2004 essentially reclassified andro as an anabolic steroid, making it illegal for use as a performance enhancer.

Heavy use of andro can produce side effects similar to those associated with other anabolic steroids. Andro can actually decrease testosterone production in men and increase production of the female hormone estrogen. It can also cause acne, shrinking of the testicles, and reduced sperm count. In women side effects of andro can include acne as well as the onset of masculine characteristics such as deepening of the voice and male-pattern baldness.

EPHEDRA. Ephedra is an herb that has been used in Chinese medicine—where it is known as *ma huang*—for thousands of years. An American version widely used by early settlers in the Southwest was called Mormon or Squaw tea. The main chemical constituent in ephedra is ephedrine, which is a powerful stimulant, similar to amphetamines. It also contains another chemical called pseudoephedrine, which has long been used as a nasal decongestant but has recently come under tighter regulation because of its role in manufacturing illegal methamphetamine. Besides its use by athletes as an energy booster, ephedra has been used as an ingredient in popular over-the-counter weight-loss pills. It has also been used by people seeking to stay alert for late-night studying or socializing activities; until recently, it was an ingredient in many popular energy drinks.

Ephedra has been linked to serious side effects, such as strokes, seizures, and heart attacks, and many people have died as a direct result of its use. Ephedra can also cause elevated blood sugar levels and irregular heart-beats. It may be addictive when used over time. In February 2003 the Baltimore Orioles pitcher Steve Bechler (1979–2003) died of heatstroke after a spring training workout. Ephedra toxicity was identified as a contributing factor in his death. Bechler's death sparked renewed efforts by the U.S. Food and Drug Administration (FDA) to take action on ephedra. In December 2003 the FDA banned ephedra from being sold over the counter as a dietary supplement. However, in April 2005 a federal judge overturned the FDA's ban on procedural grounds. The Combat Methamphetamine Epidemic Act of 2005, signed into law in March 2006, placed strict regulations on the sale of ephedrine-containing products, including record-keeping, sale from locked cabinets behind the counter, and positive identification for purchasers.

THE BALCO SCANDAL

The cat-and-mouse game of doping and detection methods has been going on among athletes and those officiating their sports since the late 1960s. A major break-through in the effort to detect doping came in June 2003, when the track and field coach Trevor Graham turned over to authorities a syringe containing what turned out to be tetrahydrogestrinone (THG), a previously unknown ana-bolic steroid. THG was considered a designer steroid, in that it was manufactured to be undetectable by the existing methods. Lab testing methods were quickly adjusted to detect THG. U.S. government investigators soon turned their attention to the Bay Area Laboratory Co-Operative (BALCO), the California-based distributor of the drug.

On September 3, 2003, agents of the Internal Revenue Service, the FDA, the San Mateo County Narcotics Task Force, and the U.S. Anti-Doping Agency raided BALCO facilities and seized containers of steroids, human growth hormone, and testosterone. Two days later officials searched the home of Greg Anderson (1964–), the personal weight trainer of the baseball star Barry Bonds (1964–), and seized more steroids, as well as documents thought to implicate a number of high-profile athletes. Over the next few months urine samples from the U.S. Track and Field Championships were retested for THG, and several came up positive. One of those athletes was Kelli White (1977–), who had won both the 100- and 200-meter (109- and 218-yard) world championships in 2003. White was stripped of her titles and banned from competition for two years. Evidence was collected from computers and documents connecting a number of other athletes to BALCO.

Victor Conte Jr., the BALCO founder and owner; James Valente, a BALCO executive; Anderson; and the track coach Remi Korchemny (1932–) were indicted in February 2004 for distributing steroids. Later that year, Conte described on the December 3, 2004, broadcast of American Broadcasting Company's (ABC) *20/20* how he provided performance-enhancing drugs to many elite athletes, including the sprinters Tim Montgomery (1975–) and Marion Jones (1975–). Jones continued to proclaim her innocence as the scandal unfolded and sued Conte for defamation of character. She settled the suit out of court in 2006, and later that year she was cleared after her alternate blood sample tested negative for banned substances. However, the cost of defending herself was steep; according to the article "Marion Jones Running Out of Money" (*Boston Globe*, June 25, 2007), the affair cost Jones hundreds of thousands of dollars in endorsements and appearance fees, which coupled with legal fees brought her to the brink of financial ruin.

The case, however, was not over; on October 5, 2007, in the U.S. District Court for the Southern District of New York, Jones admitted to having used illegal performance-enhancing drugs during the period surrounding the 2000 Olympics in Sydney, Australia, and lying about it to two grand juries. She pleaded guilty to lying to federal agents about her use of steroids and making false statements in a check fraud case. Under pressure from the U.S. Olympic Committee, she surrendered her Olympic medals (three gold medals and two bronze from the 2000 Olympics). She was suspended from all track and field competition for two years, including competition in the 2008 Summer Olympics, and was retroactively disqualified from all events dating back to September 1, 2000. U.S. District Judge Kenneth Karas sentenced her in January 2008 to six months in prison, 200 hours of community service, and two years of probation after her prison term for lying to federal agents about her steroid use and the check fraud case. She began her prison sentence on March 7, 2008, and was released on September 5, 2008. Several other high-profile track and field athletes received bans in the wake of the BALCO scandal, including the sprinters White, Montgomery, and Chryste Gaines (1970–).

The BALCO scandal also brought fines and suspensions for a handful of professional football players: Chris Cooper (1977–), Barrett Robbins (1973–), and Dana Stubblefield (1970–). Elliot Almond and Peter Carey note in "Bonds, Marion Jones Alleged to Have Received Steroids" (Knight-Ridder/Tribune News Service, April 25, 2004) that Bill Romanowski (1966–) was reported by the *San Jose Mercury News* to have been implicated by Conte, but Romanowski retired before the NFL could take any formal action against him. Romanowski later admitted to having used steroids during his playing career.

In March 2005 a congressional committee held hearings on the issue of steroids in baseball. A number of legislators mocked Major League officials for the sport's weak policy and feeble efforts to deal with the problem. Many of those who testified came out looking bad, including the former home-run champion McGwire, who was evasive when asked whether his power-hitting abilities were chemically aided. Other current and former baseball players who testified included Jose Canseco (1964–), Curt Schilling (1966–), Sammy Sosa (1968–), Rafael Palmeiro (1964–), and Frank Thomas (1968–).

In October 2005 Conte was sentenced to four months in prison and another four months of house arrest. Anderson received three months each of prison time and home confinement. Valente and Korchemny were given probation, Valente for three years, and Korchemny one year.

HEALTH RISKS OF STEROID USE

Steroid abuse has been linked with a wide range of health hazards, both physical and mental. Among the physical problems are liver and kidney tumors, high blood pressure, elevated cholesterol levels, fluid retention, and severe acne. Some studies have associated steroid use with serious cardiovascular problems, including cardiomyopathies (inflammation of the heart muscle), irregular heart rhythm, development of embolisms (blockage of an artery by a clot or particle carried in the bloodstream), and heart failure. Men sometimes experience symptoms such as shrunken testicles, reduced sperm count, baldness, breast development, and increased risk of prostate cancer. Among women, growth of facial hair, male-pattern baldness, menstrual cycle disruptions, and deepening of the voice have all been reported. Adolescents who use steroids run the risk of halting their growth prematurely, as their bones fuse ahead of schedule. Another problem for teenagers is that steroids cause muscles to grow but do not strengthen the tendons that connect these muscles to bones. This can increase the risk of injury.

Emotional/psychological problems stemming from abuse of steroids include extreme mood swings, depression, paranoid jealousy, delusions, and impaired judgment. Sometimes these steroid-induced mood swings lead to violent behavior, a condition popularly referred to as "'roid rage."

STEROID USE AND YOUTH

Data from Lloyd D. Johnston et al.'s *Monitoring the Future, National Results on Adolescent Drug Use: Overview of Key Findings, 2008* (May 2009, http://www.monitoringthefuture.org/pubs/monographs/overview2008.pdf), an ongoing study of behavior among secondary school students, college students, and young adults, suggest that steroid use among young people peaked in the early part of the 21st century and has been tapering off since then. (See Figure 1.1 in Chapter 1.) According to Johnston and his colleagues, 2.2% of 12th graders in 2008 had used steroids at some time, while 1.4% of 10th graders and 1.4% of 8th graders had done so. Among 12th graders, 1.5% reported having used steroids in the past year. Less than 1% of 10th and 8th graders had done so.

PERFORMANCE-ENHANCING DRUGS IN COLLEGE SPORTS

The NCAA Committee on Competitive Safeguards and Medical Aspects of Sports regularly compiles the results of the association's drug-testing program. The most recent available data as of 2009 were published in *NCAA Drug-Testing Results 2004–05* (July 6, 2006, http://www.ncaa.org/wps/wcm/connect/cd3516004e0b8a179961f91ad6fc8b25/NCAA_DT_0405report.pdf?MOD=AJPERES&CACHEID=cd3516004e0b8a179961f91ad6fc8b25). According to the NCAA, positive steroid tests among intercollegiate athletes have declined steeply in recent years. Forty-nine student athletes tested positive for steroids in year-round testing in 2004–05, compared with 93 positive tests in 2000–01. Table 9.1 shows drug testing results by division for selected years from 1993 until 2005. This table shows that even though steroid use has declined dramatically, dropping by nearly half in Divisions I and III and nearly three-quarters in Division II, amphetamine use has increased just as sharply, more than doubling in Division III and nearly doubling in Divisions I and II. Table 9.2 indicates that the decrease in steroid use has been most evident among white athletes, dropping from 2.6% to 1% between 1993 and 2005 among that group, though white athletes' amphetamine use had the highest jump as well; it more than doubled, from 2.1% to 4.6%. Table 9.3 and Table 9.4 break the results down by gender and sport. Table 9.3 shows that the pattern of increased amphetamine use among male college athletes held across each of the sports listed (with baseball, football, and tennis the highest at 3.9% in 2005), whereas steroid use declined among male basketball, football, tennis, and track and field participants. As shown in Table 9.4, the pattern of

TABLE 9.1

Drug use among college athletes, by division, selected years 1993–2005

Drug	Division I				Division II				Division III			
	1993 (n=1,422)	1997 (n=6,123)	2001 (n=8,776)	2005 (n=8,543)	1993 (n=681)	1997 (n=3,254)	2001 (n=4,867)	2005 (n=4,341)	1993 (n=409)	1997 (n=4,537)	2001 (n=7,520)	2005 (n=6,493)
Amphetamines	2.1%	2.5%	3.2%	4.0%	2.0%	3.3%	3.3%	3.8%	1.9%	3.7%	3.7%	4.6%
Anabolic steroids	1.9%	1.2%	1.6%	1.2%	4.3%	1.1%	2.5%	1.2%	1.9%	1.3%	1.4%	1.0%
Ephedrine	N/A	3.0%	2.4%	2.4%	N/A	4.2%	4.1%	2.6%	N/A	3.8%	2.5%	2.6%
Nutritional supplements	N/A	N/A	46.0%	33.4%	N/A	N/A	41.5%	27.9%	N/A	N/A	39.8%	28.1%

Note: All N/A's reflect that questions regarding that drug were not asked in that particular year.
n=sample size.

SOURCE: "Table 2. Ergogenic Drug Use by NCAA Division," in *NCAA 2004–05 Drug Testing Results*, National Collegiate Athletic Association, July 6, 2006

TABLE 9.2

Drug use among college athletes, by ethnic group, selected years 1993–2005

Drug	White				African-American				Other			
	1993 (n=1,968)	1997 (n=10,850)	2001 (n=16,706)	2005 (n=14,629)	1993 (n=408)	1997 (n=1,883)	2001 (n=2,908)	2005 (n=2,765)	1993 (n=116)	1997 (n=903)	2001 (n=1,611)	2005 (n=1,954)
Amphetamines	2.1%	3.2%	3.6%	4.5%	1.8%	1.3%	1.7%	2.4 %	1.8%	3.2%	4.0%	3.4%
Anabolic steroids	2.6%	1.1%	1.3%	1.0%	2.2%	1.1%	1.5%	1.6%	1.7%	2.1%	2.2%	1.6%
Ephedrine	N/A	3.8%	2.7%	2.5%	N/A	1.2%	0.9%	2.2%	N/A	3.5%	2.4%	1.6%

Note: All N/A's reflect that questions regarding that drug were not asked in that particular year.
n=sample size.

SOURCE: "Table 4. Ergogenic Drug Use by Ethnic Group," in *NCAA 2004–05 Drug Testing Results*, National Collegiate Athletic Association, July 6, 2006

---

increasing amphetamine use and decreasing steroid use among female college athletes held across all sports listed, with 2005 amphetamine use highest among softball players at 5.2%.

STEROIDS IN PROFESSIONAL SPORTS

Every sport has its own way of testing for performance-enhancing drugs and its own policy for dealing with players who use them. The NFL requires its players to take year-round drug tests. The penalty for those caught using banned substances for the first time is a suspension that lasts four games, which amounts to a quarter of a season. The second offense results in a year-long suspension. MLB, which has the most widely publicized steroid problem among the major sports, implemented a new, much harsher drug policy in 2006. Under the new policy, a player's first positive test results in a 50-game suspension without pay. A second failed test brings a 100-game suspension. A player who tests positive three times is banned for life. In the NBA first-time offenders are suspended for five games. The NHL implemented random drug testing at the beginning of the 2005–06 season.

Football

Only several players per year fail the NFL steroid test, but there is reason to believe that many more steroid users

are getting away with it. In 2005 Onterrio Smith (1980–) of the Minnesota Vikings was suspended for a year after being caught with a device called a Whizzinator, which is designed to undermine the accuracy of a urine test. In "Steroids Prescribed to NFL Players" (March 30, 2005, http://www.cbsnews.com/stories/2005/03/29/60II/main68 3747.shtml), *60 Minutes Wednesday* reveals that three players on the Carolina Panthers had filled prescriptions for steroids before the 2004 Super Bowl. None of these players failed a drug test. Four years later it appeared that attempts to hide steroid use were still prevalent when Mark Maske in the *Washington Post* ("Weight-Loss Pills Lead to Positive Tests," October 25, 2008, http://www.washingtonpost.com/wp-dyn/content/article/2008/10/24/AR2008102403338.html?nav=rss_sports/index/nfl) reported that a "significant number" of NFL players tested positive for the diuretic bumetanide, a fluid-retention drug that is reportedly used to mask steroid use and is on the NFL's list of banned substances.

In early 2009 Steven Reinberg reported in "1 in 10 Ex-NFL Players Used Steroids, Poll Reports" (*U.S. New & World Report*, February 20, 2009, http://health.usnews.com/articles/health/healthday/2009/02/20/1-in-10-ex-nfl-players--used--steroids-poll-reports.html) that not only did a surprisingly large percentage of former players admit having used steroids during their careers, but those who

TABLE 9.3

Drug use in selected men's college sports, selected years 1993–2005

Drug	Baseball				Basketball				Football				Tennis				Track/field			
	1993	1997	2001	2005	1993	1997	2001	2005	1993	1997	2001	2005	1993	1997	2001	2005	1993	1997	2001	2005
Amphetamines	1.7%	1.9%	2.7%	3.9%	0.7%	1.3%	1.5%	1.2%	2.9%	2.1%	4.3%	3.9%	0.0%	3.0%	2.2%	3.9%	1.1%	1.6%	1.4%	3.1%
Anabolic steroids	0.7%	1.9%	2.3%	2.3%	2.6%	0.6%	1.4%	1.5%	5.0%	2.2%	3.0%	2.3%	0.0%	0.5%	0.6%	0.3%	0.0%	1.3%	1.3%	0.8%
Ephedrine	N/A	3.3%	3.2%	3.3%	N/A	1.4%	1.9%	1.0%	N/A	5.3%	3.8%	4.2%	N/A	2.9%	1.6%	1.1%	N/A	2.4%	1.8%	1.8%

SOURCE: "Table 6. Ergogenic Drug Use in Men's Sports," in *NCAA 2004–05 Drug Testing Results*, National Collegiate Athletic Association, July 6, 2006

TABLE 9.4

Drug use in selected women's college sports, selected years 1993–2005

Drug	Basketball				Softball				Swimming				Tennis				Track/field			
	1993	1997	2001	2005	1993	1997	2001	2005	1993	1997	2001	2005	1993	1997	2001	2005	1993	1997	2001	2005
Amphetamines	1.5%	1.0%	2.0%	2.9%	4.0%	4.7%	3.9%	5.2%	2.2%	4.7%	3.3%	4.4%	0.0%	2.5%	2.7%	2.6%	1.4%	2.1%	1.7%	1.9%
Anabolic steroids	1.5%	0.4%	0.7%	0.3%	1.7%	0.9%	0.8%	0.4%	0.6%	0.8%	1.3%	0.1%	2.7%	0.3%	0.0%	0.2%	2.7%	0.6%	0.6%	0.1%
Ephedrine	N/A	1.8%	1.3%	1.5%	N/A	1.1%	2.3%	2.9%	N/A	0.5%	2.2%	1.7%	N/A	1.9%	1.2%	1.2%	N/A	0.9%	1.3%	1.1%

SOURCE: "Table 7. Ergogenic Drug Use in Women's Sports," in *NCAA 2004–05 Drug Testing Results*, National Collegiate Athletic Association, July 6, 2006

reported heavy usage were more likely to have sustained musculoskeletal injuries during their active years.

Baseball

In the first decade of the 21st century, MLB has suffered from a serious steroid-induced public relations problem. Baseball had no official steroid policy before 2002. That year, as part of the collective bargaining agreement between players and owners, a plan was put in place to hold survey testing in 2003; if more than 5% of players came up positive in anonymous tests, a formal testing policy, with accompanying penalties, would be implemented the following year. When the results of the survey showed a positive rate of between 5% and 7%, the policy development process was triggered. Beginning in 2004 every player was to be tested once per year during the season. The first time a player tested positive, he was to be placed in treatment; a second positive test would result in a 15-day suspension. A fifth positive test could result in a suspension lasting up to a year.

Under the policy, not a single player was suspended. However, it was clear that performance-enhancing drugs were still being used on a large scale, and pressure mounted to toughen the policy. The 2005 season brought a new policy in which steroids, steroid precursors (such as andro), designer steroids, masking agents, and diuretics were all banned. All players would be subject to unannounced mandatory testing during the season. In addition, there would be testing of randomly selected players, with no maximum number, and random testing during the off-season. The penalties for a positive result were a 10-day suspension for the first offense, 30 days for a second, 60 days for the third, and one year for the fourth. All these suspensions were without pay. The following season, the penalties were stiffened to those noted earlier.

The question of steroid use in baseball began to arise more frequently as long-standing home run records began to topple in quick succession. In 1998 McGwire and Sosa both passed the single-season home run record of 61 set by Roger Maris (1934–1985) in 1961, hitting 70 and 66, respectively. Both players were dogged by rumors that they were assisted by performance-enhancing drugs. In 2001 Bonds extended the record to 73. In 2005 Canseco published *Juiced: Wild Times, Rampant 'Roids, Smash Hits, and How Baseball Got Big*. In it, Canseco paints a lurid picture of rampant steroid use throughout the sport and names a number of players as steroid users.

Amid the furor created by Canseco's book, Congress convened in March 2005 a series of hearings on steroid use in baseball. Several prominent players were called to testify, including Canseco, McGwire, Palmeiro, Sosa, and Schilling. Canseco reiterated his claims before the congressional panel. McGwire was elusive, saying, "I'm not here to talk about the past," whereas Palmeiro denied all wrongdoing. Palmeiro, after testifying under oath that he had "never used steroids," tested positive for the steroids in July 2005. Palmeiro was suspended for 10 games and fined $164,000.

Palmeiro was not the first high-profile baseball player to get caught using steroids. As the BALCO scandal continued to unfold, Bonds admitted during grand jury testimony in 2004 to having used steroids, though he claimed that he had done so unknowingly via an arthritis cream he thought was steroid-free. Even though baseball players test positive regularly—Palmeiro was the seventh to do so in 2005—most of them are lesser known, and their stories do not make the headlines. The first prominent baseball player to publicly admit to intentionally using steroids was Jason Giambi (1971–), who confessed that he had used performance-enhancing drugs during his stellar 2003 season, in which he hit 41 home runs. Several other high-profile players have since been forced to admit having used banned substances. In 2009 it was revealed that 104 players had tested positive for performance-enhancing drugs during testing that had taken place in 2003 as part of an agreement between the league and the MLB Players Association to determine whether mandatory testing should be implemented the following year. Under the terms of the agreement, the 2003 tests were to remain confidential. The list, however, eventually saw the light of day; among the elite players whose names appeared on the list were Alex Rodriguez (1975–), Manny Ramirez (1972–), and David Ortiz (1975–). Rodriguez publicly admitted having used banned drugs from 2001 and 2003 when he was playing for the Texas Rangers, but it has been speculated—notably in the book *A-Rod: The Many Lives of Alex Rodriguez* by Selena Roberts published in the spring of 2009—that he used steroids as far back as high school and as recently as playing for the New York Yankees beginning in 2004. Ramirez later tested positive under the new testing policy and received a 50-game suspension in 2009.

Another book sparked a further investigation in 2006. In *Game of Shadows: Barry Bonds, BALCO, and the Steroids Scandal That Rocked Professional Sports* (2006), Mark Fainaru-Wada and Lance Williams outline a series of damaging accusations associated with the BALCO affair. Fainaru-Wada and Williams focus most of their attention on Bonds, but they also implicate several other athletes, including Jones and Montgomery. Shortly after the book came out, it was announced that Allan H. Selig (1934–), the baseball commissioner, had engaged the former U.S. senator George Mitchell (1933–) to head an independent investigation into steroid use in baseball, in an effort to stave off further intervention by Congress. As Bonds was surpassing Hank Aaron's (1934–) all-time home run record in the summer of 2007, a feat he accomplished on August 7, Mitchell announced that his investigation was in its final phase. Released at the end of 2007 (*Report to the Commissioner of Baseball of an Independent Investigation into the Illegal Use of Steroids and Other Performance Enhancing Substances by Players in Major League Baseball*, Office of the Commissioner of Baseball, December 13, 2007, http://files.mlb.com/mitchrpt.pdf), the report documented the widespread use of steroids in baseball beginning in the 1980s, which involved players on every team. Mitchell noted that honest athletes were placed at a disadvantage in competing with those on steroids and that many records from the period could be invalid.

The report recommended that MLB create a Department of Investigations, work more closely with law enforcement authorities, establish an education program to explain the health risks of steroids and how to achieve some of the same results through training and nutrition, and institute mandatory, unannounced drug testing. Mitchell caused a furor by naming many Major League players reported to have used performance-enhancing drugs, as well as by suggesting that these players not be punished. "I urge the Commissioner to forgo imposing discipline on players for past violations of baseball's rules on performance enhancing substances, including the players named in this report, except in those cases where he determines that the conduct is so serious that discipline is necessary to maintain the integrity of the game."

Steroid use in baseball appears to be particularly widespread among players from Latin American countries. Joseph Contreras, in "Too Intense?" (*Newsweek*, May 27, 2006), notes that a majority of players who tested positive during MLB's first year of mandatory testing were from Latin America. Contreras quotes some insiders as pointing to the increased pressure on young players from poor countries to do well, as baseball presents one of the few potential paths out of poverty for these individuals. In "Caught Looking" (*ESPN Magazine*, May 28, 2007), Ian Gordon points to a language barrier as part of the problem, suggesting that some Spanish-speaking players may not be getting the message about banned substances in spite of the league's best outreach efforts. Players from the Dominican Republic appear to be particularly susceptible to the lure of performance-enhancing drugs. Mike Fish wrote in "Steroid Problem Reaches Critical Mass in the D.R." (ESPN, March 2, 2009, http://sports.espn.go.com/mlb/news/story?id=2763194) that according to MLB data, more than half of the major and minor league baseball players who had tested positive since 2005 hailed from that country.

Basketball

Rookie NBA players are tested up to four times per season, and veterans are subject to one random test during training camp. Prohibited substances include amphetamines, cocaine, opiates, marijuana, and steroids. Penalties range from suspensions for a number of games to a lifetime ban. As of 2009, basketball had largely avoided the kind of scandals involving performance-enhancing drugs that plagued the baseball world.

Hockey

Until 2005 the NHL had no formal antidoping policy. However, in the wake of scandals that dogged other major sports in recent years, the league unveiled its first such policy in September 2005 at a congressional hearing on drug use in professional sports. Under the new policy, NHL players are subject to a maximum of two random tests with no advance notice during the NHL season for the performance-enhancing drugs designated on the World Anti-Doping Agency's (WADA) "Prohibited List" (2009, http://www.wada-ama.org/en/prohibitedlist.ch2). A first-time positive test will result in a 20-game suspension. The suspension increases to 60 games for a second offense, and a third positive test can result in permanent suspension from the league.

Cycling

Perhaps no other sport has been tainted by doping scandals more than professional bicycle racing, particularly the sport's most illustrious event, the Tour de France. During the 1967 Tour, the British cyclist Tom Simpson (1937–1967) died on one of the climbs in the race after using large amounts of amphetamines. The first major drug scandal in cycling took place in 1998, when the Festina cycling team was thrown out of the competition after the team masseur, Willy Voet (1945–), was caught in possession of various narcotics and other banned substances, including EPO, growth hormones, testosterone, and amphetamines. In 2004 David Millar (1977–), a time-trial world champion, was banned from the tour following the discovery of banned drugs at the offices of his cycling team, Cofidis. Doping allegations have plagued the career of the American cyclist Lance Armstrong (1972–), who won his seventh consecutive Tour de France in 2005 before announcing his retirement. (Armstrong emerged from retirement to compete in the 2009 Tour, finishing an impressive third overall.) In 2002 Armstrong was linked to the sports physician Michele Ferrari (1953–), who was reputed to have developed a system for taking EPO without detection. In 2005 EPO was found in Armstrong's old laboratory samples from the 1999 Tour de France. Armstrong vehemently denied ever using banned drugs and questioned the validity of such old samples that had passed through so many hands over the years. In 2006 investigators cleared Armstrong of the charges and criticized antidoping authorities for mishandling evidence and making irresponsible accusations.

Armstrong's exoneration notwithstanding, the situation only became worse for the Tour de France. On the eve of the 2006 race, several top riders, including the contenders Jan Ullrich (1973–) and Ivan Basso (1977–), were banned from competing as a result of accusations made by Spanish police after a long investigation called Operacion Puerto. The 2006 Tour was won by the American cyclist Floyd Landis (1975–). However, shortly after the conclusion of the race, it was revealed that Landis had failed a drug test at the 17th stage of the race, with tests showing an abnormally high level of testosterone in his blood. Landis maintained his innocence, but he was nevertheless stripped of his title and fired from his racing team. He appealed the decision to strip his title, but the appeal was denied.

The doping situation at the tour continued its downward spiral in 2007. Several prominent riders either tested positive for banned substances before or during the race, or were punished for avoiding testing. They included the German cyclist Patrik Sinkewitz (1980–), who tested positive at a pre-tour training camp; Alexander Vinokourov (1973–) of Russia, who was pulled after the 15th stage for receiving an illicit blood transfusion; and the Danish racer Michael Rasmussen (1974–), who was withdrawn from the tour for intentionally avoiding a required blood test. The 2008 and 2009 Tours were relatively free of doping controversy, though Alberto Contador (1982–), the winner in 2007 and 2009, remained the subject of ongoing doping rumors that had not been substantiated as of September 2009.

STEROIDS AND THE LAW

Anabolic steroids are Schedule III–controlled substances in the United States. In October 2004 the federal Anabolic Steroids Act was signed into law. The act updated the Anabolic Steroid Control Act of 1990 in a number of ways. It amended the definition of anabolic steroids, adding THG, androstenedione, and certain related chemicals to the list of substances the law covered. The act also directed the U.S. Sentencing Commission to review federal sentencing guidelines for offenses related to steroids and provided for increased penalties for committing these offenses. It authorized the U.S. attorney general to exempt from regulation steroid-containing drugs that do not pose a drug abuse threat. Finally, the law directed the U.S. secretary of health and human services to provide grants for the development of science-based educational programs for elementary and secondary schools on the hazards of anabolic steroid use. A number of states have passed their own laws targeted specifically at curbing steroid use among youths.

Antidoping Agencies

By the end of the 20th century the global sports community recognized that it would take a coordinated international effort to bring the problem of performance-enhancing drugs under control. WADA was created in 1999 as a collaborative initiative between sports agencies and governments across the globe. WADA's role is to lead international efforts against doping in sports through public education, advocacy, research, and drug testing and to provide leadership for the efforts of agencies working against doping in individual countries. The U.S. Anti-Doping Agency (USADA), an independent nonprofit organization, was launched in October 2000 to lead this work at the national level. The USADA oversees testing, education, research, and adjudication on drug issues for U.S. athletes competing in the Olympic, Pan Am, and Paralympic games.

CHAPTER 10
SPORTS AND GAMBLING

The drive in humans to gamble on sports seems to be almost as strong as the drive to participate in them. People have been betting on the outcome of sporting events since ancient times. In ancient Rome the wealthy class wagered on chariot races, animal fights, and gladiator battles. The Romans spread their penchant for gambling across the breadth of their empire, including Britain. In the 16th and 17th centuries people throughout Europe enjoyed betting on cockfights, wrestling, and footraces. In the 18th century horse racing and boxing rose to prominence as spectator sports on which the public enjoyed gambling. The 19th and 20th centuries brought a new emphasis on team sports, and Europeans began risking their wages on rugby, soccer, and cricket games.

Colonists brought their yen for gambling on sports with them to North America. Horse racing was a particularly popular sport among those inclined toward gambling. Most forms of gambling, including sports gambling, became illegal in the United States during the 19th century, as laws changed to conform to the morals of the time. Nevertheless, it remained legal to bet on horse racing, and other sports gambling continued to flourish underground. The state of Nevada legalized gambling in 1931, but after a couple of decades it was so tainted by organized crime and other scandals that it was the subject of government crackdowns during the 1950s. A new, highly regulated version of sports betting returned to Nevada in 1975; centered in Las Vegas, this segment of the gambling industry continues to thrive in the 21st century.

Modern sports gambling in the United States can be roughly divided into three categories: pari-mutuel gambling on horse racing, dog racing, and jai alai games; legal sports betting through a licensed bookmaker; and illegal sports gambling. The third category makes up the biggest portion of sports gambling in the nation.

PARI-MUTUEL GAMBLING

Pari-mutuel betting was invented in late 19th-century France by Pierre Oller. *Pari-mutuel* is a French term that means "mutual stake." In this kind of betting all the money bet on an event is combined into a single pool, which is then split among the winning bettors, with management first taking some share off the top before distribution. The share management receives is called the takeout; the takeout rate, which in the United States is set by state law, is usually about 20% of the total betting pool. Unlike placing a bet with a bookmaker, an individual betting on a pari-mutuel event is betting against other gamblers rather than against the house. The house keeps the same percentage of the total bets regardless of the outcome of the event. Another source of revenue from pari-mutuel gambling is breakage. Winning bettors are not usually paid out to the exact penny total; rather, payouts are rounded down. The leftover money, or breakage, is usually only a few cents per bet, but it adds up to a substantial sum over the course of thousands of transactions. Breakage may be split in various ways. For example, breakage generated by California horse tracks is split among the state, the track operators, and the horse owners.

In pari-mutuel betting the total pool in a race depends on how much is bet on that race. Every bet that is placed on a particular horse or player affects the odds; as a result, the more people who bet on a particular outcome, the lower the payout is for those who bet on that outcome. Betting on a long shot offers a potentially better payout, but a lower likelihood of winning anything.

The pari-mutuel system has been used in horse racing since about 1875, but it did not become widespread until the 1920s and 1930s, with the introduction of the totalizor, a special calculator that could automatically calculate the odds for each horse in a race based on the bets that had been placed. Before the 1930s most betting on horse races was done through bookmakers. Corruption was widespread. In 1933 California, Michigan, Ohio, and New Hampshire legalized pari-mutuel gambling on horse racing mainly as a way to regulate the industry, decrease corruption, and generate revenue for the state. Many other states followed their lead over the next several years.

Historically, most pari-mutuel betting has taken place in person at the location where the event is happening. However, in recent years bets have been placed at off-track betting facilities, which were first approved by the New York legislature in 1970. Wagering via telephone or the Internet is also available in some states. Many races are simulcast to in-state and out-of-state locations, including off-track betting sites, some located in casinos. This allows bettors to engage in intertrack wagering, which means one can bet on a race at one track while being physically present at a completely different track.

The American Gaming Association (AGA) estimates in the fact sheet "Gaming Revenue: Current-Year Data" (January 2009, http://www.americangaming.org/Industry/factsheets/statistics_detail.cfv?id=7) that the total gross revenue from pari-mutuel gambling in the United States in 2007 was $3.5 billion, down from $3.7 billion two years earlier.

An increasing share of pari-mutuel wagering has been taking place at racinos. Racinos, a growing phenomenon in the gaming industry, are horse- or greyhound-racing tracks that also offer casino gaming on site. The AGA reported in its *2009 State of the States: The AGA Survey of Casino Entertainment* (2009, http://www.americangaming.org/assets/files/aga_sos2009web_FINAL.pdf) that customers spent a record $6.19 billion at the nation's racinos in 2008, a 17% increase over the previous year. Pennsylvania is the state with the most racino action; about one-fourth of that revenue total was generated there.

Thoroughbred Horse Racing

People have been betting on horse races for thousands of years. Horse racing was a popular spectator sport among wealthy Greeks and Romans. Later, knights returning to Western Europe from the Crusades brought with them speedy Arabian stallions, which were bred with English mares to create the line now called Thoroughbred. Thoroughbreds are fast, graceful runners and are identified by their height and long, slim legs. Thoroughbred racing quickly caught on among the British aristocracy, and it was soon dubbed the "Sport of Kings." The sport came to North America with the colonists; there are records of horse racing taking place in the New York area as early as 1665.

Thoroughbred racing remained popular in the United States throughout the 18th and 19th centuries. The sport was scaled back significantly during World War II (1939–1945), and after the war it remained in steep decline. The reasons for horse racing's loss of popularity in the postwar

years include competition from the rise of amusement parks and malls; the failure of the racing industry to embrace television; and the rise of other gambling opportunities, such as casinos and lotteries. However, even though attendance at horse races has declined substantially, the money continues to flow and has actually increased since the 1990s. Gary Rotstein reports in "How Slot Machines Have Saved Racetracks" (*Pittsburgh Post-Gazette*, February 25, 2007) that in 1990 the total amount bet (handle) on Thoroughbred races in the United States was $9.4 billion. In "Total Handle, Purses up for 2006" (January 16, 2007), the National Thoroughbred Racing Association indicates that in 2006 the total waging on U.S. races was $14.8 billion.

However, the recession that followed a couple of years later had a negative impact on wagering. Mike Curry in *Thoroughbred Times* (July 5, 2009, http://www.thoroughbredtimes.com/national-news/2009/July/05/Total-wagering-handle-drops-16-point-9-percent-in-June.aspx) writes that the total U.S. Thoroughbred handle for the first half of 2009 was $6.5 billion, down more than 10% from the first half of 2008. Equibase—a partnership between the Thoroughbred Racing Associations of North America (TRA) and the Jockey Club that provides a comprehensive, industry-owned database of information and statistics for the entire racing industry—reports that total wagering on U.S. races was $13.67 billion in 2008, more than $1 billion less than the previous year (January 6, 2009, http://www.equibase.com/news/releases/010609release.cfm).

According to Equibase, there are about 140 Thoroughbred racetracks in the United States. The racetracks in warm parts of the country are open throughout the year, whereas others are active only during those locations' warm months. Some are government owned, whereas others are privately held. The Thoroughbred gambling business is dominated by a handful of companies, the largest being two publicly traded firms: Churchill Downs and Magna Entertainment.

The three most prestigious Thoroughbred races together make up the Triple Crown of horse racing. These races, which take place over a five-week period during May and June each year, are the Kentucky Derby at Churchill Downs in Louisville, Kentucky; the Preakness Stakes at Pimlico in Baltimore, Maryland; and the Belmont Stakes at Belmont Park in Elmont, New York. According to the Kentucky Derby, in "Crowd of 153,563 Witness Mine That Bird Win Derby 135" (May 2, 2009, http://www.kentuckyderby.com/2009/news/2009/05/02/crowd-153563-witness-mine-bird-win-derby-135), in 2009 the betting totaled $104.5 million, an 8.7% decrease from the previous year. Most of this total was bet off-track. Jeff Lowe reported in "Handle Up, Attendance Way Down for Preakness" (*Thoroughbred Times,* May 16, 2009, http://www.thoroughbredtimes.com/racing-news/2009/May/16/Handle-up-attendance-way-down-for-Preakness.aspx) that $86.7 million was wagered on the 2009 Preakness. In "Belmont Stakes Handle, Attendance Dip" (June 6, 2009, http://www.thoroughbredtimes.com/national-news/2009/June/06/Belmont-attendance-handle-dip-with-no-Triple-Crown-on-the-line.aspx) the *Thoroughbred Times* reported that the 2009 Belmont Stakes card, including all races that took place at the track that day, drew a handle of $89.7 million.

Non-Thoroughbred Horse Racing

Even though Thoroughbreds dominate the horse-racing scene in the United States, pari-mutuel gambling is available for other types of horses as well. Harness racing, in which horses trot or pace rather than gallop and pull the jockey in a two-wheeled cart called a sulky, uses a horse called a Standardbred, which is typically shorter and more muscular than a Thoroughbred. According to the U.S. Trotting Association (March 2009, http://racing.ustrotting.com/trackside/trackfacts/trackfacts.cfm), there were 46 licensed harness-racing tracks around the country in 2009. Another type of horse commonly raced is the quarter horse, which gets its name from the fact that it excels at sprinting distances under a quarter of a mile. Finally, the Arabian Jockey Club (2008, http://www.arabianracing.org/upload/Microsoft_Word_-_Arabian_Racing_in_the_US_2008_Year_End_Summary.pdf) notes that 17 tracks around the United States featured Arabian horses, the only true purebred horses on the circuit, in 2008.

Greyhound Racing

Like horses, greyhounds have been raced for amusement and gambling purposes for centuries. Greyhound racing has been called the "Sport of Queens," probably because it was Queen Elizabeth I (1533–1603) of England who first standardized the rules for greyhound coursing (a sport in which greyhounds are used to hunt rabbits) in the 16th century. Greyhound racing was brought to the United States in the late 19th century, and the first circular greyhound track was opened in California in 1919.

Greyhound racing is not nearly as popular as horse racing, and its popularity has been declining since the early 1990s. The sport reached its peak of popularity in 1992, when, according to the Greyhound Racing Association of America (GRA-America; 2009, http://www.gra-america.org/the_sport/history.html), nearly 3.5 million people attended the 16,827 races that took place at more than 50 tracks. Nearly $3.5 billion was bet on greyhound races that year. Revenue has dropped by nearly half since then. The GRA-America (2009, http://www.gra-america.org/the_sport/tracks.php) notes that there were 40 greyhound tracks operating in 12 states in 2009. More than a third of the tracks currently in operation are located in Florida. The decline in the popularity of greyhound racing is in part due to allegations, many of them well documented, of the mistreatment of the dogs. For example, the Greyhound Protection League collects data on

cruelty and deaths related to greyhound racing and lobbies for the sport to be banned altogether.

Jai Alai

Jai alai is a sport similar to handball. Like handball, it is played on a court and involves bouncing a ball against a wall. In jai alai the ball is caught using a long, curved basket called a cesta. The Florida Gaming Corporation (http://www.fla-gaming.com/history.htm) states that the first permanent jai alai arena, or fronton, was built in Florida in 1926. Jai alai is an endangered sport in the United States. Hal Habib reported in "Jai Alai, a Sport with a South Florida Flair" (May 30, 2009, http://www.palmbeachpost.com/news/content/sports/epaper/2009/05/30/a1c_jaialai_0531.html) that $68.7 million was bet on jai alai during the 2007–08 fiscal year; 20 years earlier that figure was $430.3 million. In the United States, jai alai is confined almost entirely to Florida, where the sport retains a sizable, if shrinking, following. Most of the frontons in Florida, however, rely on revenue from other forms of gambling, such as poker, to help keep them in business.

LEGAL SPORTS GAMBLING

As of 2009 unlimited gambling on multiple sports was legal in only one state: Nevada. Nowhere else in the United States is betting allowed on all big-time sports such as professional football, basketball, or baseball. In *Hidden Revenue: Regulating the Underground Economy of Sports Betting* (February 2005, http://www.pfnyc.org/publications/2005_02_hidden_revenue.pdf), Jonathan A. Schwabish and Michael R. Simas explain that this state of affairs was essentially locked into place by the passage of the Professional and Amateur Sports Protection Act of 1992, which banned sports betting everywhere while grandfathering those states where it was already allowed in some form: Delaware, Montana, Nevada, and Oregon. However, aside from Nevada, the action is limited; it may be part of a lottery game, or fantasy leagues and office pools may be legal. In May 2009 the Delaware State Senate voted to legalize certain kinds of betting on various big-time sports; the move was vehemently opposed by the four major professional sports leagues and the National Collegiate Athletic Association (NCAA), who filed a lawsuit against Delaware claiming the state, who proposed to allow single-game betting, was in violation of the 1992 ban because it had not allowed that kind of wagering previously. Frederic J. Frommer in the Associated Press ("Delaware Sports Betting Dealt Legal Blow," August 31, 2009, http://www.cbsnews.com/stories/2009/08/31/sportsline/main5277188.shtml) reported that by August 2009 a federal court of appeals limited the betting to only parlay wagers—where the bettor must choose winners of at least three separate games in one bet—on only one sport, professional football.

In Nevada legal sports gambling takes place through licensed establishments (books) that accept and pay out bets on sporting events. Sports books are legal only in Nevada.

One must be at least 21 years old to place bets with licensed bookmakers. The AGA states in the fact sheet "Sports Wagering" (February 4, 2009, http://www.americangaming .org/industry/factsheets/issues_detail.cfv?id=16) that in 2009 there were 180 locations licensed to operate sports and/or race books, all of them in Nevada.

Bookmaking

Bookmaking is the term used for determining gambling odds and handling bets and payouts. The person doing the bookmaking is called a bookmaker or bookie. Bookmakers make their money by charging a commission on each bet; the commission is usually between 4% and 5%.

Most sports bets are based on a point spread, which is set by the bookmaker. A point spread is how much a favored team must win a game by for those betting on that team to collect. For example, if Team A is a 10-point favorite to defeat Team B, the bettor is actually betting on whether Team A will beat Team B by at least this margin. If Team A wins by nine points, then those betting on Team B are winners and those picking team A are losers. In this example, Team B has lost the game, but has "beat the spread." The point spread concept was introduced in the 1940s by the bookmaker Charles K. McNeil as a way of encouraging people to bet on underdogs. Before the point spread system, bookmakers risked losing large sums on lopsided games in which everybody bet on the favorite to win.

Nevada: The Gambling Capital of the United States

Nevada legalized gambling in the 1930s as a way of generating revenue during the Great Depression (1929–1939). The state's legislature made off-track betting on horses legal during the 1940s. Betting on sports and racing was popular in Nevada's casinos throughout that decade. At the beginning of the 1950s, however, the Nevada gambling world came under the scrutiny of Congress for its ties to organized crime. Senator Estes Kefauver (D-TN; 1903–1963) initiated hearings to investigate the matter. These nationally televised hearings drew attention to a culture of corruption and gangland activity that had settled in Las Vegas. The hearings resulted in the imposition of a 10% federal excise tax on sports betting. This tax effectively strangled casino-based sports bookmaking in Nevada.

Koleman S. Strumpf of the University of North Carolina, Chapel Hill, reports in *Illegal Sports Bookmakers* (February 2003, http://www.unc.edu/~cigar/papers/Bookie4b.pdf) that the sports books mounted a comeback in the 1970s, after the excise tax was reduced to 2% in 1974, and by the 1980s sports and race bookmaking was a booming industry, helped along by another reduction in the excise tax, to 0.3% in 1983. Bookmakers such as Jimmy "The Greek" Snyder (1919–

FIGURE 10.1

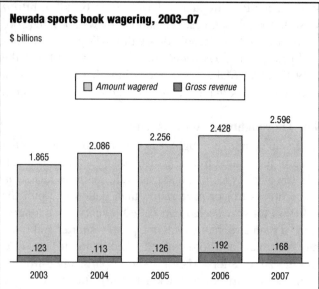

Nevada sports book wagering, 2003–07

$ billions

Amount wagered ☐ Gross revenue ■

Year	2003	2004	2005	2006	2007
Amount wagered	1.865	2.086	2.256	2.428	2.596
Gross revenue	.123	.113	.126	.192	.168

SOURCE: "Total Amount Wagered vs. Gross Revenue, 2003–2007," in *2008 State of the States: The AGA Survey of Casino Entertainment*, American Gaming Association, 2008, http://www.americangaming.org/ assets/files/aga_2008_sos.pdf (accessed July 7, 2009). Reprinted with permission from the American Gaming Association. *2008 State of the States: The AGA Survey of Casino Entertainment*, 2008. All rights reserved.

1996) became national celebrities by appearing regularly on television. Between 1982 and 1987 Nevada sports book betting increased by 230%. Betting volume began to taper off in the mid-1990s, in part due to the rise of online wagering, though it has rebounded somewhat in subsequent years. For example, the amount of revenue rose from just under $1.9 billion in 2003 to $2.6 billion in bets in 2007. (See Figure 10.1.)

Football is the biggest betting draw among the major sports. According to the AGA, in 2007 football accounted for 45% of sports book wagering, followed by basketball (26%) and baseball (20%). (See Figure 10.2.) The Super Bowl alone is a gigantic gambling event. The Nevada Gaming Control Board notes that $92.06 million was bet on the 2008 Super Bowl, the third-highest total in Super Bowl history. Figure 10.3 shows total Super Bowl betting with Nevada sports books, along with revenue from that betting, for the years 2001 through 2008. The only sports event that comes close to that kind of betting revenue is the NCAA basketball tournament, but the NCAA tournament involves 64 teams and 6 rounds of games; the Super Bowl is a single game. Industrywide, the AGA notes that about two-thirds of the bets placed legally in Nevada sports books are on professional sports. College sports account for nearly all of the remaining third; it is currently illegal to gamble on high school sports and on the Olympics.

FIGURE 10.2

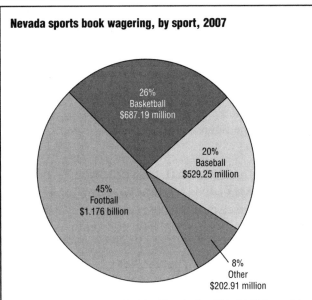

Nevada sports book wagering, by sport, 2007

26%
Basketball
$687.19 million

20%
Baseball
$529.25 million

45%
Football
$1.176 billion

8%
Other
$202.91 million

SOURCE: "What Sports Are the Most Popular Bets?" in *2008 State of the States: The AGA Survey of Casino Entertainment*, American Gaming Association, 2008, http://www.americangaming.org/assets/files/aga_2008_sos.pdf (accessed July 7, 2009). Reprinted with permission from the American Gaming Association. *2008 State of the States: The AGA Survey of Casino Entertainment*, 2008. All rights reserved.

FIGURE 10.3

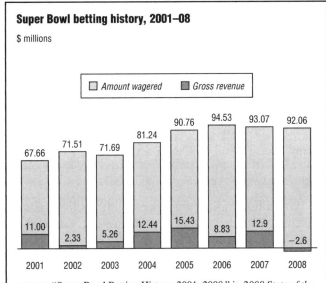

Super Bowl betting history, 2001–08

$ millions

☐ Amount wagered   ■ Gross revenue

	2001	2002	2003	2004	2005	2006	2007	2008
Amount wagered	67.66	71.51	71.69	81.24	90.76	94.53	93.07	92.06
Gross revenue	11.00	2.33	5.26	12.44	15.43	8.83	12.9	−2.6

SOURCE: "Super Bowl Betting History, 2001–2008," in *2008 State of the States: The AGA Survey of Casino Entertainment*, American Gaming Association, 2008, http://www.americangaming.org/assets/files/aga_2008_sos.pdf (accessed July 7, 2009). Reprinted with permission from the American Gaming Association. *2008 State of the States: The AGA Survey of Casino Entertainment*, 2008. All rights reserved.

ATTITUDES TOWARD SPORTS GAMBLING

In spite of gambling's reputation as a so-called vice, Americans are overwhelmingly comfortable with sports gambling, though a relatively small percentage actually participate. A Pew Research Center poll ("Gambling: As the Take Rises, So Does Public Concern," May 23, 2006, http://pewresearch.org/assets/social/pdf/Gambling.pdf) found that 67% of Americans had engaged in some form of gambling over the past year, but that only 14% of those surveyed said they had bet on professional sports in the past year, and 7% had bet on college sports. Another 5% had bet on horse racing, and 3% had wagered on boxing. Eighteen percent said they had participated in an office betting pool related to some type of sporting event, such as the Super Bowl or the NCAA basketball tournament. The Pew survey found a general downward trend in sports betting. Betting on professional sports decreased from 22% in 1989 to 14% in 2006; betting on horse racing experienced a similar decline, from 14% in 1989 to 5% in 2006. Data from the Gallup Organization appear to confirm that trend. Gallup polling conducted in January 2008 found that only 7% of Americans had bet on a professional sporting event in the past year, down from 22% in 1989. (See Figure 10.4.) Fourteen percent had participated in an office pool in 2008.

Even though not many people actually participate, a larger percentage of Americans approve of gambling in general, and sports gambling in particular. The 2006 Pew survey found that 42% of respondents approved of legalized gambling on professional sports, and 50% approved of states legalizing off-track betting on horse racing. (See Figure 10.5.)

The potential for government revenue generated by legal sports gambling is the strongest argument for

FIGURE 10.4

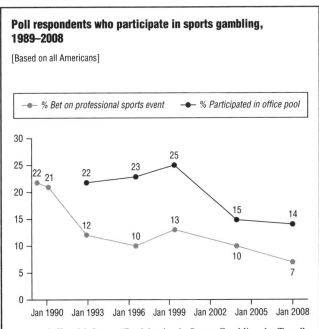

Poll respondents who participate in sports gambling, 1989–2008

[Based on all Americans]

—●— % Bet on professional sports event   —●— % Participated in office pool

SOURCE: Jeffrey M. Jones, "Participation in Sports Gambling, by Type," in *One in Six Americans Gamble on Sports*, The Gallup Organization, February 1, 2008, http://www.gallup.com/poll/104086/one-six-americans-gamble-sports.aspx (accessed July 7, 2009). Copyright © 2008 by The Gallup Organization. Reproduced by permission of The Gallup Organization.

FIGURE 10.5

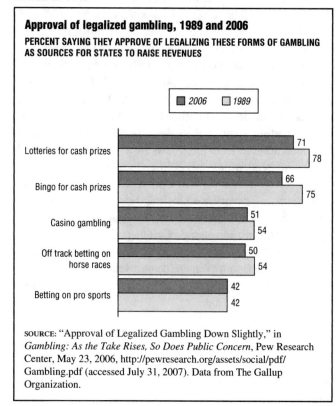

Approval of legalized gambling, 1989 and 2006

PERCENT SAYING THEY APPROVE OF LEGALIZING THESE FORMS OF GAMBLING AS SOURCES FOR STATES TO RAISE REVENUES

■ 2006   □ 1989

	2006	1989
Lotteries for cash prizes	71	78
Bingo for cash prizes	66	75
Casino gambling	51	54
Off track betting on horse races	50	54
Betting on pro sports	42	42

SOURCE: "Approval of Legalized Gambling Down Slightly," in *Gambling: As the Take Rises, So Does Public Concern*, Pew Research Center, May 23, 2006, http://pewresearch.org/assets/social/pdf/Gambling.pdf (accessed July 31, 2007). Data from The Gallup Organization.

proponents of legalizing betting on professional and college sports in states where it is currently banned. Ari Weinberg estimated in "The Case for Legal Sports Gambling" (*Forbes*, January 27, 2003) that the 1992 law that locks all states except Nevada out of the sports gambling market deprives other states of taxes of perhaps hundreds of billions of dollars in illegal sports bets each year.

ILLEGAL SPORTS GAMBLING

Even though gambling is legal in one form or another—whether in casinos, at racetracks, or on lotteries—in every state except Utah and Hawaii, illegal gambling nevertheless flourishes as well. The AGA estimates that the Nevada sports books account for less than 1% of all sports gambling in the United States. So prevalent is illicit sports gambling that it is almost impossible to calculate the dollar amounts involved. A 1999 report commissioned by Congress by the National Gambling Impact Study Commission (1999, http://govinfo.library.unt.edu/ngisc/reports/fullrpt.html) estimated that illegal sports gambling in the United States amounted to as much as $380 billion per year. The $2.5 billion wagered legally through Nevada sports books, according to the AGA, pales in comparison.

Many different activities fall into the category of illegal gambling, ranging from betting on sports outside of the legitimate, licensed bookmaking system to benign office pools. Sports gambling has a long history of association with organized crime, which ran illegal bookmaking operations across the country as early as the 1920s. After Nevada legalized casino gambling in 1931, organized crime quickly took control of the industry. When the federal government made progress in driving organized crime out of the casino business in the 1950s, the mobsters focused their efforts on bookmaking, which was not yet available in the casinos. In the 21st century a large portion of sports gambling is still believed to be controlled by organized crime figures.

FIXING, SHAVING, AND TAMPERING: SPORTS GAMBLING SCANDALS

Shady characters, including prominent organized crime figures, have always gravitated toward sports, sometimes as a means of laundering money obtained illicitly in other industries. The history of sports is rife with tales of gamblers paying off athletes to "take a dive" or miss the crucial shot. Major professional sports leagues and the NCAA have taken measures to distance themselves from sports gambling, but their efforts have not prevented a long list of sports gambling scandals from taking place in the last several decades.

Perhaps the most notorious sports gambling scandal in history was the so-called Black Sox Scandal of 1919, in which gamblers bribed several members of the Chicago White Sox to intentionally throw the World Series. A huge point-shaving scandal encompassing 7 schools and 32 players rocked college basketball in 1951. Point shaving is a type of game fixing in which players, who are usually bribed by gamblers, conspire to avoid beating a published point spread. In 1978 associates of the Lucchese organized crime family orchestrated a point-shaving scheme with key members of the Boston College basketball team. Another point-shaving scheme involving college basketball was uncovered at Arizona State University in 1994. Lesser-known scandals have taken place in the intervening years.

Many high-profile professional athletes have gotten in trouble over the years for gambling on the sport in which they participate, which inevitably creates suspicion about game fixing. In 1963 the National Football League (NFL) players Alex Karras (1935–) of the Detroit Lions and Paul Hornung (1935–) of the Green Bay Packers were suspended for betting on their own teams' games. Denny McLain (1944–) of the Detroit Tigers, the last pitcher to win 30 or more games in a season, was suspended for most of the 1970 season for associating with gamblers. In 1989 the baseball player Pete Rose (1941–), who holds the record for the most career hits, was kicked out of baseball for gambling on Major League Baseball games. He denied doing so at the time but has since admitted to betting on baseball games while serving as manager of the Cincinnati Reds. Rose's lifetime suspension has kept him out of the Baseball Hall of Fame, into which he would certainly have been inducted had his gambling activities not come to light. In 1999 the former San Francisco 49ers owner Eddie DeBartolo (1946–) was fined $1 million and suspended by the NFL for paying a $400,000 bribe to obtain a license to operate a casino in Louisiana.

The National Basketball Association (NBA) was rocked in the summer of 2007 by revelations that the veteran referee Tim Donaghy (1967–) had been involved in gambling on NBA games, including games in which he had officiated. The NBA immediately took the position that Donaghy's activities represented an isolated case and that gambling among referees was extremely rare. In August 2007 Donaghy pleaded guilty to two felony charges stemming from evidence that he had provided betting recommendations to gamblers based on inside information about game circumstances. Just days after the NBA scandal broke, professional tennis was forced to grapple with a gambling-related scandal of its own when suspicious betting patterns emerged on a match between the high-ranked Russian player Nikolay Davydenko (1981–) and the much lower-ranked Martin Vassallo Arguello (1980–) of Argentina at an Association of Tennis Professionals tournament in Poland.

Since the 1990s college sports have been at the center of some of the most visible sports gambling scandals. During the 1994–95 season two Northwestern University basketball players were caught shaving points. Two years later, 13 football players at Boston College were suspended for gambling on college football games. Other cases have involved the University of Washington football coach Rick Neuheisel (1961–), the University of Michigan basketball player Chris Webber (1973–), the Florida State University quarterback Adrian McPherson (1983–), and the University of Florida basketball player Teddy Dupay (1979–).

After decades of taking measures to avoid even the appearance of impropriety by distancing themselves from gambling entirely, there are some signs that the major sports leagues are ready to establish a cozier relationship with the gambling industry, simply because the money in sports gambling is too good to resist. A prime example are the Maloof brothers—Joseph (1955–), Gavin (1956–), and George Jr. (1964–)—who together own both the NBA's Sacramento Kings and the Palms Casino in Las Vegas. Joseph and Gavin run the Kings, while George oversees the Palms. When the Maloofs sought to buy the Kings in 1998, the NBA was willing to give its blessing provided the Maloofs quit accepting bets on NBA games in their casino's legal bookmaking operation. Before the Maloofs, there was the ITT Corporation, a conglomerate that owned three Las Vegas casinos at the time, which was allowed to purchase half interest in two New York teams: the Knicks and the Rangers. In 2005 and

2006 the National Hockey League's Pittsburgh Penguins attempted to obtain a license for a slot machine casino to raise funds to build a new stadium; the effort failed when the Pennsylvania gaming board awarded the only available license to another entity in December 2006. One of the partners in the group that won the license was the Pittsburgh Steelers running back Jerome Bettis (1972–). Bettis's participation in a proposal to open a horse track/casino/hotel complex raised some concern around the NFL, but not as much as would have been raised a few years earlier. Of course, Bettis had a good role model: the Rooney family, owners of the Steelers, also own two horse-racing facilities.

GAMBLING IN COLLEGE SPORTS

The college sports gambling cases noted earlier are probably just the tip of the iceberg. Gambling on sports, which is technically legal only in Nevada and only by adults, is extremely common among college athletes themselves. The *2003 NCAA National Study on Collegiate Sports Wagering and Associated Behaviors* (December 2004, http://www .ncaapublications.com/Uploads/PDF/2003_sports_wagering _study03918ddc-2323-446c-9fa4-2a9f40bc371f.pdf) found that in 2003 more than two-thirds (69%) of male student-athletes and nearly half (47%) of female student-athletes participated in some form of gambling in the past year; 35% of male student-athletes and 10% of female student-athletes reported having bet on sporting events in the past year, in direct violation of NCAA rules regarding sports wagering. The report includes the startling finding that 20.8% of male student-athletes and 5.7% of female student-athletes had gambled on collegiate sporting events in the past year. About 1% of football players and 0.5% of men's basketball players reported having accepted money to play poorly in a game. About 2% of men's football and basketball players said they had been asked to affect the outcome of a game.

In "A Study of Gambling Activity in a NCAA Division II Institution" (*Sports Journal*, vol. 9, no. 4, fall 2006), which focuses on gambling among students and student-athletes at the University of Western Georgia, Frank Butts finds even higher rates of gambling in general—including an astonishing 97.3% of male student-athletes having gambled in some form in the past year—but lower rates of gambling specifically on college sports.

The NCAA has long supported a complete ban on college sports gambling. Naturally, Nevada-based gambling interests strongly oppose such a measure. The gaming industry points out that the problems associated with gambling on college sports are mostly related to illegal gambling, not legitimate wagering that takes place through licensed bookmakers. For example, the AGA's 2009 "Sports Wagering" fact sheet notes that the $80 to

$90 million bet legally on the NCAA basketball tournament each year is only about 4% of the sum bet illegally.

Since 2000 some members of Congress have advocated banning college sports betting, but they have met with little success. Among the biggest proponents of banning all gambling on college sports has been Senator John McCain (R-AZ; 1936–), the unsuccessful 2008 Republican nominee for president, who first introduced the Amateur Sports Integrity Act in 2000. Initially, the bill had Nevada gambling businesses worried, but in the end it made little progress in the face of heavy lobbying on the part of the gaming industry and a lack of significant public support. McCain reintroduced the bill during the next two congressional sessions, but it met the same fate. Representative Tom Osborne (R-NE; 1937–), the U.S. House of Representatives sponsor of the bill, reintroduced a version in March 2005 (though McCain opted not to do so in the Senate at the time), just as the NCAA basketball tournament was in high gear. Gaming industry representatives working against the bill claimed that it would have a devastating effect on their business, noting that college sports gambling accounts for a sizable share—as much as one-third at some bookmaking establishments—of the total bets placed with licensed Nevada bookmakers. Tony Batt reports in "McCain Joins in on NCAA Contest Fun" (*Las Vegas Review-Journal*, March 15, 2007) that by March 2007 McCain himself had apparently softened his stance on betting on college sports; his presidential campaign Web site invited visitors to join him in picking winners in the NCAA men's basketball tournament. In August 2009, as reported by the Associated Press ("NCAA Bans Events in Some States," August 7, 2009, http://sports.espn.go.com/ncaa/news/story?id= 4382518), the NCAA approved a new policy banning championship tournaments from talking place in the few states that allow betting on individual games.

ONLINE GAMBLING

The new frontier of sports gambling is the Internet. Nobody knows exactly how much money is bet online, and the legal status of some aspects of online gambling remains ambiguous. Christiansen Capital Advisors (CCA), a gaming and entertainment consulting firm that publishes *Insight: The Journal of the North American Gambling Industry* (January 2009, http://www.cca-i.com/insight/V6i10.htm), estimates that American adults bet $5.8 billion over the Internet in 2007, while noting that it has become much more difficult to make this estimate since passage of the Unlawful Internet Gambling Enforcement Act of 2006 (UIGEA), which made it difficult for financial institutions to transfer funds to and from online gambling operations. In "Sports Wagering," the AGA indicates that online sports betting generated about $4.3 billion in revenues in 2005 (when it was much easier to collect accurate information), citing CCA as the source of its data.

Internet gambling first became available in the late 1990s, and the Nevada sports books quickly sensed that it presented a serious challenge. Many authorities argued that, based on the federal Wire Act of 1961, which was originally enacted to get organized crime out of sports betting, online sports gambling is technically illegal in the United States; however, not everybody agreed with this analysis. Moreover, most Internet gambling operations are based offshore, which complicates legal issues. The Internet knows no geographic boundaries—an online gambling operation based in Antigua can be accessed as easily from Riyadh, Saudi Arabia, as it can from Dubuque, Iowa. The U.S. government has attempted to take measures to curb online gambling, both sports betting and other types, but because these businesses are not based in the United States, enforcement is problematic. After all, these businesses are legal in the countries in which they are based.

The World Trade Organization has urged the United States to give up its attempts to ban Internet betting, but some members of Congress continue to champion legislation banning online gambling. The most active proponent of banning Internet gambling has been Senator Jon Kyl (R-AZ; 1942–), who first introduced the Internet Gambling Prohibition Act in 1997. Others in Congress argued that rather than trying to prohibit online gambling, it should instead be regulated and taxed, generating substantial revenue for state and federal governments. In the fall of 2006 the UIGEA was passed as an amendment to an unrelated bill, and signed into law by President George W. Bush (1946–). The act does not outlaw Internet gambling, but, as mentioned previously, it prohibits U.S. financial institutions from transferring funds to and from online gambling operations. The impact of the act on online sports gambling was still being assessed as of late 2009, although one immediate result was that a number of prominent online gaming establishments stopped accepting bets from U.S. customers, even though the act did not directly require them to do so. Representative Barney Frank (D-MA; 1940–), backed primarily by the online poker industry, has championed legislation to repeal the UIGEA, but as of 2009 the law remained on the books.

IMPORTANT NAMES
AND ADDRESSES

Amateur Athletic Union
1910 Hotel Plaza Blvd.
Lake Buena Vista, FL 32830
(407) 934-7200
FAX: (407) 934-7242
URL: http://www.aausports.org/

American Gaming Association
1299 Pennsylvania Ave. NW
Washington, DC 20004
(202) 552-2675
URL: http://www.americangaming.org/

Association of Tennis Professionals Tour
201 ATP Tour Blvd.
Ponte Vedra Beach, FL 32082
(904) 285-8000
FAX: (904) 285-5966
URL: http://www.atpworldtour.com/

**Bowling Proprietors' Association
of America**
621 Six Flags Dr.
Arlington, TX 76011
1-800-343-1329
FAX: (817) 633-2940
URL: http://www.bpaa.com/

Indy Racing League
4565 W. 16th St.
Indianapolis, IN 46222
(317) 492-6526
URL: http://www.indycar.com/

International Boxing Federation
516 Main St., 2nd Fl.
East Orange, NJ 07018
(973) 414-0300
FAX: (973) 414-0307
URL: http://www.ibf-usba-boxing.com/

International Olympic Committee
Château de Vidy 1007
Lausanne, Switzerland
41-21-621-6111

FAX: 41-21-621-6116
URL: http://www.olympic.org/

Ladies Professional Golf Association Tour
100 International Golf Dr.
Daytona Beach, FL 32124-1092
(386) 274-6200
FAX: (386) 274-1099
URL: http://www.lpga.com/

Major League Baseball
Office of the Commissioner
245 Park Ave., 31st Fl.
New York, NY 10167
(212) 931-7800
URL: http://www.mlb.com/

**Major League Baseball Players
Association**
12 E. 49th St., 24th Fl.
New York, NY 10017
(212) 826-0808
FAX: (212) 752-4378
URL: http://www.mlbplayers.com/

Major League Soccer
110 E. 42nd St., 10th Fl.
New York, NY 10017
(212) 450-1200
FAX: (212) 450-1300
URL: http://www.mlsnet.com/

National Alliance for Youth Sports
2050 Vista Pkwy.
West Palm Beach, FL 33411
(561) 684-1141
1-800-729-2057
FAX: (561) 684-2546
E-mail: nays@nays.org
URL: http://www.nays.org/

**National Association for Stock Car
Auto Racing**
PO Box 2875
Daytona Beach, FL 32120
URL: http://www.nascar.com/

**National Basketball
Association**
Olympic Tower
645 Fifth Ave.
New York, NY 10022
(212) 407-8000
URL: http://www.nba.com/

**National Basketball Players
Association**
310 Lenox Ave.
New York, NY 10027
(212) 655-0880
FAX: (212) 655-0881
URL: http://www.nbpa.com/

**National Collegiate Athletic
Association**
700 W. Washington St.
PO Box 6222
Indianapolis, IN 46206-6222
(317) 917-6222
FAX: (317) 917-6888
URL: http://www.ncaa.org/

National Football League
280 Park Ave., 15th Fl.
New York, NY 10017
(212) 450-2000
FAX: (212) 681-7599
URL: http://www.nfl.com/

**National Football League Players
Association**
1133 20th St. NW
Washington, DC 20036
(202) 463-2200
1-800-372-2000
URL: http://www.nflplayers.com

National Hockey League
1251 Avenue of the Americas, 47th Fl.
New York, NY 10020
(212) 789-2000
FAX: (212) 789-2020
URL: http://www.nhl.com/

National Hockey League Players Association
20 Bay St., Ste. 1700
Toronto, ON M5J 2N8
Canada
(416) 408-4040
URL: http://www.nhlpa.com/

National Sporting Goods Association
1601 Feehanville Dr., Ste. 300
Mt. Prospect, IL 60056
(847) 296-6742
FAX: (847) 391-9827
E-mail: info@nsga.org
URL: http://www.nsga.org/

National Thoroughbred Racing Association
2525 Harrodsburg Rd.
Lexington, KY 40504
(859) 223-5444
1-800-792-6872
FAX: (859) 223-3945
E-mail: ntra@ntra.com
URL: http://www.ntra.com/

Nevada Gaming Commission and State Gaming Control Board
1919 College Pkwy.
Carson City, NV 89706
(775) 684-7750
FAX: (775) 687-5817
URL: http://gaming.nv.gov/

Professional Bowlers Association
719 Second Ave., Ste. 701
Seattle, WA 98104
(206) 332-9688
FAX: (206) 654-6030
URL: http://www.pba.com/

Professional Golfers' Association of America
100 Avenue of the Champions
Palm Beach Gardens, FL 33418
(561) 624-8400
URL: http://www.pga.com/

Sony Ericsson Women's Tennis Association Tour
One Progress Plaza, Ste. 1500
St. Petersburg, FL 33701
(727) 895-5000

FAX: (727) 894-1982
URL: http://www.sonyericssonwtatour.com/

Special Olympics
1133 19th St. NW
Washington, DC 20036
(202) 628-3630
FAX: (202) 824-0200
URL: http://www.specialolympics.org/

Sporting Goods Manufacturers Association
8505 Fenton St., Ste. 211
Silver Spring, MD 20910
(301) 495-6321
FAX: (301) 495-6322
E-mail: info@sgma.com
URL: http://www.sgma.com/

U.S. Anti-Doping Agency
1330 Quail Lake Loop, Ste. 260
Colorado Springs, CO 80906-4651
(719) 785-2000
1-866-601-2632
FAX: (719) 785-2001
URL: http://www.usantidoping.org/

U.S. Bowling Congress
621 Six Flags Drive
Arlington, TX 76011
1-800-514-2695
URL: http://www.bowl.com/

U.S. Golf Association
PO Box 708
Far Hills, NJ 07931
(908) 234-2300
FAX: (908) 234-9687
URL: http://www.usga.org/

U.S. Olympic Committee
One Olympic Plaza
Colorado Springs, CO 80909
(719) 632-5551
URL: http://www.usoc.org/

U.S. Tennis Association
70 W. Red Oak Ln.
White Plains, NY 10604
(914) 696-7000
URL: http://www.usta.com/

Women's National Basketball Association
Olympic Tower
645 Fifth Ave.
New York, NY 10022
(212) 688-9622
FAX: (212) 750-9622
URL: http://www.wnba.com/

Women's Professional Soccer
1000 Brannan St., Ste. 401
San Francisco, CA 94103
(415) 553-4467
FAX: (415) 553-4459
URL: http://www.womensprosoccer.com/

Women's Sports Foundation
1899 Hempstead Turnpike, Ste. 400
East Meadow, NY 11554
(516) 542-4700
1-800-227-3988
FAX: (516) 542-4716
E-mail: info@womenssportsfoundation.org
URL: http://www.womenssports
foundation.org/

World Boxing Association
PO Box 377
Maracay, 2101 Estado Aragua, Venezuela
02-44 663-1584
FAX: 02-44 663-3177
E-mail: info@wbanews.com
URL: http://www.wbaonline.com/

World Boxing Council
Cuzco 872, Colonia Lindavista
Mexico City D.F., 07300 Mexico
52 (55) 5119-5274
E-mail: info@wbcboxing.com
URL: http://www.wbcboxing.com/

World Boxing Organization
First Federal Bldg., Ste. 711-714
1056 Muñoz Rivera Ave., Ste. 711
San Juan 00927 Puerto Rico
(787) 765-4444
FAX: (787) 758-9053
URL: http://www.wbo-int.com/

RESOURCES

Much of the information in this volume pertaining to sports participation originated in surveys conducted by two industry organizations—the Sporting Goods Manufacturers Association (SGMA), which is the trade association for sporting goods manufacturers, and the National Sporting Goods Association (NSGA), the trade group for sporting goods retailers. The SGMA releases the annual *Sports Participation Topline Report*, as well as other reports on specific aspects of sports participation. The NSGA conducts its own survey research on participation, as well as industry research on nationwide sales of sporting goods.

The *Statistical Abstract of the United States: 2009* (U.S. Census Bureau) includes information on attendance at sporting events. The Census Bureau obtains these data from a variety of sources, including the major sports leagues and private market research companies. *USA Today*'s online database of sports salaries was also an important source of information.

Polling data provided by the Gallup Organization were key in assembling information on the preferences of sports fans, including trends related to race, gender, age, and geography.

"Sports and Television" (2004) by the Museum of Broadcast Communications provided information on the history of sports on television. Another key source on this topic, as well as other aspects of sports media, was *The Business of Sports* (2004), edited by Scott R. Rosner and Kenneth L. Shropshire. The *Business of Sports* provides comprehensive coverage of all economic aspects of the sports industry. Besides sports media, the book includes essential information on the financial structure of professional team sports, college sports, and the Olympics. Also, the *SportsBusiness Journal* and Bloomberg News Service provided additional information on the broadcast contracts of major sports.

Nonprofit advocacy and public education groups provided substantial information for this volume. The Center on Alcohol Marketing and Youth provided data on alcohol advertising during sports programming. The Women's Sports Foundation offered research on gender equity in sports. Another key source of information on gender equity was *Women in Intercollegiate Sport: A Longitudinal, National Study—Thirty-One Year Update, 1977–2008* (2008) by Linda Jean Carpenter and R. Vivian Acosta.

The National Collegiate Athletic Association (NCAA) provided a wealth of data on many aspects of college sports. Key NCAA publications that contributed information include the *1981–82—2007–08 NCAA Sports Sponsorship and Participation Rates Report* (Denise DeHass, 2009), the *2005–06 NCAA Gender-Equity Report* (DeHass, July 2008), the *1999–00—2006–07 NCAA Student-Athlete Race and Ethnicity Report* (DeHass, August 2008), and the *2004–06 NCAA Revenues and Expenses of Divisions I Intercollegiate Athletics Programs Report* (Daniel L. Fulks, March 2008). Information on eligibility rules for college athletes was found in the NCAA's *2008–09 Guide for the College-Bound Student-Athlete* (2008).

The independent research company Plunkett Research offered information on revenues of the major professional sports. Team-by-team revenue and valuation figures were provided by *Forbes*, and *SportsBusiness Journal* provided data on sales of licensed merchandise. *Forbes* was also an important source of information on sports team values and revenue. Most of the information about the structure and workings of the major sports leagues came from the leagues themselves. Likewise, information about the PGA Tour, the Association of Tennis Professionals Tour, the National Association for Stock Car Auto Racing, the various boxing organizations, and other nonteam sports was obtained from the Web sites of these organizations. Revenues from Sports Venues, a company specializing in directories and other publications about the sports venue industry, also provided helpful information.

The International Olympic Committee (IOC) provided a wealth of information about the structure and workings of the Olympic movement. One important IOC report, the *Marketing Fact File: 2008 Edition* (December 2007), offered detailed information on Olympic financial matters, including sources of revenue and how it is distributed.

Steroid Abuse in Today's Society (March 2004), by the U.S. Drug Enforcement Administration, provided valuable information about steroids.

The American Gaming Association and the Nevada Gaming Commission and State Gaming Control Board were useful sources of information on legal sports gambling. The Pew Research Center provided information about the prevalence of and attitudes toward gambling. Christiansen Capital Advisors provided research on Internet sports gambling.

INDEX

Page references in italics refer to photographs. References with the letter t *following them indicate the presence of a table. The letter* f *indicates a figure. If more than one table or figure appears on a particular page, the exact item number for the table or figure being referenced is provided.*

A

Aaron, Hank, 44

ABA (American Basketball Association), 50

Academic standards, 72–73, 81–82, 84–85

ACL (anterior cruciate ligament) injuries, 112

Acute injuries, 111

Advertising. *See* Sponsorship and advertising

AFL (American Football League), 47–48

African-Americans
diversity in major sports, 55–56
fans, 22–23
National Basketball Association, 52
tennis, 15

Age issues
National Basketball Association, 51–52
Olympics, 102

Alcohol advertising, 37–39

Ali, Laila, 66

Ali, Muhammad, 66–67

All-Star Game (baseball), 33

All-Star Game (basketball), 35

Allen, Mel, 32

Amateur sports, doping in, 9–10

Amateur Sports Act, 103

Amateur Sports Integrity Act (proposed), 136

Amateur *vs.* professional status
college athletes, 72
Olympics, 105
tennis, 62

American Basketball Association (ABA), 50

American Football Conference, 46

American Football League (AFL), 47–48

American League (baseball), 44

American Professional Football Association (APFA), 47

American Psychological Association (APA), 112–113

American Youth Soccer Organization, 20

Anabolic Steroid Control Act, 121, 128

Anabolic steroids, 9–10, 43, 46, 120–121

Ancient civilization, 99–100, 129

Anderson, Greg, 122

Androstenedione, 121

Anterior cruciate ligament (ACL) injuries, 112

Antidoping agencies, 128

Antitrust laws, 44, 73

APA (American Psychological Association), 112–113

APFA (American Professional Football Association), 47

Appleby, Stuart, 60

Armstrong, Lance, 127

Arrests, 52

Artest, Ron, 41

Association of Tennis Professionals (ATP), 4, 62–63

Athletic directors, 78

ATP (Association of Tennis Professionals), 4, 62–63

Attendance
auto racing, 28
baseball, professional, 24–25
basketball, professional, 25, 27
basketball, women's professional, 53
Boston Marathon, 29
football, college and professional, 28t
football, professional, 27
by frequency, 29t

hockey, professional, 28
professional sports, 2–3
selected sports, 1990–2007, 30t
soccer, professional, 28

Auto racing
attendance, 3, 28
NASCAR, 63–64
open-wheel cars, 64
overview, 4
television, 5, 36

B

BAA (Basketball Association of America), 50

BALCO (Bay Area Laboratory Co-Operative) scandal, 8–9, 106, 122–123

Baseball, professional
attendance, 2, 24–25
doping, 9, 121, 123, 126–127
fans, 22, 24(*f*2.1), 25*f*
gambling, 134–135
history, 44–45
labor issues, 45–46
overview, 3
race/ethnicity, 22, 55–56
structure and administration, 43–44, 44(*t*4.1)
team values and revenue, 44(*t*4.2)
television, 5, 32–33
violence, 41
World Series advertising, 37

Baseball, youth, 87, 113

Basketball, college
gambling, 135–136
race/ethnicity, 79
women coaches, 78, 87*t*

Basketball, professional
attendance, 2, 25, 27
doping, 127
fans, 26*f*

gambling, 135
history, 49–51
overview, 3–4
salaries and salary cap, 51t
stadiums, 57
structure and administration, 49, 49t
team values and revenue, 50t
television, 5, 34–35, 35t
video games, 39
violence, 40–41
Basketball Association of America (BAA), 50
Basso, Ivan, 128
Bay Area Laboratory Co-Operative (BALCO) scandal, 8–9, 106, 122–123
Bechler, Steve, 122
Beijing Olympics, 2008, 99, 104–106
Belmont Stakes, 130–131
Bettis, Jerome, 135
"Big 6" conferences, 71t
The Biggest Loser (television show), 115
Billiards, 14–15
Bird, Larry, 27, 50
Black Sox scandal, 44, 134
Blake, James, 15
Bleiler, Gretchen, 20
Blount, LeGarrette, 40
Board of Regents of the University of Oklahoma, NCAA v., 34, 73
Body image, 110
Bombing, Olympic Park, 101
Bonds, Barry, 9, 43, 45–46, 122, 126
Bone health, 109
Bookmaking, 10, 132
Boston College, 135
Boston Marathon, 29
Bowling, 1, 14–15
Boxing, 4, 64–67
Boycotts, Olympic, 8, 101
Brain injuries, 111–112
Brand, Myles, 80
Brown, Larry, 50
Bryant, Kobe, 27, 34, 50
Budge, Don, 62
Burnout, 112
Burress, Plaxico, 40–41
Bush, George W., 77, 115, 136
Byers, Walter, 72

C

Camacho, Héctor, 66
Camp Shriver, 106
CAMY (Center on Alcohol Marketing and Youth), 37–38
Canadian Broadcasting Corporation, 54
Canseco, Jose, 123, 126
Car racing. *See* Auto racing; NASCAR
Carnegie Foundation for the Advancement of Education, 72

Carpenter, Jake Burton, 19
Carpentier, Georges, 66
Carroll, Pete, 6
CART (Championship Auto Racing Teams), 64
Casinos, 131–132, 134–135
Centennial Olympic Park bombing, 101
Center on Alcohol Marketing and Youth (CAMY), 37–38
CERA (continuous erythropoietin receptor activator), 121
CFA (College Football Association), 34
Chacón, Shawn, 40
Challenge Tour, 61
Champ Car Series, 64
Champions Tour (golf), 60
Championship Auto Racing Teams (CART), 64
Charlotte Speedway, 63
Chase for the Cup, 64
Chastain, Brandi, 55
Chicago, Illinois, 106
Chicago White Sox, 44, 134
Children. *See* Youth
Childress, Josh, 51
China
    gymnastics team, 102
    steroid labs, 121
Chronic injuries, 111
Cincinnati Reds, 44
Coaches
    college sports, 6
    diversity, 56
    women, 78, 87t
Cobb, Ty, 44
Codes of conduct, 40
Cognitive development, 112
Coleman, Aubrey, 40
Collective bargaining
    Major League Baseball, 46
    National Basketball Association, 51
    National Football League, 48
    National Hockey League, 54
College basketball. *See* Basketball, college
College Football Association (CFA), 34
College sports
    alcohol advertising, 39
    Division I athletic expenses, by gender, 85f
    Division I college sports participation, by gender, 84f
    Division I scholarship spending, by gender, 86f
    doping, 123–124, 124t–125t
    expenditures and revenue, 79–81
    female student-athletes per college, 82f
    gambling, 131–132, 134–136
    gender equity, 76–77
    male student-athletes per college, 83f

men's championship sports participation, 77f
men's championship sports teams, 79f
men's participation, 75t
men's teams per college, 81f
most popular women's sports, 86t
NCAA Division I-FBS revenue and expenses, 91t
NCAA Division I-FBS revenue sources, 92t
overview, 5–6
participation, 69, 70(t6.1), 74–75
race/ethnicity, 78–79, 88t, 89f–90f
recruitment practices, 7, 81–82, 84–85, 93t–94t
team names and mascots, 40
Title IX, 77–78
women coaches, 78, 87t
women's championship sports participation, 76f
women's championship sports teams, 78f
women's participation, 74t
women's teams per college, 80f
See also Specific sports
College Sports Television (CSTV), 34
Combat Methamphetamine Epidemic Act, 122
Commercialism in college athletics, 72
Committee on Infractions, NCAA, 72
Competition in youth sports, 112
Congressional hearings, 56–57, 123, 126, 132
Constitutional Compliance Committee, NCAA, 72
Consumer spending on sporting goods, 3t, 20–21, 23(t2.13)
Contador, Alberto, 128
Conte, Victor, Jr., 122
Continuous erythropoietin receptor activator (CERA), 121
Corporate sponsors of stadiums, 57
Coubertin, Pierre de, 8, 100
Court cases
    NCAA v. Board of Regents of the University of Oklahoma, 34, 73
    Radovich v. National Football League, 48
Coyle, Harry, 31
Creatine, 121
CSTV (College Sports Television), 34
Cycling, 9, 119, 121, 127–128

D

Daly, John, 41
Dasse, Bonnie, 106
Davydenko, Nikolay, 135
Daytona 500, 28, 64
De La Hoya, Oscar, 67
Deaflympics, 107
Dean, Dizzy, 32

DeBartolo, Eddie, 135
Delaware, 131
Demonstration sports, Olympic, 99
Dempsey, Jack, 66
Detroit Tigers, 45
Developmental tours, 61
Developmentally disabled children, 106–107
Diploma mills, 84
Disability compensation, 49
Disabled persons, 106–107
Ditka, Mike, 49
Diversity. *See* Race/ethnicity
Diversity Plan, 15
Domestic violence, 41
Donaghy, Tim, 52, 135
Doping
    BALCO scandal, 122–123
    baseball, professional, 43, 46, 126–127
    basketball, professional, 127
    college sports, 123–124, 124*t*–125*t*
    cycling, 127–128
    drug types, 120–122
    football, professional, 124, 126
    health issues, 123
    history, 119–120
    hockey, professional, 127
    legislation, 128
    Olympics, 8, 105–106
    overview, 9–10
    youth, 10*f*, 123
Dress code, 52
Drug testing. *See* Doping
Dubai World Championship (golf), 61
Duke University men's lacrosse team, 73–74
Duncan, Tim, 52
Dupay, Teddy, 135
Duval, David, 60

E
EA (Electronic Arts), 39
East German swim team, 120
Economic downturn
    attendance, impact on, 2–3
    consumer spending on sporting goods, 20
    high school sports, impact on, 7
    horse racing revenue, 130
Economic issues
    alcohol advertising, 37–39, 38(*f*3.2)
    college sports, 6
    college sports expenditures and revenue, 79–81
    college sports gambling revenue, 135–136
    Division I athletic expenses, by gender, 85*f*
    Division I scholarship spending, by gender, 86*f*

gender equity in college sports, 76–78
greyhound racing revenue, 131
high school athletics, 84
high school sports, professionalization of, 7
horse racing revenue, 130–131
illegal gambling, 11
legal gambling, 10
luxury suite prices, 56*t*
Major League Baseball team values and revenue, 43–44, 44(*t*4.2)
National Basketball Association, 49, 50*t*, 51
National Basketball Association salary cap, 51*t*
National Basketball Association television contracts amounts, 35*t*
National Basketball Association
    television contracts amounts, 35*t*
National Football League, 46, 48
National Football League revenue, 47
National Football League team values and revenue, 46, 46(*t*4.3)
National Football League television contracts, 5*t*
National Hockey League, 53, 53(*t*4.9)
NCAA Division I-FBS revenue and expenses, 91*t*
NCAA Division I-FBS sources of revenue, 92*t*
Nevada sports book wagering, 132*f*, 133(*f*10.2)
Nevada sports book wagering revenue, 132
Olympics, 8, 103–104
pari-mutuel gambling revenue, 130
prize money disparities, 62
salaries, 45
sporting goods sales, 3*t*, 23(*t*2.13)
stadiums, 56–57, 56*t*
Super Bowl betting revenue, 133(*f*10.3)
taxing gambling, 133–134
televised sports revenue, 31
Women's National Basketball Association, 53
Elderly, exercise among the, 110–111
Electronic Arts (EA), 39
Els, Ernie, 60–61
Endorphins, 110
Enron, 57
Entertainment and Sports Programming Network (ESPN), 32–33
Ephedra, 122
EPO (erythropoietin), 121
Equity in Athletics Disclosure, 75
Erythropoietin (EPO), 121
ESPN, 32–33
Europe, 48, 50–52
European Tour (golf), 61
Exercise
    adults, 113–114, 114*f*–115*f*
    benefits, 109–111

    calories burned, 110*t*
    high school sports participants, 84
    race/ethnicity, 116*f*
    youth, 117*f*–118*f*
Expenditures
    college sports, 79–81
    Division I athletic expenses, by gender, 85*f*
    Division I scholarship spending, by gender, 86*f*
    gender equity in college sports, 76
    NCAA Division I-FBS revenue and expenses, 91*t*
    sporting goods, 3*t*, 23(*t*2.13)
Extreme sports, 17–20, 22(*t*2.10), 36

F
Fans
    baseball, 24(*f*2.1), 45
    basketball, 26*f*
    basketball players, relationship to, 35
    boxing, 67
    favorite sports, 2(*t*1.1), 21–22, 23(*t*2.14), 23(*t*2.15), 26*t*
    football, college, 25*t*
    football, professional, 24(*f*2.2)
    football *vs.* baseball, 25*f*
    geography, 23–24, 27*t*
    race/ethnicity, 22–23
    Super Bowl viewership, 33–34
    See also Attendance
FDA (Food and Drug Administration), 122
Ferrari, Michele, 127
Figure skating, 100
Films, boxing, 65–66
FitTV, 115
Florida, 131
Food and Drug Administration (FDA), 122
Football, college
    attendance, 28*t*
    fans, 25*t*
    gambling, 135
    NCAA, 73
    television, 34
    violence, 40
Football, professional
    attendance, 2–3, 27, 28*t*
    BALCO scandal, 123
    doping, 119–120, 124, 126
    fans, 24(*f*2.2), 25*f*
    gambling, 134–135
    history, 47–48
    labor issues, 48
    overview, 3
    retired players, 48–49
    revenue, 47
    structure and administration, 46–47, 46(*t*4.4)
    Super Bowl advertising, 36–37

Super Bowl viewership, 38(*f*3.1), 38*t*
team values and revenue, 46(*t*4.3)
television, 5, 5*t*, 33–34
video game licensing, 39
violence, 40–41
Foreign-born players, 50–51, 56, 127
Foudy, Julie, 55
Fractures, 111
France, William, Sr., 63
Frank, Barney, 136
Frazier, Jacqui, 66
Free agency
    Major League Baseball, 45
    National Football League, 48
Friedman, Benny, 47
Furyk, Jim, 60

G

Gaines, Chryste, 123
Gambling
    basketball, professional, 52
    college sports, 72, 135–136
    greyhound racing, 131
    horse racing, 130–131
    Internet, 136
    jai alai, 131
    legal gambling, 131–132
    overview, 10–11
    pari-mutuel, 129–130
    participation, 133(*f*10.4)
    scandals, 134–135
    sports book wagering, 132*f*, 133(*f*10.2)
    Super Bowl, 133(*f*10.3)
Games, video, 39
Garcia, Sergio, 61
Gehrig, Lou, 44
Gender
    college sports equity, 76–77
    Division I athletic expenses, 85*f*
    Division I college sports participation, 84*f*
    Division I scholarship spending, 86*f*
    high school sports participation, 82–83, 94(*t*6.14), 96*t*, 97*f*
    male student-athletes per college, 83*f*
    men's college championship sports participation, 76*f*
    men's college championship sports teams, 79*f*
    men's college sports participation, 75*t*
    men's teams per college, 81*f*
    National Sporting Goods Association Survey data, 17
    popular high school sports for boys, 95(*t*6.16)
    popular high school sports for girls, 95(*t*6.17)
    popular women's sports, 86*t*
    prize money, 62–63

race/ethnicity of female collegiate athletes, 90*f*
race/ethnicity of male collegiate athletes, 89*f*
student-athletes per college, 82*f*
television viewership, 39
Title IX, 77–78
women coaches, 78, 87*t*
women's college championship sports participation, 76*f*
women's college championship sports teams, 78*f*
women's college sports participation, 74*t*
women's sports participation, 20*t*–21*t*
women's teams per college, average number of, 80*f*
General managers, 56
Geographic regions, 23–24, 27*t*
George, Tony, 64
Giambi, Jason, 126
Gillette Cavalcade of Sports (television show), 5, 31
Golf, professional, 4, 59–62, 60*t*
Golf participation, 15
Goodell, Roger, 40
Goosen, Retief, 61
Graham, Trevor, 9, 122
Grand Slam (golf), 59, 60*t*
Grand Slam (tennis), 62–63, 63*t*
Grange, Red, 47
Gravity Games, 36
Greece, ancient, 99–100
Greyhound racing, 131
Gridiron Greats Assistance Fund, 49
Guns, 40–41

H

Hagler, Marvin, 66
Hamm, Mia, 55
Hammon, Becky, 102
Harrington, Padraig, 61
Hawk, Tony, 19
He Kexin, 102
Health
    benefits of exercise, 109–111
    doping, 9, 121–122
    high school sports participation, 83–84
    injuries, 111–113
    participation, impact of, 8–9
    steroid use, 123
    youth sports participation, 85, 87
HealthierUS initiative, 115
Healthy People 2010 campaign, 114–115
Hearings, congressional, 56–57, 123, 126, 132
Hicks, Thomas J., 105
High school sports
    benefits, 83–84
    boys, 95(*t*6.16)

girls, 95(*t*6.17)
overview, 6–7
participation, 82–83
participation, by demographic characteristics, 96*t*
participation, by parents' education level, 98*f*, 98*t*
participation, by sex, 95(*t*6.15), 97*f*
participation, by sex and race/ethnicity, 94(*t*6.14)
recruitment issues, 7, 51–52, 81–82, 84–85, 93*t*–94*t*
See also Youth
Hispanics, 56
History
    auto racing, 63–64
    baseball, professional, 44–45
    basketball, professional, 49–51
    boxing, 65–66
    college sports, 71–74
    doping scandals, 9–10, 105–106
    football, professional, 47–48
    gambling, 129
    golf, professional, 59–60
    hockey, professional, 54
    horse racing, 130
    Olympics, 8, 99–102, 105–106
    Special Olympics, 106
    televised sports, 31–34
    tennis, professional, 62
Hockey, professional
    attendance, 3, 28
    doping, 127
    gambling, 135
    labor issues, 54–55
    overview, 4
    structure and administration, 53–54, 53(*t*4.10)
    team values and revenues, 53(*t*4.9)
    television, 5, 35–36
Hockey Night in Canada (television show), 54
Hogan, James, 71
Holmes, Larry, 66
Hornung, Paul, 47, 134
Horse racing, 130–131
House of Representatives, U.S., 56–57
Hout, Byron, 40

I

IAA (Intercollegiate Athletic Association), 71
IBF (International Boxing Federation), 66
ICSD (International Committee of Sports for the Deaf), 107
Illegal gambling, 11, 134–136
Image and public relations
    baseball, 126
    basketball, 52

bowling and billiards, 15
boxing, 65
Indianapolis 500, 28, 64
Individual sports, 1–2, 14–15, 14(*t*2.2)
   See also Specific sports
Indy Racing League (IRL), 4, 28, 64
Injuries
   common types, 111*t*
   prevalence, 111–112
   retired football players, 48–49
   risk of, 8–9
   youth sports, 87, 113
Inline skating, 18
Intercollegiate Athletic Association (IAA),
   71
International Boxing Federation (IBF), 66
International Committee of Sports for the
   Deaf (ICSD), 107
International Federation of PGA Tours,
   60–61
International Olympic Committee (IOC)
   banned substances, 119
   doping, 9
   revenue, 103–105
   Special Olympics, Paralympics, and
     Deaflympics, 107
   sports selection, 99
   structure and administration, 8, 102–103
International Paralympic Committee (IPC),
   107
International Pro Hockey League, 54
International Tennis Federation (ITF),
   62–63
International Winter Sports Week, 100
Internet
   college football, 34
   gambling, 11, 136
   Olympics, 104
IOC. *See* International Olympic Committee
IPC (International Paralympic Committee),
   107
IRL (Indy Racing League), 4, 28, 64
ITF (International Tennis Federation),
   62–63
ITT Corporation, 135

J

Jackson, Janet, 37
Jackson, Stephen, 40, 52
Jai alai, 131
James, LeBron, 27, 34, 50
Japan Golf Tour, 61
Jennings, Brandon, 51–52
Jeter, Derek, 45
Jiang Yuyuan, 102
John Madden Football (video game), 39
Johnson, Ben, 105, 120
Johnson, Magic, 27, 50
Johnson, Michael, 106

Jones, Marion, 106, 122–123, 126
Jordan, Michael, 27, 34, 50

K

Karas, Kenneth, 122
Karl, George, 50
Karras, Alex, 134
Kefauver, Estes, 132
Kelly, Chip, 40
Kennedy Foundation, 106
Kentucky Derby, 10, 130
King, Billie Jean, 62
Klitschko brothers, 67
Knee injuries, 111–112
Korchemny, Remi, 122
Kramer, Jerry, 49
Kucinich, Dennis, 56–57
Kyl, Jon, 136

L

Labor relations
   Major League Baseball, 45–46
   National Basketball Association, 50–51
   National Football League, 48
   National Hockey League, 54–55
   professional sports, 4
Lacrosse, 14, 20, 22(*t*2.11), 22(*t*2.12)
Ladies Professional Golf Association
   (LPGA), 4, 61–62
Landis, Floyd, 9, 128
Landis, Kenesaw, 44
Language issues, 127
Latin American baseball players, 127
Laver, Rod, 62
Lawsuits, 66
Layden, Elmer, 47
Layne, Bobby, 47
Lee, Robert W., 66
Legal gambling
   college sports, 135–136
   greyhound racing, 131
   horse racing, 130–131
   Jai alai, 131
   Nevada, 131–132
   Nevada sports book wagering, 132*f*,
     133(*f*10.2)
   overview, 10
   pari-mutuel gambling, 129–130
   Super Bowl betting, 133(*f*10.3)
Legislation
   Amateur Sports Act, 103
   Amateur Sports Integrity Act (proposed),
     136
   Anabolic Steroid Control Act, 121, 128
   Combat Methamphetamine Epidemic
     Act, 122
   Equity in Athletics Disclosure, 75
   Muhammad Ali Boxing Reform Act
     (proposed), 65

   Professional and Amateur Sports
     Protection Act, 131
   Unlawful Internet Gambling
     Enforcement Act, 11, 136
   Wire Act, 136
Licensing
   Major League Baseball, 43–44
   NASCAR, 63
   National Basketball Association, 49
   National Football League, 46
   National Hockey League, 53
   Olympics, 104
   video games, 39
Liljenwall, Hans-Gunnar, 119
Linton, Andrew, 119
Literature, boxing in, 65
Logan, Jud, 106
Long-distance running
   Boston Marathon, 29
   stress injuries, 111
Louis, Joe, 66
LPGA (Ladies Professional Golf
   Association), 4, 61–62
Luxury boxes, 47, 56
Luxury tax
   Major League Baseball, 45–46
   National Hockey League, 54

M

MacCracken, Henry M., 71
Madden NFL (video game), 39
Major League Baseball
   attendance, 2, 24–25
   doping, 9, 121, 123, 126–127
   fans, 22, 24(*f*2.1), 25*f*
   gambling, 134–135
   history, 44–45
   labor issues, 45–46
   overview, 3
   race/ethnicity, 22, 55–56
   structure and administration, 43–44,
     44(*t*4.1)
   team values and revenue, 44(*t*4.2)
   television, 5, 32–33, 35*t*
   violence, 41
   World Series advertising, 37
Major League Soccer, 28, 55
Maloof brothers, 135
Management, 56
Mancini, Ray, 66
Marathons, 29
Martin, Christy, 66
Martin, Ed, 73
Mascots, 39–40
Matthew, Catriona, 62
Mays, Willie, 44
Mayweather, Floyd, Jr., 67
McCain, John, 65, 136
McGwire, Mark, 10, 45, 121, 123, 126

McLain, Denny, 134
McNeil, Charles K., 132
McPherson, Adrian, 135
Mental health
    benefits of exercise, 110–111
    doping, 9
    high school sports participation, 6–7,
        83–84
    participation, impact of, 8–9
    youth sports participation, 85, 87,
        112–113
Mexico, 121
Michigan Study of Adolescent Life
    Transitions, 110
Middle-aged persons, 112
Millar, David, 127
Million Dollar Baby (film), 66
Mine That Bird, 10
Minnesota Twins, 56–57
Mitchell, George, 126–127
Mixed martial arts, 67
Mobsters, 134
Montgomery, Tim, 106, 122–123, 126
Montreal Olympics, 1976, 120
Morris, Darrin, 66
Mountain Dew, 36
Muhammad Ali Boxing Reform Act
    (proposed), 65
Munich Olympics, 1972, 101

N

Naismith, James, 49–50
Names
    stadium, 57
    team, 39–40
NASCAR
    attendance, 3, 28
    history, 63–64
    overview, 4
    television, 5, 36
Nash, Steve, 50
National Alliance for Youth Sports
    (NAYS), 113
National Association for Stock Car Auto
    Racing. *See* NASCAR
National Basketball Association (NBA)
    attendance, 2, 25, 27
    doping, 127
    fans, 26f
    gambling, 135
    history, 49–51
    overview, 3–4
    salaries and salary cap, 51t
    stadiums, 57
    structure and administration, 49, 49t
    team values and revenue, 50t
    television, 5, 34–35, 35t
    video games, 39
    violence, 40–41

National Basketball League (NBL), 50
National Boxing Association (NBA), 66
National Broadcasting Corporation (NBC)
    baseball, 32
    Beijing Olympics, 2008, 104
    The Biggest Loser (television show), 115
    college football, 34
    history of televised sports, 5, 31
    National Hockey League, 35
National Center for Chronic Disease
    Prevention and Health Promotion, 115
National Coalition on Racism in Sports and
    Media, 40
National Collegiate Athletic Association
    (NCAA)
    academic standards, 81–82
    "Big 6" conferences, 71t
    college sports participation, 74–76
    college sports participation, by race/
        ethnicity, 88t
    Division I athletic expenses, by gender,
        85f
    Division I college sports participation,
        by gender, 84f
    Division I scholarship spending, by
        gender, 86f
    Division I-FBS revenue and expenses, 91t
    Division I-FBS sources of revenue, 92t
    doping, 123–124
    expenditures and revenue, 79–81
    female student-athletes per college,
        average number of, 82f
    football attendance, 28t
    gambling, 131, 135–136
    history, 71–74
    male student-athletes per college,
        average number of, 83f
    men's championship sports participation,
        76f–77f
    men's championship sports teams, 79f
    men's sports participation, 75t
    men's teams per college, average
        number of, 81f
    overview, 5–6
    race/ethnicity of athletes, 89f–90f
    recruitment practices, 7, 84–85, 93t–94t
    sports sponsorship, by sport and division,
        72t
    structure and administration, 69–71,
        70(t6.2)
    television, 34
    women coaches, 78
    women's championship sports teams,
        78f
    women's college sports participation,
        74t
    women's teams per college, average
        number of, 80f
National Federation of State High School
    Associations (NFHS), 6
National Football Conference, 46

National Football League (NFL)
    attendance, 2–3, 27, 28t
    doping, 119–120, 124, 126
    fans, 24(f2.2), 25f
    gambling, 134–135
    history, 47–48
    labor issues, 48
    overview, 3
    retired players, 48–49
    revenue, 47
    structure and administration, 46–47,
        46(t4.4)
    Super Bowl advertising, 36–37, 37t
    Super Bowl viewership, 38(f3.1), 38t
    team values and revenue, 46(t4.3)
    television, 5, 5t, 33–34
    video game licensing, 39
    violence, 40–41
National Football League, Radovich v., 48
National Golf Foundation, 15
National Hockey League (NHL)
    attendance, 3, 28
    doping, 127
    gambling, 135
    labor issues, 54–55
    overview, 4
    structure and administration, 53–54,
        53(t4.10), 52t4.9)
    team values and revenue
    television, 5, 35–36
National Institute of Arthritis and
    Musculoskeletal and Skin Diseases
    (NIAMS), 111
National League (baseball), 44
National Sporting Goods Association
    (NSGA) survey, 17–20, 18t–20t
Nationwide Tour (golf), 60
Native American mascots, 39–40
NAYS (National Alliance for Youth
    Sports), 113
NBA. *See* National Basketball Association;
    National Boxing Association
NBA Live (video game), 39
NBC. *See* National Broadcasting Corporation
NBL (National Basketball League), 50
NCAA. *See* National Collegiate Athletic
    Association
*NCAA v. Board of Regents of the University
    of Oklahoma*, 34, 73
Nevada, gambling in. *See* Legal gambling
New York Yankees, 32, 45, 57
NFHS (National Federation of State High
    School Associations), 6
NFL. *See* National Football League
NFL Europe, 48
NFL Players Association (NFLPA), 48
NFLPA (NFL Players Association), 48
NHL. *See* National Hockey League
NIAMS (National Institute of Arthritis and
    Musculoskeletal and Skin Diseases), 111

Nifong, Mike, 73–74
Non-Thoroughbred horse racing, 131
Northwestern University, 135
Nowitzki, Dirk, 50
NSGA (National Sporting Goods Association) survey, 17–20, 18t–20t

O

Obama, Barack, 105, 115
Obesity, 109–110, 115
Office pools, 133, 133(f10.4)
Oller, Pierre, 129
Olympic partners (TOP) program, 10–4105
Olympics
  amateur *vs.* professional status, 105
  BALCO scandal, 122
  basketball, 50
  boxing, 67
  doping, 9, 119–120
  overview, 7–8
  revenue, 103–105
  scandals, 101–102
  site selection, 105
  sports included, 7t
  structure and administration, 102–103
  summer game sites, 100(t7.3)
  summer sports, 100(t7.1)
  winter game sites, 101t
  winter sports, 100(t7.2)
  women's basketball, 52
  women's boxing, 66
Online gambling, 136
Organized crime, 134
Ortiz, David, 43, 126
Osborne, Tom, 136
Osteoporosis, 109
Otto, Ed, 63
Outdoor sports, 15–17, 16t–17t
Overuse injuries, 111, 113

P

Pacquiao, Manny, 67
Palmeiro, Rafael, 123, 126
Paralympics, 107
Pari-mutuel gambling, 10, 129–130
Parker, Tony, 50
Participation
  college sports, 69, 70(t6.1), 74t–75t
  college sports, by race/ethnicity, 78–79, 88t
  Deaflympics, 107
  Division I college sports, by gender, 84f
  extreme sports, 17–20, 22(t2.10)
  female student-athletes per college, 82f
  gambling, 10, 133, 133(f10.4)
  gender, 17
  high school sports, 6–7, 82–83, 94(t6.14)
  high school sports, benefits of, 83–84

  high school sports, by demographic characteristics, 96t
  high school sports, by parents' education level, 98f, 98t
  high school sports, by sex, 95(t6.15), 97f
  individual sports, 14–15, 14(t2.2), 15t
  lacrosse, 20, 22(t2.11), 22(t2.12)
  male student-athletes per college, 83f
  men's championship college sports, 77f
  National Sporting Goods Association data, 1–2
  outdoor and water sports, 15–17, 16t–17t
  Paralympics, 107
  popular high school sports for boys, 95(t6.16)
  popular high school sports for girls, 95(t6.17)
  popular women's college sports, 86t
  ratings, by sport, 2(t1.2)
  soccer, 20
  Special Olympics, 106
  team sports, 13–14, 14(t2.1)
  ten-year history, 18t
  women, 20t–21t
  women's championship college sports, 76f
  women's college sports, 74t
  youth, 17, 19t, 85, 87
Patrick, Danica, 64
Patsy T. Mink Equal Opportunity in Education Act (Title IX), 6, 77–78
Pay-per-view, 65, 67
Pep, Willie, 31
Performance-enhancing drugs. *See* Doping
Pettigrew, Antonio, 106
PGA (Professional Golfers' Association), 4, 59–60
Phelps, Michael, 99
Pitchers, 113
Pitching, 87
Pittsburgh Steelers, 136
Point spread, 132
Politics, 8, 100–101
Pool, 14–15
Poppen, Sherman, 19
Preakness Stakes, 130–131
President's Council on Physical Fitness and sports, 115
Prize money
  golf, 62
  tennis, 62–63
Professional and Amateur Sports Protection Act, 131
Professional Golfers' Association (PGA), 4, 59–60
Professional sports
  alcohol advertising, 37–39, 38(f3.2)
  attendance, 2–4
  doping, 9, 124, 126–127
  gambling, 131–133, 133(f10.4), 134–135

  history of televised sports, 5
  television, 31–32
  violence, 40–41
  See also Specific sports
Proposition 48, 73
Psychological issues. *See* Mental health
Public funding for stadiums, 56–57
Public opinion
  baseball, 24(f2.1)
  basketball as favorite sport, 26f
  college football, 25t
  favorite sports, 2(t1.1), 23(t2.14), 23(t2.15), 26f
  football, 24(f2.1)
  football *vs.* baseball, 25f
  gambling, 133–134, 133(f10.4), 134f
Public relations. *See* Image and public relations

R

Race to Dubai, 61
Race/ethnicity
  baseball, professional, 44–45
  basketball, professional, 49, 52
  boxing, 67
  college sports, 78–79, 88t
  diversity in major sports, 55–56
  doping, 124t
  exercise, 114–115, 116f
  fans, 22–23
  female collegiate athletes, 90f
  high school sports, 82, 94(t6.14), 96t
  male collegiate athletes, 89f
  mascots, 39–40
  Olympic boycotts, 101
  soccer, professional, 55
  tennis, 15
Racetracks, 130–131
Racinos, 130
Racquet sports, 1, 4, 14–15, 15t
Radovich v. National Football League, 48
Ramirez, Manny, 9, 43, 126
Rankings, boxing, 65
Rasmussen, Michael, 128
Recruitment, college sports, 72, 81–82, 84–85, 93t–94t
Reese, Albert, 73
Retired players, 48–49
Revenue
  alcohol advertising, 38(f3.2)
  baseball, professional, 32–33, 44(t4.2)
  basketball, professional, 35, 35t, 49, 50t
  basketball, professional women's, 53
  college sports, 73, 79–81, 91t–92t
  college sports gambling, 135–136
  football, professional, 5t, 33, 46, 46(t4.3)
  golf, professional, 60
  greyhound racing, 131
  hockey, professional, 53, 53(t4.9)

horse racing, 130
legal gambling, 10
luxury boxes, 56, 56*t*
Nevada sports book wagering, 132, 132*f*, 133(*f*10.2)
Olympics, 103–104
stadium names, 57
Super Bowl advertising, 36–37
Super Bowl gambling, 133(*f*10.3)
televised sports, 31
Revenue sharing
luxury suites, 56
Major League Baseball, 45–46
National Football League, 47
National Hockey League, 54
Robbins, Barrett, 123
Roberts, Selena, 126
Robinson, Jackie, 22, 44, 55
Rodriguez, Alex, 9, 43, 45, 126
Roman Empire, 100
Romanowski, Bill, 123
Rome, ancient, 129
Roosevelt, Theodore, 71
Rose, Derrick, 73
Rose, Pete, 134–135
Rozelle, Pete, 47
Rozelle Rule, 48
Rudolph, Eric Robert, 101
Ruth, Babe, 44

S

Sabathia, CC, 45
Salaries and salary caps
college coaches, 6
Major League Baseball, 43, 45–46
National Basketball Association, 49–51, 51*t*
National Football League, 46, 48
National Hockey League, 53–54
Women's National Basketball Association, 53
Salt Lake City Olympics, 2002, 101
Sample, Steven B., 6
Sanity Code, 72
Scandals
BALCO, 122–123
Black Sox, 44, 134
boxing, 65
college recruitment practices, 84–85
doping, 9–10
International Boxing Federation, 66
Major League Baseball, doping in, 43, 46
National Basketball Association, 52
National Collegiate Athletic Association, 72–74
Nevada gambling, 132
Olympics, 8
Schilling, Curt, 123, 126

Seattle SuperSonics, 57
Segregation, 44
Self-esteem, 110
Selig, Allan H., 44, 126
Seniors Tour (golf), 61
Sexual health and behavior, 110
SGMA (Sporting Goods Manufacturers Association) survey, 13–15, 14*t*–15*t*
Shin splints, 111
Shriver, Eunice Mary Kennedy, 106
Simpson, Tom, 127
Sinkewitz, Patrik, 128
Site selection, Olympics, 101, 103, 105
Skateboarding, 18–19
Skeletal injuries, 111
Ski resorts, 19
Skyboxes. *See* Luxury boxes
Smith, Onterrio, 124
Snowboarding, 19–20
Snurfers, 19
Snyder, Jimmy "The Greek," 132
Soccer, professional, 28, 55
Soccer participation, 20
Social outcomes, 6–7, 83–84
Soft-tissue injuries, 111
Soldier Field, 106
Sony Ericsson Tour, 63
Sorenstam, Annika, 61
Sosa, Sammy, 45, 126
Sotomayor, Sonia, 45
Southeastern Conference, 34
Southern Methodist University, 73
Spalding, Albert G., 103
Special Olympics, 106–107
Specialization in youth sports, 87
Spectator sports. *See* Fans; Specific sports
Sponsorship and advertising
alcohol, 37–39, 38(*f*3.2)
NASCAR, 63–64
Olympics, 103–105
stadiums, 57
Super Bowl, 33, 36–37, 37*t*
televised sports, 5, 31
Sporting Goods Manufacturers Association (SGMA) survey, 13–15, 14*t*–15*t*
Sporting goods sales, 2, 3*t*, 20–21, 23(*t*2.13)
Sprains, 111
Sprint Cup, 64
Stadiums, 56–57
Stanley, David, 73
Stanley, Frederick A., 54
Stanley Cup, 35, 53–54
State boxing commissions, 65
States
antidoping legislation, 128
high school sports participation, 82
Statistical information
advertising (Super Bowl), 37*t*

alcohol advertising on sports television, 38(*f*3.2)
attendance of selected sports, 29*t*–30*t*
basketball fans, 26*f*
calories burned through sports and exercise, 110*t*
college football fans, 25*t*
college sports participation, 70(*t*6.1)
college sports participation, by race/ethnicity, 88*t*
Division I athletic expenses, by gender, 85*f*
Division I college sports participation, by gender, 84*f*
Division I scholarship spending, by gender, 86*f*
doping among college athletes, 124*t*–125*t*
exercise among adults, 114*f*
exercise among adults, by age and sex, 115*f*
exercise among youth, 117*f*–118*f*
exercise participation, by race/ethnicity, 116*f*
extreme sports participation, 22(*t*2.10)
fans, by geography, 27*t*
favorite sports, 2(*t*1.1), 23 (*t*2.14), 23(*t*2.15), 26*t*
female collegiate athletes, by race/ethnicity, 90*f*
female student-athletes per college, 82*f*
football attendance, 28*t*
football fans *vs.* baseball fans, 25*f*
gambling participation, 133(*f*10.4)
high school sports participation, by demographic characteristics, 96*t*
high school sports participation, by parents' education level, 98*f*, 98*t*
high school sports participation, by sex, 95(*t*6.15), 97*f*
high school sports participation, by sex and race/ethnicity, 94(*t*6.14)
individual sports participation, 14(*t*2.2)
lacrosse participation, 22(*t*2.11), 22(*t*2.12)
Major League Baseball fans, 24(*f*2.1)
male collegiate athletes, by race/ethnicity, 89*f*
male student-athletes per college, average number of, 83*f*
men's championship college sports participation, 77*f*
men's college championship sports teams, 79*f*
men's college sports participation, 75*t*
men's teams per college, average number of, 81*f*
National Basketball Association salary cap, 51*t*
National Basketball Association team values and revenue, 50*t*

National Basketball Association television contract amounts, 35t

National Football League fans, 24(f2.2)

National Football League team values and revenue, 46(t4.3)

NCAA Division I-FBS revenue and expenses, 91t

NCAA Division I-FBS sources of revenue, 92t

NCAA membership, 70(t6.2)

Nevada sports book wagering, 132f, 133(f10.2)

outdoor sports participation, 16t–17t

participation, rated by sport, 2(t1.2)

popular high school sports for boys, 95(t6.16)

popular high school sports for girls, 95(t6.17)

popular women's college sports, 86t

public opinion on gambling, 134f

racquet sports participation, 15t

sporting goods, consumer spending on, 3t

sports participation trends, 18t

steroid use among young people, 10f

Super Bowl betting, 133(f10.3)

Super Bowl viewership, 38(f3.1), 38t

team sports participation, 14(t2.1)

women's championship college sports participation, 76f

women's college championship sports teams, 78f

women's college sports participation, 74t

women's sports participation, 20t–21t

women's teams per college, 80f

youth sports participation, 19t

Stern, David, 51–52

Steroids, 9–10, 10f, 43, 46, 120–121

Stock car racing
    attendance, 3, 28
    history, 63–64
    overview, 4
    television, 5, 36

Strikes
    Major League Baseball, 45
    National Football League, 48
    National Hockey League, 54

Structure and administration
    Major League Baseball, 44(t4.1)
    Major League Soccer, 55, 55t
    National Basketball Association, 49, 49t
    National Collegiate Athletic Association, 69–71, 70(t6.2), 73
    National Football League, 46–47, 46(t4.4)
    National Hockey League, 53–54, 53(t4.10)
    Olympics, 102–103
    Women's National Basketball Association, 52, 53(t4.8)

Stubblefield, Dana, 123

Studies, reports, and surveys
    Michigan Study of Adolescent Life Transitions, 110
    SGMA survey, 13–15, 14t–15t

Sullivan, James E., 103

Summer Olympics. See Olympics

Super Bowl
    advertising, 36–37, 37t
    attendance, 27
    championship, 47
    gambling, 132, 133(f10.3)
    television, 3, 5, 33–34, 38(f3.1), 38t, 48

SuperSonics, 57

Swimming team, East German, 120

T

Taxes
    gambling, 133–134
    luxury taxes, 45–46, 54

Team names and mascots, 39–40

Team sports
    attendance, 2–4
    National Sporting Goods Association data, 1–2
    participation, 13–14, 14(t2.1)
    youth participation, 17

Teixeira, Mark, 45

Television
    alcohol advertising, 37–39, 38(f3.2)
    auto racing, 36, 64
    baseball, professional, 32–33
    basketball, professional, 34–35, 35t
    boxing, 65–67
    college football, 34
    college sports, 72–73, 80
    exercise, 115
    extreme sports, 36
    football, professional, 5t, 33–34, 47–48
    gender and viewership, 39
    history of televised sports, 5, 31–32
    hockey, professional, 35–36, 54
    Olympics, 8, 103–104
    Super Bowl, 36–37, 37t, 38(f3.1), 38t

Tennis
    participation, 15, 15t
    popularity, 1
    professional, 4, 62–63, 135

Terrorism, 101

Testosterone. See Doping

Teter, Hannah, 20

Tetrahydrogestrinone (THG), 122

Texas Tech, 73

Theodosius, 100

THG (Tetrahydrogestrinone), 122

Thomas, Frank, 123

Thoroughbred horse racing, 130–131

Tilden, Will T., II, 62

Title IX, 6, 77–78

Toms, David, 60

Tour de France, 127–128

Travel teams, 87

Triple Crown, 130–131

Tyson, Mike, 65–67

U

Ullrich, Jan, 128

Unitas, Johnny, 47

University High School, 84

University of Memphis, 73

University of Michigan, 73

University of Southern California, 6

Unlawful Internet Gambling Enforcement Act, 11, 136

U.S. Anti-Doping Agency (USADA), 128

U.S. Auto Club (USAC), 64

U.S. Bowling Congress, 15

U.S. Boxing Association (USBA), 66

U.S. Lacrosse, 20

U.S. Olympic Committee (USOC), 103, 107

U.S. Open (tennis), 62–63

U.S. Tennis Association, 15

USAC (U.S. Auto Club), 64

USADA (U.S. Anti-Doping Agency), 128

USBA (U.S. Boxing Association), 66

USOC (U.S. Olympic Committee), 103, 107

V

Valente, James, 122

Vassalo Arguello, Martin, 135

Vick, Michael, 40

Video games, 39

Viewership. See Television

Vinokourov, Alexander, 128

Violence
    among athletes, 40–41
    boxing, 65
    college football, 71
    National Basketball Association, 52

Virginia Slims Tour, 62–63

Voet, Willy, 127

W

WADA (World Anti-Doping Agency), 105, 128

Wade, Ed, 40

Wanamaker, Rodman, 59

Water sports, 16–17, 16t–17t

WBA (World Boxing Association), 65–66

WBC (World Boxing Council), 66

WBO (World Boxing Organization), 66

Webber, Chris, 73, 135

Webster, Mike, 49

Weight control, 110

Weightlifting, 119

WHA (World Hockey Association), 54

White, Kelli, 106, 122–123

White, Shaun, 19–20

Wie, Michelle, 61–62
Williams, Serena, 15, 39
Williams, Venus, 15, 39
Wimbledon Championships, 62
Wingfield, Walter C., 62
Winston Cup, 64
Winter Olympics. *See* Olympics
Wire Act, 136
WNBA (Women's National Basketball Association), 3–4, 56
Women
    boxing, 66
    championship college sports participation, 76*f*
    college championship sports teams, 78*f*
    college coaches, 87*t*
    college sports equity, 76–77
    college sports participation, 74–76
    doping, 120
    doping among college athletes, 125(*t*9.4)
    exercise, benefits of, 109
    injuries, 112
    LPGA Tour, 4
    managers, 56
    professional golf, 61–62
    professional soccer, 55
    sports participation, 20*t*–21*t*
    student-athletes per college, average number of, 82*f*

tennis, professional, 62–63
Title IX, 6, 77–78
Women's National Basketball Association, 3–4
women's teams per college, average number of, 80*f*
Women's Tennis Association, 4
Women's National Basketball Association (WNBA), 3–4, 52–53, 53(*t*4.8), 56
Women's Professional Soccer (WPS), 55
Women's Tennis Association (WTA), 4, 63
Women's Tennis Council, 63
Women's United Soccer Association, 55
World Anti-Doping Agency (WADA), 105, 128
World Boxing Association (WBA), 65–66
World Boxing Council (WBC), 66
World Boxing Organization (WBO), 66
World Hockey Association (WHA), 54
World Series
    advertising, 37
    Black Sox scandal, 44, 134
    championship, 43
    television, 32–33
World Trade Organization, 136
WPS (Women's Professional Soccer), 55
Wright, Chalky, 31
WTA (Women's Tennis Association), 63

X
X Games, 36

Y
Yao Ming, 50
YMCA (Young Men's Christian Association), 49–50
Young Men's Christian Association (YMCA), 49–50
Youth
    doping, 10
    exercise, 114–115, 117*f*–118*f*
    extreme sports participation, 17–20
    health impact of participation, 8–9
    injuries, 111–113
    lacrosse, 20
    mental health, 110
    National Sporting Goods Association data, 1–2
    participation, 17, 19*t*, 85, 87
    soccer, 20
    steroid use, 10*f*, 123
    televised extreme sports, 36
    See also High school sports

Z
Zaharias, Babe Didrikson, 61
Ziegler, John, 119